The Turn Against the Modern

The Critical Essays of Taoka Reiun (1870–1912)

Asia Past & Present: New Research from AAS

Published by the Association for Asian Studies (AAS) "Asia Past & Present" features the finest scholarly work from all areas and disciplines of Asian studies. For further information, visit **www.asian-studies.org**.

- "Teaching Japanese Popular Culture" edited by Deborah Shamoon and Chris McMorran
- "East Meets East: Chinese Discover the Modern World in Japan, 1854–1898. A Window on the Intellectual and Social Transformation of Modern China" by Douglas R. Reynolds with Carol T. Reynolds
- "A Scholarly Review of Chinese Studies in North America" (e-book), edited by Haihui Zhang, Zhaohui Xue, Shuyong Jiang, and Gary Lance Lugar
- "Changing Lives: The "Postwar" in Japanese Women's Autobiographies and Memoirs," by Ronald P. Loftus
- "Memory, Violence, Queues: Lu Xun Interprets China," by Eva Shan Chou
- "Scattered Goddesses: Travels with the Yoginis," by Padma Kaimal
- "South Asian Texts in History: Critical Engagements with Sheldon Pollock," edited by Yigal Bronner, Whitney Cox, and Lawrence McCrea
- "Beating Devils and Burning Their Books: Views of Japan, China, and the West," edited by Anthony E. Clark
- "To Die and Not Decay: Autobiography and the Pursuit of Immortality in Early China," by Matthew V. Wells
- "Collecting Asia: East Asian Libraries in North America, 1868–2008," edited by Peter X. Zhou
- "Prescribing Colonization: The Role of Medical Practices and Policies in Japan-Ruled Taiwan, 1895–1945," by Michael Shiyung Liu
- "Tools of Culture: Japan's Cultural, Intellectual, Medical, and Technological Contacts in East Asia, 1000s to 1500s," edited by Andrew Edmund Goble, Kenneth R. Robinson, and Haruko Wakabayashi
- "Modern Short Fiction of Southeast Asia: A Literary History," edited by Teri Shaffer Yamada

THE TURN AGAINST THE MODERN

THE CRITICAL ESSAYS OF TAOKA REIUN (1870–1912)

RONALD P. LOFTUS

ASIA PAST & PRESENT

Published by the Association for Asian Studies, Inc.
Asia Past & Present: New Research from AAS, Number 14

The Association for Asian Studies (AAS)

Formed in 1941, the Association for Asian Studies (AAS)—the largest society of its kind, with approximately 8,000 members worldwide—is a scholarly, non-political, non-profit professional association open to all persons interested in Asia.

For further information, please visit www.asian-studies.org.

© 2017 by the Association for Asian Studies, Inc.

All Rights Reserved. Written permission must be secured to use or reproduce any part of this book.

Published by:

Association for Asian Studies, Inc.
825 Victors Way, Suite 310
Ann Arbor, MI 48108 USA
www.asian-studies.org

Library of Congress Cataloging-in-Publication Data

Names: Loftus, Ronald P., author.
Title: The turn against the modern : the critical essays of Taoka Reiun (1870–1912) / Ronald P. Loftus.
Description: Ann Arbor, Michigan : Association for Asian Studies, Inc., 2017. | Series: Asia past & present: new research from AAS; number 14 | Includes bibliographical references and index.
Identifiers: LCCN 2017038882 | ISBN 9780924304859 (pbk.) Subjects: LCSH: Taoka, Reiun, 1870-1912. | Japan--Biography. | Japan—Civilization—1868-1912.
Classification: LCC CT1838.T33 L64 2017 | DDC 952/.02—dc23
LC record available at https://lccn.loc.gov/2017038882

To Professor Nishida Masaru

Teacher, Scholar, Mentor, and Friend

Contents

Acknowledgments / xi

Preface / xii
Situating Taoka Reiun / xvii

1. **Overview** / 1

   Reiun and Kôtoku Shûsui / 3
   Becoming a Straggler / 8
   Antimodernism / 11
   Finding the Self / 14

2. **Youth and Early Education** / 19

   Elementary School / 22
   Osaka Middle School / 27
   Bureaucratic Reforms of 1885 / 28
   Illness / 31
   Tokyo / 34

3. **"Better Consciousness": Schopenhauer and the Self in Modern Japan** / 37

   Miyake Setsurei and the Search for Equivalence / 40
   Taoka Reiun's Early Essays, 1892–1894 / 43
   "The Position of Eastern Thought in
   the Nineteenth Century West" / 58
   Understanding the Movement of Thought from East to West / 73
   Contesting Western Civilization / 77
   More on Schopenhauer's Philosophy / 79
   Conclusion / 84

4. Literary Criticism: The Seinenbun Years / 87

   The Sino-Japanese War and the New Japan / 91
   The Legacy of Kitamura Tôkoku and the Turn
      from Politics to Literature / 92
   Reiun and the Inward Turn / 95
   Finding Compassion / 100
   The Environment and Spirituality / 104
   Reiun and the Dark Side of Society / 106
   The Emergence of Social Problems (*shakai mondai*) / 110
   Yokoyama Gennosuke and Matsubara Iwagorô / 110
   A Voice from a Different Quarter: Takayama Chogyû / 113
   The Meaning of *Seinenbun* / 116

5. Hibunmeiron: The Attack on Modern Civilization / 123

   The Years before *Tenko* / 127
   Tsûyama and a Love Affair / 131
   Tenko: Sounding Heaven's Drum / 135
   Love Suicides / 140
   "The Coming Revolution" / 141
   A Call for Social Revolution / 144
   Max Nordau / 146
   Edward Carpenter / 147
   Looking Back / 154
   Dark Undercurrents / 155
   "The Roots of Contemporary Evils" / 161
   "My Socialism" / 164

6. Seeking Rebellion: Taoka Reiun and the
   Meiji Restoration / 167

   An Impasse: Ishikawa Takuboku and the Need
      to Investigate Tomorrow / 167
   "At Nagatamura" / 170
   Uncovering Rebellion / 176
   On the Character of the Meiji Restoration / 177
   Progress as "Rebellion": An Image of Historical Change / 184
   The Problem of Progress in Japanese Historical Consciousness / 188

7. **The Final Years: Toward a New Vision for Women, Society, and the Individual / 195**

  Finding Projects: Narrativizing the Self / 199
  Translating Schopenhauer / 199
  An Allegory for Humanity / 200
  A Call for Women's Liberation (*joshi-kaihôron*, 女子解放論) / 201
  Engels, Morgan, and Bebel / 204
  Chikamatsu, Carpenter, and the Institution of Marriage / 207
  Final Days / 210

8. **Last Thoughts: On Defending the Modern Self / 213**

  Struggles and Contradictions / 216
  Movement of Thought / 217
  Finding Meaning through Engagement / 218
  Becoming a Subject of Modernity / 220

Notes / 223

Bibliography / 291

Index / 309

Acknowledgments

There are many people to thank. I was very fortunate to be mentored by two scholars in Japan: Kano Masanao, modern Japanese history; and Nishida Masaru, modern Japanese literature. In addition to professors Kano and Nishida, my dissertation adviser, Professor Peter Duus, was an important guide and model for me. Thoughtful, open-minded, but always rigorous, he pushed me in directions that helped me grow and mature as a historian. Professor Tsuzuki Chûshichi, an internationally renowned expert on Edward Carpenter's life and works, very generously assisted me with his time and insights and shared his wonderful collection of primary materials. Sarah Frederick of Boston University also provided useful insights about the appeal of Carpenter's writing in Japan and was generously willing to read portions of my manuscript. Barbara Molony, Jan Bardsley, and Julia Thomas were all very helpful in responding to some of my ideas or queries and offered sound advice. While I was working on the manuscript, I began a correspondence with Professor Sho Konishi of Oxford University. He kindly invited me to offer an Evening Seminar at St. Anthony's College in October 2015. The rich discussion that we had there and the comments offered by Professor Konishi and the faculty and graduate students at Oxford helped advance the clarity of this manuscript. I also benefited from conversations with Oguma Eiji of Keio University about intellectuals in pre- and postwar Japan.

My colleagues at Willamette University have always supported me and encouraged me to develop as a scholar. In Chinese Studies, Juwen Zhang and Huike Wen helped me identify passages from the Chinese texts that Reiun quotes so frequently, as did Xijuan Zhou in the Religious Studies Department when it came to references to Buddhist materials. Miho Fujiwara and Tomoko Harpster were always available to help me with the translation of difficult passages into Japanese. My history colleagues Seth Cotlar, Leslie Dunlap, and Cecily McCaffrey offered wonderful suggestions. Also Stephen Patterson in Religious Studies and Michael Strelow in the English Department gave excellent advice on my project as it evolved. Pamela Smith ably assisted with manuscript preparation at all stages of the project, for which I am very grateful. The two anonymous readers of the manuscript offered many excellent comments and suggestions, which I believe have made the final version stronger. Of course any shortcomings remain, in the end, my own responsibility.

Family members Josh and Jen, Mike and Katy, and their children, Leah, Casey, Luca, Jackson, Emmett, Will, and Cannon, helped me think about my arguments in ways they will never know. They are always a great inspiration.

Preface

Writing a biography is a delightful challenge. There is delight in knowing that biography can be at "the heart of all living history."[1] When done properly, the subject's story becomes entwined with its broader social context, a process that Karl J. Weintraub refers to as connecting the "self" to its "circumstances."[2] But, as Gabrielle M. Spiegel reminds us, there is also a tremendous challenge historians face when reconstructing the past: how to uncover the "fragmented inner narratives" that subjects leave behind and coax them "to emerge from their silences."[3] If we neglect either one of these—the teasing out of these fragmented narratives or the process of forging connections between them and the larger story of the times—then something important will be lost. Fortunately, despite some gaps in the record, materials on the life and writings of the literary and cultural critic Taoka Reiun (1870–1912) are surprisingly rich, including hundreds of critical essays and a published memoir. Moreover, his story is a particularly valuable one to tell because he lived during those important years when Japan was fully engaged with the process of becoming modern. Coming of age as he did in the 1890s, he witnessed Japan's emergence as an industrializing capitalist society and a colonial power. Therefore, what he experienced, and how he wrote about it, can offer fruitful insights into the times in which he lived.

In many of his essays, Reiun specifically addressed the way industrialization and capitalism were transforming Japanese life, and he attacked the principles underlying modern civilization—what he referred to as *bunmei*—as severely flawed and limited in scope. He was concerned about the emergence of an impoverished underclass and the social impact of commercialization and commodification on Japan. By itself this would be more than sufficient to constitute a substantial critique of the times, but he did not stop there. He also wrote about the way "modern subjectivity"—something that has been labeled "one of the—if not the—defining issues of modern and postmodern cultures"—was something significant that needed to be explored.[4] Reiun frequently employed such terms as *ga* (我), *jiga* (自我), and *jiko* (自己) to talk about the self, and he pushed his readers to look at the *subjective* side of human knowledge or experience, which was the *shukanteki* (主観的)—something he wanted to see evaluated every bit as favorably as the *objective*, or *kyakkanteki* (客観的)—side.[5] To Reiun, the problem with the intellectual construct of *bunmei* was not only that it was too narrow and instrumentalist but also that it assumed that the western historical experience was universal. That is why Reiun favored what he called a more subjective view, one that began with the self and penetrated to the heart of things, allowing for a truer, deeper portrayal of the human experience.

While this point is central to understanding what Taoka Reiun has to say, it is also important to be aware that it may not be only the fact of subjectivity, or the exact *nature* of that subjectivity, that is important, but also *how* that subjectivity is grasped, and the manner in which it is defended. As Charles Altieri suggests, subjectivity does not lie only "in the content of the beliefs, or in the history that formed them, but in something specific *to the way that they are held*. What makes an internal state subjective is not the beliefs per se, but the sense of ownership, or sense of responsibility, involved in holding it as one's own."[6] In other words, it is not only the act of turning inward and experiencing the world through the self that is important; it is also the stance that one takes, the way one goes about becoming sufficiently self-reflexive to claim "ownership" of the experiences and to be responsible for them. This kind of awareness was something that grew in importance to Reiun as he grappled with identifying the best way for Japanese to live in the late 1890s and early 1900s. Often regarded as a maverick and a contrarian, the stance Reiun adopted was a defiant, contentious one. But he also navigated with great creativity a pathway that took him deep into the past and into contact with the great philosophical writers of ancient India and China, and then back out again to contemporary times. In an age when most Japanese were flocking to recent western canonical texts, Reiun became an Asianist. A careful reader of Zhuangzi and the *Daodejing*, he wanted to be as aware as possible and to get the most out of the times in which he lived.[7]

It may seem anomalous that a young Japanese critic would choose to hark back to Daoism in order to grapple with modernity and the notion of modern subjectivity. His most active years as a writer and critic coincide with the period in which Japan appeared on the world stage as a newly industrializing nation, defeating China in a war in 1894–95 and Russia in 1904–5, which marked the first instance in which a major western power had been vanquished by a nonwestern one. As Japan emerged as an imperialist power in its own right, most Japanese rejoiced in the great strides forward the country was taking as an economic and military power; Japan was clearly becoming a country to be reckoned with in East Asia. There was a rush among Reiun's contemporaries to embrace social Darwinism and imperialism, so when he turned to the wisdom of ancient China and India he was calling for a pause, a breather. But was he taking a step backward? Was he turning away from an embrace of the new?

Reiun did not think so, especially if one's conception of progress is not limited to the western one. Born just two years after the Meiji Restoration, he grew up in a world that was filled with new institutions, new opportunities, and new ideas. It was the era of *bunmei-kaika* (civilization and enlightenment), but all this seemed to entail was building up industry and creating a powerful modern army by borrowing and adapting previously tested western models. Although *bunmei-kaika* may have looked like it could offer Japan a great deal in the 1870s, by the 1890s there were signs that disillusionment was setting in. Reiun was concerned that people needed to anchor their experiences in something real, something concrete, not just someone else's conception of what it means to become modern.

What did becoming modern mean to Reiun? Some degree of consensus exists today among historians that becoming modern entails such things as the spread of literacy, the application of a more scientific and technological perspective to economic and political development, the application of inanimate forms of energy to production processes, and the initiation of an industrial revolution based on a secular and practical education system. In turn the growth of a market economy occurs along with the development of a consumer culture, and the diffusion of at least some institutions of representative government.[8] In brief becoming modern means coming to grips with the consequences of the two great revolutions in modern history: the French and the Industrial. But the question remains: must the process conform to only one pattern? There is mounting evidence that this is not the case. While the nineteenth century was clearly the age of the nation-state, and historical narratives were usually written from this perspective, the twenty-first century has mounted a serious challenge to this perspective. Historians are coming to see transnationalism and modernity as intimately connected. In fact, modernity is considered "the single most powerful transnationally transmitted idea in the era since 1800."[9] Ideas do not recognize national boundaries, and much of the story of *The Turn Against the Modern* is about how and when ideas flowed back and forth between Europe and Asia and how writers and critics adapted and reconfigured these ideas to fit both new and established worldviews and practices.

During the 1870s and 1880s, there can be little question that Japan was experiencing a substantial political, economic, and social transformation. A small group of young samurai leaders, most still in their thirties, managed to orchestrate the overthrow of the feudal regime and even to eliminate the old neo-Confucian four-class system. They created new political, financial, and educational institutions and these generated new opportunities for the citizenry. As a result, popular aspirations and expectations soared. Young people dreamed of rising to high office, much like the heroes of the Restoration had done, and they looked forward to having a voice in national political and economic affairs. But by the early 1880s the opportunities for doing so had dwindled substantially. In response to this narrowing of opportunities, there arose an important grassroots political movement rooted in natural rights theory known as "the popular rights movement" (*jiyûminken undô*), whose proponents introduced concepts such as freedom, liberty, and individual rights into Japan and wanted to see political power more widely and evenly distributed. While this movement held out the promise of another avenue for engagement with modernity—participatory democracy—before young men like Taoka Reiun had reached their adulthood this dream had lost most of its luster. However, in the 1890s a new world of literary and social criticism beckoned, a place where individuals could read, think, and express their ideas in the newly founded magazines and journals, ideas that drew on indigenous knowledge and practices while also incorporating new worldviews from outside Japan.

Reiun entered this world after attending a variety of educational institutions, many of them new, ending up in the Chinese Studies Department of Tokyo Imperial University. He then worked for various newspapers and small literary journals as a critic, where he discovered his voice, and explored ideas in the fields of literature, philosophy, religion, and history. Given to introspection, his favorite German philosopher was Arthur Schopenhauer (1788–1860), although he read his Fichte, Schelling, Nietzsche, and Hegel, too, along with the poetry of Lord Byron and Heinrich Heine. What he did that most of his contemporaries did not, was construct a critical project that engaged both contemporary and past writers from the western tradition alongside major philosophers from Asia in a new and creative way in order to reflect on what it means to be modern. Much of contemporary discourse around the world is still about what it means to become modern; Taoka Reiun situated himself squarely in the midst of this discourse in the 1890s and the early 1900s.

On more than a few occasions, though, the government took exception to Reiun's critical essays and banned them upon publication. Out of eight of his volumes of essays, four were banned. He was even imprisoned for a few months for "slandering an official" who he claimed was receiving kickbacks from textbook publishers. Deprived of the ability to make a good living as a social and cultural critic, Reiun left Japan and traveled to China on three separate occasions, living there for as long as two years on one of them. When he returned to Japan in 1907, he was alarmed to find that his country seemed to be turning into a police state (*keisatsu no kuni*).[10] At times he experienced disruptions and uncertainty in both his personal and professional lives, but he never gave up and he never relented. Undaunted, Reiun wanted to discover for himself and his readers what was going on in the world and what mattered most. *The Turn Against the Modern* situates his writings and experiences in their appropriate historical context and seeks to understand why he objected to certain fundamental aspects of modern life. This study also explores the intellectual and philosophical foundations on which he built his critical insights and shows how he wove them together in fresh new ways, ways that suggest a mind critically engaged in what it means to become modern.

Situating Taoka Reiun

A late Meiji thinker who is often identified with "antimodernist" thought, Reiun spent his life publishing in small journals, which often operated on the margins of discourse. I first encountered his work when I was still a dissertation student, reading secondary sources in Japanese in order to orient myself to the era in which he lived. Historians such as Irokawa Daikichi and Kano Masanao devoted several pages in their sweeping intellectual histories of the Meiji period to Reiun, and both saw him as an important voice, one that challenged the premises of the western version of modernity that was dominant in Japan. I had the great privilege of meeting both of these scholars in person, and Professor Kano was kind enough to mentor me during my dissertation research years. Another important scholar, Maruyama Masao (1914–96), in his 1960 essay "Loyalty and Treason," situated Reiun among a small group of prewar writers and critics who understood what it meant to construct a strong sense of individuality and to stand up to the Meiji state.[11]

Two other scholars are very important in the field of Taoka Reiun studies. The late Professor Ienaga Saburô (1913–2002) was the first to publish a major monograph about Taoka, *The Career of an Unfortunate Thinker: Taoka Reiun, the Person and His Ideas*.[12] An inexpensive paperback designed for the mass market, there was some hope that a "Reiun boom" might ensue. The boom never materialized, but Reiun's name certainly did become much more familiar to scholars in the 1950s and 1960s. Ienaga had stumbled on Reiun's name during the war years, when the freedom of scholars to research and write was curtailed, and since Reiun's work had suffered a similar fate in the early 1900s, his name caught Ienaga's eye. Out of curiosity, Ienaga followed up in the National Diet Library and the Meiji Newspaper and Magazine Archive of Tokyo University, looking into prewar authors whose works had been banned by the government. He found many of Reiun's works on this list, and since he knew virtually nothing about him, he began to dig up what information he could find. In fact he played off of the title of Reiun's own autobiography, *Sakkiden* (A Record of Misfortune), for the title of his book on Reiun, using the same Chinese characters for *sakki* (数奇) with their more standard reading of *sûki*. With this book, Ienaga succeeded in chiseling an image of Reiun as someone who overcame substantial obstacles in his life, wrote fiery, contestatory essays, and more often than not had his writings censored. Therefore, he was effectively cast as an unfortunate victim of the prewar Japanese state. This was an important beginning for "Reiun studies," but it is now clear that a much more nuanced view of his life and writings is possible.

The other important Reiun scholar is Nishida Masaru (1931–), professor emeritus of modern Japanese literature at Hôsei University, who is still hard at work on Reiun's writing, preparing the final volumes of his "complete works" for publication. Perhaps due to his different disciplinary approach, Nishida takes strong exception to certain aspects of Ienaga's portrayal of Reiun, especially the latter's insistence on taking some of Reiun's references to the Meiji emperor literally. Ienaga concludes that Reiun was a man of Meiji who, not unlike the novelist Natsume Sôseki, accepted the monarchy and even felt affection for the Meiji emperor. Particularly at issue is a line by Reiun from an August 1912 piece, "From Nikkô," in which, on learning of the emperor's death, he seemed to chide a local newspaper for not publishing a special edition on this solemn occasion. Putting aside the question of whether Sôseki himself was a man of Meiji who admired the emperor, Nishida argues that Ienaga misses the deep irony of Reiun's words, pointing out that in none of the other nineteen installments of "From Nikkô," nor in any of Reiun's other writings from 1912, is any mention made of the emperor at all. Nishida supplies ample contextual evidence for his position and argues convincingly that everything Reiun stood for during his lifetime went against the social and political hierarchy of the late Meiji state, which was centered on the monarchy.[13]

Professor Nishida has written extensively on Reiun over the past sixty years and is indubitably the leading expert on Reiun's work. He has published editions of his selected works with very thorough explanatory essays appended and is in the final stages of compiling and annotating his complete works. Currently five volumes of a projected seven have been published, and the sixth is scheduled to appear in 2017. Professor Nishida was teaching a seminar on Taoka at Hôsei University in the early 1970s, and he generously invited me to attend. He became a friend and lifelong mentor, and his insights into Taoka's life and writings have been indispensable to this project. Each of the published volumes of Reiun's complete works includes extensive notes and detailed information on original publication dates and other specifics. In his 1993 book *Kindai wa hitei dekiru ka?* (Can We Deny the Modern?)—which is not particularly focused on Reiun—Nishida argues that Reiun's grasp of Laozi and Zhuangzi exceeded that of postwar critic Karaki Junzô (1904–80).[14]

In the field of Japanese studies there is often an underlying assumption that the collective ethos in Japan leaves little room for the healthy development of an individual self and that obligations to the group and duty take precedence over individual freedom. This characterization of Japanese culture as group oriented rather than centered on the individual is clichéd, but, as is the case with many clichés, it contains a degree of truth. But it does not necessarily follow that individualism or a healthy interest in the self did not exist in prewar Japan. In the years just after World War II, there was a heated debate among Japanese intellectuals about "subjectivity," known as the *shutaiseironsô* (主体性論争), which evinced concerns about the prewar "self" and why it had not proven strong enough to resist the power of the state, especially in the form of the ideological framework of the emperor system. Film director Kurosawa Akira (1910–98), when making his first postwar film in 1946, *No Regrets for Our Youth*, wanted to feature "an independent woman with a strong sense of self" because the prewar years had taught him that without a strong sense of self and some individual autonomy people are powerless in the face of the state.[15] Maruyama Masao, who was a leading voice in the postwar debate on subjectivity, also felt that if an autonomous individual lacks a sense of independence and agency, a spirit of resistance is difficult to foster. This study of Taoka Reiun shows that even in the difficult prewar years it was possible for writers and critics to develop a strong sense of self, one with the potential for historical agency. In his essays, we encounter the voice of someone who valued autonomy, who was intent on exploring his own subjectivity and on generating a self that would be capable of resisting authority and defending itself.

In thinking about these kinds of issues in modern Asian intellectual history, the work of the historian Joseph Levenson inevitably comes to mind. His classic study *Liang Ch'i-cha'ao and the Mind of Modern China* (1967) is a model for portraying how the life of an individual critic can be situated in its historical context. An accomplished Confucian scholar and a journalist of considerable influence, Liang Qichao (1873–1929) was depicted by Levenson as someone who was emotionally tied to his tradition—Confucianism—but also incapable of denying that "value" and meaning were currently being generated elsewhere, outside the Confucian order, and this troubled him. As Levenson saw it, everyone naturally "has an emotional commitment to history and an intellectual commitment to value," and the aim for individuals is "to make these commitments coincide."[16] When this becomes impossible, Levenson argued, writers experience tension, and in order to come to terms with this tension they need to find some firm ground on which to stand. Liang, less than three years younger than Reiun—and with whose writings Reiun was quite familiar, as evidenced by the numerous times Liang's name crops up in his essays—wrestled mightily with this tension. We can see his dilemma as intrinsic to the process of becoming modern, for modernity regularly catapults critics and intellectuals into unfamiliar terrain and forces them to find their way without a road map. If Liang felt compelled to search for ways to make China seem equivalent to the West, Reiun did something analogous, although he turned some of the arguments on their head. Why, he asked, were so many important writers in the West just now discovering how much there was to admire about the great religious and philosophical traditions of Asia, particularly those of ancient China and India? To Reiun this was a sign that a significant transformation in western thought was under way. Modern civilization was experiencing its own existential crisis, one to which ancient Chinese and Indian thought might make a valuable contribution; ignoring this fact would be perilous.

In the end, not until the years following World War I did Liang resolve his tension by coming to see the West much as Reiun did, as a place where science, empirical inquiry, and materialism were dominant but lurking beneath the surface was an undeniable falsity or deceit. Liang came to understand that, whereas western science may be able to "tell the truth about matter" by breaking it down into its smallest units, it had to tell "a lie about reality" while doing so.[17] Science could not tell people what is really important: what the nature of the human experience could and should be like. Science may have made the West materialistically powerful, Liang reasoned, but it had also made it "spiritually bankrupt."[17] Reiun, who died half a dozen years before Liang came to this realization, had learned this truth for himself by the early 1890s. One of his favorite themes when he began writing was that the western scientific view of reality lacks depth and comprehensiveness. It has no ideals, no capacity to care for the fate of fellow human beings. Embedded in all its materialism lurks a destructive egotism and an economic greed that leads to disappointing social inequities. The modern may glitter on the outside, he was fond of saying, but on the inside you can find much to distrust.

To become modern is now recognized as a universal experience, and it is usually accompanied by intense personal and social change that can feel very disruptive at times. Jean-Jacques Rousseau, whom Reiun greatly admired, characterized these kinds of changes as a "whirlwind," while the contemporary critic Marshall Berman described them in 1980 as a "maelstrom." He notes that people enmeshed in modernity are witness to cycles of "perpetual disintegration and renewal, of struggle and contradiction, of ambiguity and anguish."[19] By the 1990s, scholars such as Anthony Giddens were referring to modernity as "a careering juggernaut" always threatening to spin out of control and wreak havoc.[20] How does the individual fare in the face of this kind of tumultuous change? Obviously, the individual is to a large extent thrust back on him- or herself, and this is why subjectivity becomes such a cornerstone of the modern experience. But at the same time the self was turning out to be something considerably more complex, and more divided, than when the term was first employed by Rousseau and later the romantics. Nature was first thought to have offered solace and repose for the individual self, a refuge where the hegemonic power of reason and rationality could be balanced by a healthy dose of interiority. But by the late nineteenth century this vision of the modern self was becoming more difficult to sustain. Advances in the biological sciences, fascination with the "unconscious," and the growth of post-Schopenhauerian and Nietzschean philosophy all but demolished simplistic notions of compatibility between inner nature and reason.

As Berman reminds us, then, modernity brings with it a divided legacy. "To become modern," he writes, "is to find ourselves in an environment that promises us adventure, power, joy, growth, transformation of ourselves and the world—and at the same time, that threatens to destroy everything we have, everything we know, everything we are."[21] *The Turn Against the Modern* takes this view of modernity as a lens through which to better perceive and understand what it meant to become modern in late-nineteenth- and early-twentieth-century Japan. Although the metaphors depicting modernity as a "whirlwind," a "maelstrom," or a "careering juggernaut" may not have offered Reiun much solace, they would have been instantly recognizable to him. So the story of how Taoka Reiun confronted and wrestled with modernity and came to see himself as a maverick and a contrarian is the central focus of this book. Among the questions it poses are the following. What specific angle did Reiun adopt on the nature of the paths to modernity that stretched before his country? To which authors was he most drawn, and how did he fashion his own take on modernity out of the diverse sources with which he worked? How did he view literature, and what did he think its role in modern society should be? What was his vision for Asia in the early twentieth century? Why was the self so important to him as a bastion from which the individual could confront modernity? And what sort of stance did he feel modern Japanese should assume in the face of the "maelstrom" that was swirling around them? In answering these questions, there emerges a clear portrait of someone who consciously assumed a contrarian stance and grappled with the very essence of what it means to become modern. It took courage and ingenuity to offer the vision of society, history, the individual, and community that he embraced. And, while he was neither recognized nor rewarded in his lifetime for what he accomplished, he should be remembered today as someone who reflected deeply on his experiences and his times and contested much of what he was being asked to accept uncritically. In doing this, he embraced a vision of history, society, and the future that marks him as an original and creative thinker, one whose understanding of the nature of the human experience remains vital and alive today.

1

Overview

> [T]he central event of the last century for the majority of the world's population was the intellectual and political awakening of Asia and its emergence from the ruins of both Asian and European empires.
>
> Pankaj Mishra, *From the Ruins of Empire*

History always favors the stories of those larger-than-life figures such as Saigô Takamori, Sakamoto Ryôma, or Fukuzawa Yukichi. But to the extent that the experiences of men and women such as Kinoshita Naoe, Yokoyama Gennosuke, Fukuda Hideko, Taoka Reiun, Ishikawa Sanshirô, Ogawa Usen, and Takamure Itsue are overlooked, the historical record will remain incomplete. Aren't the stories of men and women who lived through Japan's most tumultuous years, who fought for things they believed in, and who wrote about what they were experiencing as Japan plunged into its encounter with modernity, of equal importance? Yet all too often these voices, these "fragmented inner narratives," are overlooked when the past is reconstructed. If we are not quite sure where to situate people, unfortunately, we often leave their stories out of the historical record altogether.

Of course history always has its master narratives to fall back on, and clearly the most compelling one for modern Japan is the story of how modernity itself was experienced. In the history of nonwestern societies, however, it is almost always the western version of modernity that is assumed to be operative, and historical narratives that veer away from this assumption are all too easily overlooked. But, as Pankaj Mishra reminds us, sometimes it is the stories of the individuals who fall outside the mainstream that matter the most, for in them "the lines of history converge"; yet it is their stories—and Mishra concentrates on figures such as Jamal al-Din al-Afghani (1838–97), Liang Qichao (1873–1929), and Rabindranath Tagore (1861–1941)—that offer "a broad view of how some of the most intelligent and sensitive people in the East responded to the encroachment of the West (both physical and intellectual) on their societies."[1] Taoka Reiun's story must also be read in the context of people like this because he, too, searched, wandered, and explored the intellectual and philosophical landscape around him while struggling to make sense of his world. However, as a consequence of his wanderings—intellectual and spiritual, as well as physical—he has too often been relegated to the margins of history as a "forgotten thinker" or an "antimodernist."[2]

Writing about Japanese history in this pivotal late-nineteenth- and early-twentieth-century period, Sho Konishi makes the important observation that the western version of modernity had become "solidified as the master narrative for . . . modern Japan" and that "the people, thoughts, and practices that do not fit this logic have often been forgotten or categorized as products of anti-modern, nativist counter-urges against the Western gaze."[3] Konishi would argue for replacing that master narrative with "a view of modern global history . . . [that incorporates] simultaneously existing, multiple imagined and lived ideas of progress, or 'modernities' absent [any] teleological and hierarchical ordering" of them. Simply put, these "modernities" are, in Konishi's words, "the ways in which progress and civilization have been imagined and lived," and these are precisely the kinds of modernities that most interested Taoka Reiun.[4] Reiun's journey reminds us that there never was a single way to imagine the experience of becoming modern; his world was replete with rich alternatives, and he relished exploring them. When at times he wrote as a pan-Asianist, he was challenging the intellectual legitimacy of western hegemonic discourses. As Cemil Aydin notes, pan-Asianists, like pan-Islamicists, were modernists who believed in the power of globalization but could not accept the notion that the "more imperialistic, aggressive and racially and religiously exclusive" West had anything to do with their own "racial or religious inferiority." Rather, "The flexibility of the concepts of Asian, Eastern, and Islamic civilizations . . . allowed non-Western intellectuals to inject their own visions and subjectivity into these notions of European provenance."[5] Part of Reiun's way of injecting his own vision and subjectivity into this discourse was to engage issues that were relevant to all of humanity, not just the citizens of a single nation-state.

The arguments of Mishra, Aydin, and Konishi converge to offer a valuable perspective on Japanese writers and critics during the late nineteenth and early twentieth centuries who harbored a vision of how to realize a modern society based on paradigms other than the dominant western one. As members of a loose confederation of like-minded people, they shared certain values and visions of the future. Like many of them, Taoka Reiun developed a multifaceted view of history and society, one that took the past into consideration but also envisioned rich possibilities for a future in which individuals—both men and women—could live cooperatively and independently in an emerging global

Figure 1.1. Taoka Reiun. Photo courtesy of Nishida Masaru

society. While he saw the nineteenth-century relationship between the West and non-West as characterized by conflict, expropriation, and domination, Reiun pinned his hopes for the future on a new syncretic global order—universalist yet respectful of local cultures and needs. Precisely how he arrived at the various positions he took along the way is the main subject of this book, but we can begin by noting something about his background.

Reiun and Kôtoku Shûsui

Reiun was born in what is now Kôchi City on the island of Shikoku on November 21, 1870. Within a few years of his birth, his hometown would become the political and intellectual center of the popular rights movement, and this affected his upbringing and early education a great deal. In this way, he was like his close friend, the socialist-anarchist Kôtoku Shûsui (1871–1911) with whom he was visiting nearly forty years later, in late May 1910, when Kôtoku was arrested for high treason and subsequently hanged. At the time, Reiun was visiting the Yugawara hot springs in Kanagawa Prefecture, overlooking Sagami Bay, where he was seeking relief from the spinal meningitis that would soon end his life prematurely. He had been staying at the Nakanishi Inn with his friend Masaoka Geiyô (1881–1920) but decided to move to the Amanoya Inn where Kôtoku was hard at work on what would turn out to be his final manuscript, *Kirisuto massatsu ron* (On the obliteration of Christ). Also needing some solitude in order to finish some of his own writing projects, Reiun wound up in a room next to Kôtoku's, and the two visited often. It was in early June (Reiun recalls it as the third, but it was probably the first) that Kôtoku decided to get up early and board a train for the three-hour trip to Tokyo to speak with his editors. While waiting for a rickshaw to pick him up at the inn, he sat in Reiun's room and chatted. He left a little later, but at the station he encountered officials from the prosecutor's office in Tokyo who brought him back to Yugawara where he was held for interrogation at the local jail. Soon a Kanagawa police officer and a couple of local policemen showed up at the inn and asked Reiun to accompany them to the station for questioning as well; once there he was put in a room by himself. It was an early summer day with clear skies, and he could hear the croaking of frogs outside.

After some time, he was finally asked a few questions and then released. He asked to speak to Kôtoku before leaving, but his request was denied. As he was about to depart, however, he heard Kôtoku call out "Sayônara" from the rear of the station. He did not know that this would be the last word he would ever hear his friend utter. Kôtoku was tried in secret and hanged along with ten others due to his affiliation with an anarchist plot to assassinate the Meiji emperor.[6]

Kôtoku and Reiun were similar in many respects but also different. Kôtoku was an important figure of the Left in late Meiji Japan, a socialist who later embraced anarchism. A veteran of the popular rights movement as a young boy, he joined with Sakai Toshihiko (1870–1933)—with whom he would later translate the *Communist Manifesto* into Japanese—Abe Isô (1865–1939), and Kinoshita Naoe (1869–1937), the latter two having come to socialism through the Christian socialist movement, to form the Heiminsha (Commoner Association) in 1903 so that he could publish an antiwar newspaper opposing the Russo-Japanese War. This came on the heels of Kôtoku joining with many of these same people to form Japan's first Socialist Democratic Party in 1901, although the government promptly dissolved it hours after it was formed. Even though Reiun himself was neither opposed to the war with Russia at that time (he later admitted that he had been shortsighted) nor formally affiliated with any of the early socialist groups, he nevertheless considered himself a socialist. As Kôtoku's friend, he contributed articles to the *Heimin shinbun* in support of the antiwar cause, and he regularly associated with people in both the socialist and antiwar movements.

Reiun remained a maverick, though, insistent on going his own way. As his friend the writer Tokuda Shûsei characterized him in a foreword he wrote for Reiun's autobiography, "He was definitely a one-of-a-kind personality.

On the one hand, he possessed a heart like no other; on the other, in an age governed by an intense revolutionary spirit, he was a maverick. He was a devoted reader, a serious and sincere explorer in the world of ideas, and he remained throughout his life a fierce critic who called for the destruction of the existing system and its replacement with a [universal] humanist society (人類社会)."[7] Since both Kôtoku and Reiun were from the same part of Japan, the former feudal domain of Tosa—which was the birthplace of the popular rights movement—they shared the rebellious spirit for which that region is renowned. They both lost their fathers early, Kôtoku only a year after he was born, Reiun when he was in high school. Raised as a true child of the popular rights movement, Kôtoku left home at age seventeen and the next year moved into the home of Nakae Chômin, a leading proponent of natural rights theory, and was his student for the next five years.[8] Kôtoku said of his early years:

> I was born in Tosa and thus from earliest childhood became fascinated by the doctrines of liberty and equality. I felt the deepest grief as I witnessed the post-Restoration downfall of the fortunes of my family and relatives. The lack of funds for education was mortifying for me; I felt this to be an injustice of fate. Among the books I read were Mencius, the histories of European revolutions, [Nakae] Chômin's *San suijin keirin mondô* [A Discourse by Three Drunkards on Government], Henry George's *Social Problems* and *Progress and Poverty*. These are the origins of my becoming an ardent democrat and going on to develop a deep interest in social problems.[9]

Reiun had also been deeply affected by the popular rights movement, and he, too, had read his Locke, Mill, and Rousseau. But he claimed that he lacked the character to be a real socialist like Kôtoku. Somewhat tongue-in-cheek, he commented in his autobiography:

> My socialism, if we have to call it that, was extremely simple: sympathy for the poor and nothing more. As far as breaking down capitalism and analyzing it from an economic perspective, that just wasn't me. Resistance to the powerful, sympathy for the weak: this was the cornerstone of my thought. If I learned anything from socialism, it wasn't from Karl Marx or Kropotkin; rather, it came from [writers such as] Victor Hugo and Tolstoy. In other words, my beliefs were not rooted in science so much as in the kind of artistic socialism I absorbed from novels. Kôtoku was more of an orthodox socialist, so he was led naturally to a position against the [Russo-Japanese] war. At that time, I tended more toward a pro-war stance, which is why I say that I really lacked the character to be considered a genuine socialist. However, when Kôtoku founded the *Heimin shinbun* (平民新聞)

out of the courage of his convictions and based on his resolute character, I promised him that I would come up to Tokyo and contribute some articles to help launch his new paper. When I arrived at the editorial offices in the Yûrakuchô area of Tokyo, I not only found him a little less heroic and larger than life than I remembered, but also more inclined toward a puritanical stance. He seemed to be bent on some kind of crusade for moral reform.

The day we met was actually the emperor's birthday, so we had a rare opportunity to spend half a day in the Sukiyabashi area drinking and enjoying ourselves. When it was time to go and we left the restaurant, we could see the glow from a sea of lanterns just off to our right; this was because the foreign minister was hosting a fancy party at his residence.[10]

As the two radical friends step out of a small drinking establishment, noticing over their shoulders the glow of lanterns from a fancy garden party at the foreign minister's residence, it is clear that two different worlds are on display. In one, war is celebrated; in the other, it is something to which a small group of Christians and socialists try to muster opposition, congregating in their small editorial offices crammed with portraits of Karl Marx, Friedrich Engels, William Morris, Emile Zola, August Bebel, and Leo Tolstoy. But clearly, to Reiun, Kôtoku was a man of considerable stature. He had studied hard and displayed the courage of his convictions; he was probably the most articulate and influential left-wing thinker of his day. Comparing himself unfavorably to his friend, Reiun acknowledged his own lack of rigor when it came to the study of socialism. He never took a systematic or scientific approach, he claimed; rather, he was just someone who loved his Tolstoy and his Victor Hugo, someone who always sided with the poor and downtrodden. He was less a student of socialism or anarchism than someone who tried to practice his basic principles in everyday life.

However, there was much more that linked these two young men than separated them, and the irony comes into play at the end of the passage described above in which they are looking over their shoulders at the ostentatious display of a high government official, something neither one of them could endorse. In 1901, when Kôtoku published his first major work on imperialism, *Imperialism: The Monster of the Twentieth Century* (*Nijûseiki no kaibutsu: Teikokushugi*) Reiun reviewed it favorably and wrote that he and Kôtoku shared a distaste for narrow-minded patriotism, militarism, expansionism, and, of course, imperialism itself—finding all these things to be inimical to the interests of the people, as well as antithetical to peace and human morality and dignity.[11] Instead, they favored a more peaceful, global, humanitarian, and egalitarian view of the world. Two years later, in 1903, when Kôtoku published *The Essence of Socialism* (*Shakaishugi shinzui*), Reiun also reviewed it in glowing terms, claiming that it "envisioned a way to realize the highest ideals of which humanity and human nature are capable," and he stated that he would have no problem with following the path it outlined.[12] In this sense, Kôtoku and Reiun were clearly linked by common values and sensibilities, part of that loose association of likeminded people who shared a vision of the future that differed substantially from what a majority of their contemporaries embraced.[13]

Reiun would no doubt be quick to say that both he and Kôtoku acquired their passion for liberty and equality when they were immersed in the popular rights movement as young boys. The cities of Kôchi and Nakamura were places where enthusiasm for individual liberties and natural rights theory ran deep. Between the late 1870s and the early 1880s, these ideas permeated the air they breathed and shaped their ideals and beliefs. But by the end of the 1880s—when Reiun was entering the Chinese Studies Department at Tokyo Imperial University getting ready to launch his career as a literary and social critic in the manner of romantic poet and critic Kitamura Tôkoku (1868–94)—much of the spirit of the popular rights movement had waned and a certain disillusionment had set in.[14] Popular outpourings of political opposition in the early 1880s had been ruthlessly crushed by the government with military force, and leading activists in the movement had either been killed or arrested or had sold out. Backroom deals were made, opposition leaders co-opted, and a new, very conservative constitution was in the works, promulgated or bestowed on Japanese imperial subjects in 1889. It was not what the proponents of "popular rights" had in mind. More drawn to natural rights theory, they hoped to see individual rights and civil liberties become more firmly rooted in their society.

Reiun and many others of his generation were not only familiar with Rousseau, Locke, and Mill, but were conversant with the basic ideas found in socialism and even anarchism as well because, after all, "anarchism, in the first quarter of the 20th century, was the largest anti-systemic movement in almost all parts of the world."[15] Perhaps even more important, "[A]narchism was born of the Western and modern world, yet at the same time it was a denial of these things . . . [for] anarchism was a denial of modernity and Western domination."[16] There can be little doubt that this was a large part of its appeal to individuals like Reiun. Not long before his death in 1912, Reiun wrote in one of the supplements to his autobiography that "freedom has its roots in disorder," and the word he chose for "disorder" was *muchitsujo* (無秩序), a term that suggests how widely vocabulary from the anarchist movement was circulating at that time.[17] In its own way, anarchism, broadly conceived, was turning the modernist project upside down by offering people who cared (or dared) to explore it an alternative way to conceptualize history, progress, modernity, and the West.[18] In Japan, especially in and around the time of the Russo-Japanese War, this dynamic intellectual and discursive community endorsed a kind of antielite idealism that drew many Japanese writers and activists into its fold—as many as six thousand individuals Konishi estimates—sometimes embracing utopian communalism, sometimes Christian ethics, sometimes pacifist antiwar values but generally being attracted to non-state-centered forms of civic engagement.[19] It is often suggested that studying these kinds of communities, with their "distinctive and highly articulated sensibilities, attitudes, and world views," can offer valuable insights into the ways individuals and small groups grappled with the complex forces of political, economic, and social change.[20]

Obviously, Reiun fit into this group very well, for alternative ways of exploring both the past and present were precisely what he was looking for. He began writing and publishing in late 1892, just a few years after he arrived in Tokyo, when he was only twenty-one years old, around the same time that Kôtoku was beginning his career as a journalist. Reiun and his friends in the Chinese Studies Department at Tokyo Imperial University had put together a little journal called *Tôa zeirin* (East Asia Forum) and he published there, as well as in more established outlets such as *Kokumin shinbun*, *Nihonjin*, *Shigai*, and *Shûkyô*. Widely read in literature, philosophy, religion, and Chinese thought, Reiun greatly admired the Upanishads and Vedas, along with the works of romantics like Rousseau, Byron, Carlyle, Schopenhauer, Fichte, Schelling, Emerson, and Thoreau. He was so eclectic that at times it is difficult to pinpoint exactly what it is about his writings that makes them so appealing other than to say that his interests ranged widely and that he was able to generate a picture of history and the world that was radical in its implications. It was radical in the sense that it envisioned substantial human and social transformation, and it moved his readers from the outside to the inside, from the past to the present, and across time and cultures. Given this kind of sweep and movement in his thought, it is not surprising that Reiun's writings have resisted facile categorization.

Becoming a Straggler

Reiun spent most of his career eking out a meager existence, moving from small journal to small journal, taking jobs at newspapers just to pay the bills, and traveling to China to teach Japanese language when other options dwindled. Although he may have fallen outside the intellectual mainstream of the day, Reiun offers something genuinely intriguing precisely because he stands on the margins of discourse. From this vantage point, he was able to come up with some penetrating insights into the world around him. If readers of a biography need to be convinced that the subject had "influence," then clearly, yes, Reiun's writings did have a substantial impact. When he passed away on September 7, 1912, some three hundred writers and critics attended a memorial for him in the Yanaka section of Tokyo the next day. Moreover, when his autobiography, *Sakkiden* (数奇伝), was published in hardbound form, some nineteen fellow critics and friends wrote forewords. On this occasion, his best friend, Shirakawa Riyô, wrote, "*Sakkiden* can never be considered Reiun's story alone. The 'misfortune' of which he wrote was part of a fate in which we all shared, something in which we all secretly took some pride. . . . In other words, Reiun was the representative figure for our group." (*SD*, 447) While he may have been much less a representative figure than a unique one, in terms of stature and widespread impact on his times, he did not rise to the level of a Fukuzawa Yukichi, although this study suggests that in most instances there was more depth and substance to Reiun's commentaries on the world and the times in which he lived than we can find in Fukuzawa. But whether or not we hail him as a representative figure of his day, because he so thoroughly encapsulated all the "twists and turns of a thought process working itself out," his work should be of particular interest to historians.[21]

Disrupted by health and other issues, the trajectory of Reiun's early life and education was far from ordinary. While he eventually did attend the most prestigious educational institution of his day, neither his route there nor his official status at Tokyo Imperial University could be considered the norm for the times. A marked man after his imprisonment for "insulting an official," many of his written works were banned upon publication by the authorities. Moreover, unable to make a living, he had to leave Japan for China on several occasions, an experience that surely transformed his perception of the world. Living a hand-to-mouth existence for most of his life, he died of illness in 1912; in his own words, he was a kind of straggler, a *rakugosha* (落伍者). By this he meant that he was out of step with the times; his literary style, his ideas, his hopes for literature, his way of looking at the world, all of these were "old school" by his own reckoning.[22]

But the content of his ideas was never old-fashioned; he pushed boundaries and got to the heart of what it means to become modern, and in doing so he produced a radical critique of his times. For the most part, he read, thought, and wrote with little concern about being accepted or acknowledged for his beliefs. Perhaps that is why he was always willing to go against the grain and favored contesting modernity rather than accepting it uncritically, as most of his peers were doing at the time. Instead, he immersed himself in ancient Indian and Chinese texts, exploring mysticism, literature, and philosophy, as his way of tackling questions about the modern self and its orientation in the world.

He admired progress and was at times fascinated by technology, but he also saw much to distrust. He did not think the wholesale adoption of western ideas and influences should go uncontested in Japan. He believed that the Vedas, the Upanishads, the *Daodejing*, Zhuangzi, and *Yijing* or *Book of Changes*, not to mention the philosophy of Arthur Schopenhauer (1788–1860), all had something to offer contemporary Japanese. He became convinced that the world would be a better place if more people were willing to explore what was inside them. As a writer who pushed his readers to think about the deeper truths that are invisible to most of us, he was not afraid to take stands that were unpopular.

As a critic, Reiun published thousands of pages of essays, edited compilations of the Chinese classics, published a memoir, and probed an astonishingly broad range of ideas. Mesmerism, hypnotism, the occult, theosophy, and the philosophical writings not only of Schopenhauer but of Plato, the Stoics, Kant, Fichte, Schelling, and Nietzsche, as well as the work of romantic poets such as Byron and Heine, mystics such as Jakob Böhme and Jeanne-Marie Guyon, and, of course, Laozi, Zhuangzi, and esoteric Buddhists. Later Reiun would delve into such books as Eduard von Hartmann's *Philosophy of the Unconscious*, Edward Carpenter's *Civilization: Its Cause and Cure*, Max Nordau's *The Conventional Lies of Our Civilization* and *Degeneration*, Henry Lewis Morgan's *Ancient Society*, Engels's *The Origin of the Family, Private Property and the State*, and August Bebel's *Women and Socialism,* from which he gleaned many ideas about women's liberation and gender equality. As for his personality, although he was small of stature, he was marked by a decided intensity. When he moved to the city of Mito in Ibaraki Prefecture in 1898, his arrival was much anticipated by the other reporters at the *Ibaraki Newspaper* because he had been in the Tokyo literary world for longer than anyone else there. On meeting him for the first time, one colleague described the volatility of the piercing eyes behind his metal-framed glasses yet acknowledged a feeling of comfort while in his presence because of his generous nature and warmheartedness.[23]

Antimodernism

Given his predilection for classical Asian philosophy and his rejection of much that was underlying modern civilization, most Japanese historians consider Reiun to be a *hankindaishugisha* (反近代主義者) or "antimodernist." Ienaga Saburô was probably the first to affix this label to him, which he did as early as 1953 when he published an article in *Rekishigaku kenkyû*, "Historical Reflections on Antimodernism."[24] This categorization is quite understandable, for Reiun portrayed himself this way in his autobiography.

> At that time I embraced the notion of rejecting civilization (*hibunmei*). So-called contemporary civilization represents the development of the human faculty for clever reasoning (*chikô*, 智巧), which I believed had removed human beings from their natural state and forced them to enter upon a life that is morally corrupt and physiologically unwholesome. The philosophy of Laozi and Zhuangzi had provided me with the foundation for this belief. Early on I had been influenced by the philosophical systems of Schopenhauer and [Eduard] von Hartmann as well. However what gave my ideas their concrete form of expression were, among others, Carpenter's attack on modern civilization and Max Nordau's *The Conventional Lies of Our Civilization* and *Degeneration*. My own attack on civilization (*hibunmeiron*) began with the appearance of my flagship journal, *Tenk*o [Heaven's Drum]. (*SD*, 670)

No doubt this is a fair self-assessment, as far as it goes. But one could also argue with equal plausibility that Reiun was so much a part of modernity, the very thing he supposedly opposed, that he was inseparable from it. After all, as Marshall Berman notes, modernists

> are at once at home in this world and at odds with it. . . . [T]hey deplore modernization's betrayal of its own human promise. Modernists demand deeper and more radical renewals: modern men and women must become subjects as well as objects of modernization; they must learn to change the world that is changing them, and to make it their own.[25]

In his eclecticism and contrariness, Reiun was definitely at odds with his times, and he constantly sought, as Berman suggests, those ever "deeper and more radical renewals" in the world around him. Moreover, because of his preoccupation with subjectivity, he clearly wanted his readers to feel that they could become *subjects,* as well as objects, of modernization. He deplored modern civilization's failure to live up to its own promises, and for that he insisted on attacking its underlying premises. He understood that the notion of modernity was not a single, hegemonic entity but one that incorporated a variety of possible trajectories for human history. While he enjoyed looking back to the earliest days of human thought and creativity, back to the days of the Upanishads, the Vedas, and the ancient Chinese philosophy of Laozi and Zhuangzi, it was not out of a nostalgia or a wish to return to a simpler, more primitive past; rather, it was a strategy to find a grounding in which the modern person could become an autonomous individual capable of embracing a productive existence.[26]

In the final pages of his autobiography, Reiun looked back on some of the different discursive spaces he had occupied during his career.

> When it comes to my ideas and outlook, *I was always inclined to go against the grain* and oppose whatever trend was popular at the time. When everyone was enthusiastically embracing western thought, I became a proponent of nationalism. When people favored internationalism, I supported the state. I rejected materialism in favor of spiritualism. While others embraced individualism, I was touting selflessness. When the glitter of modern civilization drew people in, I heralded the value of returning to nature and critiquing civilization. When everyone in the literary world was turning to realism, I called for left-leaning socially conscious literature. Instead of naturalism, which became a major trend, I called for an embrace of the original premises of romanticism. So there may be an element of contradiction in the course of the development of my ideas, but when it comes to opposing whatever the popular trends were, I was remarkably consistent. Whenever I walked past the Imperial Palace, I was the type of patriotic soul who would secretly doff my cap and surreptitiously offer the incumbent a bow. But *if a slight change in my stance* emerged since my younger days, it would have to be a kind of resistance to the oppressive nature of the pseudo patriotism that was laced with a smarmy servility to officialdom. That was basically because it was just part of my nature to refuse to follow the trends that were popular at the time just to go along with everyone else. Instead, *I enjoyed going against the grain and being a contrarian*. I suppose that is why my life and my career were basically so unhappy and unfulfilling. (*SD*, 713–14, italics mine)

At times a master of understatement, what Reiun refers to as a "slight change in my stance" was actually something rather profound, as later chapters will show. As he moved his critique beyond the narrow confines of the literary world to contest the whole idea of modernity, his essays took on a more radical tone. But we cannot fail to notice a striking ambivalence in this passage, as well, when Reiun suggests that, while he might make the occasional outward gesture of respect to the incumbent of the Imperial Palace, it did not necessarily follow that he would turn a blind eye toward the oppressive nature of the modern state. In fact his act of singling out "the oppressive nature of pseudo patriotism" and the "servility to officialdom" that he observed around him certainly lends credence to Nishida's claim that Reiun was no admirer of the monarchy. In his study of antimodernism in America between 1880 and 1920, T. J. Jackson Lears underscores the fact that this kind of ambivalence was not uncommon when individuals grappled with modernity. Someone might become completely caught up in his or her enthusiasm for material progress in one moment while also expressing the most profound doubts and fears about it in the next. Lears goes on to point out that antimodernism "was far more than a response to the effects of market capitalism; it contained a critique of modern culture applicable to all secular, bureaucratic systems whether socialist or capitalist. The antimodern impulse stemmed from revulsion against the process of rationalization first described by Max Weber: the systemic organization of economic life for maximum productivity and of individual life for maximum personal achievement."[27] Reiun harbored similar doubts about the value of an overly rationalized, scientific worldview, and the fact that it was being put forth as a model for Japan to emulate was a cause for even greater concern in his eyes. It pushed him to rail against the whole idea of nineteenth-century western civilization with its emphasis on economic rationalization, narrow utilitarianism, and crass profit seeking.[28]

While it may not be startling news to say that rapid historical change is often accompanied by instability, confusion, and even anomie, the very fact that a critic like Reiun was able to depict himself in his memoir as someone willing to be a maverick and go against the grain, and someone who had to pay the price for this by becoming a "straggler," provides some direct evidence not only for his awareness of what was taking place around him but also for his inclination to reflect on and narrativize his experience. Reiun understood that being a contrarian had its costs, and with many of his books and articles banned or censored, he was forced to choose his words very carefully. That is why, buried inside his sarcastic claim that he was just an ordinary, run of the mill, patriotic citizen who might doff his cap in respect to the occupant of the Imperial Palace, there lurks a determination to mount a firm "resistance to the oppressive nature" of the pseudo patriotism of the modern state.

The few photographs that we have of Reiun highlight his contrarian nature: he appears disgruntled, disheveled, and irritated. He often wrote with a sense of urgency, as though he was agitated, and his criticism could be quite pointed.

The rhetorically contentious stance that he adopted explains why he could write about paying lip service to the monarchy by doffing his cap jauntily as he passed by the palace when he clearly neither trusted nor respected the institution. Heavily influenced by all the Chinese texts that he read, his syntax was hard edged, and his style offered resistance to readers rather than inviting them in. When choosing his Chinese characters—kanji—he always went with the most complex and difficult ones. Especially late in his career, when he came across things he did not like, he "cursed" and "reviled" them. He wrote with a substantial chip on his shoulder and consequently was often vituperative and inflammatory in his tone.

Finding the Self

Recalling Berman's comments on the tendency of modernists to be at odds with their world, one can appreciate that this was the strategy Reiun adopted in order to survive the "maelstrom" or "careering juggernaut" that is modernity. He constantly reminded his readers in the midst of his tirades against the modern condition that there is always value in focusing on the inner self, for that self is a source of freedom and autonomy. "When it came down to it," Reiun wrote, "all I ever really wanted to do was keep the self at the center of all I did. What I valued most was the self, and I couldn't embrace any sort of ideology or theory that would operate as a filter between me and that self" (SD, 662).

This kind of inward turn was a process that had been going on in Europe at least since the age of the romantics, during which nature was hailed as the source of genuine feelings and pure, unmediated experience. But the late nineteenth and early twentieth centuries were requiring something more: the turn inward was now toward a self that lay "outside the circle of the single, unitary identity," a self that is more fragmented, more complex and more multilayered, reflecting the reality that everyday experience had become.[29] By the early twentieth century, older romantic notions about exploring the self were being revisited with a greater intensity and sense of purpose. The stakes were higher now that societies were being profoundly transformed by industrialism and capitalism. As Lears writes, "By the end of the nineteenth century, the self seemed neither independent, nor unified, nor fully conscious, but rather interdependent, discontinuous, divided, and subject to the play of unconscious or inherited impulses."[30]

Reiun saw the modern self in very much the same way, which is precisely why he came to see himself as an outcast, a misfit, and a "straggler." He

Figure 1.2. Reiun (bottom center) in his student days.
Photo courtesy of Nishida Masaru.

intensified this impression in *Sakkiden*, which was serialized in a leading journal as his life was drawing to a close. The title, which can be translated as "A Record of Misfortune," alludes to the "misfortunes" that plagued his short life, and we saw that some of his closest friends believed he was expressing something common to all of their lives when he touched on this theme. But when musing about the reasons why an "ordinary" person such as himself should even be writing an autobiography—he knew that he was no Saint

Augustine or Rousseau—Reiun points out that these modern times were not the age of the hero but rather the age of the ordinary person. Unfortunately, this meant that it was also an age of conformity and mediocrity. It was the age of machines, the age of reducing things to the lowest common denominator in order to assess their value. This was not an age of lofty ideals but one of petty calculations: "It's a paradise for the ordinary man, and that's why Nietzsche had to issue his call for a Superman. [For a critic to] confront times like these is very rare. That is why I don't feel all that guilty about publishing my autobiography; in this age of mediocrity, I believe that an ordinary person like myself has the same right as some larger-than-life hero to tell his story" (SD, 473–75).

More than ushering in some heroic or golden age, Reiun realized that modernity was making promises it could not keep. But it was also creating an age in which there was a place for the story of an ordinary person who goes against the grain and is willing to stand his ground and contest the forces that would obstruct the path to personal freedom. Being a contrarian, though, is rarely a guarantee of popularity or success. Reiun acknowledged as much toward the end of *Sakkiden* where he points to the times when darkness plagued him and he turned to an exploration of his inner self, which may be why he was drawn so strongly to Schopenhauer's works. This darkness continued to haunt him when he was ill and slowly dying. He ruminated about lost love and the way his propensity for fanciful daydreams made it impossible for him to feel at home in the noisy, tumultuous everyday world of this detached, utilitarian, and rationalized modern era. "Distant from that world," he writes:

> I was able to see *my disrupted, fragmented self* and confront it; I was at once like a *first-person observer* and a *third-person observer*. I stood outside myself and could look at my actions objectively as though they were laid out before me on the chopping block. I could criticize my actions and ridicule them; if I felt charged with emotion about what I was seeing, then that third-person perspective allowed me to observe things through cooler, more detached, more intelligent eyes. But I was never able to put everything together and see a complete picture of myself as a single entity. . . . So there were always parts of me that were filled with sadness and loneliness. (SD, 742, italics mine)

Observing a disrupted and fragmented self from a first-person stance, venturing deeply into the self and exploring one's interiority with all its dark places, and then being able to stand back and recapture the whole experience from a third-person stance—these are among the core elements of modern subjectivity. In that sense, for a Japanese writer to be expressing himself this way in 1911 is noteworthy. When he refers to his "first-person stance," his language anticipates contemporary philosopher Charles Taylor's remarks in *Sources of the Self: The Making of Modern Identity* (1989): "What is new in the post-expressivist era is that the domain is within, that is, it is only open to a mode of exploration which involves *the first person stance*. This is what it means to define the voice or impulse as 'inner.'"[31] Reiun clearly wanted his readers to see that his essays were all about ways of exploring interiority and grappling with inner truths and their relationship to the outer world as constituted by family, society, nation, and the global community. He somehow understood that the modern self is something to be conceived of more as process than an entity, and this process is rooted in self-reflexiveness.

At times, though, he would despair whether writing, reflecting, and being a critic were really doing enough. He writes in *Sakkiden*:

I began to feel that making my living by reading books and writing might end up being meaningless. All the elevated discourse in the world is, in the end, an empty exercise that has little to do with actually affecting the lives of real people. The number of people in the world who are starving grows daily, but can philosophy help them fill their empty stomachs? The number of people cast out in the freezing cold these days is also on the rise, but can literature provide them with a single stitch of clothing to help keep them warm? Trying to discuss how we find our pathway to truth, how does that help a starving person?. . . . In the end, aren't ideas simply a form of wordplay? Don't we find in that little dance we do with our written characters something that gives us pleasure but really has little to do with the everyday lives of ordinary people? Isn't it just a luxury we indulge in, something that is hardly necessary for humanity? The law is supposedly a constant, but how does it help alleviate the misery we see right in front of our eyes? Our writing is supposed to be enduring, but do we ever really help a single person in the world in which we live? Right now our country is rife with poor, weak, and discarded citizens, but are they not all our brothers and sisters, part of the same humanity that we all share? Working on behalf of our fellow human beings, isn't that what gives our lives some real meaning? So, when will people like us, who are not making any other real contribution to our fellow human beings who need it the most, throw away our books and get rid of our writing brushes and start doing something real? I think that is when we will be able to see for the first time *a self that has meaning*. (SD, 688, italics mine).

Especially later in his life, when Reiun wrestled with the tension between thought and praxis, he walked a fine line between belief in the value of probing, thinking, and writing and the nagging feeling that there must come a time when individuals have to act, when they must exercise agency in order to bring about historical change. It is natural to suffer doubts about how much good one may be doing in the role of writer or critic, but notice how quickly he directs the narrative back to the topic of looking inward and discovering one's real self. In the end, he wanted to be able to encounter "a self that has meaning," and he was coming to believe during his final years that this meant one had to be an engaged self. If there was one thing that drew him to the world of discourse and kept him in it, surely this was it. There may come a time when action is called for, but before this happens people need to know who they are, and they need to find a firm grounding for their inner selves in concrete social reality.

The Turn Against the Modern is one person's story about coming to terms with modernity and discovering how the modern self is constituted. Individuals face decisions every day about what to do and how to live. Understanding the process of grounding oneself in the world while remaining aware of what is going on in the world outside the self is both a challenge and a worthwhile undertaking. It is easy to assume that this kind of exploration of interiority in the midst of substantial social change never occurred during the prewar period, but Taoka Reiun's story suggests otherwise.

2

Youth and Early Education

> My early youth fell right in the middle of the period when the winds of the popular rights movement whistled and blew like a tornado.... The youth of Tosa approached the theory of popular rights with near religious ardor. It was impossible for young people like myself to avoid becoming caught up in this whirlwind.
>
> Taoka Reiun, *Sakkiden*

Indeed, the winds of the popular rights movement did blow "like a tornado" through Reiun's hometown, Kôchi, and generated a whirlwind whose effects were difficult to escape. The popular rights movement got its start in 1874, rapidly generating notions about individual liberties, natural rights, and the idea of a constitution. Essays by political thinkers such as Locke, Spencer, Mill, and Rousseau were regularly translated and introduced in local newspapers, and the heated discussions that ensued made for very heady times. A young boy during these years, Taoka Reiun could not avoid becoming completely caught up in the spirit and rhetoric of the movement. Reiun was born Taoka Sayôji, the third son of a low-ranking samurai family. He was a small child and was never very healthy; apparently he did not begin to walk until he was more than two years old.[1] For the first seven years of his life, Sayôji lived a sheltered existence as the baby of the family. His weak physical constitution, frequent fainting spells, and bouts of illness undoubtedly contributed to the feeling that he had to be treated with special care. He recalled that "in my early years, my world revolved mainly around the goings-on in the house, and my only real friends were the members of my family."[2] About the time that he was ready to enter elementary school, a fourth son was born, and Reiun went to live in a small cottage nearby with an aunt. This woman, who had served a lady of the Kyoto court before the Restoration, gave him her full attention and more than ample affection, so that far from feeling demoted he felt that his special status in the family was enhanced.[3]

It is difficult to accurately pinpoint the Taoka family's socioeconomic status. Reiun surmised that his great-grandfather was a merchant or businessman and his grandfather a poor farmer. So his was not a family steeped in a rich heritage. But somehow his father had attained *shizoku* (lower ranking) samurai status just before the Meiji Restoration. In the service of a *karô*'s (house elder's) retainer,[4] this gave him "sufficient status to claim the title of *shizoku* and likewise to wear the swords." (SD, 485) Furthermore, the newness of the family's samurai status gave Reiun the best of both worlds, for, although he felt "unequalled pride" in his samurai status, he was not encumbered by it. He notes:

> Our household has no impressive genealogy.... Apparently until my great grandfather's generation we were pure *chônin* [townsmen or merchants] but then in my grandfather's time we became poor peasants. In this respect, it was my father who was the real founder of our household. So there was no false sense of pride in our ancestors or pedigree around the house. Just as the house was new, built by Father with his own hands, in our family there was no dark and brooding past to be concealed and no burdensome family codes and regulations to obstruct or restrict us. Even though my father was appointed to samurai status, since he was only in the service of a lower retainer—more like an employee with a rice allowance as compensation—there was never any question of taking great pride in this or putting on aristocratic airs. The atmosphere in which we were raised was completely open and forthright, without any of the oppression of custom and tradition. (SD, 716–17)

Later Reiun would portray the family as a source of oppression, especially for women, so it is interesting that he feels his upbringing occurred in an open atmosphere free of the oppressive hand of tradition. Reiun recalls his father as a serious person but never one who was obstinate or uncultured. He was active in village affairs, read poetry in his spare time, and enjoyed composing light, humorous essays when time allowed. He helped rebuild the local theater when it burned down, so Reiun had a free pass, one that allowed him to attend performances whenever he wished. Moreover, although he felt that hanging a pawnshop license outside the entryway to their house was something degrading and quite beneath his father, he denied that it pointed to any despicable "*chônin* nature." He defended it as the only way his father could finance the education of his four sons (SD, 730–31). Basically, Reiun's father comes through as a quiet, hardworking, unassuming man who never extolled the virtues of moneymaking or looked down on the poor or less fortunate. A reflexive, inner-directed type, he was always generous and lenient with his children. Reiun contrasted his own impatience and short temper, his dissipation and lack of self-control, with the father he admired (SD, 724–25). Moreover, he believed that the one flaw in his father's character had become the cornerstone of his wayward son's personality. He explained it like this.

Although my father was generous and lenient, I remember hearing my grandmother telling my mother of his tendency to dislike and take no satisfaction in anything done by someone other than himself. For my father, this distrust of anything not done by him became a source of internal fortitude and courage and the basis of his belief in his ability to control his own destiny through diligence and hard work. In me this same quality produced nothing but self-denial, discontent, or self-indulgence. (*SD*, 724–25)

What was an insignificant idiosyncrasy in his father's character, a flaw that was more than balanced by his many virtues, in Reiun's character became the "psychological basis" for his outlook and approach to life. He lamented:

My distrust of everyone, my dissatisfaction with everything, my discontent with the times—can't this all be seen in terms of this character trait . . . which was rooted deep in my being? My lack of religious faith, my unsubmissive nature when it came to politics, my inability to recognize any history outside the immediate present, my unwillingness to recognize any authority outside myself, my belief that originality and creativity can only arise from independent judgments, my belief that freedom can only be found in disorder (*muchitsujo*)—the roots of these ideas, too, can all be traced to this inability to accept the validity of what someone else does.

The self (*ga*, 我) that I established and nurtured, my opting for a path that was contrary to what everyone else accepted, my inability to get close to other people—in short, the essence of my career of misfortune—wasn't this also a product of the same characteristic? (*SD*, 724–25)

What has enduring value, Reiun suggests, is not to be found in what others do or say but in what is rooted in the individual self's own experiences. In his case, it meant being independent and unsubmissive, going against the grain, being a maverick and contrarian, and preferring disorder to an overly bureaucratic and regimented order. Regardless of what Reiun might like us to believe, however, this willfulness and stubborn nature was only one side of his character. He was also an extremely shy, retiring boy. He rarely ventured outside and made friends or played freely with children his own age. As soon as he learned to read, he retreated into the world of books and magazines as often as he could, and this was unquestionably a factor in his later attraction to the literary world.

Reiun attributes his painfully bashful nature to the fact that he was born the third son in the family, which naturally meant that all expectations were that he would be a girl. This left him, he felt, physiologically a male but psychically female in nature. It not only made him timid and shy but accounted for his sentimentality, his ability to empathize, and his general softheartedness. He claimed that he never took part in the kind of mischief young boys traditionally engage in if it involved harm to an animal or even an insect. He offered the view that his attraction to socialism in later years was primarily due to "the sympathy (dôjô, 同情), the compassion I felt growing out of my own weakness, which was easily projected onto the weak and the poor" (SD, 490).[6]

Elementary School

Until 1877, when he entered elementary school, Reiun had led a very sheltered existence, one that reinforced his basic shyness and strengthened his tendency toward introversion. Going to school was when, as he put it, he "first encountered the cold winds of the real world" (SD, 733). On the first day, when his older brothers left him outside his classroom and proceeded to their own, he broke into tears and was unable to last the day. Although he eventually made the adjustment, he recalled with acrimony the experience of being victimized by a bully, which marked his first encounter with the "oppressive side of human nature and the agony it can cause" (SD, 732). There was apparently an older boy in the class who had been demoted and picked on the younger pupils, especially Reiun, who was quite small. Reiun claimed to have been permanently scarred by this experience, which presumably dragged on for some time.

> [A]lthough I may have lacked the courage to resist out in front, inside, where I was so accustomed to having my own way, my reaction was strong. Moreover, the awareness of my powerlessness in this situation added to my discontent. I had to keep the anger and discontent that burned within me locked inside and was unable to express it openly, although all the while I felt this outrageous trampling underfoot of freedom and independence unbearable. That equality and freedom became pillars of my personal philosophy and code of beliefs, and that I always felt a sense of solidarity with the weak and downtrodden, was the result of the bitterness that this experience deeply ingrained in me. (SD, 733)

These tendencies were only strengthened by the experiences he underwent in his early education. Reiun entered the local village elementary school in 1877 but found the ideas and methods of instruction there to be strictly of the old *terakoya* (temple school) variety. He recalled, "Among the teachers, there was not a single one who had received any formal teacher training" (SD,

500). A heavy emphasis on calligraphy stood out in his recollections, perhaps because it caused him considerable difficulty. Otherwise it was standard fare, with Chinese texts introduced in class (but more commonly pursued at the teacher's house after school hours) and later at home with his father. Also, in about his third year, just as a local newspaper, the *Kôchi shinbun* began to be published, his father's younger brother, Kimura Susumu (1843–1901) left a government post, returned to Kôchi, and began to tutor Reiun in English.[7] Although he claimed that learning English was quite painful for him, he apparently gained some ability rather rapidly.

Local organizations that became building blocks for Japan's first political associations were the Risshisha or "Self-Help Societies"; part of their energy went into the establishment of educational institutions that would help prepare future generations to effectively function in the new world of the Meiji era.[8] One school, which was more or less an English academy, was set up in Kôchi under the direction of Kataoka Kenkichi, with the assistance of Baba Tatsui (*SD*, 513). It collapsed shortly thereafter when its founders were arrested and imprisoned in 1877 as a result of their plot to support Saigô Takamori in his rebellion against the government, and it was not reopened until nearly five years later, in May 1882, known then as the Kôchi Kyôritsu Gakkô or "Kôchi Community School." Although working with primary sources in English constituted the basis of the program, according to Reiun the curriculum was more diversified than in its days as strictly a language school, featuring readings in history, geography, and mathematics (*SD*, 516). When Reiun saw a bulletin announcing that works by Mill and Spencer would be used as texts in the top classes, his heart "leapt violently in anticipation." He beseeched his father to let him withdraw from the village elementary school and enter this new, most progressive educational facility (*SD*, 519).

By all accounts it was a stimulating experience for him. The other pupils were basically of middle school age, but Reiun's ability in English was sufficient to allow him to enter at an intermediate level where he found himself amid older boys whose grounding in the Chinese classics and other areas of scholarship far exceeded his own. It may well be that Reiun's proclivity to go against the grain had its roots in his early years in Kôchi, where the influence of political thinkers such as Ueki Emori (1857–92) and Nakae Chômin (1847–1901) was widespread. The students explored the idea of a constitution for modern Japan, introduced the theory of natural rights, and translated original works by such writers as Rousseau and Locke.[9] As noted in the epigraph that opens this chapter, Reiun's youth occurred right in the middle of the period, and he could not help becoming caught up in it (*SD*, 506). In another era, children might have concentrated on swordplay or other games, but in Reiun's Kôchi, the most popular form of play was pretend political discourse. Toward the end of 1881 or early 1882, Reiun joined a branch of one of the many *sha* (political associations) that had sprung up with the growth of the Risshisha in the late 1870s (*SD*, 509). Among other activities, these groups sponsored series of public speeches on relevant topics in which Reiun also participated. Since at that time students were prohibited from taking part in political discussions, rather than labeling themselves accurately, such meetings had to be held under the banner "Discourse on the Arts and Learning" and the like. Reiun recalled his participation in this way.

> Those were the days in which the question of popular rights was in the air, and being discussed openly; so accordingly it was the period in which discussion was most widespread, particularly in the form of speeches, which were the single most popular form of political discussion. Studying and practicing oratorical methods was more or less an essential process for a young person living in Tosa in those days. . . .
>
> Looking back now, I really have to feel ashamed, but even I was infected by the popularity of this kind of activity, and now and then I would even mount the podium and stand before the public. Since students had been prohibited from the outset from participating in political debates and rallies, we invariably would hold our meetings under the banner of discourses on arts and learning. The place was the elementary school's calligraphy room. I guess it was widely recognized that it was an academic discourse in name only, for there were always about three police officials keeping us under surveillance. They would always pull up seats near the podium, set up their official lanterns on their table, and transcribe our speeches. The audience usually numbered about thirty or forty people.
>
> Among those making speeches, I was the very smallest. I was at an age where, when I stepped up on the platform, only my head was visible above the table. And, although literally I was standing up and engaging in the art of public speaking, I really didn't have any orderly pattern of argument hidden away anywhere in my mind, so usually the first thing I said was totally incoherent. Soon I'd be at the point where I had no idea what I'd just said, or what I should say next, and there were instances when I just left the podium in the middle of my talk, completely tongue-tied. Personally, I always felt sorry for those policemen who had to sit there diligently transcribing all this childish nonsense. (*SD*, 511–12)[10]

It is a humorous anecdote but one that reminds us that this was a milieu in which political discourse was not only highly prized but also something subject to close scrutiny by the authorities. Reiun's tendency to identify with the poor and downtrodden, to want to contest things, and to believe in freedom and the importance of individuals being allowed to develop their own abilities—these were all nurtured by the tumultuous years of the popular rights movement.

While there can be no doubt that attending Kyôritsu Gakkô was a valuable experience, in a seeming reversal of priorities, Reiun left the school in the summer of 1883 and accompanied his elder brother to Osaka, where he entered the government-operated Osaka Middle School in September. Directly under the control of the Mombushô (Ministry of Education), this school later became the Dai San Kôtôchûgakkô (Third Higher Middle School) and ultimately the nucleus for Kansai University, established with the aim of competing with Tôdai or Tokyo Imperial University as a top-ranked university. Firmly enmeshed as it was in the emerging nationwide educational system, it represented more or less the opposite extreme from the Kyôritsu Gakkô run by the Risshisha in terms of educational facilities. However, as a "model school" it also represented one of the best educational opportunities available to someone in Reiun's position: "Among the teachers there were people with masters of arts and bachelors of arts earned during study abroad, and there were several graduates of the normal school for middle school teachers. . . . This was something unprecedented in the middle schools of that period" (*SD*, 513).

What prompted Reiun to leave the Kôchi Kyôritsu Gakkô, which he had been so anxious to attend just a year earlier ("I placed all my aspirations on that school and resolved to quit the village elementary school and become a pupil there" [*SD*, 516]) in favor of a government-run school in Osaka? In his autobiography, Reiun linked the move with the Imperial Rescript announcing the plan to establish a constitution, writing:

> The political ardor that had permeated the generation of youth so captivated by the popular rights movement gradually subsided with the Imperial Rescript announcing the establishment of a Diet, and our interests and ambitions began to be diverted into the classrooms and lecture halls. It became the popular thing to do among us young people to leave the village and set out for the capital to acquire more learning. Those who couldn't get permission from their parents took great pride in their willingness to act in emulation of the great Restoration *shishi* and escape from their homes secretly in order to accomplish their goals. (*SD*, 516)

This would suggest that the resolution of the political crisis of 1881 in favor of the oligarchs with the announcement of their intention to inaugurate a constitutional government was a source of disillusionment to the youths who had been politicized by the movement for popular rights.[11] Still to come were the violent political eruptions led by popular rights movement activists against the government in the early 1880s and the conservative bureaucratic reforms of the mid-1880s. But in the meantime, there was a strong sense of anticipation, of a need to prepare for the impending challenge of making the new parliamentary system work, that motivated Japanese youth. As the novelist Tokutomi Rôka had the progressive young teacher Komai Sensei (who somewhat resembles Nakae Chômin) tell Kikuchi Shintarô, the hero of his novel *Footprints in the Snow*:

> Japan won't be able to get by on the platitudes they've fed us with till now. The race will go to the swift, not the empty-headed! The real testing time in politics will come after the Diet gets going in 1890—and everything, not only politics: the more opportunities for the really able. Now is the time for true patriots to prepare themselves, Kikuchi, without counting the cost: and by true patriots, I mean every single loyal citizen in every walk of life who has a mind to serve his country.[12]

It was probably on the basis of a similar belief that Reiun plunged into the available organizational and educational facilities in Kôchi. The best way to continue the spirit of the popular rights movement, then, was to get a good education and be prepared to act as a watchdog to keep the government honest.

What was disillusioning, however, were the intraparty disputes surrounding Itagaki's announcement of his intention to travel abroad and ultimately the vicious interparty dispute that raged between the Liberal Party, or the Jiyûtô and Okuma's Progressive Party, the Kaishintô (*SD*, 516). It may be that the effect of these disputes at the local level so discredited the party movement that the future of Kyôritsu Gakkô was brought into question. The overall atmosphere of the era was even more disillusioning because of what followed. In the early 1880s, a more radical element in the movement emerged and brought the demands of poor people and farmers to bear on the situation, and this led to confrontations with the Meiji government, many of them violent. There were half a dozen of these so-called *gekka-jiken* (violent uprisings), and the government put them all down with force. Pitched battles were followed by arrests, trials, jail sentences, and even executions. Reiun would later tell the story of these "Meiji rebels" in 1909, near the end of his life, in his book *Meiji hanshinden* (Biographies of Meiji Rebels).[13] Whatever the precise circumstances, with one brother studying at a preparatory school in Tokyo and the other at a merchant marine academy in Osaka, and with most of his friends leaving for study elsewhere, it seemed important to Reiun to do likewise. He tells us:

> Ablaze with passion and commitment, I threatened my parents that if they didn't grant me permission, I would set out on my own. My parents strongly believed that I should wait until I was fifteen, but eventually they acquiesced, and I was given permission to accompany my brother and study in Osaka. (*SD* 521)

Osaka Middle School

Such was the spirit with which the twelve-year-old Reiun left home in the summer of 1883. In the company of his older brother, he boarded a steamship sailing for Kobe and embarked on his first journey away from home. The next three years were very significant in Reiun's development. He was to remark later, "Perhaps this was the most pleasant and cheerful period of my entire life" (*SD*, 519).

Circumstances at the school combined to have a very healthy, positive impact on his personality, for he had been painfully shy and not very self-confident as a child. His sheltered upbringing, partially attributable to his weak physical constitution, had done little to provide him with the basic tools necessary for successful social interaction. Although his involvement with the popular rights movement in Kôchi helped crack the shell that encased him, his relative youth (young men in their early twenties also participated in this group) had made him more an observer than a participant. At the Kyôritsu Gakkô, as well, where he was younger than most, he was probably more often in the wings than at center stage.

He entered the Osaka Middle School as a first-year student, but his prior experience at the Kyôritsu Gakkô served him well academically. For example, English, in which he possessed some degree of facility, was taught "from the ABCs" up, and likewise mathematics was still at a fairly rudimentary level, so for Reiun, the curriculum at the Osaka school was, in his own words, "like pulling an empty cart downhill." This did not mean that he was completely unchallenged, however. The teachers were good, and by and large the other students were of high caliber, so Reiun's competitive instincts did not remain completely dormant. He was not at the top of his class; his roommate in the first year, Yamagata Isô, held that honor. (*SD*, 519).[14] But Reiun was usually a close second and was generally well regarded by his classmates for his academic abilities.

Since it was a boarding school, this kind of status carried over into the all-important social life of the dormitory. Reiun tells us that the living quarters were separated into "boys' " and "young men's" dormitories, with the dividing line being age fifteen. Reiun was of course in the boys' dormitory, where the atmosphere was generally warm and supportive. Regulations were lax, and students could freely assemble in each other's rooms for discussion and amusement. Once or twice a week they were allowed to go into town with their spending money to make any necessary purchases. Since academic pressures were not overwhelming, Reiun found that he had a good deal of surplus energy to pour into "social activities," which apparently consisted of pranks and a good deal of schoolboy mischief. In his own words, he became "quite the troublemaker" (*SD*, 521). By all accounts, these early years at Osaka saw a genuine blooming of his previously brooding, introverted personality. He felt that the "shadow of gloom," which had been hanging over him since his early youth, was finally beginning to lift (*SD*, 530–31).

However, this nurturing environment was altered in a way that had near disastrous effects for the young man. At some point during his last year at the middle school, his brother, who was attending a maritime academy, had to leave to spend some time at sea. As a result, Reiun's aunt came from Kôchi so someone would be responsible for him, and he moved out of the dormitory and into a little cottage with her. There was no problem adjusting to this, as he made new friends among the other day students and widened the horizons of his activities by attending poetry sessions with older fellow students, as well as outings to the *rakugo* halls and elsewhere. But when his aunt returned to Kôchi and Reiun moved back into the dorm, because he had reached the statutory age limit, he wasn't allowed to reenter the boys' dormitory where most of his friends were. This rankled him since there were people already in the dorms who had passed the age limit. But because he was coming back after living outside, the school authorities stood their ground.

Bureaucratic Reforms of 1885

While this was a little disappointing, what constituted a more disturbing state of affairs were the changes in dormitory life that grew out of the *kansei-kaikaku* (bureaucratic reforms) of 1885. In preparation for the promulgation of a constitution and the establishment of a parliamentary government, Itô

Hirobumi created a system of peerage and appointed a cabinet as part of a general restructuring of government. Reiun would later consider this move a complete betrayal of the ideals of the Meiji Restoration and for this reason would repeatedly call for a more radical and thoroughgoing revolution. These bureaucratic reforms, carried out in 1885, were not limited to a few changes in functions or titles at the top. They represented a thorough reordering of the bureaucracy down to its lowest levels. For example, Futabatei Shimei (1864–1909), the author of Japan's "first modern novel," became disillusioned and resigned when the nature and goals of the foreign language institute of which he was a member underwent a change and the director was replaced as a part of this reform. It can be effectively argued that this experience played an important role in the creation of his first novel, *Ukigumo*, in which the hero's world collapses when he suddenly loses his minor post in the bureaucracy as a result of the 1885 bureaucratic reforms.[15] But there was really more to it than this. While Futabatei was a student at the Tokyo School of Foreign Languages, learning to read and speak Russian, he was introduced to Russian populist literature as a key component of the program. Therefore, his method of translating the West and its modernity was very different fare from the "civilization and enlightenment" (*bunmei-kaika*) approach that had been common in the previous decade. Futabatei's aim was to give his readers "a new, modern sense of the 'social' as a historically and spatially specific problem in need of a solution" and he sought to evoke in his translations "sympathy and compassion for those of another nation, language, and culture."[16] Moreover, it is probably no coincidence that one of his students, Yokoyama Gennosuke (1871–1915), became one of the first "social scientists" to investigate "social problems" (*shakai-mondai*) in Japan. As we will see, Taoka Reiun shared Yokoyama's concern about the new industrial poor emerging in Japanese cities in the 1890s and referred to him by name in his writings on literature on several occasions.

These reforms had a direct impact on Reiun as a result of the educational philosophy and policies of the new minister of education, Mori Arinori (1847–1889).[17] An enigmatic public figure of the Meiji era who was assassinated in 1889, Mori was described by his contemporary, Okuma Shigenobu, in the following manner.

> As an earnest advocate of national education, he believed in the theory that pupils should be educated for the benefit of the State, and that schools should bring up young men for the sake of the country. In an age when liberty, cosmopolitan civilization and the thought of Mill and Spencer as

well as the doctrines of Christianity were advocated, and when the State was regarded as one of the necessary evils, he devoted himself in his capacity of Minister of Education to manufacturing faithful subjects of the State, and he regarded military education as the best means to that end.[18]

Because Osaka Middle School was a model school directly under the supervision of the Mombushô (Ministry of Education), it was among the first to feel the effects of the new provisions, and the atmosphere of the school changed overnight. Reiun recalled Mori's impact this way.

> His approach to instituting a new education system was extremely high-handed. In his view, the schools were training grounds for the military and each student a potential soldier. His idea of discipline was to oppress the students. Military drills and calisthenics became part of the curriculum, and the dormitories were organized like military barracks. There was roll call every morning and evening, and students were prohibited from entering each other's rooms. . . . Freedom of the dorm residents to come and go was severely restricted, and the dorm supervisors were constantly on the scene, interfering in even the most trifling matters. (SD, 533)

In a word, most of what had made life pleasant for Reiun at the Osaka school was transformed overnight. Surely none of the students was greatly pleased by these kinds of changes, but Reiun must have felt that much of what he was living for was being threatened. Although nothing could be done to alter the situation, Reiun's response was that of a contrarian: he led some of his fellow students in nocturnal mischief to vent their frustration and express their dissatisfaction. For example, after the dorm supervisor had made his rounds to check that everyone was in bed, and went back to his own bed, Reiun and others would run noisily up and down the hall. When the supervisor leapt out of bed to see what was up, they would return to their own beds and feign sleep. Similarly, since he found marching in the military fashion to the sports fields for calisthenics distasteful, Reiun would sometimes duck out of the formation as they marched, counting off in cadence, and spend the afternoon trying to stay out of sight. Apparently he was not overwhelmingly successful since he was frequently caught and disciplined.

The basic form of punishment was to prohibit the student from leaving the dormitory during his free time. This meant that if a student was given a one-day restriction, he would have to go to a small room adjacent to the supervisor's room and stand there every minute that wasn't spent in class or at the dining hall. The maximum amount of restriction time one could accumulate was fifteen days. Anything over that resulted in expulsion. It is an indication of the depth of Reiun's reaction to these changes that he soon accumulated the maximum. He tells us that he managed to avoid expulsion only because summer vacation intervened (*SD*, 533). At this point Reiun returned to Kôchi, with no sense of triumph, for he was seriously ill with a stomach ailment and on the verge of a nervous collapse. He spent the next two years in the prefectural hospital, and following that another year and a half at home recuperating. He lamented in *Sakkiden*, "The *kansei-kaikaku* [bureaucratic reforms] indirectly made me the victim of a serious stomach ailment. From that point on, my life plunged into darkness" (*SD*, 536).

The basis for such a claim lay in circumstances arising from the punishment meted out to Reiun for his mischievous activities, his little acts of resistance. Apparently he became a symbol of resistance to other boys in the dormitory, and since he was prohibited from going outside, they took it upon themselves to secretly supply him with cakes purchased outside, every day. To support Reiun and defy the authorities, students would sneak up the stairs when the supervisor wasn't looking and pass the cakes to him in his little cell. The combination of lack of exercise and too many sweets between meals, coming at a time when he was experiencing stress, left Reiun with a fairly serious stomach disorder. The pressures and frustrations of the last month at school initiated a cycle of frequent regurgitation, probably brought on by nerves. When this nervous illness worsened and he could scarcely keep anything down, he was forced to enter the hospital. Apparently the people in his household did not believe he would be returning from the hospital, indicating that whatever the precise nature of his illness it was indeed serious (*SD*, 555).

Illness

Although our knowledge of Reiun's life between the summer of 1886 and the beginning of 1890 is limited, we know that these were not easy years. The long period of hospitalization led the young Reiun to turn inward again. As a result, the melancholic strains evident in his early youth and his tendency to engage in a brooding kind of introspection came to the fore once more. He lost much of the ground he had gained during his years at Osaka in developing a sense of self-worth and a personality capable of successfully interacting with others. In place of the normal activities that might absorb the energies of a sixteen- or seventeen-year-old boy, the years of isolation left Reiun little choice but to explore his inner self. He felt later that the illness had actually provided him with a valuable lesson in matters connected with interiority.

That is, he realized later that the years of physical incapacity had offered him an opportunity to observe and become aware of his inner self without having to wrestle with the desires that so often plague people and prevent them from attaining such awareness. Therefore, he concluded, "[I]n this sense, physical illness does not mean that the spirit is likewise afflicted. On the contrary, physical illness liberates the spirit from interference by corrupt worldly desires. (*SD*, 555)

But from this we should not conclude that the period of his illness was a time when he could take pleasure in this awareness. Rather, his understanding of the lesson only came later, when he became more directly experienced in confronting the world of the ego and its selfish desires. In the years during which he was sick, he turned inward because the outer world had become "severely oppressive and filled with gloom. . . . I could find nothing in the outer world to stir my heart or motivate my mind. As a result, I had to turn inward and search for something there" (*SD*, 555).

Moreover, all this took place in an atmosphere of confusion and frustration. Anxious to get well again, he became increasingly impatient as time wore on. The feeling that the world was moving on without him, that his friends were pushing on and making their careers while he was languishing, naturally plagued him throughout his illness. At times his impatience and frustration, by affecting his nerves and his whole mind-set, only succeeded in further hindering his recovery. Hence he suffered the confusion and disorientation of having no sense of when, if ever, he would get back on his feet.

In fact Reiun's apprehension about being left behind was not unfounded. Meiji society was very much in flux as the curtain rose on its third decade. The stirrings of what would become vital new forces in journalism, political criticism, literature, and the intellectual life of the nation in general could be felt everywhere. Tokutomi Sohô's enormously popular *The Future of Japan* was published in October 1886, shortly after Reiun entered the hospital, launching its young author on a skyrocketing journalistic career.[19] In the following year Tokutomi established the Min'yûsha publishing house in Tokyo and began publishing the widely read magazine modeled on *The Nation* called *Kokumin no Tomo* (The Nation's Friend),which firmly established him as the most important opinion leader of his day and attracted many young people to him.[20] Futabatei Shimei, for example, turned to fiction from journalism after he quit the foreign language institute following the bureaucratic reforms and published in 1886 the first installment of his novel *Ukigumo*. With the prospect of a new wave of literature on the horizon, there were deep stirrings in the worlds of journalism and literary criticism. Although career opportunities in politics and government had definitely narrowed by this time, the example of Tokutomi and the growth of newspapers and journals meant that Tokyo had lost little of its allure as a place where a young person could make his or her mark.

No wonder, then, that bedridden Taoka Reiun grew impatient and frustrated. Of course, he was probably not completely idle during his illness, but we have no record of what he might have been reading (SD, 560). He did mention that an uncle taught him the fundamentals of haiku composition at this time and that this was one way he passed the hours (SD, 542). His brother in Tokyo also sent him copies of the magazine *Nihonjin*, which was published by the Seikyôsha (another publishing house established to rival Tokutomi's Min'yûsha) beginning in April 1888, and he was aroused by the views he read there. Founded by Miyake Setsurei (1860–1945) and Shiga Shigetaka (1863–1927), it essentially staked out the ground untrammeled by Tokutomi: a brand of cultural nationalism that argued that the rush to embrace westernism would have its costs if indigenous traditions were neglected or ignored.[21] By and large, though, this was an extremely difficult, angst-ridden period for Reiun. His emotional condition suffered a severe shock when, on the first night he returned home from the hospital, his father had a stroke and died the following morning without regaining consciousness. The date was March 20, 1888; Reiun was seventeen years old. He had returned specifically to take part in the festivities honoring his older brother's announcement of betrothal, and after a spirited evening his father fell into a coma from which he never recovered.

Reiun's affection for his father, as noted above, was considerable. Moreover, he saw his father's primary motivation in life as the desire to provide an adequate education for his sons. He had foregone simple pleasures for himself and even pursued what Reiun believed were activities far below his station in order to secure his aim of educating his children. Understandably, these feelings further intensified Reiun's impatience with being sick, generating an urge to prove his worth by fulfilling his father's expectations and acquiring a solid education. Although a full recovery would still take almost another two years, the death of his father, coming in the midst of perhaps Reiun's most vulnerable period, crystallized in the young man an awareness that the time had come to take his life in his own hands and do with it what he could. These experiences had been a sobering confrontation with reality, a painful lesson in the truth that the warmth and security of childhood do not last forever.

Reiun began to approach his illness in terms of "mind over matter" and initiated his own recovery program, which included daily bathing in the cold water of a nearby stream at daybreak. Of this he wrote, "I don't suppose this had much effect on my health, but spiritually I gradually felt my courage and confidence returning. I secretly resolved to go to Tokyo to study." So it was a very circuitous path, but if Reiun were to get back into the race, he needed to catch up with his classmates and friends, most of whom were preparing to enter the university. It was with such a sense of urgency that Reiun left his home in January 1890 and embarked on his first journey to the capital.

Tokyo

Much later, near the end of his life and in the final pages of his autobiography, Reiun reflected on the circuitous route that his education took.

> Sometimes it seems that my conduct strayed from a normal path and was in danger of falling into extreme and erratic patterns, and one would have to say that my academic career in no way resembled anything close to an accepted path. Going back to my elementary school days, I never really completed any formal programs. Just about a year before I was to have graduated, I withdrew in order to get a private education at the community school affiliated with the popular rights movement. But then I left this school, too, after only a year, in order to attend a middle school in Osaka. When I entered the middle school run by the Ministry of Education, I was exposed to a standardized educational curriculum for the first time. Moreover, I was being educated by the most progressive middle-school teachers of the day. But, once again, I had to withdraw from this school, this time for health reasons. More was the pity because I basically had to drop out of school during several of my most important adolescent years.

> And, let's face it, the School of Fisheries from which I eventually graduated was, as its name would suggest, really more of a vocational training program for apprentices; so while it was a certified vocational school within the system, it was really nothing more than a practical training course. So, for someone like myself who had fallen behind in terms of the regular educational system, if I wanted to get back on track and enter a genuine academic program, the best option for me was to try a shortcut by applying to enter the university as a "special student" (*senkasei*). Since I really wanted to get into the best school I could but had these lingering doubts about the worthiness of my academic preparation due to my irregular background, I figured that the path of least resistance was to apply to the undersubscribed Chinese Studies Department as a special student. If you were able to pass a test on a section of *The Analects*, all you had to do was attend lectures

for three years and you could become certified to teach in a middle school without having to pass an examination. So I went for it.

My education, then, from elementary school all the way up through college, was thoroughly and completely irregular. Since my ideas, then, were not backed up by sufficient preparation and I lacked the authority that comes from being solidly grounded in a rigorous curriculum, I tended to fall back on my own views, and sometimes my biases could not help but surface. On the other hand, if we find in my essays some frankness and a bold vision that is not bogged down by pedantry or constricted by superficiality, then maybe this is the gift I received from an unorthodox education. (*SD*, 736–37)

Never having fully succumbed to regimentation in either his intellectual or daily life, Taoka Reiun managed to survive with a capacity for "bold vision" and the "frankness" to express what was on his mind. Moreover, he did what he needed to do. If his education was a bit unorthodox, he nevertheless succeeded in getting himself to Tokyo and into Tokyo Imperial University, the nation's top school, albeit as a "special" student. There he found himself in a marginalized department with marginalized student status, but he was there. This was the heyday of interest in everything western, so few students were drawn to studying the Chinese classics. What he was unable to gain from a broad and deep education, he made up for by falling back on the resources he generated when he was probing his inner depths. The result was that he wrote frankly and without pretension; he wrote from the heart. Nevertheless, he carried with him the burden of a series of sobering experiences that had undoubtedly affected the way he looked at the world. Somewhat disillusioned and hardened, as he prepared to leave his youth behind he was already marked by a maturity beyond his years.

3

"BETTER CONSCIOUSNESS"
SCHOPENHAUER AND THE
SELF IN MODERN JAPAN

The better consciousness in me lifts me into a world where there is no longer personality and causality nor subject and object.

Schopenhauer, Manuscript Remains

A certain wise man in search of immortality, turned his sight inward and saw the self within.

Katha Upanishad

The disciples said to Jesus, "Tell us how our end will be." Jesus said, "Have you discovered the beginning, then, that you now seek the end? For where the beginning is, there the end will be. Blessed are those who will stand at the beginning, and they will come to know the end and will not taste death.

The Gospel According to Thomas

In the whole vast universe there is nothing higher than I. All the worlds have their rest in me, as many pearls on a string.

The Bhagavad Gita

Reiun arrived in Tokyo in January 1890. For the next year and a half he attended the new School of Fisheries and Maritime Life (Suisan Denshujo). It was not an interest in the curriculum that particularly drew Reiun to this school but the fact that he could complete the equivalent of a high school course in only a year and a half. Besides, the new school was soliciting students, and it offered him a pretext for leaving home and journeying to Tokyo (*SD*, 542–43). According to his own account, little of consequence took place during his first year and a half in Tokyo. At school he had no difficulty with the coursework but was inept when it came to practical applications of the subject matter. His scores on the examination prior to graduation were "perfect" on the theoretical side and "zero" on the applied dimension. He claimed that they gave him a token reexamination and passed him "out of pity" (SD, 545–46).¹ Yet his experience at the school served him well, for he took the entrance examinations and was admitted as a special student to Tokyo Bunka Daigaku, later known as Tokyo Imperial University. He began to study there in the fall of 1891 and completed his course in Chinese studies in the summer of 1894. His interest in Asian thought brought him into contact with some other young Chinese studies enthusiasts, who became his lifelong friends: Sasagawa Rimpû (1870–1949), Shirakawa Riyô (1874–1919), and Fujita Kenpô (also Toyohachi, 1869–1929). Along with their poet-friend, Nakano Shôyô (1867–94), who composed in the Chinese style (漢詩), they nicknamed their lodgings "Cave of the Night Demons" (夜鬼窟) and were known for their long nights of intense discussion and drinking. Together they cofounded Reiun's first scholarly journal, *Tôa zeirin* (East Asia Forum) and devoted themselves to the serious study of all things Asian. When Reiun died in Nikkô in 1912, Shirakawa erected a pair of commemorative stone monuments at the Jokôji temple, one to represent his best friend, Reiun, and the other for himself, symbolizing the way the two men had stood side by side in the world as brothers.²

Within a year after he entered Tôdai, during the fall of 1892, Reiun began publishing short pieces in various journals, particularly *Nihonjin*. He was no doubt under the influence of that journal's editor, Miyake Setsurei (1860–1945), who had studied eastern and western thought at Tôdai a few years earlier. Miyake was one of the leading spokespersons for the *kokusui-hozon* (preservation of national essence) movement, which was popular during this period. It had arisen as a counter to Tokutomi Sohô's enthusiastic embrace of the western notion of progress and Herbert Spencer's belief in social Darwinism. Already present in these early essays were the basic elements that shaped the development of Reiun's ideas over the next twenty years: the *kokusui-hozon* brand of nationalism; an interest in Chinese thought, particularly that of Laozi and Zhuangzi; and, finally, his affinity for the ideas of the German philosopher Arthur Schopenhauer. In Schopenhauer's work, Reiun found ideas and a way to think about the self that engaged him for the rest of his life.

The late 1880s were considered a significant transitional period in Japan. As Kenneth B. Pyle describes "Japan's historical predicament":

> Somewhere in the terrain of the late 1880s and early 1890s lies a major watershed in modern Japanese history. On one side lies a Japan occupied

with domestic reform; a curious, self-critical, uncertain Japan; a Japan still in the making, preparing for the future, impelled by a robust and often naïve optimism; above all, an experimental Japan, open to the world, trying new institutions, testing new values, intent on reordering her society and government. On the other side lies a Japan with a renewed sense of order and discipline in her national life; a Japan less tractable, less hospitable to social reform, less tolerant of new values; a self-esteeming Japan, advertising her independence and destiny; above all, a Japan with a heightened sense of her own unity and exclusiveness.[3]

Politically, prior to the mid-1880s Japan was, indeed, looking for appropriate ways to create a more open, participatory society, but this search, in the form of the popular rights movement, was brought to a virtual halt in 1885 through a mixture of brute force and more subtle forms of coercion. In literature, too, writers were exploring new genres and searching for new forms of language with which to express Japan's visions and ideals. Writers and critics could sense that a new phase was on the horizon, but by 1890 only the faintest outlines were discernible. With the collapse of the grand coalition movement (*daidô-danketsu*) among the political parties in 1889, signaling for all intents and purposes the end of the popular rights movement, the idealism generated by that movement was replaced with disillusionment and even cynicism. The Diet, which held its first session in 1890, was viewed as a meaningless show by many young people. Yanagida Izumi, an expert on Meiji literature, describes this period as follows.

> In terms of Meiji history, the period of the Meiji '20s (1887–97) is generally referred to as the *kokusuishugi* era. Japan became materially prosperous, the national state structure was firmly established, and there was a general feeling of security coupled with a growing sense that Japan was beginning to acquire sufficient strength to effectively compete with the West. Some of the confidence in relation to the West that had been lost at the time of the Restoration was recovered, and people were able to assess Japan's strengths, and to examine the traits that had made Japan what is was.

> But if we penetrate this surface a bit and look at what was really going on in society, we find that the people were far from feeling secure; there was a resurgence of reactionary, conservative feelings, and it was clear that the *hanbatsu* system of "rule by clique-based power" rooted in the old feudal domains was not going to be swept aside. There were collisions on vertical fronts between the haves and the have-nots, and the tension level between the government and the people was high. . . . This deep unrest gave rise to much hostile criticism and many acts of resistance.[4]

This criticism, he goes on to point out, is the voice of Meiji youth, the young writers and critics who had been born in the Meiji era.

> Who were they opposing? Their elders, who they believed had lost their progressive spirit and were starting to become complacent. The Meiji Restoration had been a significant transformation. The *shishi*—the loyal patriots—of that period were the young revolutionaries who offered their lives and careers to achieve progress for their nation, their society, and the people. They sought at all costs to build a new Japan that was not submissive to the West. But within ten or fifteen years, they had accomplished most of these aims and were now sitting firmly on the seat of authority, surrounded by a plethora of material things. . . . They gradually lost their progressive spirit. . . . The popular rights movement has posed a significant challenge, but by the 1890s, with a Diet that functioned in name only, scarcely a hint of the great ideals of the Restoration remained and few traces of the revolutionary spirit of the *shishi* could be found anywhere.[5]

This was the dilemma with which Reiun would contend for much of his career: Japan had evinced signs of a progressive spirit when the old feudal order was overthrown, but by the late 1880s what had become of it? The popular rights movement had raised the hopes of his generation, but where was that hope now? How could his generation find its voice and revive the "revolutionary spirit" that had so conspicuously dwindled?

Miyake Setsurei and the Search for Equivalence

Miyake Setsurei, leading thinker and spokesman for the *kokusui-hozon* brand of cultural nationalism to which Reiun was drawn, encouraged his readers to be independent of mind and called upon the Japanese people to become more self-reliant, both collectively and individually. One of the characteristics that made Miyake an appealing figure to the youth of the Meiji period was his image as a fearless and outspoken critic. In the early days of his journal, *Nihonjin*, he would write like this.

> If a country is lacking a spirit of independence and self-reliance, not only will all the other countries inevitably scorn it, but also it will be unable to maintain its own national polity (*kokutai*). Therefore, if we wish to be an independent and self-reliant people beholden to no one, we must cultivate our special heaven-sent gifts and develop our creative capacity so that we do not become mere slavish imitators content to lick up the dregs of others. In other words, if this country wants to preserve its character indefinitely, then the positive aspects of these special attributes must be fostered, and our self-reliance must be preserved.[6]

Miyake is perhaps best known for his articulation of the belief that the Japanese must recognize their weaknesses but at the same time refine and strengthen their positive points in order to make a meaningful and lasting contribution to world civilization. His nationalism was a form of cultural nationalism because he thought in broader terms than just the nation-state, something that Taoka Reiun would also do. Much of his writing was aimed at fostering national pride among the Japanese in order to combat their tendency to feel ashamed or inadequate in the face of western civilization. As Kano Masanao expressed it, the overall significance of the *kokusuishugi* nationalist thinkers lies in their persistent search for a way to nativize the modernization experience so that it would not entail total submission to a foreign culture.[7]

It is not difficult to see the links between a concern for individual identity and a commitment to developing a national or cultural identity. In Reiun's case, his drive to define and assert the individual self can be seen as the underlying force behind his interest in this brand of cultural nationalism. There is clearly a connection between the appeal of such ideas in Japan at this time and the influence of the popular rights movement. Matsuda Michio argues that the introspection and self-reflection that were so characteristic of Meiji nationalism in the later 1880s and early 1890s could not have taken place if the basis for individual self-reflection had not been established by the popular rights movement. Therefore, he singles out the most important feature of that movement for modern Japanese history in this way.

> It was the sudden appearance of the spirit of individualism. It was the awakening of the human spirit. For people who had been treated like animals by the Tokugawa government, it was essential that they recover their basic humanity. Indeed, it was because of this great awakening that the nationalism of the 1890s was possible. . . . I wish to stress the importance of the popular rights movement as preparation for the nationalism of the 1890s.[8]

In other words, without the concern with individual liberty and identity sparked by the popular rights movement, there could not have been the widespread concern for collective identity in the late 1880s. Therefore, Reiun's search for equivalency between the historical experiences of Japan and Europe was clearly rooted in the popular rights movement and was an extension of his interest in the modern self.[9]

That Reiun chose to identify with the *kokusui-hozon* group tells us something about his tendency to go against the grain, as well as his attitudes toward social inequities. After all, the nationalist publications, such as *Nihon* and *Nihonjin*, acted as watchdogs for the interests of the neglected elements in Meiji society, often publishing exposés of living conditions among the poor and downtrodden. In 1888 they participated in exposing the harsh working conditions and maltreatment of laborers at the Takashima Coal Mine.[10] In 1890 *Nihon* ran one of the earliest exposés of living conditions among the poor slum dwellers of Tokyo and Osaka.[11] Both publications tried to demonstrate government culpability, or at least to establish its failure to act positively, as part of their overall attack on government policies. These publications had a radical tinge, which is reflected in the numerous occasions on which the government responded by shutting them down.[12] Rejecting a submissive posture and standing up against injustices in both the domestic and international arenas was important to both Miyake and Reiun, and this was probably an important reason why Reiun was drawn to Miyake in the first place.[13]

Reiun had been reading *Nihonjin* before he arrived in Tokyo, and according to *Sakkiden*, he continued to do so while a student at the School of Fisheries. Presumably, he initiated contact with Miyake and the *Nihonjin* group shortly after he became a student in the Department of Chinese Studies at Tôdai (*SD*, 549). Just at this time, a subtle shift was occurring in Miyake's outlook, which in the end greatly influenced Reiun's development as a thinker and critic.[14] Although Miyake did not want to completely abandon hope for the legacy of popular rights in Japan, the party movement repeatedly revealed its inability to become a genuine force opposed to an oligarchic government. So, in his disillusionment, Miyake began to reduce the domestic political content of his nationalism in favor of a broader, deeper, more philosophical approach. In 1889 he published his synopsis of modern western thought, *Tetsugaku kenteki* (Vignettes in Philosophy), which treated the ideas of Bacon, Hobbes, Locke, Hume, Kant, Fichte, Schelling, and finally Hegel. This was followed in 1892 by the appearance of *Gakan shokei* (我観小景, A Small Portrait of My Views), a book that offered his own view of the universe interwoven with arguments for the fundamental congruence of the ideas of Laozi and Daoism with the philosophical system of Arthur Schopenhauer.[15] By bringing together Schopenhauer and Laozi in order to demonstrate the comparability and equivalency of their ideas, Miyake argued that Schopenhauer's open admiration of eastern thought, particularly that of Buddhism and the Vedas and Upanishads of ancient India, made him an important figure in stimulating western interest in Asian philosophy. The idea behind Miyake's work must have made a particularly strong impression on Reiun, for he subsequently delved deeply into Schopenhauer's thought and consistently sought to demonstrate the basic similarity between this philosophical system and the ideas of Daoist thinkers such as Laozi and Zhuangzi.[16]

Taoka Reiun's Early Essays, 1892-1894

After Reiun graduated from the Department of Chinese Studies in 1894, he joined with his friends and colleagues Sasagawa Rimpû, Shirakawa Riyô, Fujita Kempô, and Nakano Shôyô to form an institute and publish the journal *Tôa Zeirin*, which was devoted to the study and dissemination of information about Asia. In this endeavor, Reiun and his colleagues were emulating Miyake, who had inaugurated a similar journal, *Tôhô kyôkai hôkoku* (Report of the East Asian Society) some years earlier. In fact Miyake endorsed Reiun's project and contributed an article to the first issue.[17] *Tôa Zeirin* lasted for only four issues, but it is worth noting because it clearly reveals how committed Reiun was to trying to realize Miyake's ideal of establishing equivalence between eastern and western philosophy. Reiun may have been following in Miyake's footsteps, but the way he went about selecting the texts on which he would focus, as well as the wide range of readings that he integrated into his overall project, suggests that he was not only unique and insightful but also creative and innovative in framing his arguments.

On "Su Dongpo" and "Zhuangzi's 'Free and Easy Wandering'"

In his autobiography, Reiun recalled the joy he experienced when he published his first essay as a professional critic on the Song dynasty poet Su Dongpo (1037–1101).[18] Indeed, he should have celebrated, for it is a very long, detailed treatment of the poet that takes up almost seventy printed pages in his complete works. Written largely in the Chinese style (*kanbun*), it was published in Taguchi Ukichi's magazine *Shigai* (August 1893) under the title "Sotôba," the Japanese rendering of Su Dongpo's name (SD, 562–67).[19] Although it is a very comprehensive essay on the poet, it does not contain all the references to eastern and western philosophy that would become the hallmark of Reiun's early essays, so, while there will be more to say about this essay momentarily, we should first look at his subsequent essay, "Sôshi no shôyôyû," (On Zhuangzi's "Free and Easy Wandering"), which appeared in *Shûkyô* [Religion] in June 1894. This essay merits close attention for here he delves deeply into Daoist, Indian, and Buddhist thought, as well as Schopenhauer's ideas and the insights of many others. Twenty-five pages in length, it is a substantial essay in which Reiun not only displays a grasp of Zhuangzi's paradoxical style of philosophical inquiry but also makes the case that readers need to appreciate the *Laozi* and Daoist philosophy in general in order to grasp the nuances of Zhuangzi's essays.[20] In order to frame his argument, as any budding researcher would, Reiun opens the first four or five pages of his essay with quotations from Chinese scholars and commentators on "Free and Easy Wandering," such as the eminent Daoist alchemist Tao Hongjing (451–536), the great Buddhist recluse Zhi Daolin (314–66), and Lu Deming (556–627), a Tang dynasty scholar. Also figuring prominently in this part of the essay are the works of Lin Xiyi (1193–1221), the leading Song interpreter of Zhuangzi; Zhang Zai (1020–77), a Northern Song philosopher of yin-yang and *Yijing* studies; and the Southern Song contemporary and rival of Zhu Xi, Lu Xiangshan (1139–92), a scholar influenced by Daoism who founded the school of the "universal mind." Reiun also cites Lin Xizhong (ca. 1628–97) of the Qing dynasty but reserves a special place for the early critic Guo Xiang (ca. 252–312) because of the way he distilled the essence of Zhuangzi's thought into the notion of self-transformation (自得), which incorporated a sense of "spontaneous realization" of the individual by "doing what one has to do." For Guo Xiang, the key was "the perfection of one's nature in the fulfillment of one's duty (任) to society," and by singling his interpretation out, Reiun was displaying a flair for adapting classical Chinese ideas to a contemporary situation in which one must account for both the singular, creative individual and the world, or the social arena, in which he or she must operate.[21]

After opening his essay with this impressive survey of supporting materials and establishing himself as well versed in the existing scholarship on Zhuangzi, Reiun turns to an extensive discussion of Daoism, starting with a small quotation from the first verse of the *Daodejing*, the opening lines of which are so well known: "The Dao that can be talked about is not the true Dao; Names can be named, but not the Eternal Name." But Reiun does not quote these familiar lines, drawing instead on the following ones, which allude to boundaries.

故常無欲以觀其妙/常有欲以觀其徼.

Thus, to be really objectless (無欲) in one's desires is how one observes the mysteries of all things.

While really having desires is how one observes their boundaries.[22]

Objects in the universe have both inner and outer aspects, and both need to be considered. To be *muyoku* (無欲, *wuyu* in Chinese) is to be without the desire to possess and control objects, and this enables one to see their "inner essence," or "the mysteries of all things."[23] There is a certain reciprocity that functions like a "swinging gateway" between these two realms of inner and outer experience: our perceptions shape our thoughts and actions, and they in turn shape our perceptions.[24] According to the *Daodejing*, the humanity's problem begins with "naming" (名) things and thereby discriminating among them.[25] Livia Kohn notes, "Good and bad, joy and anger, right and wrong, liking one and disliking another—these attitudes represent the fundamental error of human existence in the world."[26] To the extent that one insists on fixing and naming phenomena, the deeper understanding of reality will become more elusive. As Ames and Hall see it, "the fluid immediacy of experience precludes the possibility of exhaustive conceptualization," which is precisely what the process of naming brings about.[27]

Below are the six additional quotations from the *Daodejing* in the order in which they appear in Reiun's essay.

> Ch. 13: 吾所以有大患者, 爲吾有身. (Excerpt)
>
> These are a response to the question why should we welcome humiliation or misfortune if it befalls us? The answer given is:
>
> Because our selves are the very source of our misfortune.
>
> If we have no self, how can we experience misfortune?

If the self becomes unencumbered by attachments, if we can rid ourselves of distinctions, then we will not have to worry about misfortune befalling us.[28]

> Ch. 4: 道沖而用之或不盈. 淵兮似萬物之宗. 挫其銳, 解其紛, 和其光, 同其塵. 湛兮似或存. 吾不知誰之子. 象帝之先.
>
> The Dao is like an empty bowl, which in being used, can never be filled up.
>
> Fathomless, it seems to be the origin of all things.
>
> It blunts all sharp edges, it unties all tangles, it harmonizes all lights, and it unites the world into one whole.
>
> Hidden in the deeps, yet it seems to exist forever.
>
> I do not know whose child it is; it seems to be the common ancestor of all, the father of things.[29]

Being very deep, the Dao "prefigures" all things and, "Within the rhythms of life, the swinging gateway opens and novelty emerges spontaneously to revitalize the world."[30]

> Ch. 6: 谷神不死. 是謂玄牝. 玄牝之門, 是謂天地之根. 綿綿若存, 用之不勤.
>
> The spirit of the Fountain dies not.
> It is called Mysterious Feminine.
> The Doorway of the Mysterious Feminine is called the Root of Heaven and Earth.
> Lingering like gossamer, it has only a hint of existence;
> And yet when you draw upon it, it is inexhaustible.[31]

The dark, the feminine, is mysterious, but it is "the root" of existence, and once you draw upon it, the "spirit," the life force that it provides, is inexhaustible.

> Ch. 10: 生之, 畜之. 生而不有, 爲而不恃, 長而不宰. 是謂玄德.
> (Excerpt)
>
> Rear your people! Feed your people!
> Rear them without claiming them for your own!
> Do your work without setting any store by it!
> Be a leader, not a butcher!
> This is called hidden Virtue.[32]

To work and accomplish things without claiming any reward or recognition—this is the challenge to the Sage who would be engaged but never attached to the results of accomplishments.

> Ch. 14: 視之不見, 名曰夷. 聽之不聞, 名曰希. 搏之不得, 名曰微. 此三者不可致詰. 故混而爲一. 其上不皦, 其下不昧. 繩繩不可名, 復歸於無物. 是謂無狀之狀, 無物 之象. 是謂惚恍. 迎之不見其首, 隨之不見其後. (Excerpt)
>
> Look at it but you cannot see it. Its name is *Formless*.
> Listen but you cannot hear it! Its name is *Soundless*.
> Grasp it, but you cannot get it! Its name is *Incorporeal*.
> These three attributes are unfathomable; therefore they fuse into one....
> Confront it and you do not see its face!
> Follow it and you do not see its back![33]

Because by nature the Dao cannot be reduced to the basic categories of cognitive understanding, the Laozi constantly reminds readers that we are dealing here with something beyond the realm of ordinary sensory perception or typical modes of categorization.

Ch. 56: 知者不言, 言者不知. 塞其兌 閉其門 挫其銳 解其紛 和其光 同其塵. 是謂玄同. (Excerpt)

> He who knows does not speak.
> He who speaks does not know.
> Block all the passages!
> Shut all the doors!
> Blunt all edges!
> Untie all tangles!
> Harmonize all lights!
> Unite the world into one whole!
> This is called the Mystical whole.[34]

Again, as in the opening lines of the text, the reader is reminded of the limitations of language and cognitive knowledge for helping people live their everyday lives. That Reiun would end his excursion into the *Daodejing* by returning to this concept of "mystical unity," or the "Mystical whole" (謂玄), shows the value he places on "seeing" that which is not immediately visible to the human eye and of listening when the inner voice speaks; it is clear that the entire theme of uniting everything into one whole is among the things that interest Reiun the most about *Zhuangzi*. He is arguing, as do many of the commentators on the *Zhuangzi*, that in order to interpret this text correctly, one must read it in close connection with the *Daodejing*.

If Reiun's purpose in these opening pages is to demonstrate to the reader his grasp of classical Chinese thought and the broad intellectual context in which it should be read, it is significant that he goes straight to the two canonical Daoist texts. But he does not limit himself to these two; we also find the *Analects* quoted five times and the *Yijing*, the Chinese *Book of Changes*, several times. And, on at least two occasions, quotes appear from Song philosopher Zhou Dunyi's (1017–73) commentary on the principle of the "Supreme Ultimate" (太極), or the "Supreme Polarity," drawn from his essay "Explanations of the *Taiji* Diagram" (*Taijitu shuo*, 太極圖說).[35] From the *Analects*, passages about ren (仁) seem to interest Reiun the most: "Desiring to take his stand, one who is *ren* helps others to take their stand; wanting to realize himself, he helps others realize themselves. Being able to take what is near at hand as an example could perhaps be called the method of *ren*" (6.30), and "The scholar with great aspirations and the person of *ren* will not pursue life at the expense of *ren*" (15.9).[36]

Reiun's essay on Zhuangzi also makes reference to other Chinese thinkers such as the early Daoist Yangzi and some of the better-known classical thinkers such as Mengzi, Mozi, Xunzi, and Wang Yangming. Furthermore, he takes this occasion to introduce his readers to Schopenhauer's thought, setting for himself the task of demonstrating its fundamental congruence with Daoist philosophy. Moreover, he connects Schopenhauer's thought with Plato's notion that the universe consists of eternal, changeless "Forms" or "Ideas" that contain the essence of material things before he moves on to discuss Descartes ("I think, therefore I am"), the Stoics (whose cosmopolitanism sought to unite all human beings), the Epicureans, Spinoza, Leibniz, Kant, Pedro Calderón ("Man's greatest crime is to have been born"), and finally Buddhist texts such as the *Awakening of Faith*, the Diamond Sutra, the Heart Sutra, and the Sutra on Emptiness or Sūnyatā.[37] In this manner, in just a few pages, he takes his readers on a tour of the myriad approaches to human understanding of the world that share in common the importance of looking inward and probing the depths of the human experience.

In the *Awakening of Faith* (起信論), we find a statement to the effect that the mind exists in two aspects: either as the One Mind, or the Absolute (*tathata*, "Suchness"); or in terms of phenomena (*samsara*, "birth and death"), in which all things are differentiated. If one is freed from illusions, then there will be no appearances (*lakshana*) of objects, and things will transcend all attempts at verbalization, description, and conceptualization.[38] Reiun ties these perceptions not only to early Brahmanical traditions and Yogācāra, or "Mind-Only" Buddhism but to Laozi's first stanza about being without desire as well.[39] From the Diamond Sutra, Reiun quotes the lines "when people begin their practice of seeking to attain total Enlightenment, they ought to see, to perceive, to know, to understand, and to realize that all things and all spiritual truths are no-things, and, therefore, they ought not to conceive within their minds any arbitrary conceptions whatsoever."[40] Emptiness is the true nature of reality. Reiun also discusses Buddhist terms such as atman (真我), one's supreme or eternal self, one's natural or given inner self (自性), and satya, the most sacred truth as originally found in the Upanishads (Tat twam asi, or "That Art Thou," which means that the self is coterminus with the ultimate, cosmic reality) and which is also present in Buddhism's Four Noble Truths, as well as in ideas about the Three Realms or Planes of Existence (三界).[41]

Reiun was far from done at this point. While Asian philosophical and religious traditions clearly have much to offer the modern reader, countries and regions are not the most meaningful units here. In western romantic philosophy and literature, Reiun also found a like-mindedness to which he gravitated. After a brief quote from the romantic poet Lord Byron ("The tree of knowledge has been pluck'd—all's known") he continues with two passages from the New Testament, 1 John:15–16:

> [15] Do not love the world or anything in the world. If anyone loves the world, love for the Father is not in them.
>
> [16] For everything in the world—the lust of the flesh, the lust of the eyes, and the pride of life—comes not from the Father but from the world.

and Matthew 16:24–25:

> [24] If any man will come after me, let him deny himself, and take up his cross, and follow me.
>
> [25] For whosoever will save his life shall lose it: and whosoever will lose his life for my sake shall find it.

If John admonishes readers to not love the world, he is speaking as good Daoists do about not attaching oneself to all the desires the world contains—they are not part of a spiritual journey. Accordingly, to speak as Matthew does about denying the self and losing one's life in order to actually find it—this resonated with what Reiun was encountering in Schopenhauer, namely, that the small self, or the "will," has to be "turned," quieted, and ultimately denied; it must be transcended in order for the true self to be uncovered. Reiun concludes his essay with the exhortation, "All phenomena are a product of our subjectivity; people who are confused about this are the sinners; those who become aware of it are gods, they are saints or magi; they are bodhisattvas. Know the one mind!"[42] Plato had seen the inner mind, the soul, as had the Vedantic writers before him; early Christians had sought it out, as had Buddhists.

What stands out among Reiun's perceptions at this time is something that he continued to believe in throughout his career: philosophers in ancient China and India had come to understand some very important principles, including that there is an underlying force in the universe of which human beings are unique in possessing the capacity to come to know. They do this by observing the inner workings of the self and by emptying themselves of desires or ceasing to "attach" to them. Therefore, it made perfect sense for Reiun to quote Zhuangzi (who was actually attributing the words to Liezi列子) to the effect that "Therefore I say, the Perfect Man has no self; the Holy Man has no merit; the Sage has no name."[43] Ego, merit, and fame—these are no more than artificial human constructs; the movement toward perfection is a movement away from these and toward selflessness. As Kohn notes, "Zhuangzi begins with the conviction that human beings do not feel at home in the world," largely because of the workings "of their rationally determined minds." It is up to humans, therefore, to free themselves from all these artificial mental categories and, in effect, "reorganize" their consciousness.[44] Zhuangzi understood that people discover their "true selves" only after they have abandoned the illusion of identity. This is what Reiun—who also never felt at home in his world—found appealing in "Free and Easy Wandering," and he wanted his readers to see how Chinese critics of old, as well as Daoists, Christians, romantics, Schopenhauer, and Buddhists, had all addressed this same point from a variety of perspectives. This is less cultural relativism than an appreciation that certain truths about the human experience are universal and can be shared by all.

It is clear from this essay that Reiun had not only read his Chinese classics and Schopenhauer very carefully but had also understood that Schopenhauer's philosophy, coming through Leibniz and Spinoza as it did, adhered closely to Kant's work because he argued that Kant's "thing-in-itself" was something that *could* in fact be known even though Kant himself did not think so. Kant considered what appeared to the senses, what was knowable, to be "phenomenon," while the unknowable was "noumenon."[45] Schopenhauer created a word for what Kant believed was unknowable, and it was *will*. Quoting Schopenhauer's line "Necessity is the kingdom of nature; freedom is the kingdom grace," Reiun points out that all the Indian philosophers, along with Laozi and Zhuangzi, had addressed this notion of knowing the unknowable, and when Schopenhauer spoke of quieting the power of the *will*, this was his way of revealing this unknowable. For anyone who realized this, it became the ultimate expression of freedom from the power of the will.[46] In a word, the "true self" is essentially selfless, and the individual who has succeeded in quieting the *will* has learned how to live without attaching to everything. As Stephen Cross points out, there is something that "hovers in the background of all [Schopenhauer's] writings . . . from the early *Manuscript Remains* to the essays in *Parerga and Paralipomena*," and this is "the idea of something ultimately real and infinitely desirable that lies beyond the will and stands to it as an opposite pole."[47] Initially, Schopenhauer referred to this "opposite pole" as the "better consciousness," although he would later abandon the term.

It is impressive that the twenty-three-year-old Reiun was capable of such a nuanced appreciation not only of Chinese thought and philosophy but also esoteric Buddhism, as well as western philosophy and religion. There can be little question that this kind of reading project went well beyond what was required for his certification at the Chinese studies program at the university, and it underscores just how dedicated and creative he was in establishing his discursive project. Just some twenty-five years earlier, Schopenhauer himself had updated his "Essay on Sinology"—something with which Reiun was not likely to have been familiar—and demonstrated that, although his knowledge of Daoism was still rather sketchy (though he does, in fact, mention the *Daodejing* by name), he was able to argue that it was fundamentally congruent with Buddhism but had been largely superseded by it.[48] Reiun, who was not willing to accept the notion that becoming modern meant following a western path only, found affirmation for his position in the ideas of the great thinkers in the Asian tradition, and he tried to demonstrate their congruence with the thought of western philosophers who were sufficiently farsighted to be open to these "eastern" teachings.

What is interesting here is the way Reiun consciously constructed the argument that in these ancient texts, as well as in Schopenhauer, not only could one discover something useful for life in Japan of the 1890s, but also one could learn that the greatest hope for the future lay in a world in which the best of Asian and western knowledge could be fused or synthesized into a new universal, global perspective. In this he was not only being creative, but he also exhibited considerable agency in his choice of writers and texts on which to focus his energies. Whether he was fully cognizant of it or not, Reiun was actively engaged in what Akira Iriye calls a "conceptual decentering of the west, as well as a denationalizing of history" as he developed "a conception of the unity of humankind that shared the same aspirations and dilemmas throughout the world."[49] This was both a powerful and an effective way to ground himself in the world of discourse, and while he was not alone in his efforts—there were others in the socialist-anarchist circles, in religion and philosophy, and among seekers of deeper understanding who shared his proclivities—he was unique in the way he articulated his vision.

Bashô

In the essay on Su Dongpo, Reiun was developing his ideas on the nature and role of a great poet. He believed that poets had a special way of perceiving the universe, and this was what made their work so important to humanity. Later he developed these views more fully in his essay on haiku poetry ("Haikai kanken," December 1893) and especially in his study *Bashô* (February 1894).[50]

In a word, it was the poet's capacity for compassion or "sympathy," a favorite term of Schopenhauer's, *Mitleid*, which Reiun rendered as *dôjô* (同情). He quoted with deep approval the Song poet's assertion that wherever he looked throughout this world, he could see no one that he did not love (*SD*, 566–67).

The mark of the great poet for Reiun, then, was the ability to effect direct, intuitive perception, to become free, if only for a moment, from the vicelike grip of the will. The true poet could capture this experience in verse so that it could be rekindled to live again in others. The poet stands with the key to the secrets of the universe in hand, and when speaking conveys pure nature, something for which "clever skills" and logical systems of reasoning are useless.[51] Reiun distinguished this way of the poet from the approach of the modern scientist, who investigates the universe in terms of its various interlocking relationships and presents us with a general outline of how things work that is abstracted from these observations. The poet, by contrast, uses his or her emotions to go directly to the heart of the universe and perceive it simply as it is. For example, Reiun quotes the Byron line "I live not in myself, but I become Portion of that around me, and to me High mountains are a feeling."[52] The "ordinary" separation between the observing subject and its object dissolves, and the poet, the subject, becomes one with the observed object. As Reiun saw it, never was this principle given better expression than by Bashô, who was famous for saying:

> Go to the pine if you want to learn about the pine, or to the bamboo if you want to learn about the bamboo. And in doing so, you must leave your subjective preoccupation with yourself. Otherwise, you impose yourself on the object and do not learn. Your poetry issues of its own accord when you and the object have become one—when you have plunged deep enough into the object to see something like a hidden glimmering there. However well phrased your poetry may be, if your feeling is not natural—if the object and yourself are separate—then your poetry is not true poetry but merely your subjective counterfeit.[53]

Reiun believed that Bashô's ability to view the universe in this way derived largely from his acceptance of death.[54] For Bashô death was a part of life, and so there really was no such thing as death in the universe. For the poet, a person of compassion who has experienced *mono no aware* (the pathos of things), everything becomes a living being, and this is made possible because of the presence of sympathy or compassion in the poet. Reiun identified this kind of compassion in Bashô's poetry as the quality that distinguished it from the poetry of superficial writers who were unable to penetrate the depths of human feeling and therefore could not move their readers.[55] For it is through the mechanism of sympathy or compassion that even the lifeless comes alive to stir our emotions. Therefore, in a verse by Bashô about an old withered tree or dying summer grass we can experience our transient nature and at the same time our oneness with all things.[56]

In reference to the importance of compassion (*dôjô*), Reiun is able to appreciate with Schopenhauer the power of art to liberate us from the slavery of the will. This is because, as a person "loses himself" in perception, he or she becomes a "pure knowing subject" with no sense of the individual self, so that knowledge no longer exists in service of the will.[57] But obviously this can only be a temporary release. Permanent alteration necessitates a means of cultivating that state, and it is here that the idea of *Mitleid*—sympathy or compassion in the sense of "knowledge of the suffering of others"—must come into play. Only action that is rooted in compassion has real moral value.[58]

"Bi to zen" (On Beauty and Goodness)

Reiun's interpretation of Schopenhauer's aesthetics was given more comprehensive treatment in another article published in *Shûkyô* in August 1894, "Bi to Zen" (On Beauty and Goodness).[59] After a lengthy introduction discussing how nature has been a source of solace and comfort for humans that "lulls doubt and destroys sorrow," Reiun takes the reader through quotes from Schiller and Goethe, including the observation, "In true love there remains neither I nor me, mine, to me, thou, thine and the like." This quote is attributed to Jakob Böhme, but it also appears in volume 2 of Schopenhauer's *The World as Will and Representation*, where it is attributed to Madame Guyon and supposedly influenced by the Vedas, although this is unlikely.[60] Reiun follows this with another quote from Schopenhauer stating that "every individual, completely vanishing and reduced to nothing in a boundless world, nevertheless makes himself the centre of the world and considers his own existence and well-being before everything else. In fact, from the natural standpoint, he is ready for this to sacrifice everything else; he is ready to annihilate the world in order to maintain his own self, that drop in the ocean, a little longer."[61] This is human egoism taking hold.

In this essay, Reiun describes humans in terms of organisms equipped with sensory apparatuses designed to receive stimuli from the environment, which serve as signals to initiate action in support of one's life system. Therefore, these external impressions are always received and then processed in terms of what is necessary for the promotion of self-interest. This, then, is how the will is set in motion on a daily basis.[62] But the impressions we receive from art are not in this category. When we contemplate art, there is no sense of gain or loss, so our will is not activated. As a result, without will there is no sense of distinction between subject and object. When we are conscious of the individual self in relation to the object, then we have thoughts in relation to that object, and this gives rise to desire. But if we are without such thoughts, the small self merely becomes a part of the larger, universal self.[63] In this state, humans are spared the pain that arises inevitably from desire, for the latter always imagines that it can find fulfillment, which is only an illusion. Desire is rooted in the future, an unreal time that is always coming. Reality is experienced by people living in the present, and only people who live in the present are really living.[64]

Again, two quotations from the *Laozi* appear, one from chapter 14, from which we saw an excerpt in the essay on Zhuangzi where the Dao was *Formless*, *Soundless*, and *Incorporal*.

視之不見、名曰夷．聽之不聞、名曰希．搏之不得、名曰微．此三者不可致詰．故混而爲一．其上不皦、其下不昧．繩繩不可名、復歸於無物．是謂無狀之狀、無物 之象．是謂惚恍．迎之不見其首、隨之不見其後。執古之道、以御今之有．能知古始、是謂道紀．

These three attributes are unfathomable;
Therefore, they fuse into one.
Its upper side is not right:
Its underside is not dim.
Continually the Unnamable moves on,
Until it returns beyond the realm of things.
We call it the formless Form, the imageless Image.
We call it the indefinable and unimaginable.
Confront it and you do not see its face!
Follow it and you do not see its back!
Yet, equipped with the timeless Dao,
You can harness present realities.
To know the origins is initiation into the Dao.[65]

Initiation into the Dao can open up individuals to a deeper understanding of the present, so that "present realities" can be harnessed; this view was fundamental to Reiun's understanding about what is possible for modern individuals.

The other quotation is an excerpt from chapter 21.

惚兮恍兮、其中有象.　恍兮惚兮、其中有物.　窈兮冥兮、其中有精, 其精甚眞、其中有信

It is a passage that describes the Dao as elusive and evasive.

> Elusive and intangible, yet within it are objects.
> Deep and obscure, yet within it is the life force (精).
> The life force is very real, and within it is certainty.[66]

In this second quote, we find language that captures how elusive and intangible this ancient Way can be, yet it contains an essence, a spirit, or "life force" (精), and it is "very real" or genuine (眞). The verse goes on to say that because it is genuine (眞) one can have belief or "certainty" (信) within it. If such certainty exists, then one can be firmly grounded in reality. The challenge is learning how to uncover this spirit, this "life force," and thereby become connected to a truer, deeper reality.

Reiun's commentary on these two quotations informs us that "this language captures the subjective state of no-self" and that this state was precisely what the philosophers of old sought in their deepest meditations. Simple as it may sound, however, the problem is that we, too, easily forget that we can live in that selfless subjective state—what the contemporary philosopher Milton K. Munitz calls "Boundless Existence"—and instead allow our lives to fall back into the illusion of object-centered, ordinary reality.[67]

As we have seen, Reiun believed that poetry (and art) can play the role of suspending the power of the will so that we can experience life without the impulses, or the desires, that drive our existence. Therefore, he continues his essay with further quotations from the likes of Goethe, Schiller, Milton's *Paradise Lost*, Plato, Byron, Frederick Harrison, Emanuel Swedenborg, and Jakob Böhme, arguing that the selfless state that can be brought on by beholding beauty is nothing less than a path to the "divine," of which human beings have been in pursuit since the beginning of time.[68] From Plato's *Phaedrus* he quotes a passage about the Muses, who, from the time of their birth, need no sustenance; they just sing continually, without food or drink, until they die, and then they ascend to the heavens to entertain the Deities.[69]

Another place to discover the path to oneness is in nature. As Schiller expresses it, "Blessed is the man! Blessed I must praise him, in the quiet of the countryside hall, away from the life confused circles, childish lies on the breast of nature."[70] But the most important way to transcend the small self, the ego, is to be found in the practices of humanity toward other human beings. "All love is compassion (*dôjô*)" he quotes from Schopenhauer. A central teaching of the Upanishads is "Tat Tvam Asi" Thou art that), which basically means that the self is not separable from the ultimate or true reality; they are one and the same. Many religious teachings advocate that if we treat others as we treat ourselves, if we refrain from violence and take measures to reduce suffering in the world, if we avoid egoism and thoughts directed toward revenge, we can naturally cultivate a strong sense of sympathy or compassion. This, Reiun argues, is a principle recognized by philosophers of both East and West, from Plato to the Gospels ("let him deny himself and take up the cross"), and is even found in the Diamond Sutra.[71] As the *Laozi* puts it in chapter 28, this is precisely how one retains one's power, or efficacy (德), and is able to return to the state of a newborn babe whose mind is not yet riddled with distinctions. When the false self is left behind, one returns to a state of true selflessness.[72]

Bryan Magee astutely characterizes this as "practical mysticism," that is, a mysticism based on the understanding—achieved through long and hard inner observation—that everyone shares the same inner experience of will.[73] With what Christopher Janaway refers to as an "intersubjectivity," compassionate individuals are able to "transcend an egocentric standpoint" and treat the suffering of others as their own.[74] If humans are able to leave behind the world of "distinctions," where choice and desires arise, and recognize the unity of all things, they will be able to break the cycle of cause and effect, of karma, and discover that compassion is the key to pure love. *Mitleid*—sympathy or compassion—is therefore the root of all virtue.[75] We will see in greater detail in the next chapter how this concept of sympathy emerges as a cornerstone of Reiun's literary criticism.

"Heinrich Heine"

In the same month that his essay on *Bashô* appeared in Taguchi Ukichi's magazine *Shigai*, Reiun began serializing a five-part essay on the romantic poet Heinrich Heine in *Nihonjin*.[76] A pioneering work in the field of Japanese research on Heine, it is of interest for what it tells us about Reiun. As others have pointed out, the similarities between events in the life of the German poet and those that later befell Reiun, such as misfortune in love, a frustrated revolutionary spirit, and recurring ill health, make this early essay almost prophetic.[77] He saw Heine as having "the most poetic nature among all poets, but because of this, he tasted life's bitterness much more than others." He refers his readers to a passage from Schopenhauer where the philosopher points out, near the end of *The World as Will and Representation*, "The person in whom genius is to be found suffers most of all."[78] A feature of Reiun's treatment of Heine that bears note, however, is his placement of the poet in a stream of resistance to the increasing mechanization of the nineteenth century, which situated him squarely in the company of Schopenhauer and von Hartmann in philosophy and Byron in poetry.[79] In depicting Heine as a restless figure who, discriminated against as a Jew and ultimately pressured into apostasy for the sake of an academic career—in other words, as one who had tasted the bitterness of life—Reiun gave vent to his distaste for modern western civilization, a theme that continued to grow in importance for him. Stimulated but later disillusioned by the July Revolution in France (1830), Heine symbolized to Reiun the spirit of the revolution, doomed to repression by the forces of reaction.[80]

This revolution did not belong solely to the political realm, however; it transgressed the realm of the human spirit, something reflected in Heine's concern with the universal human condition and how easily human existence could be reduced to a series of shallow, empty formalities. Heine sought to counter this emptiness with his poetry of feeling.

> He lived his life for love. He cried for love and laughed over love. He loved man to the point of slighting God: he loved human nature to the point of begrudging this world. He loved freedom so that he was willing to sever his ties with his homeland. He fought for humanity. He wanted to liberate all mankind from the bonds of oppression.[81]

As a poet who could perceive the "human paradox" in its totality, Heine could at times weep openly for mankind, at other times laugh with abandon, and at still other times simply stare in mute wonder and amazement. Nonetheless, he was a fighter; his aim was human liberation. The times called for resistance and contestation; Heine did not shrink from this calling. Not unlike Bashô, he celebrated the joys of human existence without ever denying the pain and sorrow that flow through life and are central to the human experience. More than anything, Heine stood as a comment on his times.

> The nineteenth century is the scientific era, the age of widespread mechanization in which faith gives way to skepticism and low worldly knowledge. Idealism has been replaced by utilitarianism, and the spirit of awe and reverence for great works of art has withered in the face of materialistic scholarship and learning. A scientific outlook has replaced spirituality, and along with this, the world of the true genius and the poet has been forsaken. So the first one to face this nineteenth century, and sense

the discord between materialism and the world of ideals, was Byron, who was stirred by pessimism over the human condition. Next to take up the fight was Heine, but it was a battle he could not win.[82]

Reiun discovered in poets like Byron and Heine a bridge that links ideas found in ancient and contemporary literature and philosophy with a critique of modern civilization. Reiun's praise for and admiration of Heine were based on what the poet stood for: the willingness to do battle in order to see human emotions triumph over the mechanical side of human nature, something that had grown uncontrollably along with modern, utilitarian, and mechanized civilization. For Reiun further testimony of Heine's genius was the fact that, like Byron, he was someone who, at the beginning of the nineteenth century, could perceive accurately what lay ahead in the modern experience, which for Reiun meant a deep dissatisfaction with the antispiritual, materialistic, and mechanistic character of modern western civilization.

"The Position of Eastern Thought in the Nineteenth-Century West"

These early essays tell us a great deal about what Taoka Reiun was reading and thinking about during his college years and beyond, and how he was starting to put ideas from diverse traditions together to generate his critique of the modern. Obviously, he was widely read in the area of western philosophy, and he proved very adept at integrating this reading with his understanding of ancient Chinese thought along with the Upanishads and Vedas. Schopenhauer's works clearly offered him a gateway into a wide variety of readings in European intellectual history, and he was reading Schopenhauer in a careful and dedicated manner at a time when his significance was not yet fully appreciated by most western philosophers. But from Schopenhauer, Reiun gained a grasp of medieval European philosophy, and of how central Descartes was to the western philosophical tradition, as well as an understanding of the revolutionary impact the Enlightenment, especially in the form of Rousseau's thought. But he also demonstrated a capacity to put all these ideas to use in formulating a critique of the world in which he lived. He had read his romantic poets and thinkers, such as Goethe, Carlyle, Fichte, Schelling, Schiller, and Byron, as well as Thoreau and Emerson. And he did not neglect the Greeks either, referring not only to Socrates, Plato, and Aristotle but also to neo-Platonists such as Plotinus, as well as the Stoics and Epicureans. Finally, he had clearly absorbed much about mysticism, referring often to the writings of Böhme, Swedenborg, Mme. Guyon, Sebastian Franck, Meister Eckhart, and so on. Schopenhauer's work may have introduced him to many of these intellectual currents, but if so it is an indication of how closely he was reading the philosopher and how willing he was to follow Schopenhauer's leads. All in all, it was an impressive reading program for a young Japanese critic in his early twenties, one that required not only intelligence and creativity but a great deal of initiative to bring all of these voices and texts together in order to construct his own worldview and articulate his vision.

But, as impressive as these early essays are, in December 1894 Reiun published an even more remarkable essay on what he perceived as the most recent and meaningful trends in nineteenth-century western thought, trends that seemed to be reorienting European thought in a new direction. His goal was to alert his readers to this fact and make them appreciate more fully the value of Asian thought in the context of global intellectual history. A tour de force, "Jûkyûseiki ni okeru Tôyô no shisô" is intriguing for what it reveals about how well informed Reiun had become about current intellectual trends in Europe and America.[83] Ever on the alert for positive assessments of Asian traditions that could be used to balance all the praise being heaped on the accomplishments of modern western civilization, Reiun discovered the work of western writers and thinkers who were part of a strong reaction, fueled by romanticism, against materialism and positivism in early-nineteenth-century Europe. In the inaugural issue of his journal *Tôa Zeirin* he asked, "How can inhabitants of an Asian nation, who have been so affected by the achievements of Asian civilization, be so indifferent and uninterested in this vast region stretching from the Himalayas to the Pacific Ocean?"[84] After tracing the impact of eastern thought on many European thinkers, he concluded on a note that would be amplified in subsequent periods: "People often say that the nineteenth century is the age of conflict between eastern and western civilizations: the materialistic civilization of the West is being imported by the East, while the spiritualistic civilization of the East is pouring into Europe. So won't we see with the coming of the twentieth century the rise of a new civilization based on the total synthesis of eastern and western civilization, which will permeate the entire globe?"[85] Here is a strong assertion of the value of resisting the intrusion of western culture by strengthening the consciousness of Asia's rich cultural heritage, but with the ultimate goal of creating a new civilization out of a fusion of the two.

Although "Jûkyûseiki ni okeru Tôyô no shisô" is a relatively short article, occupying fewer than ten pages in Reiun's complete works, it is a virtual catalog of all the recent events that were milestones in the introduction of Asian thought into the nineteenth-century West. As he expresses it:

So far, the intercourse between East and West has been little more than the West taking advantage of the easygoing and generous nature of Asians for its own material gain. . . .[But] over time, as knowledge of the East has spread more widely, the attraction has gradually shifted toward the metaphysical and spiritual realms. At the very outset of the nineteenth century, the famous French traveler Anquetil-Duperron, who had earlier translated the classic Zoroastrian text the *Zend-Avesta*, published in 1801 a translation from the Persian into Latin of the Indian classic text the Upanishads. Relying on a difficult and fragmentary text that Dara Shukoh had translated from the Sanskrit into Persian, Anquetil-Duperron managed to produce a readable Latin text that successfully transmitted the core ideas of the Upanishads. By rendering the text into Latin rather than French (there was a French version but it was never published), Anquetil achieved the widest distribution of these ideas throughout Europe, something that enabled its deep and lasting impact on the European mind, especially in the field of philosophy.[86]

This "deep and lasting impact" to which Reiun alludes is, of course, a reference to how significantly Abraham-Hyacinthe Anquetil-Duperron's translation affected Schopenhauer's major work, *The World as Will and Representation*, which had appeared as early as 1818 but only became widely appreciated after 1860. With interest in Schopenhauer on the rise, Reiun was starting to see a profound shift in the degree and direction of western interest in Asia.

Although we might well recognize the appearance of Schopenhauer's philosophy as the first shimmering light of mysticism's dawn, Mr. Schopenhauer was able to do little more than initiate the process. We know that in his later years, Mr. Schopenhauer had begun to conduct experiments with mesmerism; we can only wonder what scholarly achievements he would have produced had he been granted a few more years of life. At any rate, the late nineteenth century clearly witnessed a strong reaction against materialism everywhere, which probably reached its peak at this time. People were evidently weary of skeptical thought that could offer no solace. They turned instead toward mystical and spiritual views. . . . This phenomenon resulted from increased contact between India and the West, and a growing interest among westerners in things Asian. This interest was facilitated by the founding of the Royal Asiatic Society in London (1823) and its rapid growth under the dynamic leadership of [Thomas] Colebrooke. . . . Further, Max Müller began publishing his multivolume set of translations, *The Sacred Books of the East*, containing the classic texts from Asia's leading religious traditions. Following in rapid succession, Arnold published his *The Light of Asia*, [and] Sinnett his *Esoteric Buddhism*, so that the European mind was soon inundated with impressions of eastern mystical thought.

Moreover, in 1875 we have the founding of the Theosophical Society in New York, followed by the creation of a Madras branch in India in 1880. Soon there radiated forth some 400 branches (175 in India, 89 in the United States, and 70 in Europe) of this organization, the purpose of which was to disseminate information on eastern thought and to study seriously the principles of esoteric knowledge. So, in effect, this, too, constituted a frontal assault on European materialism. There were allies in this campaign, such as the followers of [Emanuel] Swedenborg and members of spiritualist groups who joined the chorus denouncing materialism. Their combined force was starting to change the face of European thought and religion. Moreover, in 1889, a major scholarly conference was held in Paris to assess the impact of eastern philosophy on European civilization, which provides further evidence for the force behind this powerful wave.[87] Even such a prominent voice as that of the leading spokesman for the realistic novel [Émile] Zola could say:

The current trend is definitely in the direction of a return to mysticism. In a tumultuous century such as the present one, in which so much has been destroyed, this sudden upsurge in faith is surprising. How do we explain such a current? Science, which was supposed to replace religion, was unable to deliver on its promises. It was only natural that disaffected people would turn toward religion.

Likewise, [Charles Jean Marie] Letourneau comments that:

In the west, the emphasis is clearly on material progress while in the east, by contrast, the emphasis is on spiritual enlightenment. Consequently, they are rich in ideals, while we excel in commodities. Their spirituality cools the friction generated by material progress, though it is insufficient to douse the flame entirely.[88]

This is an impressive catalog of landmark events in the history of the diffusion of ideas from East to West, the likes of which will not be seen until 1950 when Raymond Schwab published *La Renaissance Orientale*. It is worthwhile to break down some of these epic moments to which Reiun is pointing such as the founding of organizations like the Theosophical Society and the Royal Asiatic Society, Thomas Colebrooke's role in transmitting Indian thought to Europe, the popularization of Buddhist ideas by Alfred P. Sinnett, and many more. While not an exhaustive list, I will highlight below several things that Reiun stressed in his article.

The Theosophical Society

The Theosophical Society was founded in 1875 by Madame Helena Petrova Blavatsky (1831–91) for the purpose of exploring spirituality and the occult. The organization is much maligned today, but it did have a very significant impact in its day. Her book, *The Secret Doctrine* (1888), introduced to European readers such unfamiliar Buddhist concepts as māyā, karma, reincarnation, and meditation. Blavatsky and her society popularized the idea of an ancient universal truth underlying all things that could be found in the teachings of Buddhism, as well as transmitted by people of insight such as herself.

After its founding in 1875, the Theosophical Society grew rapidly, with branches appearing all over India, Ceylon, America, and Europe. Calling for a universal brotherhood without the distinctions of race, creed, sex, caste, or color, it was dedicated to the study of ancient religions, especially Buddhism.[89] Reiun considered the society to be a sign of a burgeoning western interest in Asian philosophy and mysticism. Mme. Blavatsky herself had even traveled to Ceylon, where she formally studied Theravada Buddhism. Stephen Batchelor reminds us, "However eccentric and dated the ideas of the Theosophical Society may appear today, in the first decades of its existence they attracted an enormous and respectable following."[90] He goes on to describe a lecture by Annie Besant in 1911 at the Sorbonne where more than four thousand people were packed into an amphitheater and many more had to be turned away.[91] Also, he notes, "The composer Schoenberg and the painters Kandinsky and Mondrian were all card-carrying Theosophists."[92] Rudolf Steiner (1861–1925), the holistic educator and student of esoteric traditions, was a Theosophist for a time, as was the great Irish poet William Butler Yeats, who joined the Theosophical Society first in Ireland in 1885 and later in London again; he remained attracted to the occult for many years thereafter.[93] He wrote to a friend in 1892 that "the mystical life is the centre of all that I do & all that I think & all that I write. It holds to my work the same relation that the philosophy of Godwin held to the work of Shelley & I have all-ways considered myself a voice of what I believe to be a greater renaissance—the revolt of the soul against the intellect—now beginning in the world."[94] The importance of the mystical life, the *atman*, the soul, and the place of the higher self among spiritual seekers—these were among the teachings that Reiun believed eastern philosophy could offer the world, and the Theosophical Society was doing its part in spreading the word.

Alfred Percy Sinnett (1840-1921)

Reiun also noted the significance of Alfred Percy Sinnett, who worked closely with the Theosophists. His *Esoteric Buddhism* (1883) was organized around the principle that every major religion has its esoteric teachings, which are kept hidden from all but the initiates. In the case of Buddhism, these secret teachings derived from the Brahmanical teachings that had been around for a very long time, even before the Buddha's birth. Sinnett writes:

> This secret knowledge, in reality, long antedated the passage through earth-life of Gautama Buddha. Brahmanical philosophy, in ages before Buddha, embodies the identical doctrine which may now be described as Esoteric Buddhism. Its outlines had indeed been blurred, its scientific form partially confused, but the general body of knowledge was in possession of a select few before Buddha came to deal with it. Buddha, however, undertook the task of revising and refreshing the esoteric science of the inner circle of initiates, as well as the morality of the outer world.[95]

Since he had studied the Vedas and Upanishads, Reiun was probably well aware of this, but he was pleased to underscore its significance in his essay. Sinnett elaborated on the secret nature of these doctrines in his other popular book, *The Occult World* (1888). He writes:

> [M]odern metaphysics, and to a large extent modern physical science, have been groping for centuries blindly after knowledge which occult philosophy has enjoyed in full measure all the while. Owing to a train of fortunate circumstances, I have come to know that this is the case; I have come into some contact with persons who are heirs of a greater knowledge concerning the mysteries of Nature and humanity than modern culture has yet evolved; and my present wish is to sketch the outlines of this knowledge, to record with exactitude the experimental proofs I have obtained that occult science invests its adepts with a control of natural forces superior to that enjoyed by physicists of the ordinary type, and the grounds there are for bestowing the most respectful consideration on the theories entertained by occult science concerning the constitution and destinies of the human soul.[96]

No doubt there was something about such an antimaterialistic "secret" doctrine that appealed to seekers in the West as well as Reiun.[97]

Sir Edwin Arnold (1832-1904)

Reiun also wanted his readers to appreciate the significance of Sir Edwin Arnold's work, *The Light of Asia*, a long, lyrical poem inspired by the life of the Buddha. Originally published in 1879, it was extraordinarily popular in Europe and America, selling nearly a million copies, and was translated into six languages. "I have put my poem into a Buddhist's mouth," Arnold wrote in the preface, "because to appreciate the spirit of Asiatic thoughts, they should be regarded from the Oriental point of view." And the long poem contains such soaring language as this to describe the Buddha's moment of enlightenment.

> [H]e saw by light which shines beyond our mortal ken
> The line of all his lives in all the worlds,
> Far back and farther back, and farthest yet,
> Five hundred lives and fifty . . . —thus Buddha did behold
> Life's upward steps long-linked, from levels low
> Where breath is base, to higher slopes and higher
> Whereon the ten great Virtues wait to lead
> The climber skyward . . .
> Lo! The Dawn
> Sprang forth with Buddha's Victory! In the East
> Flamed the first fires of beauteous day, poured forth
> Through fleeting folds of Night's black drapery.[98]

With powerful imagery and rhetorical flourishes like this, it is not hard to see how this epic poem had such wide appeal, even though, for the most part, it is forgotten today.

Thomas Colebrooke (1765-1837) and the Royal Asiatic Society

Another text to which Reiun refers in his essay on nineteenth-century thought is *On the Religion and Philosophy of the Hindus* (1858) by Thomas Colebrooke, a young astronomer who went to India at age seventeen, learned Sanskrit, and translated several works into English. One who believed in the value of studying other languages and cultures at a time when most of his countrymen did not, Colebrooke helped found the Royal Asiatic Society and thereby ensured the future of the serious, systematic, and scientific study of other cultures. An essay of his on the Vedas that appeared in the German Asian studies journal, *Asiatick Researches* caught the attention of the young Schopenhauer and helped lead him toward further study.[99] This willingness to learn languages and found institutes and journals for exploring Indian philosophy was something that Reiun respected about these pioneering individuals who were introducing eastern thought to the West.

Eduard von Hartmann (1842-1906)

Likewise, Reiun refers admiringly to Eduard von Hartmann's *The Philosophy of the Unconscious*, an all but forgotten work today but one that was very popular and enjoying its tenth printing in the 1890s. It aimed to bring a rigorous scientific methodology to a philosophical understanding of the unconscious. He considered his own work to be the culmination of Arthur Schopenhauer's pioneering accomplishments in the world of philosophy, only von Hartmann claimed that his work was grounded in modern science. In his own way, von Hartmann was convinced that discovering and exploring the unconscious was another path to "divine inspiration," the "inner light," or "inner intuition," in other words, the mystical experience that religions had long sought.[100]

Arthur Schopenhauer (1788-1860)

Of course, the single most important figure in all of this for Reiun is Arthur Schopenhauer. Although *The World as Will and Representation* (1818, (hereafter *WWR*) was almost completely ignored by philosophers and critics when it first appeared, by the latter half of the 1800s, Schopenhauer's work was gaining a much wider readership. Although he is usually overlooked as a "philosopher of pessimism" in the West today, his work is enjoying a resurgence that has resulted in a burgeoning number of scholarly publications on him over the last twenty-five years.[101] In the preface to the most recent English translation of *WWR* from Cambridge University Press (2010), editor Christopher Janaway characterizes Schopenhauer's place in western thought as follows.

> Schopenhauer is one of the great original writers of the nineteenth century, and a unique voice in the history of thought. His central concept of the will leads him to regard human beings as striving irrationally and suffering in a world that has no purpose, a condition redeemed by the elevation of aesthetic consciousness and finally overcome by the will's self-denial and a mystical vision of the self as one with the world as a whole. He is in some ways the most progressive post-Kantian, an atheist with profound ideas about the human essence and the meaning of existence that point forward to Nietzsche, Freud and existentialism. He was also the first major Western thinker to seek a synthesis with Eastern thought. Yet at the same time he undertakes an ambitious global metaphysics of a conservative, more or less pre-Kantian kind, and is driven by a Platonic vision of escape from empirical reality into a realm of higher knowledge.[102]

Clearly, Schopenhauer's contribution to both eastern and western thought is substantial, but for most contemporary readers there is probably not a high degree of familiarity with either his name or his philosophical works. His name may summon up vague images of a philosophy of "pessimism," although few will know exactly what is meant by this term. Arguably, Schopenhauer has been too easily dismissed as a pessimist simply because he argued that the world and the individual subject who imagines it are nothing more than projections of the human mind, simply a part of māyā, "dreamlike constructions with no basis in reality."[103] Since this perception and the terminology that is used may also bring to mind Buddhism, some readers might make the connection between Schopenhauer's philosophy and the insights of the great Shakyamuni (the Buddha), who lived sometime during the fifth century BCE. Schopenhauer was well aware of a strong correspondence between his doctrines and the Four Noble Truths of Buddhism, which feature the ideas that life inevitably involves suffering, that suffering is caused by desire or cravings, that these cravings can be overcome, and that the elimination of these desires will lead to liberation.[104] In trying to situate concepts like māyā and explain them in the context of western metaphysics, Schopenhauer more than any other writer in the early nineteenth century succeeded in placing some of the core concepts of ancient Indian philosophy, including Buddhism, squarely before European readers for the first time. For this he was highly esteemed by Taoka Reiun, something that should come as no surprise given that, in the early 1890s, Reiun had already authored numerous essays on the topics of mysticism, the sublime, and the quest for deeper truths and philosophical understanding.

If Schopenhauer's name brings to mind neither pessimism nor Buddhism, then perhaps some readers might associate it with a brand of aesthetic theory that places art and music in a philosophically significant category that offers access to the sublime. His influence on figures such as Nietzsche, Wagner, Brahms, Freud, Wittgenstein, Mann, Rilke, Proust, Tolstoy, Borges, Mahler, Langer, and Schönberg is usually mentioned in this context. But other than these three areas, most people do not know a great deal about Schopenhauer, and those who read his work carefully are few. But Taoka Reiun was certainly one who did.

If we want to understand why Schopenhauer held so much appeal for Reiun, we only have to look at the preface to the first edition of *WWR*, where he makes clear the high value he placed on what he knew and understood of eastern philosophy. He explains to his readers what would be helpful to have as background before reading *WWR*, starting, of course with both Kant and Plato.

> Thus, for the purpose of my discussion, I do not presuppose that the reader has a complete knowledge of any philosophy besides that of *Kant*. But if in addition the reader has spent time in the school of the divine *Plato*, then he will be much more prepared for and receptive to what I have to say. And if he has even shared in the blessing of the *Vedas*, which have been made accessible to us through the *Upanishads*, and which to my mind, is the chief advantage of this still-young century enjoys over the previous one (and in fact, I expect the influence of Sanskrit literature to have as profound an effect

on us as the revival of Greek literature had on the fifteenth century)—so, as I was saying, if the reader has also already received and been receptive to the consecration of the Indian wisdom, then he will be in the best position to hear what I have to say to him.[105]

No doubt, this passage was music to Reiun's ears. The appearance in the 1800s of initially fragmentary but later increasingly more complete works on Asian thought struck Schopenhauer as one of the most significant occurrences of the century. He believed, as this passage asserts, that the discovery of Sanskrit literature was likely to spark a renaissance as profound as the impact of Greek literature on the development of western civilization. This was high praise, indeed. In the *WWR* there are at least half a dozen references to the Vedas and Upanishads, and several references to yin-yang thought and the *Yijing* as well.[106] It was just this kind of forceful and articulate insertion of eastern philosophy squarely into the mainstream of the development of western thought that most excited Reiun.

Schopenhauer argued for a direct line of transmission in western philosophy from Plato to Kant. In his appendix to *WWR*, an essay called "Critique of the Kantian Philosophy," Schopenhauer notes that "*Kant's greatest merit is to distinguish between appearance and the thing in itself*—by providing that the *intellect* always stands between us and things, which is why we cannot have cognition of things as they may be in themselves."[107] Kant is famous for having coined the term *thing-in-itself*, and Schopenhauer sought to explain in the same appendix how Plato's ideas and Kant's notion of the thing-in-itself were connected.

> With complete originality and in an entirely novel way, Kant discovered, from a new angle and along a new path, the same truth that Plato tirelessly repeats . . . that the people who are chained firmly in the dark cave would not see either the true, original light, or real things, but rather only the dim light of the fire in the cave and the shadows of the real things that pass by this fire behind their backs: they would think that shadows were reality and true wisdom consisted of determining the succession of the shadows. The same truth, presented in yet another, completely different way, is also a principal doctrine of the Vedas and Puranas; this is the doctrine of māyā, which simply means what Kant called appearance in connection with the thing in itself. . . . Kant not only expressed this same doctrine in a completely new and original manner, but also made it into an established and incontrovertible truth through the calmest and most sober presentation, while both Plato and the Indians only grounded their claims in a general world-view, articulating these claims as direct expressions of

their consciousness, and presenting them more mythically and poetically than clearly and philosophically.[108]

Although Schopenhauer delivers a somewhat backhanded compliment to both "Plato and the Indians," who favor more intuitive, mythic, or poetic modes of expression, we can assume that the main point that grabbed Reiun's attention was Schopenhauer's situating of the Vedas and Upanishads alongside and on an equal footing with two of the greatest names in western philosophy, Plato and Kant. This is clearly what Reiun wanted his readers to see.[109] He could declare that if they wanted "incontrovertible truth" all they had to do was go back to ancient Indian and Chinese thought. It is all there. Plato had first argued for the insubstantial nature of what we see with our eyes: it is no more than shadows flickering on a cave wall compared to the brighter, fuller, and more engaging "complete reality." In this he was little different from the authors of the Vedas and Upanishads, and this validation was very important to Reiun. The question arises, though: what sort of access to Indian and Chinese ideas did Schopenhauer actually have in the early 1800s?

The Role of Anquetil-Duperron (1731-1805)

To answer this question, one has to look back, as Reiun himself did, to the pioneering efforts of the French scholar Abraham-Hyacinthe Anquetil-Duperron, who traveled to India in order to unearth and translate authentic sources from the East and introduce them to the West. For this reason, Reiun spends considerable time discussing Anquetil-Duperron's work, as he was the first person to translate fragments of the Zoroastrian text, the *Zend-Avesta*, and then, following this, fragments from the Upanishads from Persian into Latin. This publication provided European readers with access to the Vedas for the first time. We now can be certain that it was in precisely this format that the young Schopenhauer encountered the Upanishads—or the *Oupnek'hat*, as Anquetil-Duperron rendered it. It was in the winter of 1813–14 in Weimar, presumably at the urging of a young orientalist with whom Goethe was quite familiar, Friedrich Majer (1771–1818). Majer was working with Julius Klaproth (1783–1835), founder of *Asiatisches Magazin*, a journal disseminating information about the East, which appeared only briefly in 1802–3. Schopenhauer borrowed several issues of *Asiatisches Magazin* on December 4, 1813, and studied them carefully for several months, returning them on March 30, 1814. As the scholar Urs App suggests, "[I]f Schopenhauer did not let these two volumes sleep for four months in a corner of his Weimar room we can assume that the *Magazin* also contains his earliest known reading matter in the field of Indian philosophy."[110]

Library records also indicate that he checked out Anquetil-Duperron's translation of the *Oupnek'hat* from the Weimar Library on March 26, 1814, and returned it on May 5.[111] Moreover, in 1815–16 Schopenhauer carefully studied the first nine volumes of *Asiatick Researches*, the journal of a research society of British Sanskrit scholars founded in Bengal in 1784, and took some forty-five pages of notes.[112] Not only did Schopenhauer check out these volumes of *Asiatick Researches*, which contained articles on the *Bhagavad Gita* and Buddhism, but he had also attended classes at Gottingham back in 1811 taught by Professor Arnold Hermann Ludwig Heeren, an Indologist, who gave survey lectures on Chinese history. What Schopenhauer discovered during these years was that much of what he found in the Upanishads matched his own philosophy, which he had derived from Plato and Kant. In fact, he wrote, "I confess that I do not believe that my teaching could ever have come into being before the Upanishads, Plato, and Kant cast their rays simultaneously into one man's mind."[113] Schopenhauer made it clear just how indebted he felt to Asian philosophy, especially the Upanishads, when he wrote, in *Parerga and Paralipomena*:

> The Upanishads are the production of the highest human wisdom and I consider them almost superhuman in conception. The study of the Upanishads has been a source of great inspiration and means of comfort to my soul. From every sentence of the Upanishads deep, original and sublime thoughts arise, and the whole is pervaded by a high and holy and earnest spirit. In the whole world there is no study so beneficial and so elevating as that of the Upanishads. The Upanishads have been the solace of my life and will be the solace of my death.[114]

These powerful words of praise obviously made an indelible impression on Reiun. It is well known that Schopenhauer kept a copy of Anquetil-Duperron's Latin translation of the *Oupnek'hat* open on a nightstand in his study and that he invariably consulted it before sleeping.[115] Based on the Persian translation by Prince Dara Shukoh (1615–59), with its overlay of Sufi mysticism, when it first appeared it "fell on fertile ground in early 19th-century Germany where the writings of Jakob Böhme, Madame Guyon, Plotinus, and Schelling were ardently studied and discussed."[116] The idea of a mystical awakening to the oneness of everything in the universe had a profound and lasting impact on Schopenhauer's work, enabling him to connect the two versions of experience that he had pointed to in his writings: the world as "representation," or the world of empirical consciousness, and the world that was made directly known to the self, to the individual subject, as "will." As Schopenhauer states very clearly, "the solution to the riddle of the world is possible only through te proper connexion of outer with inner experience."[117]

Among all the objects in the universe, Schopenhauer asserted, there is *only one* object—namely, our physical body—that is given to us in two entirely different ways. It is given as representation (i.e., objectively, externally) and as will (i.e., subjectively, internally). But he was quick to point out that he arrived at his philosophy independent of any direct influence by Buddhist texts.

> If I wished to take the results of my philosophy as the standard of truth, I should have to concede to Buddhism pre-eminence over the others. In any case, it must be a pleasure to me to see my doctrine in such close agreement with a religion that the majority of men on earth hold as their own, for this numbers far more followers than any other. And this agreement must be yet the more pleasing to me, inasmuch as in my philosophizing I have certainly not been under its influence. For up till 1818, when my work appeared, there was to be found in Europe only a very few accounts of Buddhism, and those extremely incomplete and inadequate, confined almost entirely to a few essays in the earlier volumes of the *Asiatic Researches*.[118]

It is true that there was very little scholarship available on Buddhism at the time Schopenhauer was avidly searching for it, but he did discover an essay in yet another journal, this time one from France, *Journal Asiatiques*, that provided some of what he was looking for. Written several decades earlier by a French scholar named Deshauterayes, it provided a brief overview of the Buddha's life and teachings. Schopenhauer came across it in Berlin in 1826 after it had finally been published.[119]

Friedrich Max Müller (1823-1900)

By the time Reiun was writing his essay in the 1890s, the situation described by Schopenhauer regarding the paucity of materials on Asia available in Europe had changed dramatically; publications on Asia were proliferating, which is precisely the phenomenon to which Reiun was trying to call attention in his article. For example, thanks to the pioneering efforts of another figure Reiun singled out for mention in his essay, the philologist Friedrich Max Müller—who had edited a huge fifty-volume set of translations of key Asian religious texts known as *The Sacred Books of the East*—all the key religious and philosophical texts from Asia were now being made available. This was something that impressed Reiun for what it had to say about the fact that all the writers and thinkers he was discussing in his essay were willing to explore ideas and worldviews different from their own and to grapple with the important reality that lies just beyond the limits of human perception. The very fact that all these works were available to a young writer like Taoka Reiun in early 1890s Japan suggested to him that there was a significant new trend in western thought unfolding, one that would supplement, if not challenge, the western intellectual paradigm. This new current in western thought clearly suggested that there could be movement from East to West, that Asian thought could and should have a strong appeal in the West, and that the challenge for the next century would be to fuse and harmonize the best ideas from both civilizations. Reiun's capacity, even in the early 1890s, to begin to think transnationally and transculturally, and to envision a future world in which nation-states are not the most significant units, is part of what makes his intellectual journey so fascinating.

Franz Anton Mesmer (1734-1815) and James Braid (1795-1860)

Reiun had mentioned Schopenhauer's interest in hypnotism and mesmerism in terms of their potential to aid our understanding of will. In an essay published less than a month after "The Position of Eastern Thought in the Nineteenth Century West" appeared, Reiun wrote about Franz Anton Mesmer and James Braid; the latter is often called the father of modern hypnotism, but many would push that discovery back to Mesmer. Mesmer became convinced that the human body featured a magnetic force or fluid that connected all living things and all living human beings to one another. Today he is remembered for his attempts to cure neurological and psychological conditions with magnetic plates, and so his work has been fairly well discredited. While this kind of "scientific" work may be easily dismissed, even scoffed at, today, at the time "mesmerism" was still a very popular form of treatment, and people took the phenomenon quite seriously. In fact it was considered to be cutting edge.

James Braid, a Scottish surgeon, had seen some of Mesmer's demonstrations. He was not as impressed with the magnetism theory, but he was curious about the state into which Mesmer's subjects were put, a state he would later call "hypnotism." Braid worked successfully with hypnosis to alleviate pain in patients with spinal cord injuries, as well as stroke victims and persons with chronic rheumatoid pain, skin conditions, and sensory impairment.[120] After the appearance of his major work on hypnotism, *Neurypnology* (1843), Braid was contacted by scholars with knowledge of Hindu yogic traditions who urged him to investigate, which he did, eventually publishing *Magic, Witchcraft, Animal Magnetism, Etc.* (1852).[121] Reiun discovered an article on Braid's investigations of Indian antecedents to hypnotism called "New Hypnology," which he cited in his January 1895 article "On Divinity and Mysticism" (Shimpikyô no sesshin o ronzu).[122]

Eugene de Vogüé (1831-1902) and Gabriel Monod (1844-1912)

Reiun was also struck by trends in France that had authors such as Zola and Letourneau commenting on eastern and mystical influences on contemporary Europe, as noted above, but he was also intrigued by articles by Viscount Eugene Melchior de Vogüé such as "The Neo-Christian Movement in France," which appeared in *Harper's* magazine in January 1892, and by the historian Gabriel Monod writing about "The Political Situation in France" (1893) in *The Contemporary Review*. Both were discussing the emergence of Neo-Christian groups in Europe that responded to the growth of materialism by turning to eastern philosophy and religion, as well as vegetarianism, mesmerism, and hypnotism. De Vogüé wrote of a sense of "eternal mystery" returning to the souls of young intellectuals in France, who were seeking the "deep roots that the real has in the invisible." Likewise, Monod waxed poetic about "a longing for something nobler and greater," observing that in France there was evidence of "a certain fermenting dissatisfaction—a yearning for an unknown ideal. . . . Our age has lost faith and admits no other source of certainty than science, but at the same time, it has not been able to resolve, as positivism would wish, not to reflect and remain silent about what it ignores."[123] Since it is precisely to these things ignored by science that Reiun wishes to draw his readers' attention, he welcomes such remarks by eloquent spokespersons.

Rousseau (1712-1788), Emerson (1803-1882), and Thoreau (1817-1862)

Finally, in his essay on "The Position of Eastern Thought in the Nineteenth century West," Reiun includes the voices of three of his favorite western authors: Jean-Jacques Rousseau, Ralph Waldo Emerson, and Henry David Thoreau, quotations from whom can be found scattered about many of his essays and appearing as epigraphs in others. He admired Rousseau as a pioneer of the "inward turn" and the transcendentalists for their deep appreciation of eastern thought.[124] Overall, his point in the article on the place of eastern thought in the West was to alert his readers that, while his own society and culture seemed intent on abandoning its past and traditions in favor of borrowing all that was new and modern from the West, there were well-regarded thinkers outside Asia who understood how important eastern thought could be. Reiun's message to his fellow Japanese was as if to say, "Wait a minute! Look what some of the leading minds in the West are starting to realize about ancient Chinese and Indian thought. Aren't these westerners moving toward the East in order to see what ancient Asian philosophy and religion can offer the world in such a millennial moment?" What is remarkable is that Reiun had managed to put his finger on the pulse of some very important trends in contemporary European thought.[125] In just ten pages he outlined almost all the important recent developments in the movement of eastern thought toward the West. Moreover, he found in figures like Anquetil-Duperron and Schopenhauer individuals who were in the center of this flow of ideas, and he admired them for their role as cultural mediators.

Understanding the Movement of Thought from East to West

Clearly Reiun was doing something more than just reading a variety of critics and philosophers; he was putting them together in new ways, so that these texts could engage in conversation with one another, and in doing so he pushed his readers into new, unmapped territory. Moreover, in creating a new discourse, he was substantially ahead of his time. Even as recently as fifty years ago, there was hardly an equivalent understanding of *how* this whole process of transmitting ancient Indian and Chinese ideas to Europe had occurred during the previous century. The earliest comprehensive work on the subject was Raymond Schwab's *La Renaissance Orientale* (first published in French in 1950), a study that discusses many of the same individuals and issues that Reiun took up some sixty years earlier.[126] Of course, Edward Said's classic Orientalism, which came along almost thirty years after *La Renaissance Orientale*, in 1978, had a substantial impact on the field of Asian studies. We need only recall that Said viewed "orientalism" as "a kind of intellectual authority over the Orient within Western culture" (19) which is "premised upon exteriority, that is, the Orientalist poet or scholar, makes the Orient speak, describes the Orient, renders its mysteries plain for and to the West (20-21)." "In general, it was the West that moved upon the East, not vice versa."[127]

Stephen Batchelor echoed this view sixteen years later, in 1994, in *The Awakening of the West*.

> In the European imagination Asia came to stand for something both unknown and distant yet also to be feared. As the colonizing powers came to identify themselves with order, reason and power, so the colonized East came to be perceived as chaotic, irrational and weak. In psychological terms, the East became a cipher for the Western unconscious, the repository of all that is dark, unacknowledged, feminine, sensual, repressed and liable to eruption.[128]

Therefore, the standard interpretation was that the only way for the West to know the East was to incorporate it and appropriate its knowledge—as part and parcel of the imperialist process—into the familiar terms and framework rooted in western thought much the way that a knowing subject incorporates its object. This approach is obviously quite the opposite of what the Japanese haiku poet Bashô advocated when he wrote "if you want to know about the bamboo, go to the bamboo; if you want to know about the pine, go to the pine."[129] In other words, if you truly want to know and understand an object, you must go to it, meet it on its own terms, and make a sincere effort to understand it and even become one with it. Reiun was interested in discovering western seekers and thinkers who seemed capable of accepting eastern ideas on their own terms.

In a work that largely denounces the West's efforts to appropriate the East in economic as well as cultural terms, Said's account of Anquetil-Duperron is instructive. He did not regard Anquetil-Duperron the same way he viewed the other, more imperialistic or colonialist "orientalizers" on whom his book focuses and of whom he was highly critical. Anquetil-Duperron had actually traveled on his own to India in 1755 and remained there until 1761; he was not part of any official government mission. Moreover, while there he studied languages and engaged scholars in conversation as he searched for more information about the Upanishads, and worked collaboratively on a translation project. Said's major complaint about orientalists is that they could only come to terms with the East by viewing it through a lens of western understanding, so that their understanding "is premised on exteriority, that is, on the fact that the Orientalist, poet or scholar, makes the Orient speak, describes the Orient, renders its mysteries plain for and to the West."[130] Although scholars can never completely leave behind the cultural baggage they bring to their projects, Anquetil-Duperron, in his own way, did something much more like going to the pine, or to the bamboo, instead of simply trying to incorporate what he was studying into a preexisting worldview. He reached out to meet another culture on its own terms. As he wrote to a friend:

> To deepen the understanding of the history of ancient peoples, to elaborate the revolution which peoples and languages undergo, to visit regions unknown to the rest of the people where art has preserved the character of the first ages: you will perhaps remember, with distress and sighing about my follies, that these subjects have always been the focus of my attention.[131]

It is clear that Anquetil went about his quest for the "recovery and renewal of ancient wisdom" with an earnestness, a seriousness of purpose, and a sense of humility that was not typical of orientalists who only sought to appropriate.[132] While Schwab's book provides a great deal of information on Europe's discovery of Asia in the eighteenth century, it appeared in a much earlier time, and while it was superseded by *Orientalism*, Said's book itself is now nearly forty years old. A much more recent and compelling work is Urs App's *The Birth of Orientalism* (2010), an incredibly rich source on the eighteenth-century European contact with non-Islamic Asia. App makes it clear that:

> The birth of modern Orientalism was not a Caesarean section performed by colonialist doctors at the beginning of the nineteenth century when Europe's imperialist powers began to dominate large swaths of Asia. Rather, it was the result of a long process that around the turn of the eighteenth century produced a paradigm of change. . . . [O]ur case studies reflect not only evolving images of Asia's religious landscape but also a *transformation of the worldview of the perceivers*. In the course of the eighteenth century, Europe's dominant ideological matrix experienced a deepening crisis, and its hitherto unassailable biblical foundations showed ever more threatening fissures.[133]

Reiun was not only attuned to these emerging "fissures" in the foundations of European thought; he was also keenly interested in the way the "worldview of the perceivers" was being transformed by this East-Eest cultural contact. It was a powerful epiphany for Reiun, who was sitting in his small study in far-off Tokyo and yet somehow was still able to grasp the significance of what he was reading. Coming out of the *kokusui-hozon* movement, Reiun might well have developed a conservative stance. But he clearly moved well beyond any strictures that this movement might have imposed on him both intellectually and ideologically. He experienced this not only when he was immersing himself in the reading of eastern and western texts alongside each other but also when he traveled to China in 1899, 1900, and again in 1905. As he recorded in his autobiography about his time in Shanghai in 1899:

> The year I spent in Shanghai was not without consequence for me. I was not terribly stimulated by teaching Japanese to Chinese students, but in terms of my ideas, the stimulus I received was profound. When I went to China, I was still under the sway of a rather narrow type of nationalism (*kokusuishugi*). Now I was someone who had come of age during the late 1880s when there was a healthy current of reaction going on against the wholesale importation and worship for everything western. Moreover, at that time, the field I was pursuing at the university was Chinese studies, so I was: primed to become enamored of the classics; this meant that I tended to see only the strong points of my own country and could even be led down

the path to dreams about my own country rising to world-class status. So that was the kind of narrow worldview that I embraced.

But Shanghai was one of the great world ports and within the confines of a four-square-mile area, it was its own little cosmos, with people from all over the world brought together in a small republic. The black, yellow, and white races all living together.... So I learned very quickly that I had been looking at the world like the proverbial frog in a well, [and] my horizons were instantly broadened. I came to appreciate how large the world really was and that people should not only be citizens of nation-states; they needed to start living as members of the broader human race and to learn to do the correct and morally upright thing for humanity as a whole. (SD, 607–8)

Transcending the narrower, more nationalistic side of *kokusui-hozon*, Reiun found himself in a world that allowed him to imagine the possibilities of transnational communities that placed their highest priority on independence and freedom of choice. Of course we can still find today substantial traces of this kind of appeal for a synthesis between eastern and western values about which Reiun wrote. One only has to peruse the religion or occult sections of bookstores to see all the material that is now available on such subjects as martial arts, yoga, shiatsu massage, feng shui, acupuncture, kung fu, tai chi, Chinese herbal medicine, Zen, Daoism, the *Book of Changes*—it is all there. But what Reiun was honing in on was a special moment in Europe's discovery of Asian religious and philosophical texts that he felt was especially worth noting. He was drawn to such things as Zen, mysticism, art, aesthetics, beauty, poetry, philosophy, hypnotism, spiritualism, and mesmerism because they invited readers to consider the value of Asian thought. He struggled to understand why the ideas associated with *bunmei-kaika*, with their fascination with western thought and culture, should be privileged above something as valuable and insightful as early Chinese and Indian thought.

Reiun used what he learned about the European response to Asian philosophy and religion to make the case that it was a mistake for Japanese to turn their backs on the contributions Asia could make to western thought. Western civilization was materialistic and bankrupt, he believed, but Japanese were blindly following the western lead in the Meiji era in order to strengthen the material base of their economy and military. Of course all this material progress was well and good, but at what cost? To what extent was the utilitarian, highly commercial, profit-oriented, pragmatic, purely objective worldview inimical to a subjective, inner-directed, spiritual understanding of the universe? That was the question Reiun posed for his readers. Better that individuals ground themselves in a genuine spiritual reality than sacrifice their souls on the altar of material progress.

Contesting Western Civilization

As part of the process of placing the two civilizations on an equal footing, Reiun did not hesitate to express his reservations about modern western civilization. In a short piece published in *Tôa Zeirin*, "Ridiculing the Nineteenth Century" (Jûkyû-seiki o Azakeru) he taunts those who would be impressed with the alleged accomplishments of modern civilization. "Ah, nineteenth century," he begins, "you boast of your civilization, but is it really such a blossoming flower? To be sure, you have electricity and the power of the steam engine, but what of virtue and morality?"[134]

> Is it true that your civilization is that of the common man? To be sure it can be said that your skills brought down the feudal class structure of the eighteenth century, but in its place can you deny that a great gulf between the rich and the poor has been erected? You helped liberate people from the oppression of the previous century, but don't you know that the coercive power of economic might is far more potent than that of violence? Your civilization serves the rich man well, but isn't it only used to adorn the world of the rich? Your glowing street lamps . . . shine on your elegantly dressed sons out for a stroll, but what good are these to the starving worker, who huddled in his dreary hovel deep in the heart of the slums, blows on his numb hands and arms on a frosty night, and who still cannot find sleep when his flickering candle is finally extinguished. Doesn't your civilization suffer from the evil of having all the financial power drained by an elite at the top, while the lower echelons are left uncared for? Doesn't your civilization rob the worker of his job and give it to that which is so much more agreeable to you, the machine?[135]

He takes to task a system that would tax workers to the very limit while letting the leisure classes off lightly. He contests a worldview that takes pride in its system of law but renders its justice virtually unavailable to those who cannot afford the price of costly appeals. He chastises a system that produces inadequate social services, mediocre art, cities, and smoke-belching factories; a system that infringes on nature and stifles the vision of poets and philosophers; and an educational system that is geared toward the sciences and tries to force everybody into identical molds.

This contestatory vision of nineteenth-century western civilization was something Reiun retained intact throughout his life. He considered the whole notion of modernity as the triumph of a utilitarian, materialistic, instrumentalist view of the world, and he believed that it should not go uncontested. The themes he touched on here reappeared subsequently when he launched his frontal assault on modern civilization after the turn of the century. In his earliest writings, though, and in his essays as a literary critic, Reiun's interest in civilization was more indirect.

At this stage, he was most concerned with understanding how an individual's inner life interacted with and was shaped by life in society and the world. How do humans perceive the world around them? How do they interpret themselves and others? How do they define what is important, what is of value to them? In some ways, Reiun did take his cues from the nineteenth-century European romantic writers and thinkers that he admired. He felt himself reacting against the trends of his times much the way romantics like Byron, Heine, and Thoreau did. But, at bottom, he embraced his own conception of "the modern" as an ideal in which individuals develop a stable, autonomous self and on this basis move their societies forward. No one has yet attained perfection in this process, and, although western societies may be ahead of Japan, progress is relative. By looking at the value of Asia's past as a rich heritage of thought and human understanding, Reiun could establish grounds for equivalence.

Reiun had noted in his description of his intellectual proclivities that he was someone who preferred to go against the grain. When others were busy being drawn to naturalism or realism, he spoke up for a reinvigorated version of romanticism. As Peter Gay points out, "Romantics set a tone for rebellious nonconformity," which was then carried over into the stance taken by many disaffected moderns.[136] In fact, many scholars agree that the "crisis of representation" that has come to define the nature of the literary and philosophical movement we call "modernism" has its roots in nineteenth-century romanticism.[137] The idea that the romantic perspective represents a new way of looking at the self is hardly news; it goes all the way back to the pioneering work of the social psychologist George H. Mead, author of *Mind, Self, and Society* (1934). But it is also kept very much alive today by such contemporary critics as Charles Taylor and Charles Altieri.[138] Nevertheless, if not surprising, it is at least very interesting that a young critic in Japan in 1890 would come to see the world in this way.

More on Schopenhauer's Philosophy

Finally, since Schopenhauer's thought was so central to the development of Reiun's ideas, it may be worthwhile to spend a little additional time before concluding this chapter examining more closely Schopenhauer's basic ideas and the way he believed that he was not only pushing Kant's understanding to its logical conclusion but was also solving the metaphysical dilemmas that Kant's philosophy had left unanswered.[139] Kant, he believed, had established a new basis for understanding how the human mind functions, and Schopenhauer, a great admirer of Kant, wanted to build on his predecessor's philosophical system. As he would later write in *Parerga and Paralipomena*, "[M]y philosophy is only his [Kant's] thought out to the end."[140] Schopenhauer's biographer, Rüdiger Safranski, explains how Kant's unresolved problem gave Schopenhauer his starting point and allowed him to go straight back to Plato and the metaphor of the shadows on the cave wall.

> Plato lit for him the torch which Kant had denied him. Time and again he read the parable of the cave from the *Republic*: We are in a dark dungeon. Behind us burns a fire, even further behind us lies an exit into the open. We are chained up, we cannot turn our heads, we gaze at the wall facing us. There we follow the shadow play of the objects which are carried past the fire behind us. If we were able to turn we should see the real objects and the fire; if we were actually free and stepped out of the dungeon we should be in the sun, and only then would we be within the truth....[T]his was the way into the open, into the sun, to participation in being.[141]

Cross explains succinctly how the power of this metaphor allowed Schopenhauer to place his work in the long line of thought about the metaphysics of human understanding that incorporated ideas from the nonwestern tradition.

> All through his life he drew strength from the belief that the ideas he had formulated were essentially at one with the ancient wisdom of India, as well as with that of Plato. Time and again he draws attention to this in his writings. Why is this? It is because it meant that his doctrines were unlikely to be merely his own subjective inventions but belonged to a great tradition of human wisdom; that the European philosophical tradition, after centuries of wandering in the dark, had, in the person first of Kant and then of Schopenhauer himself, come at last, and with a new and startling clarity, upon the same fundamental insights—that all plurality is apparent, that all individuals are manifestations of a single, uniquely real essence—that had in distant ages been perceived by Plato, by the sages of the Upanishads, and by other great minds of the past.[142]

Reiun admired Schopenhauer's desire to add to Kant's insights his own conviction that the individual is capable of directly experiencing the "thing-in-itself." Therefore, by implication, anyone is capable of turning around and seeing the parade of people and objects, or, even better, of stepping out of the cave and into the sunlight. Thus, it seemed obvious to Schopenhauer that the "possibility of freedom which thus expresses itself is man's greatest prerogative,"[143] and it was on this basis that he could write in his *Manuscript Remains*, "I am the man who has written *The World as Will and Representation* and has given a solution to the great problem of existence. . . . I have solved the problem and have fulfilled my mission."[144] Although he would later abandon the term in his published works, Schopenhauer's notebooks contain frequent references to something he called "a better consciousness," which is to be distinguished from "empirical consciousness," and by which he meant "a state that transcends ordinary experience, allowing human beings to gain access to something timeless and universal, to leave behind their everyday concerns for peace from all striving, and enjoy face-to-face cognition of the truest and most permanent aspect of reality."[145]

Schopenhauer is labeled a pessimist, but should this central insight of his legitimately be considered pessimistic? Clearly it offers the genuine hope of release from the controlling power of the will. This notion of a "better consciousness"—the idea that beyond ordinary consciousness there lies a higher or 'better' state in which the human mind can see beyond mere appearances into something more real—speaks to what Mannion describes as a "form of transcendence which is intuitively grasped and which takes the individual 'beyond' his or her normal day-to-day and egoistic concerns."[146] As Schopenhauer's epigraph expresses very succinctly, "better consciousness" can lift one "into a world where there is no longer personality and causality nor subject and object."[147] Reiun clearly understood what Schopenhauer meant by this, and he believed that it was to this better consciousness that humans could and should aspire.

Scholars have wondered whether Schopenhauer should be considered a system builder like the philosophers he admired most, Plato and Kant. Schopenhauer would undoubtedly have responded with an unequivocal yes.[148] In a conversation with a visitor he once observed that there were really only three noteworthy philosophers in history—the Buddha, Plato, and Kant—and since he believed that his own system completed Kant's pioneering work, he obviously would have placed himself in that esteemed company.[149] What was his system then? Stated in the most simple terms, he divided his principal work, *WWR*, into four parts so that he could consider his subject from each of two vantage points and in each of two different ways: the world as representation, first consideration; the world as will, first consideration; the world as representation, second consideration; and the world as will, second consideration.[150] Central to Schopenhauer's system, then, is his insight that the world has a double aspect, that is, it can be experienced both as will (*Wille*) and as representation (*Vorstellung*). So the opening lines of the first section of *WWR* are:

> "The world is my representation": this is a truth valid with reference to every living and knowing being although man alone can bring it into reflective, abstract consciousness. If he really does so, philosophical discernment has dawned on him. It then becomes clear and certain to him that he does not know a sun and an earth, but only an eye that sees a sun, a hand that feels an earth: that the world around him is there only as representation, in other words, only in reference to another thing, namely that which represents, and this is himself. . . . Therefore, no truth is more certain, more independent of all others and less in need of proof than this, namely that everything exists for knowledge, and hence the whole of this world is only object in relation to the subject, perception of the perceiver, in a word, representation.[151]

In a word, "The mind or intellect comes first, and the world it perceives, the world of representation, is totally dependent on it."[152] According to Schopenhauer's second basic proposition, this objective world, the world as representation, is only one side of what human beings can experience, and the "outward" side at that. He says, "The world has an entirely different side which is its innermost being, its kernel, the thing-in-itself." To this he affixes the label *will*.[153] As he notes:

> In the First Book we consider the world from this side alone, namely in so far as it is representation. . . . We will make up for its one-sidedness in the next book by means of another truth that is not so immediately certain as our present point of departure . . . a truth that must be very serious and alarming, if not terrifying to anyone, a truth that can and must be maintained by him as well, namely this: "The world is my will."[154]

Sophia Vasalou makes the very important observation in her study of Schopenhauer that his principal accomplishment was taking Kant's "inward turn" to a second, deeper level, where "we could look within us to discover, not only the forms conditioning the appearance of the world, but the very inner nature of the appearing world: the thing-in-itself. And this we could do by looking inward to the *psychological facts of our self-experience* . . . to which the forms of our knowledge did not (or did not wholly) condition our access."[155] In chapter 8, we will see that Reiun, too, was drawn to understanding "the psychological facts" of our experience because they could help individuals discover the appropriate "psychological path" from which to defend themselves (see *SD*, 477). This is also why Günter Zöller can claim that Schopenhauer opened up "a radically different understanding of what is the core of the human being designated by the word *self*, of what constitutes the form of human existence referred to as the *better self*, and what it means for the *self* to underlie the world and everything in it."[156] These notions about coming to terms with a new and radical understanding of the self and being able to confront "the psychological facts of our self-experience" were by far the most important things that Reiun was gleaning from Schopenhauer's works, and they gradually became central to all his writings because of the new vistas they opened up for him.

For Schopenhauer, *will* is a blind striving that enslaves people to an endless cycle of desire that can never be satisfied, which is why he is labeled a pessimist. But where Schopenhauer's view differs considerably from pessimism, and where it held special significance for Reiun, was in the unique position that it affords human beings, the only form of creation that has the capacity of *knowing*, and hence becoming liberated from will. Schopenhauer admits that no meaning in life could be uncovered "if the investigator himself were nothing more than the pure knowing subject. But he himself is rooted in that world, and thus he finds himself in it as an individual—in other words, that is to say his knowledge, which is the conditional supporter of the whole world as representation, is nevertheless given entirely through the medium of a body."[157] He goes on:

> It is just this double knowledge of our own body which gives us information about that body itself, about its actions and movements following on motives as well as about its suffering through outside impressions, in a word, about what is, not as representation, but as something over and above this, and hence what it is in *itself*. We do not have such immediate information about nature, action, and suffering of any other real objects.[158]

This "double knowledge," this unique human capacity to know will, to penetrate the veil of illusion, or *māyā*, and to quiet the will's power, gives the modern self its special place, for it is something other than mere "representation" because it can be known as it is, "in itself." By denoting the self in this way, Schopenhauer takes a step beyond a pessimistic statement of the world as illusion and into a realistic or active mysticism that sees the world as an arena in which humans can discover the true nature of their being.[159] Denial of the will need not mean obliteration of the self as so many western readers of Schopenhauer have feared; like the idea of noncoercive action (*wuwei*) in Daoist thought, it simply means that the individual is no longer caught in the web of identification and attachment to the outer world of representation. As Charles Muses puts it:

> The denial of the will can emanate no quietist aura, bears no implication of stagnation or repression. Denial is rather the most active assertion of the will that can be, eclipsing all selfish assertions with its power: for it takes the will to deny the will. This redirection is the difficult solution of the very master-problem itself.[160]

At the core of Schopenhauer's system, then, lies a potential for individuals to correctly perceive and understand the world around them, and it is to this aspect of his philosophy that Reiun was so powerfully drawn. This was a universal truth, not limited to some regions or some eras only. As Gerard Mannion puts it:

> Schopenhauer's method depends upon the underlying unity of being which was to be the foundation of his ethics and hence the inspiration for his compassion, which Schopenhauer took over from Christianity and Buddhism and pronounced as the highest virtue. The questions concerning self therefore reciprocally relate to the questions concerning the wider world, with other beings and, indeed, what lies beyond.[161]

This concern with a wider world, with all human beings regardless of class, race, or nationality, with the "unity of being," and with "what lies beyond"—these are all important elements in how Reiun was able to transcend the limitations of his own time and come to think globally and transhistorically. By seeing the inner self and outer world operating in a reciprocal relationship, and seeing the possibility of an exchange between self and other with the individual self acting as a gateway, Reiun was able to appropriate from Schopenhauer an integrated system that provided him with the materials necessary to construct and defend this new view of the world from the self outward. It was a prudent choice, for it allowed Reiun to gain much—especially an appreciation for "sympathy" or "compassion"—without having to sacrifice large pieces of his cultural identity in order to do so. Once it is recognized that the inner nature of another person is really made up of the same substance as our own, then we cannot help but empathize and have compassion for and with him or her.[162] Therefore, it is not solely the "inward turn," the moment when the inner self and the will are observed, that allows the individual to overcome its power; nor is the suspension of subject-object duality that occurs when contemplating great art the only other option. There is also the possibility of practicing compassion in everyday life, or following the so-called humble path.[163] This is how we can bring about that "better consciousness" of which Schopenhauer wrote, and Reiun's ability to grasp this is one of the things that makes his critique of his society and the times so penetrating.

So for Reiun, and probably most Japanese at the time, the issue of whether Schopenhauer was a pessimist was not really important. Scholars trained in western philosophy might recoil from Schopenhauer's comment that "the actual, positive solution to the riddle of the world must be something that the human intellect is wholly incapable of grasping and conceiving" (*WWR*, 2:185), but to anyone well versed in Zen, the *Daodejing*, the *Yijing*, or Indian thought, this insight would present few difficulties. Schopenhauer was simply pointing out the obvious limitations of human cognition while reinforcing the value of observing the inner processes of the individual. In the early 1890s this emphasis on turning inward, on discovering the inner self, clearly struck a responsive chord in Meiji youths like Kitamura Tôkoku (1868–94) and Taoka Reiun, much as it had appealed to the youth of Europe a few decades before.[164] A glance at the content of Reiun's early essays reveals this clearly, as he constructs brief sketches of such figures as Zhuangzi, Laozi, Bashô, Su Dongpo, and Heine and discusses religion, aesthetics, and the pursuit of the sublime. He also wrote a number of articles on mysticism because this was the obvious way to connect the "wider world" with "what lies beyond," to borrow Mannion's phrasing. Reiun constructed his vision of the world, and of human experience, on the foundation of these philosophical insights, for which he drew on both East and West in a highly creative fashion. This is one of the things that caused him to stand apart from his peers.

Conclusion

In the years just before and after the Sino-Japanese War, there was intense yearning among Meiji youth to explore the world of the inner life, to be on the path of spiritual growth, and there was an interaction of this wish with the drive toward concrete achievements in the "real" world. This drive was doubtless part of the legacy of the Meiji Restoration, a product of the high expectations that had been awakened by historical change. Just as in Europe in the early nineteenth century, in Japan in the early 1890s, "There was much soaring ambition, much insatiable desire for experience, for self-expression, for the heroic stance (often supported with glowing rhetoric) for Promethean persistence against adversity or torment, and simply for notoriety. . . . There was a desire to break the chains of tradition, to achieve new forms of freedom and the possibility of creating anew."[165] Young critics like Tôkoku and Reiun were starting to wonder whether art, particularly literature, could function as a mediating force to help resolve the tension and restore some stability to one's sense of self. Raised on tales of Restoration heroism and exposed early to the ideals of the popular rights movement and the near-absolute belief in the value and possibility of self-improvement that had permeated Meiji society in the early years, these young men could not escape a longing to follow in the *shishi* tradition and perform acts in the public interest.[166] But the environment they encountered was one in which the public arena had increasingly come under the control of a select minority, so that public roles, whether in the central government bureaucracy or the political parties, became virtually inaccessible to all but a few possessing the correct credentials and connections.

This is what felt new about the world of 1890s Japan. Crowded with articulate young writers trying to work out the implications of their frustrating position, there was a palpable restlessness. Someone like Fukuzawa Yukichi (1835–1901), the leading *bunmei-kaika* advocate of his day (the 1860s and 1870s), could not help but feel contentment and take great pride in his country's performance in the Sino-Japanese War. It stood as a monument to the distance Japan had traveled since the Restoration. The sense of crisis that had driven the men of Fukuzawa's generation had made it imperative that Japan become a strong nation as soon as possible, and the victory in this first foreign war seemed to say that the initial storm had been weathered. But for young men in Reiun's generation, who had not personally experienced the sense of foreign crisis in the last years of the Tokugawa period, the time seemed appropriate to take full stock of the implications of the path on which the country was embarking and to question the nature and goals of *bunmei-kaika*, which had been so central to Fukuzawa's worldview. It was time to ponder instead what kind of world, what kind of life, *bunmei-kaika* was actually bringing about for the citizens of modern Japan.

It was in the years immediately after the Sino-Japanese War that the voices of the people in Reiun's generation first began to be heard. But, as Pyle reminds us, it was a world that was "less tractable, less hospitable to social reform, less tolerant of new values." It was also a world with less occupational opportunity, fewer outlets for political engagement, and, as Reiun had experienced in the Osaka Middle School, more emphasis on order and discipline in national life. What members of Reiun's generation shared was a tendency to be more introspective and conscious of their particular historical dilemma, which had surfaced in the wake of the collapse of the popular rights movement. Many young people had invested their ideals in this movement, and, in turn, the movement had shaped their values and consciousness. When the movement disintegrated, many were thrown back on themselves, with both their self-consciousness and their awareness of their predicament heightened.

Likewise, Reiun's perceptions of history were starting to change. If they had previously been based almost exclusively on the western model of "the rise and development of the nation state toward a Western modern form of political and economic history," other options were now starting to be explored.[167] What if it turned out that in the West the view of history and the place of the individual in society were not rooted solely in a monolithic, pragmatic, utilitarian worldview? Was there perhaps room for a more complex, multifaceted vision? This seemed quite possible to someone like Reiun, who found that there were many writers in the West willing to challenge simplistic notions about the nature and value of progress. Moreover, it gave rise to an enduring interest in the modern self and its place in the world.

4

Literary Criticism
The Seinenbun Years

Who sees all beings in his own Self, and his own Self in all beings, loses all fear. When a sage sees this great Unity and his Self has become all beings, what delusion and what sorrow can ever be near him?

Isa Upanishad

Boundless compassion for all living things is the firmest and surest guarantee of pure moral conduct, and needs no causitry. Whoever is inspired with it will assuredly injure no one, will wrong no one, will encroach on no one's rights; on the contrary, he will be lenient and patient with everyone, will forgive everyone, will help everyone as much as he can, and all his actions will bear the stamp of justice, philanthropy, and lovingkindness.

Schopenhauer, *On the Basis of Morality*

That is merely literary that has no other object than to please. Minor literature has a didactic object. But the greatest literature of all—the literature that scarcely exists—has not merely an aesthetic object, but in addition a creative object: that of subjecting its readers to a real and at the same time illuminating experience. Major literature, in short, is an initiation into truth.

Katherine Mansfield in A. R. Orage, *On Love*

At twenty-five years of age, Taoka Reiun emerged as a literary critic of considerable force in the years immediately after the first Sino-Japanese War. Ever the contrarian, someone who was more than willing to ruffle feathers and go against the grain, he pushed his readers and challenged them. The ideas that grabbed his attention most forcefully show that he was a person with substantial insight and vision, someone able to penetrate beyond the more obvious and superficial questions and dig deeper, into the heart of what was going on in the world around him. He gained a reputation as an extremely precocious critic whose brush produced frank and stinging attacks on some of the leading figures of the literary and journalistic world. It was a result of his writings as editor and chief critic for *Seinenbun* (青年文, Literary Youth), a small journal inaugurated in 1895, that his name first became widely known in Japan. A collection of his essays from this period sold more than twenty thousand copies, not an inconsequential circulation figure for Japan at that time.

The opportunity to take on editorial responsibilities for a new literary journal came to Reiun almost as a calling, although I have no doubt that if a journal dealing with contemporary thought or ideas or issues in society and philosophy had been available he would have been equally comfortable. According to his autobiography, his friend and former roommate at the Osaka Middle School, Yamagata Isô, contacted him in January 1895 about writing for *Seinenbun* when Reiun was staying at his older brother's home outside Tokyo for the New Year holiday.[1] Yamagata's older brother was the founder of *Shonen'en* (少年園), a magazine for young people that was later succeeded by *Bunkô*. They were interested in publishing a companion journal to feature literary criticism oriented toward the youth market. Reiun was asked to join the editorial staff and write a monthly column of literary criticism, "Jibun" (時文, Contemporary Writing).[2] During his period as literary critic, Reiun's belief in the value of literature—for the individual, society, and mankind as a whole—was near absolute. How seriously Reiun took this position is clear from a statement made near the end of his life.

> When I first began to write for my journal *Seinenbun* fifteen years ago, I pursued my vocation full of youthful ardor and with great confidence in myself and in the value of literature as a way of learning about life. To this end I devoted my complete being with utter sincerity, so that it was unavoidable that at times my thoughts were crudely expressed, not unlike those of a child. Nevertheless, underlying this childlike quality was a deathly seriousness tinged with a burning passion.[3]

And in his autobiography he recalled:

> In those days, literature was for me a sacred enterprise. When it came time to draft my literary column "Jibun" at the end of each month, I would always rise early and sit facing my desk, making my body tranquil to prevent my mind from wandering, and I would eat only a little for fear of dispersing my energy. And during a brief rest after my meal, I would look at nothing except perhaps some ancient poetry, so that just as I felt my energy welling up I could with almost pious reverence put my brush to paper. Consequently, although I make no claim that my writing from that period is worth noticing, the fact that it expressed my deepest and most

sincere feelings, straight from my heart, may make it worth something. (*SD*, 569–70)

As we shall see, Reiun found in literature a real possibility for affecting the world through its impact on human consciousness. If readers could learn more about the world around them, and experience what goes on in the hearts and minds of others, they were bound to be better for it. It is the writer's job to transmit experience through narratives: fiction, nonfiction, memoirs, and criticism. Ideally, these narratives should allow the reader to share in an original experience; or, even better, writer and reader should move along a trajectory together, in tandem. In such a view, then, there was little that literature could not do; it could alter human consciousness, create unity in the social mind, and thereby affect real change. To Reiun "literature" during these years provided a framework that allowed him to integrate his thoughts and express his beliefs around a coherent theme.

Yet within two years *Seinenbun* had been discontinued. Reiun wrote for other periodicals for a while and then left the literary world, retreating to the mountains and a post as a middle school teacher in Tsûyama where he was fairly unhappy. While there he had an unfortunate love affair with a young apprentice geisha, and as a result he had to leave the middle school position. He worked with his friends on another journal, *Kôko Bungaku*, where he published numerous essays, until he joined the staff of the *Yorozuchôhô* newspaper for six months (where he first met and worked closely with Kôtoku Shûsui). He then left for the city of Mito, northeast of Tokyo, to join the staff of the *Ibaraki* newspaper, where he met the anarchist painter and illustrator Ogawa Usen (1868–1938), with whom he would later collaborate. Usen tried to make his art—drawings, paintings, and *manga*—reflect the everyday lives of ordinary people.[4] Reiun's friendship and collaboration with both Kôtoku and Usen provide convincing evidence of his affinity for philosophical and artistic anarchism. He enjoyed thinking about a decentered world in which the simple, everyday things in life could be appreciated. As it turned out, Reiun did not stay at *Ibaraki* very long, soon leaving for a year in Shanghai where he accepted a teaching position at a Japanese language school. It was during his year in Shanghai that he met some of the late Qing reformers who had worked closely with Kang Youwei and Liang Qichao.

Reiun's life after his stint on *Seinenbun* must have felt very unsettled, and often his feelings of disillusionment were quite pronounced.[5] He seemed to be in search of an ideal to substitute for his short-lived belief in the power and potential of literature. His frustration at this point is clearly reflected in a number of articles he wrote on the theme of youth and the need for a continual regeneration of ideas. In an essay published in *Nihonjin* in January 1897, the same month the last edition of *Seinenbun* appeared, he offered the following critique of Japanese youth in the aftermath of the Sino-Japanese War.

> Youth is vital and energetic. The spiritual flame of progressiveness ever burns deep within. The young think only of pressing on and perennially improving: they do not know about conserving. They really do not yet know the world . . . so they are without doubt: they only bravely press on to follow the beacon of their hopes. Consequently, they are totally earnest and utterly sincere. . . . If something is damming up and holding back the flow of the national spirit, it is only the young that can remove the obstruction.
>
> Meiji. The years go by and now it has been some thirty years since the Restoration. The youths who once wore their hair long and free flowing are now approaching old age. And how clear it is that their vitality, which was so instrumental in effecting the Restoration-Revolution, has now degenerated significantly. Like old people, they take their pleasure by snatching a brief moment's rest. There is no point in searching for the spirit of Meiji youth in these quarters. A nation's spirit is always on the verge of stagnation.
>
> But in times such as these the only ones who can resolutely step forward and succeed in reversing the trend of stagnation are the youths of the period. But what about the young of today? Are they energetic? Does a progressive spirit burn in their souls?[6]

Reiun's doubts on this point were explicit. He recoiled especially from the marked utilitarian streak and the strong materialistic outlook that were apparent among Japanese of his day. The drive for worldly success and material prosperity meant, for Reiun, destruction of the whole notion of being devoted to an ideal. Who can entertain the concept of self-sacrifice if he is driven by a commitment to self-gain? The denizens of the literary world were hardly removed from this influence. Writers who had opportunity stretched open before them were content to do only what was necessary to sustain their careers and acquire fame and reward. Where was there room for deep poetic insights into the times and the individual's inner life in this discursive space? Accordingly, Reiun would have little truck with their so-called realism, for in all their "realistic observations" of the world around them, there was never any serious intention of penetrating beyond the surface of that reality. As the epigraph by Katherine Mansfield that opens this chapter suggests, literature must have a creative as well as an aesthetic object. It needs to penetrate life, to subject its readers to "a real and at the same time illuminating experience," and to initiate them into truth. The literature that followed the Sino-Japanese War was not living up to this standard.

Although by mid-1896 Reiun was no longer confident that the Japanese literary world was capable of producing a writer who could bring readers face-to-face with real experiences and initiate them into truth, he did not abandon his interest in seeing this come about. He still wanted to see widespread changes in the outlook of the Japanese people, but he felt he needed to broaden his critique to address the modern condition in its entirety. This chapter examines Reiun's writings over a two-year period in considerable detail, as they are noteworthy on at least three counts. First and foremost, they offer us a view of interesting literary developments during a very important period in modern Japanese history, and this view is presented through the eyes of one person who had distinct beliefs as to what was necessary and possible for Japanese writers to achieve at this time. Second, by exhibiting a fundamental concern over newly emerging social problems, and by demanding that literature become more socially conscious, Reiun's essays reflect the impact on Japan of the rapid industrialization that was just getting under way. In this sense, he was among the earliest critics of modern Japanese capitalism. Finally, in his attempts to define what should be the concern of Japanese writers, and in his choice of writers who most fully lived up to his expectations, we have a reasonably accurate guide to the aspects of life and experience that were most important to Reiun. To state a conclusion in advance, what was a primary concern for Reiun was the question of what writers needed to do in order to achieve a deeper understanding of the modern self and its relation to society. Engagement, commitment, and compassion, these were his watchwords.

The Sino-Japanese War and the New Japan

There can be little doubt that Japan's first foreign war as a modern nation-state was a momentous and psychologically stirring event for the citizenry. The surge of national and cultural pride was discernible during and immediately after the war.[7] Moreover, the stimulus to industrial development generated by the demand for munitions and other war matériel, along with the large indemnity and the possession of Taiwan as a colony that Japan's victory brought about, combined to propel Japan's first major spurt of industrial growth. Watsuji Tetsurô, who grew up during this period, reflected on the impact of the Sino-Japanese War in the following way. The Restoration dramatically altered the national political scene, and by eradicating the *han*, the feudal domains, change was brought down to the provincial level. But it was the onset of the Industrial Revolution, which began just after the war, that actually altered life in the villages.⁸

It was against this backdrop that a new Japan was being born. By the end of the Russo-Japanese War in 1905, Japan's first industrial revolution was fully under way, a new middle class was emerging, while an industrial proletariat was also becoming clearly visible.⁹ As Asukai Masamichi has pointed out, nowhere was this feeling more clearly evident than in the world of journalism, where virtually overnight new magazines and newspapers came into being or experienced a rapid expansion of their circulation.¹⁰ Moreover, within the literary world, this shifting of gears was symbolically expressed by one publishing house's consolidation in 1895 of two previous publications into a single, larger magazine, *Taiyô* (The Sun), which soon became a prestigious journal and a great financial success.¹¹ In Professor Kano's estimation, *Taiyô*'s large-scale and eclectic character guaranteed it widespread appeal, which in turn made the magazine an ideal forum for the bourgeois ideals of the newly-emerging middle class. It became the symbol of Japan's first industrial revolution.¹² This latter point elicited Uchida Roan's observation that with the appearance of *Taiyô* "proof that a magazine could also be a respectable business venture was firmly established."¹³

The Legacy of Kitamura Tôkoku and the Turn from Politics to Literature

Economic motivation alone, however, is not adequate to explain all the intensified activity in the journalistic world. There was a genuine and widespread feeling that all was not right in Japan. Yes, the victory in war brought about a heightened sense of national unity, and many young people felt that the time was right to carry over the momentum from this victory to create a new, truly modern national literature. However, finding writers who were willing to take up this challenge was more complicated than one might think. Just before the war, there had already been a powerful statement made by the writer and critic Kitamura Tôkoku (1868–94), often regarded as the founder of modern Japanese romanticism. He was also the prototype for young men whose passions were stirred by the popular rights movement but who turned away from politics and toward literature (*seiji kara bungaku e*, 政治から文学へ) in the 1880s after the movement had lost its power to inspire young people. As Meiji youths became increasingly disaffected with politics they turned inward and sought to become writers and critics, adopting the new social role of the *bungaku seinen* (literary youth). Tôkoku stands out because he was a pioneer in charting the problems of his day and remains a pivotal figure in Japanese intellectual history. He was young, talented, and committed. Deeply involved in the popular rights movement as a youngster, he consciously turned away from the world of politics and looked for solutions in religion, literature, and himself. As one writer put it:

> Tôkoku was the first writer in Japanese history to explore seriously the nature and potentialities of the self and to try to integrate a philosophy of self into an overall view of life. By reason of this new view of life, centered upon self and his theory of the inner life (*naibu seimei*), Tôkoku was one of the first really modern Japanese writers. There is a sharp break between him and those who had gone before, just as there is a remarkable continuity between him and those who came after. By anticipating in his work the themes and problems that were to occupy later writers, he well deserves the title of forerunner, which has been given him by Japanese critics.[14]

Under the influence of writers such as Byron, Carlyle, and Emerson, Tôkoku introduced some novel perspectives to Japanese readers and seemed to be able to articulate what many others felt but could not put into words themselves. Although he definitely anticipated themes that later appeared in Reiun's work, Tôkoku's relationship with Reiun was more that of a colleague than a precursor.[15] Both were trying to work out similar problems, albeit in slightly different contexts and with different nuances. Tôkoku was a Christian who came to religion by way of his passionate love for the woman he married when he was only twenty years old, making his life experiences very different from Reiun's. Much of his writing was concerned with the theme of romantic love. Moreover, he was a writer who created both fiction and poetry, while Reiun was basically a nonfiction writer, a cultural and literary critic. Reiun never showed much interest in Christianity or any other organized religion. His involvement with love and members of the opposite sex came after he had left the literary world, and these were hardly ideal relationships. With his interest in philosophy and ancient Chinese thought, he came at things very differently from Tôkoku, and yet the two unquestionably shared some common discursive ground.

Specifically, they both reacted strongly against the leading figures in the literary world at that time, the novelists Ozaki Kôyô and Kôda Rohan, because instead of looking forward and challenging their readers, they seemed to be harking back to the literature of the Genroku period (1688–1704) in general and of Saikaku in particular, resurrecting themes of chivalry (*kyô*) and purity (*iki*),[16] along with the fine flowery style that was characteristic of the era. Since Futabatei Shimei had abandoned Japan's "first modern novel" unfinished in the summer of 1889, the Kôyô-Rohan genre of literature was able to move into a position of uncontested dominance in the newly emerging literary world of the 1890s. Kitamura Tôkoku, however, expressed profound doubts about the value of this kind of literature in view of the demands facing modern Japan. In one essay he expressed concern over the neglect of the principles that Tsubouchi Shôyô had espoused in *Tosei Shosei Katagi*,[17] and spoke directly about Kôyô's *Irozange* (1889).

> Mr. Kôyô is very skillful at depicting old-fashioned *ninjô* (human emotions) but in the end such cleverness remains only a clever skill, and one can hardly detect a single special feature emerging from within.[18]

Tôkoku recognized the importance and the power of love in the universe and agreed that it should be a function of literature to explore this mystery.

> [B]ut I never understood that novelists were supposed to stop there. . . . If you lack the capacity to entertain a really deep view of the universe, then you will find it difficult to become a great literary figure.[19]

Why, he asked, could he never be satisfied with this kind of literature?

> It is because all I can make out is a lot of writing aimed at pleasantly passing the time. . . . The day has come when we need people who are indignant. These writers are fine at idle chatter, but they do not have a single tear to shed.[20]

He continued:

> [I]sn't there a single poet or novelist who is conscious of the age in which we live? Isn't there among these eloquent writers one who can shed an honest tear for his country? To be sure, their sentences are rich and powerful, their characters clean and pure, but, as for my emotions, they were not budged even once.[21]

Tôkoku expected something more out of literature than mere entertainment; he wanted passion, deep emotions such as the romantics had manifested. Clearly, there is a link between romanticism and modernism, the former being a precursor to the latter. Without the romantic emphasis on looking inward and seeking one's authentic, natural self, it is difficult to imagine what Peter Gay refers to as the "climate of thought, feeling, and opinion" that characterizes modernity ever coming about.[22] As old ways of thinking about human beings, nature, and the world began to crumble, people were anxiously seeking new approaches to life. For young writers like Tôkoku, simply going back to the past and reviving a literary style of an earlier era would not suffice. Emotions, feelings, and expressions of an authentic self had to be present.[23]

By the 1890s, the times were calling for a different approach to literature, and it was becoming increasingly clear that the up-and-coming writers in Japan would have to break out of these older molds and unite the new streams of experience into an articulate and insightful national literature. This was an appeal that Reiun would voice repeatedly in the years after 1895. Unfortunately, Tôkoku was unable to be a part of that discourse because after a serious bout with mental illness, on a May evening just three months prior to the outbreak of the Sino-Japanese War, he hanged himself from a tree in Shiba Park at the age of twenty-five.

During his brief three-year career, though, Tôkoku had effectively staked out the territory of the principal problems and dilemmas of his age. From his vantage point in the Bungakkai, his small literary group, he hoped to generate new ideas and ideals for the youth of his generation; and, as Reiun would in 1895, he aspired to unite the literary world, and ultimately the entire nation, in a surge of creative activity. But in order to be truly modern and creative, literature needed to be rooted in the real everyday experiences of individuals, and in the genuine self, as Tôkoku had so eloquently argued. As Yoshida Seiichi, a leading expert on Meiji literature, points out, though, the self at this time had an intimate relationship with social realities. Consequently, what critics were increasingly looking for was a literature with concrete social links.[24] Taoka Reiun was a critic who put forth his own clear and distinct conception of how this relationship could work.

Reiun and the Inward Turn

Reiun's version of the inward turn is apparent in the kinds of essays on poetry, aesthetics, metaphysics, and mysticism that he wrote just prior to joining *Seinenbun*. Two articles in particular, one published in *Nihonjin* (October 1894) and the other in *Shûkyô* (January 1895) addressed the topic of mysticism. He opened the *Nihonjin* article, "Mystical Philosophy" (Shimpi tetsugaku), with a paraphrase from Schopenhauer: "Mysticism and philosophy are diametrically opposed. The former explains from within, while the latter explains from without."[25]

It is clear that he is drawing here from volume 2 of *WWR*, where Schopenhauer discusses the mystics from whom he has learned so much and argues how valuable it is to discover mystical truth "in its most beautiful and richest form" such as is found "in the *Oupnek'hat*, in the *Enneads* of Plotinus, in Scotus Erigena, in passages of Jakob Böhme, and especially in the wonderful work of Madame de Guyon, *Les Torrens*, and in Angela Silesius, and finally in the poems of the Sufis."[26] Schopenhauer was well acquainted with mystical writings, and we now know from notes he kept at the time that he believed "Buddha, [Meister] Eckhart, and I teach the same thing; Eckhart in the fetters of his Christian mythology."[27] Inner experience is something real that can be accessed, and Schopenhauer did not need Christianity, with all its baggage, to do so. Philosophy was adequate to the task. Schopenhauer, as noted above, underscored the importance of "looking inward to the psychological facts of our self-experience," something that convinced Reiun of the value of his philosophy for modern times.[28] Following Schopenhauer closely, Reiun went on to discuss the historical development of western philosophy, starting with the Stoics and Epicureans and proceeding to Aristotle, Plato, and the neo-Platonists, and he mentions as well the Indian and Buddhist notions of the divine, the Three Body Doctrine (Trikaya) of the Buddha's manifestation, and the notion of the oneness of all things.

Similarly, in "On the Divine Nature of Mysticism," the longer and more substantial piece that appeared in *Shûkyô*, in 1895, he discusses mysticism as a religious experience that was sought in yoga and Zen, was described in the *Bhagavad Gita* in ancient times, and was currently being approached through philosophy and even science.[29] In terms of western mystical thought, we find him again mentioning Plotinus, Meister Eckhart, Sebastian Franck, Mme. Guyon, and Jakob Böhme, as well as the *Bhagavad Gita*, and, of course, Schopenhauer himself, from whom he was clearly gleaning much of his information. Plotinus is quoted to the effect that when we meditate, subject and object distinctions disappear, and by completely immersing ourselves in contemplation we are able to transcend time and space and experience oneness with the universe.[30] While Reiun may not have known this, Plotinus was an admirer of Indian thought, too, and in fact he was on his way to Persia to learn more when Emperor Gordian III—to whose armies he was attached—was assassinated and Plotinus was unable to complete the journey.

In "On the Divine Nature of Mysticism," Reiun also refers to one of Schopenhauer's essays in *On the Will in Nature* about animal magnetism, for here figures like James Braid and Dietrich Georg von Kieser (1779–1862) had caught the philosopher's attention, sparking his interest in this kind of emerging "scientific" investigation. Reiun's point was that with the passing of the nineteenth century, which was so caught up in skepticism and logical analysis, the time would be ripe to combine what had been learned from philosophy, mysticism, and modern science in creative new ways in order to investigate and better understand the inner world of the individual. For this is the only place where one can discover the deeper, more permanent truths of human existence. For Reiun the recent European interest in psychic phenomena, hypnotism, and Asian thought was not only proof that these were things worth exploring by contemporary Japanese but also represented an opportunity for human beings to take dramatic steps forward in uncovering the secret truths for which people had been searching throughout the ages. Moreover—and perhaps this was the most important thing to Reiun—they offered a basis on which the principles of eastern and western civilization could be merged in order to give birth to a new, more holistic global culture.

Finally, in another pair of articles Reiun wrote in late 1895, in which he commented on the recent popularity of Zen Buddhism and the renewed interest in *zazen* (sitting meditation), he expressed the fear that this interest might be little more than the latest fad, a popular trend in which people were dabbling. Were these people prepared to take seriously the opportunity to gain insights into the deeper recesses of the human mind and spirit in order to move forward with a renewed synthesis between East and West in the coming century? Japan was uniquely situated to lead such a movement, but Reiun was not convinced that the rising popularity of Zen was a reliable indicator that Japan was moving in the right direction.[31] It was time for writers and critics to start wielding a mightier pen than they had been.

Seinenbun Writings

Reiun inaugurated his literary column in the first issue of *Seinenbun* with the somber observation that the literary world was in a state of transition, undergoing seasonal change of the sort that we might see in nature. The literary world seemed to be experiencing "winter decay," and when Reiun looked out across the literary horizon, he remarked that "it is the cold and desolate spectacle of winter as far as the eye can see."[32] The war effort had brought forth nothing noteworthy in the literary sphere except a plethora of military songs (*gunka*), something Reiun could not accept as a valid form of national literary expression.[33] He longed for a national poet (*kokumin shijin*), but he was uncomfortable over the ease with which the Japanese had won the war, for he believed that only through adversity can people come to know themselves and learn to express the feelings of their innermost hearts. But if winter had set in, spring cannot be far behind. In the essay "Thoughts at the Outset of 1895 on Youth's Promising Destiny," he viewed the first twenty-seven years of the Meiji era as encompassing modern Japan's infancy and adolescence and proclaimed it the duty of youth in the postwar era to forge a mature Japanese spirit out of the best features of both eastern and western cultures.[34] He credited the *kokusui-hozon* movement with directing attention away from the mindless Europeanization of the early decades of Meiji and back to Japan's own special characteristics and its links to ancient Asian civilization—a clear acknowledgment of his debt to Miyake Setsurei and the Seikyôsha. But now, he argued, it was time to go beyond simply "preserving national essence" (*kokusui-hozon*) or even "enhancing the nation's special characteristics" (*kokusui-hatsuyô*), and get down to the serious business of creating a new civilization based on a combination of eastern and western thought. He concludes his essay with the following.

> The great task of seeing that this is achieved is the lifework, the calling of we young people. The insincere devotees of western civilization certainly cannot be counted on, nor can the decrepit conservative pedants undertake it. So it is up to us, and to achieve our goals we must come to understand both the strengths and the weaknesses of our civilization. Likewise, we must have a thorough knowledge of the West, so indeed the burden on our shoulders is great.[35]

Like Tôkoku before him, Reiun was making it clear from the outset that he wished to disassociate himself from two prominent streams found in the literary and journalistic world: the enthusiastic westernism of Tokutomi Sohô and the Min'yûsha, and the pedantry of Ozaki Kôyô and the Ken'yûsha. In a subsequent piece on Sohô, Reiun dismissed him as a third-rate thinker and writer who just happened to have been in the right place at the right time. He was such a worldly, pragmatic figure that, despite his claims of having been deeply influenced by Christianity, Reiun saw him as an irreligious man, "more like Fukuzawa than Niijima." Moreover, he could not forgive Sohô for reversing himself and actively supporting the government, so he chided him with a play on words: "It may be all right to change your theory (setsu, 説), but don't betray your honor (setsu, 節)."[36]

Similarly, Reiun was hostile to Ozaki Kôyô, founder of the Ken'yûsha and a leading literary figure of the day. Although he never questioned Kôyô's talent as a writer, and, like Tôkoku, he could credit him with a clever and effective literary style, Reiun was impatient with his superficiality and his lack of ideas and imagination. He was long on technique but short on heart and compassion. Most distasteful, however, was his willingness to sit back and profit from his writings while playing the teacher (*sensei*) role and lording it over the young writers who flocked around him to gain his patronage. In Reiun's eyes, Kôyô had passed the peak of his popularity and would soon be a figure of the past.[37] In 1895 literature was still too beholden to the old styles from the Genroku era, and literary criticism was failing to offer a new language or a comprehensive vision. Literature needed to be created anew; it needed to become energetic, and committed to social change. It had to grapple with the real questions of the day. In Reiun's estimation, that is how literature should fulfill its role in society, but it was currently failing to do so.

Concerned about the growth of materialism and a purely selfish and utilitarian spirit, Reiun was holding out for the appearance of some kind of literary *ijin* (偉人, great man) who would be passionate and sympathetic and above all with ideals.[38] In "Realism and Ideals," he explained that realism is a fine tool as far as it goes. It is capable of revealing to us the form of things, but ideals are necessary in order to penetrate into the soul, into the deeper spirit of things. Realism, therefore, must be part of any writer's arsenal, but it cannot be the sole object of his or her labors.[39] Reiun likened realism to the materials an architect might use to construct a building, but like novelists, he felt, it is the architect's job to construct a beautiful building that reaches to the stars. Drawing on a powerful metaphor of the day, he spoke in terms of smelting and wrote about the searing flames of the furnace, which reduce matter to powder and ashes. But it is ideals that have to fuel this purification process, and it is up to writers to inject the purity of their art and vision into the reality in which they are immersed. Reality, then, provides the framework, the context, for their creations, but it is their art that must infuse the text with heart and soul. Writing needs to be a quasi-religious experience in which the author experiences higher realms of human consciousness and the small self of the everyday world is lost in the boundless self of the cosmos. Part and parcel of this experience should be kyônetsu (狂熱), an intense, even frenzied passion.[40] This, Reiun felt, was the key to attaining profound insights into the human experience and to producing a literature that truly moves its readers. In Reiun's eyes, genius is always accompanied by this kind of passion bordering on madness, which is the source of truly inspirational writing. If writers lack this element, no matter how dazzling the form and structure of their sentences, their literary output will be lifeless.[41] A genuine, selfless literary figure is obviously the complete antithesis of the well-paid, complacent author who composes skillful but artless works that might entertain people but cannot stir them—which is precisely how Reiun viewed Ozaki Kôyô.

In "Literature and Religion," he also observed that, because human beings naturally seek peace of mind, they turn to religion and faith. But when you come down to it, religion is no more than philosophical truth expressed in a less concrete form. However, religious faith does involve passion, sincerity, and earnestness. Do we see any of these in contemporary society? No! We are likely to find plenty of superficiality and irresponsibility but no sign of passion, ideals, or commitment. Reiun is not interested in "religious novels" per se, but he sees poetic insight and religious emotion as closely related, so he would like to see some of this religious fervor translated into fiction.[42] These ideas were apparent in his call for writers to be discontented with the world around them.[43] In "Dai fuhei nare!" he argued that where ideals are present there is bound to be discontent because there is always a built-in conflict between the idealistic vision of poets and the realities of the world around them.

> Their ideals are continually obstructed by existing realities, and as a result there is contradiction and conflict. The heart tries to suppress the agony and dissatisfaction that inevitably grows, but it cannot. As a result, discontent deepens. Without other outlets for all this pent-up feeling, it should be gushing out in the form of poetry. And if it does, these will be poems with passion and intensity, which can move people.[44]

Honing in on this fundamental dichotomy, this contradiction in the emerging capitalist society, Reiun wondered whether Japan was capable of facing the real world with all its flaws and contradictions. The Japanese, he felt, might lack a genuine sense of pathos. When they cry, it is like the tears of an infant who can be easily distracted. Thus, Reiun saw as inevitable in the years ahead a critical growing-up process for Japan. If Japan were to step forward and assume its place in the world, then the Japanese people would have to learn to face reality. But some superficial notion of "realism" would not suffice. This would be achieved and expressed in literature only if writers could attain the view of reality that comes with profound insight into the totality of life's deepest experiences as captured in a moment of inspiration. But in order to accomplish this, writers would have to know themselves, to look within and know their souls.

Finding Compassion

Although Reiun came to be known for his frank and sometimes very pointed essays, most of his literary criticism was devoted to drawing attention to a number of young, up-and-coming authors and encouraging them to go deeper and do more. He wanted them to step out from under the shadow of Kôyô and break with convention. Old styles needed to be replaced with new stances. The most notable among these young authors were Izumi Kyôka, Kawakami Bizan, Kosugi Tengai, and Hirotsu Ryûrô, all of whom were closely associated with the Ken'yûsha. So Reiun's critique can be read as one component in an overall effort to dislodge Kôyô from his position of eminence. That is, by encouraging these writers and promoting their talents, Reiun hoped to drive a wedge between them and Kôyô, leaving the latter isolated.[45] But it would be unfair and misleading to presume that Reiun's only interest in these writers was strategic. They represented a new wave in the literary world; their novels were being dubbed *shingoku* (grave, serious) or *hisan* (miserable, wretched) because their themes revolved around great misfortune and human suffering. Odagiri Hideo has noted that the appearance of these writers' new works one after another throughout 1895 marked a turning point in Meiji literary history, for they signaled the end of the dominance of the older *gesaku*-style literature favored by the Ken'yûsha.[46] Izumi Kyôka's novels are often called *kannen* (conceptual novels) because they frequently revolved around a certain key idea, such as duty in his well-known tale *Yakô junsa* (Night Patrolman), in which a young policeman forfeits his life to save that of a man who had refused to allow him to marry his daughter.[47] As was typical of much of this *kannen*, *shingoku*, and *hisan* fiction, there was a strong sense of the inadequacy and betrayal implicit in the *bunmei-kaika* ideology, which had promised so much but delivered so little. As the historian Hirota Masaki notes, for example, since society was becoming much more divisive in the post war years, the experience of becoming modern was beginning to drive wedges between citizens in the newly emerging state structure.[48]

It is not surprising, then, that Reiun, who was concerned about Japan not living up to the promises of modernity, was excited and encouraged by the appearance of these new dark trends in literature. In what Nishida has called his "monumental statement," "The New Brilliance in Japanese Literature," Reiun gave these writers credit for ushering in a new era in Japanese literature, the most significant one since the coming of Commodore Perry.[49] Yet Reiun was not blind to the limitations of these writers, and he was often critical of their weak characterization and tendency to feature deformed or otherwise abnormal people as central characters.[50] It was his hope, however, that their efforts would constitute a beginning, a first step toward creating a new literature, a foundation on which something more substantial could be built. Moreover, his basis for supporting them was that they were realistically looking at their surroundings and dealing with what they found, even if it did not necessarily make a pretty picture. But to simply depict misfortune was insufficient. Literature needed to do more; it needed to exhibit compassion.

We saw in the previous chapter how important the concept of sympathy or compassion (dôjô, 同情, Schopenhauer's *Mitleid*) was to Reiun's philosophical grounding. He argued in the pages of his literary magazine that, along with intense or frenzied passion, *kyônetsu* (狂熱), compassion was a crucial ingredient of serious literature. By the term *compassion*, Reiun did not refer only to the capacity for understanding of and empathy with the plight of others. As he had learned from Schopenhauer, this term signified the merging of the small worldly self with the larger, universal self of the cosmos. In "Poets and Compassion" he argued:

> Poets and writers must not lack compassion, for observation that lacks compassion is superficial, and writing that lacks compassion is shallow. People with compassion can pour their heart and soul into their writing. Because they are sincere, they can genuinely make people feel something.[51]

Unlike the scientist, who views the universe mechanistically, as if it were a dead, sterile thing, the poet, through compassion, merges with the universe and makes it come alive. As a result, this view is deep compared to the shallow vision of the scientist. It is likewise sympathy or compassion that enables the upright man, the *gijin* (義人), to become a savior, someone who can offer his life without regret for the sake of the people.

> Ah, the reason no great authors have emerged is that our poets and writers lack sufficient sympathy or compassion. That a true savior has not appeared is because our authors lack sufficient compassion. But there are many people waiting for a true *gijin* to emerge in the form of a serious poet or writer. But, alas, when will one appear?[52]

Reiun saw the potential for more sympathy and compassion occurring in literature in the shift of these young writers toward tales of human misfortune, which is why he welcomed the trend. He saw sympathy and compassion underlying Ryûrô's work, and he considered Kyôka a genius capable of expressing the same thing.[53] But seemingly only one writer came close to meeting Reiun's expectations with regard to a sense of empathy or sympathy, and this was Higuchi Ichiyô (1872–96), the talented young author who died before her twenty-fifth birthday. Known for her poignant and insightful descriptions of life in the Yoshiwara (Pleasure) district, Ichiyô was a very important Meiji literary figure. In one critic's estimation, she was significant in her ability to bridge the gap between the spirit of Edo literature and the demands of modern fiction. This can be substantiated by the fact that, although her literary style and themes gave her something in common with the Ken'yûsha writers, she was warmly received by the young romantic writers at the journal Tôkoku created, *Bungakkai*, and some of her stories appeared in this journal as well. In fact, many scholars see Ichiyô as the most important writer to emerge from the *Bungakkai* circle during the years immediately after Tôkoku's death.[54] In a tribute to Reiun after his death, Sasagawa Rimpû wrote of his good friend:

> Reiun was extremely rich in compassion. He was also a genius who could recognize the quality of genius in others. He was the first person to recognize the talent of Izumi Kyôka and praise it wholeheartedly. Today Miss Ichiyô's name is loudly proclaimed throughout the literary world, but when her story "Takekurabe" was first serialized in *Bungakkai*, Reiun was the first to unqualifiedly praise her genius. *Bungakkai* may have first introduced her work to the public, but Reiun was the first to introduce the public to Ichiyô.[55]

Some might quibble with this claim, wondering if it was not a review of "Takekurabe" in Mori Ôgai's magazine *Mezamashi Kusa* by Ôgai, Kôda Rohan, and Saito Ryûkû that first placed Ichiyô in the limelight.[56] But that Reiun recognized her talents early on and continuously praised her major works, especially "Takekurabe" and "Nigorie" (Muddy Bay), can be neither questioned nor overlooked.[57] What Reiun valued highly in Ichiyô's work was her ability to depict characters from the world around her, such as prostitutes and laborers who struggled and suffered all their lives, and to do so with compassion so that they truly came alive as characters. Therefore, even though Ichiyô's language echoed the older, classical style, she infused it with new sensibilities and was able to uncover and transmit the character's innermost feelings with great skill and sensitivity. To seek out and discover human feelings in the midst of poverty and misfortune was for Reiun the mark of a compassionate genius.[58] But, as we saw above, realistic depiction was only part of the story for Reiun. He regarded it as the foundation of good literature, but he believed that there had to be more. Reiun found in Ichiyô's work to be an important statement about the dual nature of existence that is so often neglected by writers. For deep down beneath the layers of the external, social self there is a deeper, unchanging spiritual self, and Ichiyô grasped this.

Everyone possesses the external self; it is made up of our acquired attributes, the stuff of our habits, customs, and behaviors. Literally, it is our "second nature" (shûsei, 習性). However, Reiun did not want his readers to confuse this external self with the inner, spiritual self. The external self, which is like a mask we are forced to wear, is shaped by the environment. All the laws and social mores that society creates are aimed at this self. But codes and courts of law cannot address the inner person who dwells behind the mask; they do not touch our fundamental humanity. This is where a writer like Ichiyô comes in, a writer who can show that within characters whose outer selves are prisoners of the environment there always remains a second, deeper level, where the spiritual self resides.

The Environment and Spirituality

Reiun developed these ideas further in a companion piece, "Environment and Spirituality" (Kyôgû to reisei) where he stressed that the duty of writers is to not ignore this binary fact of our existence, the presence of this duality, but instead to probe it and try and depict both sides of reality—the good and the bad, the light and the dark, the inside and the outside. For this is the only way we can confront the whole truth of existence.[59] He explained it like this.

> Let's not waste time talking about whether it's the environment (境遇) that shapes our character or whether our basic natures (性) are simply the sum total of all our little habits and behaviors (習い). It is not that simple. Each of us does possess a self (自己), and that self has a soul or spirit (靈性). So we have two sides to our nature: we do have the selves that are the product of all our everyday life habits and are shaped by the environment in which we live, but we also have these inner selves, our true spiritual natures, and they are inherent. But they become so deeply buried within us, so suppressed, so twisted out of shape by social forces, that they are almost impossible to locate and uncover. Our only chance to catch a glimpse of this inner self at the darkest recesses of our being is when there happens to be a flash of illumination like a bolt of lightning splitting the darkness in two for just an instant. You had better look quickly, though, because it will be gone before you know it. But this is where we need to look because this is where our true inner nature resides. If we want to penetrate that deepest level of our being, if we want to see past the superficial self that is shaped and molded by the environment, if we want to look past that tangle of habits that we call our second nature, then we had better learn to look with the right kind of eyes; we need to be able to employ the right kind of vision. And for that we must have compassion, or sympathy (同情) in our hearts, and manifest mercy and forgiveness (寬恕) in our actions. We cannot afford to be without these elements, and this is especially true for writers.[60]

It is no easy task that Reiun sets before his readers; the inner person is elusive and difficult to grasp. It might appear suddenly, like a flash of lightning on a dark night, only to disappear again immediately.[61] It is fleeting and difficult to capture, but it represents human nature in its most genuine and essential form, so it is the only way to get at the true nature of the human experience.[62] What is especially important here is that Reiun is starting to put together a model of how an individual might exist in the world, how he or she might perceive and come to grips with the inner self. Perhaps his vision of the inner self has its roots in the days when he had to leave the Osaka Middle School and was hospitalized as a youth. Given his circumstances and inability to focus on other things, he turned inward and discovered something in his inner nature or being. He was now coming to understand that this inner self is subject to the vagaries of one's surroundings, of what he calls the "environment." But if one can spend time in observation and contemplation of how the environment, external reality, operates on the self, then one has the opportunity to raise one's awareness of the true nature of this inner self. One can see how it actually functions in real time.[63] His language in many of his *Seinenbun* essays is all about the self, about one's inner nature, one's character, even the soul. As Munitz mentions in his book on acquiring a cosmic understanding of the universe, "[I]ntensified awareness of the Boundless Existence . . . helps give life an additional dimension of meaning."[64] Reiun wanted writers and readers of his generation to probe more deeply and develop an appreciation for these additional levels of meaning.

In order to penetrate the external layers of the self that are rooted in the environment, and to make contact with the deeper, innermost part of the human experience, Reiun believed a special kind of perception is required, a key element of which is *dôjô* (compassion), the term inspired by Schopenhauer's notion of *Mitleid*. By means of compassion, the hearts of the subject and the object—the writer and the character (and the reader)—are linked. A sense of community, of solidarity, can be constructed once people appreciate that the suffering of one means the suffering of all.[65] Then the actions of the characters, their external behavior, can be viewed with empathy, forgiveness, and understanding. So to seek out the inner person that resides in even the outcast or the criminal is to affirm the good in humanity and the humaneness of all humankind. And also it brings us closer to reality, for to depict only the external self—the social self, the one constructed out of our habits and customs, everything to which we have become acculturated—is to see only one dimension of the human experience. This is not true reality; it is not all that literature can depict. In "Environment and Spirituality," though, Reiun argues that Higuchi Ichiyô was capable of delivering this kind of deep insight even though her style might read like a throwback to classical Japanese. To Reiun it was never just a matter of verb endings or syntax. Literature has to have content, it needs to be about something, and it needs to grapple with important ideas that have something to do with real life issues. In her latest work, "Nigorie" Reiun found her portraits of the inner nature of the young prostitutes so elegantly crafted and filled with such deep compassion and understanding that they were capable of moving the reader and raising the his or her awareness or consciousness. That is precisely what he wanted literature to do.

Reiun and the Dark Side of Society

In his 1897 essay "The Development of a Materialistic Civilization and Humanity," Reiun starkly criticized any developmental trajectory that values only material improvements to the neglect of the spiritual and metaphysical sides of existence. What Japan was experiencing was the polarization of society into rich and poor. A perfect case in point was the recent Ashio Mine Pollution Incident in which the mine owner and operator, Furukawa Ichibei, stood squarely on the side of the wealthy, watching as the poor suffered and disproportionately bore the burden of this lopsided approach to becoming modern.[66] Even after he began editing his own literary journal, Reiun was still an occasional contributor to *Nihonjin*. In an essay entitled "Poets and the Pessimistic View of Life," he set down some of his thoughts about the role of the poet in society.[67] Why, he begins, are so many poets pessimistic about the world? It can't be explained solely in terms of a statistical analysis of the proportion of pleasure to pain such as von Hartmann attempts to do, nor by Schopenhauer's vision of everything in the context of will, nor even by a religious hope for happiness in the world to come. Poets' pessimism is neither religious nor philosophical in origin; rather, it comes from their poetic nature. Poets do not operate under principles or reason, and they are not bound by faith; they just perceive intuitively and feel. Consequently poets are the sensitive ones who are easily moved by the world around them. Due to their sensitivity, however, the sham, deceit, and falsity of the world are difficult for them to endure.

But things weren't necessarily always this way. In ancient times, before literacy, people were simple creatures of feeling, so in a sense all were poets. But, he wrote, the nineteenth century is a world of materialism, of intellectual cleverness; it destroys poets and the poetic spirit. The nineteenth century praises analysis, thrives on meticulously breaking down the object, gouging out and exposing its particulars in minute detail, and classifying them for further reference. Such a view leaves no room for a single, sweeping intuitive grasp of the universe. The argument unfolds along lines that are now familiar, ultimately reaching the conclusion that it is no wonder poets such as Byron and Heine grew weary of the world. On the contrary, it would be difficult to understand if they had not. But until things can be set right, the poet, the sensitive observer of society, must continue to express honestly what he or she feels, even if it is only a catalog of human misery. The same code was later explicitly applied to critics and reporters when Reiun wrote:

> Critics must lead society, they must be a friend to society, they must become its guide; they must improve society; they must do their best to educate and enlighten it. If there are flaws in society, they must be pointed out, and critics must call for their rectification. If there are transgressions, they must warn of these. And it is up to them to address those issues in society that lie outside the direct purview of the law. They must be the supporters of social morality. . . . If society is imperfect, then they, too, are imperfect. But can we really say that today's critics and newspaper reporters are fulfilling their obligations to the best of their ability? Today the occupation of newspaper reporter has become something of a glory position, a prestigious occupation. But isn't this an insult to the dignity of the profession? . . . Reporters and critics must be independent and not submit to pressure from the authorities; they must not give in to the interests of the rich and the powerful.[68]

We encounter here the familiar distrust of complacency, as well as something that grew out of Reiun's perceptions of Higuchi Ichiyô's writings: the idea that there is a realm of human affairs that does not fall under the jurisdiction of society's laws, and here it is up to writers and poets to dig deep and create a complete picture of the human experience, encompassing both inner and outer realms. To these must be added another element contained in the opening lines, not quoted above, where Reiun directly links the inroads made by materialism to deterioration in the spiritual realm.

> People speak of "civilization" (*bunmei*) and "enlightenment" (*kaika*), and the splendors they promise are certainly more than enough to amaze and dazzle the beholder. But this view only takes into consideration the external world; it pertains only to the surface.[69]

Of course, to write of *bunmei-kaika* is to summon up the legacy of Fukuzawa Yukichi, who looms as a giant of his day, but by the mid-1890s he is already starting to appear to some as a critic who had gotten it wrong.[70]

That is why Reiun would later couch his critique of modernity in the form of a *hibunmeiron*, a rejection of modern civilization's underlying principles, which were so unequivocally endorsed and uncritically praised in the 1870s and 1880s. Such a belief was the cornerstone of Reiun's earlier, boldly stated appeal to writers to probe the dark side of progress, and expose the social costs of industrialization. In "Novels and the Dark Side of Society," he begins by denouncing the growth of an obscene luxuriousness and the destruction of public morality, which he sees as the cornerstones of modern civilized life. In his eyes, corruption abounds everywhere. Is it any wonder that writers and reporters are beginning to focus their attention on this dark side of society? But so far, it is only a beginning. Assuming the rhetorically exaggerated stance that would become his calling card, Reiun lashes out.

> Ah! Expose! Expose! Let us keep exposing the dark side of society! Isn't it the task of critics and reporters to criticize the corruption that lies outside the laws of society—to fix the blame, to reprove it, ridicule it, abuse it, and then suddenly to make it repent and right itself? But just to give vent to this evil, to expose this indecency and be done with it, will never be sufficient. Peoples' hearts are easily swayed, so if we stop with just exposing the unsightly, people will be easily lured and pulled into the deep pool of evil. What we need is passionate writers whose work is alive with blood and tears, who laugh on the outside but weep within. We need writers who are indignant on the outside but grieve within. It is my hope that the nation's writers, in addition to exposing society's ills, will shed tears of sympathy and weep for the sake of humanity, be wrathful for the sake of morality, and let their screams and shouts serve as the warning bell at dawn heralding the awesome thunder of chastisement.[71]

The language and imagery of this passage bristle with emotion, and their intent is clear: the truth needs to be told, and the contradictory side of human nature must be exposed. But the object is not to revel in the spectacle of it and pull humanity farther down into the morass of corruption. Rather, the purpose is to reform and redeem society. Realism just for "shock value," or for the sake of exposure, is of little or no consequence. Writers must "embrace ideals" so that ultimately they can be restored and the situation recovered.

Likewise, in a companion piece, "Writers and the Poor at the Lower Depths of Society," Reiun argues as follows.

> This so-called *bunmei-kaika* is nothing more than a civilization that favors the wealthy. Although the aristocratic classes were overthrown in the name of liberty, this only served to additionally widen the gap between rich and

poor. The elaborate machines that have accompanied the advance of this materialistic civilization have robbed the worker of his job, and the spread of luxury that has accompanied the growth of this glorious civilization has swept the poor aside and magnified their suffering and distress. The rich are made richer and the poor poorer; the rich are continuously happy, while the poor constantly suffer. In the houses with the red lacquered gates, the horses are well fed, while in the streets the number of pale beggars swells. . . .

The present civilization, in addition to seducing those of the middle strata and above into a life of vice and corruption, sweeps aside the lower classes altogether and plunges them into the dark valley of misery. Today the people at the lower depths of society are starving, but do they die? No, rather than die they are forced to steal in order to eat . . . so rather than dying of starvation, they must live bearing the label of criminal. When we compare these crimes of the lower classes to the corruption that arises from idleness among the upper classes, we must feel pity. But people do not provide punishment; they do not take to task the "big fish," who get away and pollute the waters of the upper strata of society.

Ah, is it that after all peoples' eyes can only see the light and not the dark? Moreover, their poverty is not necessarily the result of laziness, and their transgressions are not necessarily their own doing. Once you sink into the deep abyss of poverty, it is difficult to rise again to the top of the current; once you become a convict, the world never forgets it. . . . Alas, aren't those with the most wretched fate in the land, with the most pitiable lives, the members of this lower stratum of society? Yet isn't it up to the poets and writers to capture the wretchedness of their fate and to depict their pitiable lives?

Today, now that readers have at last grown weary of skillfully crafted novels about clever men and beautiful women and of epic tales about brave heroes and heroines, they are showing signs of turning to stories that deal with real problems, stories that probe human nature, and seek to unlock the secrets of the soul. Now is the time for authors to pour out their hearts and souls, to express their sympathy and compassion as they depict the wretched fate of these people. They must consecrate the fiery spirit of their inner being, channel it through their brushes and into their depictions of these peoples' pitiful lives. They must sound the deep sigh of lament for these people, whose story remains untold, and speak out on their behalf. It is time to vigorously voice their complaint to the world. After all, isn't the reason why [Victor] Hugo's pen could create the shaking and roaring of thunder and the billowing up of waves because he was indignant on account of the unheralded, because he wept over their wretched fate, and because his voice was the cry of humanity? Ah, but who is capable of doing this for Japan, who will step forward and do this for Japan?[72]

The Emergence of Social Problems (*shakai mondai*)

The crux of Reiun's literary criticism can be found in the passages that seek to expose the "dark side" of modern industrial society. What distinguishes Reiun from other literary critics of the day is the importance he attached to the emergence of "social problems" (*shakai-mondai*, 社会問題).[73] To be sure, there were other critics who called for a Japanese social novel or expressed a concern for social problems. But no other critic took it as far as Reiun, and no one else singled out the gap between the rich and the poor as the foremost issue confronting Japan in the 1890s. The Industrial Revolution was just getting under way in Japan, so the fact that Reiun could isolate this dilemma at such an early stage indicates that he was well ahead of his time.

Given the fact that Japan's industrialization was still in its incipient stages in 1895, there is a temptation to dismiss Reiun's concerns as somewhat overblown. However, a similar tendency to accentuate these kinds of problems was widespread among European writers in the early the nineteenth century as well. Jacob L. Talmon suggests that the age "was fascinated by and obsessively interested in the problems of industry."[74]

> In particular, no topic was more discussed in the 1830's and 1840's than the social question. This was centered on the industrial worker in the new urban agglomerations which had grown at a fantastic speed . . . their miserable existence and long hours, child labor, disease, unemployment, insecurity and general degradation, the desperate struggle of spinners and weavers to compete with the machine—such things loomed much larger than was warranted by the numerical proportion of proletarians to the population as a whole. They did so because men were intensely conscious of a vast transformation afoot, and because the evils of industrialism contradicted so flagrantly the expectations and claims engendered by that transformation.[75]

Since this sort of consciousness was not nearly so widespread in Japan in 1895, Reiun needs to be recognized for his perceptiveness as well as his precociousness. While other humanitarian thinkers and activists, such as Christians, socialists, and anarchists, may have shared his misgivings, few placed them as centrally in their arguments as Reiun did.

Yokoyama Gennosuke and Matsubara Iwagorô

During Reiun's tenure as a literary critic, a principal source of data about living conditions among poor laborers was the *Mainichi shinbun*, a leading Japanese daily edited by the Christian Shimada Saburô. As noted earlier, a protégé of the writer Futabatei Shimei, Yokoyama Gennosuke (1870–1915), was on the staff of the *Mainichi* at the time and under the influence of a pioneer researcher on the urban poor, Matsubara Iwagorô (1866–1935), as well as of Futabatei, who had set literature aside in search of something more concrete. Yokoyama set out to record social conditions in the wake of the Sino-Japanese War.[76] His findings were serialized in the Mainichi and elsewhere throughout 1896-97 under such headlines as "Present Conditions among Manual Laborers," "Living Conditions among Tenants," "The State of Poor People in Tokyo," "The Present State of Handicrafts," and "Labor in the Mechanized Factory." In 1900 they were assembled and published in a single volume under the title *The Lower Strata of Japanese Society*.[77] Making effective use of official government figures, as well as compiling an impressive amount of original data, the author put together a well-documented and sometimes chilling account of conditions among the poor and laboring classes. One point demonstrated by Yokoyama was that workers in modern factories had no advantages in terms of livelihood or lifestyle compared to the poor of the preindustrial society, which had been made up mainly of coolies, day laborers, rickshaw men, and the like.[78]

In addition to this publication, considerable effort was made in another book Yokoyama published around the same time, *Japan after Mixed Residence (Naichi zakkyo ato no Nihon)*, to demonstrate that recent price rises had offset any gains provided by the spurt of industrial prosperity sparked by the Sino-Japanese War.[79] Accompanying a table that showed the difference between prewar and postwar prices was the following explanation.

> If we inquire into the causes of the [price rise], we can point to the immediate factors of expanding governmental and industrial expenditures, along with the growth of general purchasing power, which in the end are nothing more than manifestations of the consequences of the war. Comparing price increases with increases in the level of wages, we see that the latter are consistently lower, which means there are grounds for maintaining that the war had a favorable impact on workers.
>
> However, the period 1895–96, with the succession of victories in the war, was a prosperous time for all, and throughout the provinces all life signs were vital. Even laborers were well off. But those industries that had arisen suddenly to meet the immediate demands of the situation began to gradually give way in the latter half of 1896, and the cry of panic was frequently heard. In places like the spinning mills, where talk of work shortages was most widespread, workers were laid off, and with the overall slump in the industrial world, the labor force is on the verge of a terrible depression. Should we in the end rejoice over the war or not?[80]

But, the author continues, since these developments have all worked to focus attention on the problems of the poor, there is room for encouragement. He notes with approval the growth of labor unions and the frequency of strikes, both primarily postwar phenomena. After all, he began his studies under the tutelage of Futabatei Shimei, and Yokoyama shared with his mentor the same deep concern for the poor and downtrodden that Futabatei had encountered in Russian literature.[81] Therefore, Yokoyama was never ambivalent about where he stood. He openly encouraged workers to organize and unite. He saw the Sino-Japanese War as a curtain rising on a new era for the labor movement, and in his eyes the coming struggle would be between worker and capitalist, between the rich and the poor.[82]

Reiun definitely admired the efforts of men like Yokoyama and Matsubara, and in a *Seinenbun* piece he specifically singled them out and endorsed their contributions.[83] But of course these sorts of "white paper" exposés were hardly the stuff of the great literature that Reiun envisioned. Yes, great literature had to be founded on reality; it had to be rooted in the conditions of life that surround readers and writers. But great literature also had to go beyond the limitations of the immediate in order to encounter truth that is universal and immortal. Therefore, Reiun could take issue with another critic's approach, even though it took social problems into account, because the call for a "national poet" (*kokumin shijin*) seemed too restrictive.[84] That is, while poets and writers should respond to their environment, to the conditions in their society and nation, this should never limit the purview of literature. For Reiun literature still had to penetrate the depths of the human experience and reach the deepest recesses of the human heart. It needed to open readers' eyes and hearts to the truth. Consequently, he could entertain no vision that dealt only with the citizens of a single nation or probed only superficial aspects of individual experiences.

True, Reiun himself had once called for a national poet, but he required that this poet first of all be a great poet. A poet who only captures the spirit of his or her times will fade with the passage of time. But when the poet makes contact with the absolute, when the poet encounters the universality of human nature, then he or she is in the presence of something immortal. Great literature is the product of this kind of contact, and it was for this and nothing less that Reiun believed writers must strive.

In taking a position such as this, Reiun was reacting with profound insight to developments in the world around him. His hopes for a Japanese Victor Hugo and obsession with the "dark side" of modern civilization were not shallow preoccupations. Rather, they were concerns rooted in a deep suspicion of the way in which wealth and materialism could corrupt human and social life by replacing ideals with the profit motive. Reiun's was a visceral reaction to a capitalist system that divides society in two, making the wealthy who occupy the top portion complacent and even degenerate while those occupying the lower strata are forced to become beggars and thieves. In his essays on the need to uncover and expose the lot of the downtrodden, Reiun was registering shock at the enormity of the transition modern Japan was undergoing. With his stress on spirituality, coupled with his frank concern for social problems, Reiun was attempting to deal with two themes that were an important part of the intellectual terrain of late Meiji Japan. He wanted writers to be angry, to be outraged, and to contest the values that modern society was imposing on people. But in the mid-1890s, in the afterglow of Japan's first victory in a foreign war, his words all too often fell on deaf ears.

Worlds Apart: The Voice of Takayama Chogyû

While in hindsight it seems clear that Reiun's insights into post war society were "spot on," his views were not the predominant ones at the time. That claim could more accurately be applied to one of his contemporaries, the widely recognized literary critic Takayama Chogyû (1871–1902). Educated at Tokyo Imperial University as a regular student, and one who enjoyed all the privileges accruing to a member of the elite), Chogyû's views were very different from Reiun's. A featured writer for the glossy, highly successful, all-purpose magazine *Taiyô* (The Sun), which boasted a circulation of nearly three hundred thousand and dwarfed much smaller literary magazines such as Taoka's *Seinenbun*, Chogyû was an ardent nationalist and supporter of the state. Chogyû and *The Sun* were at the center of the world of discourse; Reiun and *Seinenbun* were on the periphery. While Chogyû basked in the limelight, Reiun was often marginalized and isolated by the stances he adopted. In almost all respects, Chogyû's critical position was diametrically opposed to Reiun's. Unlike Reiun, who was often critical of the government and focused his attention on the displaced members of the lower strata of society, Chogyû was close to government spokesmen on domestic issues and was an advocate of Japanese particularism.[85] In many respects, the two critics seemed to come from different worlds, and for this reason they are often held up in contrast.[86]

In fact, Chogyû's rise to prominence coincides rather closely with Reiun's departure from the literary world, which serves to underscore the overall differences between the two men. The smaller, thematically specialized magazines like *Seinenbun* were not, like *Taiyô*, big business. With small circulations, magazines like *Seinenbun* were scarcely economically self-sustaining. This is why, after seriously agonizing over it, Reiun decided to leave the literary world in May 1896, although issues of *Seinenbun* that he edited would continue to appear until January 1897. Anxious to get away from it all, Reiun accepted a teaching position at a middle school in Tsûyama, tucked away in the mountains of Okayama Prefecture. Meanwhile, as Reiun was leaving the capital, Chogyû was making his way back to Tokyo from Sendai in order to assume his new post with *Taiyô*.[87]

Takayama Chogyû is best known for his advocacy of a highly particularistic brand of "Japanism" (Nihonshugi), one that stressed the special characteristics of the Japanese people (*kokumin seijô*).[88] Although Reiun is also associated with a variety of Japanese nationalism, *kokusui-hozon*—the notion of preserving the national essence and maintaining equivalency with the West—it was a far less particularistic and state-oriented variety of nationalism than what was being advocated by Chogyû. In fact Reiun was more likely to think in global terms about humanity, spirituality, and making responsible decisions that neither imperiled nor destroyed other human beings, while Chogyû, a student of Tokyo Imperial University's leading conservative thinker, Inoue Tetsujirô, who had staunchly defended the Imperial Rescript on Education when it came under attack, was not capable of thinking in these terms. Unlike Reiun, whose name is scarcely known in Japan today, Chogyû is a figure with whom many Japanese are acquainted, in part, perhaps, because his writings are often considered exemplary in terms of style and because they were popular with pre-1895 governments. In contrast, Reiun's style was gritty and difficult, and his ideas were never popular with the authorities. He did not want his sentences to make his readers comfortable or lull them into a false sense of security, so, propelled by a strong sense of urgency, he tried to stir his readers with his fiery passion.

What about the content of Chogyû's literary criticism? Here the differences with Reiun emerge clearly. Writing on the primary duty of the literary critic, Chogyû defined his version of national literature as "literature based on the national character."[89] He concluded that any writing that excluded the factor of the national character was "utterly without significance."[90] And elsewhere he observed that the highest duty of literature is to complete or fulfill the people's national character.[91] Not surprisingly, then, he found little to admire in the very novels that excited Reiun and seemed to herald the coming of a new era in Japanese literature. In a sequel to a long article on Meiji novels,

Chogyû isolated these "so-called social novels" for special treatment.[92] What kind of novels are these social novels, he queried? His answer:

> Well, although it's not easy to give a clear outline of what they are, according to what I've seen it would not be a grave error to see them as a sort of novel that builds on the reaction of the weak and the poor to the unequal distribution of wealth and power, which must be seen as an inevitable consequence of social evolution.[93]

Such an open espousal of the doctrines of social evolution was in stark contrast to Reiun's ideas. Chogyû, however, would carry it even further.

> So from this point of view, how should we look on these so-called social problems? In the first place, while we can see no earthly reason to protect those who are weak and incompetent in relation to society and the national enterprise, I think it is absolutely useless and actually harmful to the overall welfare of the state to turn to these no-accounts, who, as an inevitable result of social evolution cannot share in the power of state activities, and bestow on them gains they do not deserve. The demands of our feelings are not necessarily moral.[94]

The paramount concern for Chogyû is clearly the state. There is no room for a view of the self such as that which was a primary concern for Reiun. In Chogyû's view, the world was entering the era of the state (国家, *kokka*), and doctrines such as universalism and equality would soon be buried as "primitive illusions."[95] This arose from his belief that the state was instrumental as a means of attaining individual happiness.[96] In this view, which measured the value of things according to their contribution to the state, social novels had little to offer. Particularly repugnant was their tendency to sympathize with the unfortunate and downtrodden and to ascribe their misfortunes and even their transgressions to the effects of the environment.[97] In fact, at least by implication, the dominant classes were portrayed as the root of all social vices, about which Chogyû commented, "It is hardly necessary to argue that these kinds of novels are utterly without value. I think they should be eradicated as literature that represents an unwholesome current in social morals."[98] While he admitted the existence of social problems, and could understand that people "concerned about the world" would want to give them consideration, Chogyû was completely paternalistic in his belief that the only happiness workers deserved should be bestowed on them from above "in return for an appropriate display of submissiveness."[99] Social novels, moreover, encouraged the weak and poor to resist and urged criminals not to repent. For these reasons, in Chogyû's mind there was no reason to welcome their appearance on the literary scene. It is hard to imagine a position more diametrically opposed to Reiun's.

Chogyû's expectation that those in society's lower ranks should be submissive to their social betters contrasts sharply with Reiun's emphasis on compassion and his strong reaction to "pseudo patriotism." He had no enthusiasm for the idea of a submissive populace molded and integrated from above. In his estimation, the government was already indoctrinating pupils in the national education system in accordance with principles set down in the Imperial Rescript on Education. In an article entitled "Youth and the Current Moral Education," Reiun objected fiercely to efforts to fit people into a single, uniform mold. Young people must be free so that their spirit and enthusiasm can grow and develop. To make of them into "blind followers" dependent on superficial forms and ritualized by empty gestures of loyalty and patriotism was to destroy the spirit of youth. With alacrity he remarked "To have a single legitimate form of moral education based on vainly worshipping portraits of the emperor and attentively listening to imperial rescripts demeans and destroys youth. There is no greater cause of erosion of youthful enthusiasm. My hatred for such sham knows no bounds."[100] What to Chogyû were sacred tools for forging national unity were to Reiun merely the ingredients for creating blind pseudo patriots and sham loyalists.

The Meaning of *Seinenbun*

Reiun was uneasy about the fact that the new freedoms unleashed by the Meiji Restoration were creating individuals who were self-centered and egoistical and that this seemed to be at the very core of *bunmei* (modern civilization). These reservations surfaced clearly in a series of articles written toward the end of his days as a literary critic. One that appeared in the final edition of *Seinenbun* was "The Negative Impact of Utilitarian Civilization on Youth."[101] In it he reasoned that what made youth revolutionary by nature is a deep inner resolve rooted in utter indifference to personal gain or loss. One of the earmarks of members of Reiun's generation was that they had to search within themselves for what was no longer provided by the environment. Reiun strongly believed—and this is where the "times" were hard for him—that Japanese of his day had an extra need for inner resolve in order to deal with the impact of a materialistic view of the universe that lay at the heart of the modern scientific worldview. In the new world, there seemed to be little place for the metaphysical side of existence, for passion, and for ideals. Western materialism was fostering an attachment to individual pleasure, and so it emphasized the utility and potential profitability of everything in relation to the individual. How could people so concerned with their own losses and gains appreciate the idea of sacrificing everything for the benefit of a larger humanity?[102]

By addressing the youth of his day in such a tone and by coming back to the image of the *shishi*, the youths who had led the Meiji Restoration movement, Reiun was discovering, like many of his generation, that it was necessary to return to the spirit of the Restoration in order to uncover its deeper meaning. Because the men who carried out the Restoration had been young, Reiun attached particular significance to the role of youth in effecting change. In another article from this period, "Youth and Progress," he stated, "Progress means destruction, and destruction brings improvement. Stagnation is the enemy of progress. Revolution destroys for the sake of progress. If there is no revolution, then there is stagnation, and with stagnation comes decay. Revolution is what brings renewal."[103] But who can bring about this renewal? Only youth. The people like himself, born in the early years of Meiji, were now approaching the age of thirty, so from the point of view of their individual development, wasn't it time to effect significant change? Reiun wrote, "Youth has the vitality, the energy. Young people are the allies of progress, the children of the revolution. In Japan today, many look to youth.[104]

Underneath it all, though, Reiun was not very optimistic about the capacity of young people to live up to their responsibilities. Toward the end of his Seinenbun period, he seemed to have arrived at the conclusion that they lacked the inner fortitude necessary to accomplish their task. It was precisely these feelings that prompted one of Reiun's earliest attempts to define the spirit of the Meiji Restoration. This was an essay entitled "The Blockading of Human Talent" (Jinzai yôsoku), which appeared in *Nihonjin* in September 1896. As we will see in chapter 6, it also anticipated several themes that would occupy the young writer and critic Ishikawa Takuboku some fifteen years later.[105]

In an attempt to make use of the past to criticize the present, Reiun located the *bakufu*'s principle failure in its rigid social stratification, which meant that people of great talent were not permitted to exercise it if they lacked the appropriate lineage. A bureaucratic elite, the *bakufu* monopolized positions of authority and blocked the road upward for three hundred years. When the situation became extreme, that is, when the bakufu could no longer carry out its duties in the face of the arrival of foreign ships, the discontent that had been welling up in "men of talent" burst forth in the Meiji Restoration and made it revolutionary. Reiun noted the following characteristics of the men who carried out the Restoration: they were young, talented, and highly discontented. They were discontented because they were prevented from developing their full potential, their natural talents. Wasn't the same situation being faced again thirty years later?

> Supposedly the separation of high and low on the basis of lineage was eradicated by the restoration-revolution, but today we can see a new, different kind of clique. . . . Today it is a world of clever skills, a mechanical world of machines and apparatuses; above all, it is a material world. These trends are not something to which men of great talent can readily accommodate themselves. . . . Men of real talent don't flatter and curry favor just to please the world and fit the times. This is suitable only for the small, clever men who become petty officials.[106]

The last thirty years had seen the growth of slothfulness and a makeshift approach to life, he argued, in which principles had ceased to guide individuals' actions. People today could talk, but they did not act; they might be well adorned on the outside, but inside they lacked a true heart. To be sure, there was some discontent, but it was only over trivial things such as how to get a good job or how to become a bureaucrat. Was any of the sincerity and devotion, the courage and resolve, of the *bakumatsu shishi* to be found there? Reiun's doubts were explicit.

> Stagnation breeds decay, and waves of change bring forth vitality. In today's world talent is being blocked because society lacks vitality. The cabinets are, as always, bastions of oligarchic power, controlled by the *genrô* [elder statesmen]; the Kaishintô is still led by Okuma and the Jiyutô by Itagaki. The Ken'yûsha is still under the control of Kôyô. If a great whirlwind of change does not come soon, setting in motion great billows of activity, if society isn't soon subjected to some major shocks, then the country is bound to swell with the ranks of the disappointed and discontented.[107]

The specter of stagnation and decay that haunted Reiun was responsible for the overall tone of dismay coupled with indignation that characterized his essays toward the end of his time with *Seinenbun*. Society was in dire need of some "shocks" to set it on the correct path forward. In "Humanity," Reiun railed against those who would talk of *bunmei* and *kaika* while ignoring the fact that society was becoming increasingly polarized into the haves and have-nots thanks to industrial capitalism. Where was the humanity when the wealthy were devouring the impoverished? Writers needed to open their eyes, and then those of their readers, to this reality. It was as if Reiun were saying, "Come on, you writers, quit trying to write about romantic love and address what is really going on in the world around you!"[108]

Insofar as his frustration was a product of his deep-seated concern with the impact of modernity on Japan, these essays offer a preview of the themes that would surface in Reiun's more thoroughgoing critique of modernity itself. The difficulty of his position as he began to grow disillusioned with the literary world is suggested by the kind of essays he chose to contribute to a new journal being launched by Reiun himself along with Sasagawa Rimpû and several other colleagues. For this journal, *Kôko Bungaku*, Reiun dusted off some essays from the prewar period, added a new introduction, and offered them as a series on mysticism.[109] These were to be his "own views" on a number of basic questions. What is philosophy? What is human nature? How does the personality operate in everyday life? What are space and time? What is the role of the cosmos? His answers were basically Schopenhauerian. He kept coming back to the subject side of the subject-object equation and to thinking about the self as offering individuals the opportunity to achieve the state of no-self. The scientific view, while helpful, was ultimately too narrow, too constricting, too superficial. A penetrating philosophical view was necessary. He claimed that his view of reality, which emanated from the subject (*shukanteki shinjittai ron*), was much closer to the truth. "The universe exists only for our knowing," he would write, sounding much like Schopenhauer. "The universe appears to the self and belongs only to it. It is born with us and dies with us."[110] Concepts such as God and Buddha belong to the realm of our subjectivity; they are representations of our subjectivity in the realm of objectivity: "That is why they say 'The Kingdom of Heaven is Within You.' That is why I call it a mystical philosophy and try to see it as a true expression of the actual, of reality."[111]

By going back and picking up the threads of his earlier writings, it might seem that Reiun was in retreat, that his experience as a literary critic had ended by bringing him full circle, back to his original point of departure. That is, he was once again wrestling with a "contested duality," pitting his mysticism, on the one hand, against his social concerns on the other. An article on Indian mystical thought from this period written for *Taiyô* confirms that he was continuing to deepen his knowledge of the inner experiences in human consciousness.[112] Yet at the same time he continued to urge youth to finish what the Restoration had begun by wiping out all existing cliques and enclaves of privilege.[113] Elsewhere he openly endorsed the use of strikes and clearly voiced his support for the railway engineers and stokers of Nippon

Tetsudô in their 1898 labor dispute.[114] He also spoke out in opposition to the treatment Korean students received in Japan and helped organize a benefit concert on their behalf.[115]

Although he definitely was going through a period of reevaluation and taking stock of his ideas rather than being thrown back on his earlier position, Reiun was branching out in a variety of new directions. What was lacking in his immediate post-*Seinenbun* essays was a single coherent theme or vision that could unify his ideas. Literature had served this function for him temporarily, but he had evidently reached his limit with it. His hopes exhausted, he was shopping around for something else. In time Reiun would find that something in his critique of modernity (or "modern civilization" as he called it). Before we turn to an examination of that critique, however, a final point should be noted about the inward turn of the late 1890s and what was at stake.

In his book *The Failure of Freedom*, Tatsuo Arima makes the case:

> There is no better record, no more telling evidence, for the understanding of Japanese history in the twentieth century than the intellectual experiences which grew out of the Meiji era. The failure of Japan's effort to extend the emotional experience of emancipation beyond the level of the philosophical, the religious, and the aesthetic into the realm of social reality is part of her general failure to preserve and foster the constitutional form of government.[116]

In his eyes, any progress in the development of a modern self during Meiji was marred by the fact that it was always a self with "no clear conception of its relationship to others."[117] He lamented, "Social realities eluded their grasp; the emancipation of the self was to be sought outside actual social processes."[118] Perhaps, Arima was thinking about the case of Kitamura Tôkoku and saw his turn from politics to literature as an abandonment of hope for accomplishing something in the social or political realm. Obviously he had not read the critical essays of Taoka Reiun. In writing about Higuchi Ichiyô, Reiun had argued in favor of recognizing the importance of inner as well as outer experience. In Reiun's view, it was the inner person that comprised the essence of human experience; this is where the individual's true nature could be found. This was an inner nature that was not subject to rule by the external forces of chance and circumstance; it was something more stable, more permanent. It was the place where the capacity for self-knowledge resides. Great literature, he contended, if it was to depict truth or reality, could not neglect this realm of human experience.

But does it make sense to label this inward turn "escapist"? In view of his pioneering concern for "social problems" and the fate of the poor in industrial society, the answer has to be a resounding no. The distinguishing characteristic of Reiun's literary criticism is precisely that he insisted that writers must penetrate to the heart of existing social realities and find their subject material there. He rejected a superficial kind of "realism" if all it meant was that writers were going to simply employ some fashionable literary techniques in order to expose unpleasant situations and leave it at that. Instead, he wanted writers to discover ideals deep within themselves and then infuse those ideals into their characters. He wanted to see characters that could manifest empathy, compassion, and sympathy. This is hardly a basis for suggesting that social realities "eluded" Reiun's grasp.

On the contrary, Reiun called for a deeper, more compassionate understanding of reality. He began with the premise that existing social realities must be the point of departure for great literature. However, reality to him always implied the interaction between individuals and their environment, between objects and a perceiving subject. Although, as Schopenhauer had pointed out, reality was the sum of these two aspects, Reiun was now drawing attention to the subjective side of the equation. In part this was because it represented the human element, the repository of human emotions, especially sympathy and compassion. He had learned from Schopenhauer that the "better consciousness" to which it was possible for humans to aspire could lead one "into a world where there is no longer personality and causality nor subject-and-object. . . . All genuine *love* is compassion, and all love that is not compassion is selfishness."[119] Reiun's gripe with nineteenth-century civilization was that, by insisting on reason alone, on a rationality that was narrow and small-minded, "clever reasoning," as he would come to call it, had become the order of the day. But if one is being completely rational and clever, thinking only about one's own interests, then behavior will be rooted in selfishness. That is why he admired the world created in fiction by Higuchi Ichiyô: she brought her world to life by infusing it with emotion, with sympathy and compassion, the antithesis of selfishness and greed. This is where it was possible to discover something that was real, that was genuine and authentic, something rooted in "the psychological facts of our self-experience," to borrow Vasalou's phrase. By the same token, this is why it saddened him that Takayama Chogyû was such a darling of the literary world; for all his style and flash he offered readers little substance. To get that, Reiun argued, you had to gravitate toward art that has the capacity to lift readers above "empirical consciousness" and initiate them into the truth of a "better consciousness." It was up to literature to show readers how to stand outside themselves and view the world with clear eyes.

Reiun believed that in order to understand reality people had to learn how to correctly perceive it. However, the human organism is conditioned to be aware of only one side of reality. Reiun's great hope for literature was that it could come to the rescue and lead people toward a fuller, more accurate perception of reality. Therefore, he wanted literature to be based on the true self, a genuine self grounded in the reality of inner experience that could be projected outward. But to be concerned in this fashion with humans as real, functioning organisms who wish to know their capacity for development and understanding, is not at all the same as seeking to create a self with "no clear conception of its relationship with others." As Reiun's essays in *Seinenbun* clearly reveal, his conception of self did not fail to come to grips with the realities of the socialized self. On the contrary, his was a fully realistic vision of the self that did not deny the human capacity for inner as well as outer experience. This is the upshot of Reiun's move away from literary criticism and toward a broader cultural critique, which we will examine in the next chapter. Takahashi Tadashi writes that Reiun:

> had forcefully called for a literature that was fully prepared to critique capitalist society and nineteenth-century civilization. As he began to grope his way along this path, it was inevitable that he would break out of its narrow confines and find his way into the territory of social and political revolution where he would formulate a penetrating and thoroughgoing critique of capitalism and of a society in which the all-encompassing power of money is pervasive. But the road ahead for him would be steep, and a difficult fate would await him.[120]

Chapter 5 charts the path that stretched before him and suggests why it would become steep and difficult to navigate. For it was a path toward problems of wider significance, problems that dealt more directly with society, gender, and history, a path that could address what humanity had once been, what it had become, and what it could be.

5

HIBUNMEIRON
THE ATTACK ON MODERN CIVILIZATION

> [N]ow for the first time in History both the masses and the thinkers of all the advanced nations of the world are consciously feeling their way toward the establishment of a socialistic and communal life on a vast scale. The present competitive society is more and more rapidly becoming a mere dead formula and husk within which the outlines of the new and *human* society are already discernible.
>
> Edward Carpenter, *Civilization: Its Cause and Cure*

> Obviously, there must exist a simple thread on which everything is arranged side by side: but what is it? . . . [I]t must be the *prius* of consciousness, and the root of the tree of which consciousness is the fruit. This, I say, is the *will*.
>
> Arthur Schopenhauer, *WWR*, 2:139

> Schopenhauer acknowledges as metaphysical principle only the Will whilst Ideation is, according to him, a cerebral product in a materialistic sense . . . [and so] the Will, the sole *metaphysical* principle of Schopenhauer, is therefore, of course, an unconscious Will. . . . It must therefore be granted that Schopenhauer divined the truth, but gave it faulty expression. . . . The Unconscious has, in fact, been as clearly and exactly characterized in this old Indian book of the Vedanta philosophy (Pañcadaśa-prakarana) as by any of the latest European thinkers.
>
> Eduard von Hartmann, *Philosophy of the Unconscious*

It is often said that the modern age began in nineteenth-century Europe in an atmosphere of "unparalleled historical crisis."[1] This sense of crisis was brought on when inherited eighteenth-century beliefs in nature as orderly and humans as rational beings were being undermined by the realities of the French and Industrial revolutions. These fundamental beliefs about human beings and nature had constituted the foundation, as well as the scaffolding, on which a particular outlook on the universe, and the place of human beings in it, was rooted.² This was a nature controlled by certain laws that could be apprehended by individuals through study and learning because people possessed the capacity for reason. But the intervention of concrete historical experiences exposed the limitations of this outlook, and the feeling grew throughout the nineteenth century that reason alone could not be relied on to provide modern individuals with a full and complete picture of reality.

If not reason, then what? Imagination was the answer that many figures in the romantic movement came up with, accounting for a pronounced turn inward in Europe of the mid-nineteenth century. In place of reason, romantic thinkers wanted to substitute an emphasis on what was irrational in the human experience, that is, on the emotional, the mysterious, and the stirrings of the sub- or unconscious. American intellectuals in the 1880s and 1890s experienced something similar. As T. J. Jackson Lears writes, "Antimodern dissent often contained a vein of deep religious longing, an unfulfilled yearning to restore infinite meaning to an increasingly finite world."³ It was a way for Americans to challenge "the progressive creed" that permeated their world. Understandably Japan, which was just entering a sustained encounter with modernity, was still enthralled with rationalism and empiricism, so the appeal of this kind of serious questioning of the pitfalls of becoming modern was not widespread. But to a small number of people in the socialist and anarchist movements, and in the fields of literature, philosophy, and religion, it represented an important legacy.

Taoka Reiun was among those willing to take a serious look at these kinds of questions. Drawing on the romantics, as he frequently did, he understood how important the inward turn was for coming to terms with modernity. "Inwardness," Charles Taylor notes,

> is as much a part of the modernist sensibility as of the Romantics. And what is within is deep: the timeless, the mythic, and the archetypical. . . . But our access to it can only be within the personal. In this sense, the depths remain inner for us as much as for our Romantic forbears. They may take us beyond the subjective, but the road to them passes inescapably through a heightened awareness of personal experience.⁴

While there may be a temptation to dismiss the writings of someone like Reiun as anachronistic—for, after all, he studied classical Chinese language and Asian thought—the counterargument can also be made that this was his way of deepening a connection to the present while envisioning a more viable future. By going "beyond the subjective," as Taylor puts it, and moving toward something more akin to a "reflective consciousness," individuals are able to discover a deeper reality.⁵ From Daoism, Reiun could certainly have learned about self-cultivation and personal transformation of the sort that would produce in individuals "the quality of character that makes this world itself a better place," and they could achieve this through a certain stillness of mind that brings with it "frictionless equilibrium."⁶ Even today, western philosophers seem to appreciate that "reality is not just objective reality, and the pursuit of objectivity is not an equally effective method of reaching the truth about everything."⁷

In 1903, the year before the Russo-Japanese War began and when Kôtoku Shûsui and Sakai Toshihiko launched their antiwar journal, *Heimin shinbun*, an interesting historical moment occurred. One of Tolstoy's closest friends, Vladimir Chertkov (1854–1936), who advocated that Tolstoy's philosophy should be taken as a new religious view of the world, brought several young Japanese men to meet Peter Kropotkin in London because they were seeking to learn more about anarchist philosophy. As Sho Konishi suggests, "This private meeting of Russian and Japanese Tolstoyans on the eve of the war was indicative of the impending broader shift in Japanese intellectual and cultural life toward a historicist, or Kropotkinist understanding of anarchism, and of the role of anarchist religion in fueling that very shift."⁸ This "broader shift in Japanese intellectual and cultural life" is rooted in an understanding of anarchism that can be most productively thought of "not as a political movement marked by violent clashes with the state, but as a cultural, intellectual, and social movement," one that attracted the attention of a significant number of Japanese between 1905 and 1920.⁹ Moreover, as Konishi reminds us, "Tolstoy was by far the most translated foreign writer in the entire history of modern Japanese translation practice," and Reiun, for one, mentioned his passion for Tolstoy's work frequently.¹⁰ Steeped in spiritual values, Tolstoy provided a view of the world and history that featured a modern self, one capable of exercising individual autonomy and historical agency.

To have that ability to look within, to establish one's individual independence and become self-reliant, was a quality on which Reiun placed a high value. For more than a decade he had been asking questions about what it means to be human, to manifest one's "humanity." He wanted to know how individuals were supposed to ground themselves in reality and to find meaning in the world around them. What should people do? How should they behave? In the pages of *Seinenbun*, Reiun had argued that literature not founded on ideals lodged deeply in the writer's innermost being was somehow false, or counterfeit. Without contact with an inner life, our perception and understanding of reality is incomplete. As he argued in his essays on Higuchi Ichiyô, when judgments are based solely on what is experienced by the knowing subject situated in external reality, a reality shaped and conditioned by the environment, all that can emerge is a false, one-sided picture. If literature fails to perform at the highest level possible, it cannot lead readers to the truth. He appealed to the writers of his day to rely on their imagination, intuition, and ideals in order to see the world through sympathetic eyes, eyes that could quietly and calmly see the world as it is. With imagination and intuition, the poet could penetrate the barriers that divided the individual self. In the deeply intuitive vision that results from this clear-eyed perception of reality, the poet could bridge the divisions that plague the modern individual and transcend subject-object dualities.

However, Higuchi Ichiyô, the writer in whom he had invested most of his hopes, died of tuberculosis before her twenty-fifth birthday, and it did not seem that another Ichiyô, nor a Tolstoy or Hugo, was poised to make a dramatic entrance into the Japanese literary world. Over time Reiun came to realize that the focus of his writing needed to shift away from literary aesthetics in the direction of a comprehensive critique of nineteenth-century civilization as a whole, and of recent history in particular, as a way to better understand the nature of becoming modern. He wanted to bring attention to what was not working well in the contemporary world and to reimagine what was possible in modern social, political, and economic life. Individuals must learn how to behave more selflessly and act more responsibly. This can only occur, however, if a new kind of self emerges, a self aware of itself and capable of defending itself. As noted earlier, the "maelstrom" of modernity promises much but also "threatens to destroy everything we have, everything we know, everything we are."[11] It would require a strong, independent, autonomous self to weather this storm.

Reiun's essays attacking modern civilization—his *hibunmeiron* (非文明論)—were mostly authored during the 1903–4 period when he was on the staff of an Okayama City newspaper, *Chûgoku Minpô*. At the end of 1904, Reiun left Okayama for Tokyo where he inaugurated a new journal, *Tenko* (天鼓, Heaven's Drum), in which he presented many of the same ideas he had been working on in Okayama.[12] Although Reiun spent a brief and unproductive six months on the staff of Kuroiwa Ruikô's *Yorzuchôhô* in 1898, where he came to know Kôtoku well, his effort with *Tenko* marks his reappearance in the literary world after a seven-year absence. Unfortunately, it was not a triumphal reentry, and his stay was short-lived. *Tenko* was economically a shoestring operation from the outset, and after less than a year Reiun left Japan once again, this time for Suzhou, China, where he lived until May 1907.

The Years before *Tenko*

Between his departure from the literary world in late 1896 and the period of his attack on modern civilization, Reiun's personal life had taken a number of significant turns. Until he settled down with his job in Okayama in 1901, his life had been filled with a good deal of motion and activity. When he left Tokyo he was headed for a teaching position in Tsûyama in the mountains of Okayama Prefecture. He then left Tsûyama and returned to Tokyo and the *Yorzuchôhô* but was dissatisfied with the atmosphere and left for another newspaper job in Mito in Ibaraki Prefecture with the *Ibaraki News*. A number of radicals and anarchist thinkers could be found there, most notably the painter Ogawa Usen (1868–1938). After studying art in Tokyo, Usen had been summoned by his father to work on the family farm in Ibaraki, in the village of Ushiki, but he still regularly supplied artwork to the *Ibaraki shinbun*, where he got to know Reiun well. They shared an affinity for Daoist thinkers and writers whose advocacy of simple, back-to-nature living enhanced their appreciation for what Konishi calls "the everyday practices of ordinary people without reliance on the government . . . or identification with the nation state." He goes on to point out, "This conceptual relationship of man and nature was in sharp contrast with the constructs of man and nature in Western modernity in which human progress and civilization were measured according to the increasing departure from nature."[13] Later the two men would cross paths again both on Kôtoku's *Heimin shinbun*, where Usen was a fixture, and on Reiun's own journal, *Tenko*, where many of Usen's illustrations appeared. Moreover, in 1908 the two would collaborate on a short illustrated work, *Yûzo muzo* (The Voiced and the Voiceless), in which Reiun's words provided the voices while Usen's illustrations captured the experiences and feelings that could not be put into words, images that reflected the spontaneity and creativity of the everyday lives of ordinary people as they made tofu or created folk art.[14]

But, after only six months on the job there, Reiun accepted a position teaching Japanese language in Shanghai, where he lived for the year 1898–99. Shortly after his return to Japan, the Boxer uprisings took place, and Reiun returned to China as a reporter embedded with Japanese troops that were sent to help quell the rebellion. His coverage for his friend Shirakawa Riyô's paper *Kyûshû Nippô* was later bound and issued as a book, *Sempô Yojin*.[15] It was after he returned from China the second time, in late 1900, that he settled down in Okayama where he remained for the next four years.

There were several experiences in the period after Reiun left the literary world that merit attention. First, there was his trip to China. It is only natural that for someone who was so indebted to ancient Chinese thought this trip would be meaningful. Unfortunately, we know little about what Reiun did there other than his teaching. All we find in his autobiography *Sakkiden* is the assertion that it was in Shanghai that he was first introduced to the "breadth of the world."[16] It seems that the open, cosmopolitan atmosphere of Shanghai was a new and refreshing experience and that it took something like this to overcome some of the narrow prejudices that he claimed had carried over from his earlier association with *kokusuishugi* nationalism. It is interesting to note that, while Reiun was teaching Japanese language at the Eastern Academy of Languages (Dongwen Xueshe, 東文学舎) in Shanghai, the Chinese scholar Wang Guowei (1877–1927) read about Schopenhauer and Kant in some of Reiun's essays and was sufficiently stimulated by this encounter to explore the value of comparative East-West philosophical studies.[17] The two apparently met on several occasions, including two years later when Reiun was living in Suzhou.[18]

Professor Nishida believes that part of Reiun's motivation in going to China was a thirst for some revolutionary activity. Indeed, not long after he left Tokyo the first time, Reiun wrote Miyake Setsurei to the effect that he was interested in emulating Byron and joining the Cuban Revolution of 1898.[19] Also it is true that refugees from Kang Youwei's aborted 100 Days Reform did flee to Shanghai for asylum, and Reiun had contact with them when he settled in Shanghai in May 1899.[20] We saw in chapter 3 how important for broadening his horizons and instilling an appreciation for the cosmopolitanism his time in Shanghai was. He came to understand that the world is made up of many different peoples and races, and he developed even more strongly an awareness of the value of envisioning transnational communities and their potential for representing the future.

But it is also clear that the time he spent with the late Qing antigovernment activists associated with the Confucian reformer Kang Youwei (1858–1927) made a strong impression on him. The group included the reformist official and poet Wen Tingshi (1856–1905), the leading reform advocate Tan Sitong (1865–1898), and Tan's closest comrades Wang Kangnian (1860–1911) and

Tang Caichang (1867–1900).[21] Tan Sitong was martyred in 1898 when the Qing government executed him for his participation in the ill-fated 100 Days Reforms, so Reiun never met him. Tan could have escaped to Shanghai, but he willingly chose martyrdom. But Reiun did get to know Tang Caichang. Later, after Reiun returned to Japan and learned of Tang's summary execution in 1900, he was both shocked and saddened. He wrote a tribute to Tang in which he bid farewell to his friend by referring to his Buddhist name, "Buddha's Dust," and calling him a true man of Hunan.[22] Both Tan and Tang favored a new eclectic form of Buddhism that not only blended Buddhist ideas with Daoism, Christianity, Mozi's notion of universal love, the wisdom of the *Yijing*, Confucianism, and modern western liberalism but also offered something that Hung-yok Ip calls "interconnectivity" (通, *tong* in Chinese), which shares much with the kind of nondifferentiation that Reiun found in Schopenhauer, Daoism, and Buddhism.[23] Kang Youwei's ideal of the "Great Peace" had argued for a connection (通) between China and non-Chinese nations for which he drew on the eleventh hexagram in the *Yijing*, "Tai" (泰, Peace), which points to the harmonious interaction between the forces of *yin* and *yang*, between the "Receptive" (Earth) and the "Creative" (Heaven). The judgment is "Peace. The small departs, the great approaches."[24] Once the small self is overcome, the larger, greater self becomes manifest. In a mode of expression with which Reiun would have been extremely comfortable, Tan saw that individual human desires were:

> rooted in humans' analytical, discriminating mental mode, which was the source of various but interrelated kinds of dualism. Unable to understand the non-dualistic relationship between self and other, ordinary people clung to their selves and therefore intended to maximize their gains. Moreover, the dualistic preoccupation with self, blinding them to the non-differentiation between birth and no-birth, and that between destruction and non-destruction, led to the dualistic preoccupation with life—i.e., bodily existence.[25]

Reiun was obviously predisposed to share the questioning of this kind of dualism, although he preferred the term *clever reasoning* (*chikô*, 智巧), something he believed modernity fostered relentlessly, and he also shared with these late Qing reformers and revolutionaries the vision of a broader, more cosmopolitan community.

Interestingly, the eclectic form of Buddhism of which Tan and many of the other Qing reformers were enthusiastic practitioners was Yogācāra Buddhism, with which Reiun demonstrated some familiarity in the early

1890s. Although Yogācāra Buddhism had deep roots in Indian traditions, it was also construed as "a new knowledge system" in late Qing and early Republican China, particularly one "by which to interpret and understand science."[26] Tan Sitong, for example, tied the brain, the nervous system, and electricity together as part of *yitai* (以太, ether). One can imagine that Reiun understood well this impulse to seek ideas that could bring about a unified worldview, one that would account for both a spiritual and a mystical view, along with a modern scientific one as well. So it seems likely that he not only valued the company of these people, whom he admired, but was also stimulated by the exchange of ideas with them. At the very least, he found some confirmation for what he already believed about the possibility of equivalencies between East and West, the need to transcend the narrow limitations of a single western view of history and progress, and the need to rethink or reimagine the modern nation-state in terms of a wider, global community of world citizens.

This sense of interconnectivity also no doubt operated on him when he returned to China as a war correspondent during the Boxer incident and helped to open his eyes. He was critical of the way the army treated reporters and found that everything he wrote was censored. His dispatches from China also show that he was sympathetic to the plight of the innocent bystanders in this conflict, which was little more than an international political power play by the various countries involved. He frequently depicted scenes of the wanton destruction of property and life by the troops of various nations.[27] On the whole, we can say that he was dismayed by the realities of war to the extent that he would write, "Although I did try not to be antiwar, in the end I couldn't help it."[28]

Reiun had seen enough of western imperial expansion in Asia to issue a call for pan-Asianism as a form of resistance to the domination of this region by the white race. In an 1897 essay entitled "Tôa Daidômei" (An Asian Confederation), he wrote bluntly of the need to "resist the domination of Asia by the white race."[29] He singled out Britain's ruthless control and exploitation of India, France's takeover of Annam, and the Russian incorporation of Siberia, as well as the continual pressure it was applying in Manchuria and Korea. Germany, too, was joining the fray, taking over Jiaozhou Bay off the Shandong Peninsula and turning it into a German concession. Meanwhile, Japan was sitting idly by watching all this "out of control lawlessness by the white powers." At the very least, Reiun suggests, Japan should form an alliance with the Qing government to counter Russian influence in Korea, paving the way for a three-country pact among Japan, China, and Korea. This could be the first step in a strategy to oust Britain, France, Germany, and Russia from Asia because, apparently, "the arrogance of the white race towards the people of Asia knows no bounds."

> In the end, we should do this neither to come to the aid of the Qing dynasty, nor to support those [Chinese] people forced to wear their queues. Rather, we should do this for the sake of Asia and for the fate of the yellow race. We should lend China a hand, do the right thing, and rid Asia of the arrogant white race once and for all.
>
> Japan is a pioneer in Asia, so it should be the one to lead an eastern alliance against the incursions of the West. This is our calling, our mission.[30]

Although we may find in this passage something that is suggestive of the language of the Greater East Asian Co-Prosperity Sphere, something that was yet to come, make no mistake: Taoka Reiun was not talking about Japan establishing some kind of autarkic control over Asia, nor positioning the Japanese as the leading race exercising hegemony over other Asians. He was writing well before Japan's victory over Russia in 1905 and the 1931 Manchurian Incident, so any discussion of the need to expand the power of the state or to speak in terms of Japan's "destiny" in Asia was still a long way off. Instead, Reiun was calling for an alliance among partners in order to roll back the intrusion of western imperialism and help quell Asian feelings of humiliation. His language about the arrogance and domination of the white race is more an expression of the frustration and humiliation that Asians were experiencing in the late 1890s than anything else.

Tsûyama and a Love Affair

There was another experience of an entirely different sort that occurred just after Reiun's departure from the literary world. His destination when he left Tokyo was Tsûyama, where he was to teach in a middle school. He had hoped that getting away from Tokyo and into the solitude of the mountains would be stimulating. But apparently he found the small town a bit dark and dreary, and he did not particularly enjoy teaching.[31] A friend of haiku poet Masaoka Shiki and fellow University of Tokyo graduate Ôtani Zekû was living in Tsûyama at the time, and one evening he took Reiun to the Musashino Inn where he met Ôisô Katsu, a young apprentice geisha, and soon Reiun was in the thick of his first real love affair.[32] Unfortunately for Reiun, it was a love affair fraught with drastic consequences, and it left a profound mark on him.

She was only twenty years old and the product of a complicated and unhealthy family background, which aroused Reiun's deepest sense of empathy.[33] An illegitimate child herself, she lived with her stepmother, who treated her as little more than an economic asset. As Reiun wrote in *Sakkiden*, she was taught first how to smile and sell her charms and later her body (*SD*, 576). Prior to meeting Reiun, she had become involved with the son of a wealthy businessman. Ambitious to a fault, he had stolen his father's *hanko* (seal) and used it to borrow money illegitimately, a transgression for which he was tried and sentenced to jail. When the young man had completed his sentence, his family immediately entered him into an arranged marriage, but apparently he continued to see Katsu. It was around this time that Reiun met her, and his heart went out to this fragile person who was brought up in such a cold, unsympathetic environment. To Reiun she was his *tsukimisô na onna* (月見草な女, evening primrose), a flower that blooms only at night, because, never having known a loving family or had the opportunity to follow her heart, she had become a timid, frightened young woman accustomed to being manipulated and bullied. But when they managed to escape prying eyes and spent nights alone at an inn on the outskirts of town, as moonlight played on the tatami mats and cast eerie shadows in their room, she became warm and open to him. They recited poetry together. He claimed that their meeting could not have been a matter of chance; it was fate, or destiny, pure and simple.

Katsu's stepmother was adamantly opposed to her liaison with Reiun, for obviously he was not a person of means. She took steps to interfere in the relationship, and when it continued despite her efforts she was forced to take drastic measures. She arranged to have her stepdaughter sold to a wealthy man, even though by this time she had conceived Reiun's child. He claims in *Sakkiden* that this was the moment in his life when he learned to hate the power of money and its ability to dictate and control people's lives. As he put it, "I had never experienced until that moment how despicable money is, and at the same time I confronted the inescapable truth that wealth is power" (*SD*, 580).

Naturally, the impact of all this on Reiun was profound. It had been difficult enough to adjust to the prospects of fatherhood, but then to be stripped of it all and confronted with his economic powerlessness was highly unsettling. Shattering might be a more accurate description. There followed a brief period of last-ditch efforts to save the situation, secret letters and ultimately a final meeting between the two lovers. But it came to naught. After all this, though, Reiun could hardly go back to teaching at the middle school, for his affair had been the subject of considerable gossip; so he left Tsûyama and returned to Tokyo where a friend got him a post on the *Yorzuchôbô* newspaper. This paper was later to become one of Japan's opinion leaders, and at this time it was attracting the talent that would form the nucleus of the Idealists Band (Risôdan). This group, which was formed by Kuroiwa Ruikô around 1901, included Uchimura Kanzô, Sakai Toshihiko, Abe Isô, Kinoshita Naoe, and Kôtoku Shûsui—all people who shared concerns about industrialization in general and the Ashio Mine pollution incident in particular, but they also believed that reform must begin with the individual self and move outward.[34] Reiun came to know Kôtoku extremely well, and their friendship endured for the rest of their lives. However, Reiun had continued what he called his "dissolute" lifestyle and had been drinking heavily since the Tsûyama affair, so his behavior clashed somewhat with the sober and earnest atmosphere at the newspaper. He disliked signing an attendance sheet and played his cherished role of maverick by refusing to do so. When he wound up with a position as a reporter for the *Ibaraki News* in Mito, it was more of the same. His sake bill soon outdistanced his salary, and he had to leave town on the sly to avoid debt collectors. (*SD*, 595-604).

Back in July 1900, on his return from accompanying Japanese troops in China as part of the suppression of the Boxer Rebellion, he would write an essay in his lodgings at Shimonoseki about his son called "My Pitiable Child."[35] Just a little over two years old at this point, Reiun addressed his narrative to the son he could not know.

> My pitiable child, you are now in your third year, yet you do not know your father and your father does not know you. The man your mother calls your father is not your real father. No doubt the memory of your real father is etched deeply in your mother's heart, but this is not something you will ever see. You will continue to sleep peacefully, snuggled in the warmth of your mother's bosom, dreaming sweet dreams after nourishing yourself at your mother's breast. . . . Our beloved child, you were born bearing the burdens of our mistakes, your mother's and mine. Your mother's heart was nearly torn apart by the harsh reality of social obligations (*giri*), and because your current father possesses wealth and social standing, he was able to become your father while your real father stood by powerless in the face of his wealth. If fear was your mother's crime, then mine was being weak. But, please, do not begrudge your mother, nor hate your father. Yes, we have our faults, and we made our mistakes; the shame and the pain that we had to endure was so intense that your mother even thought of harming herself. . . .

> Now many of my friends are married, and their wives are having children; yet you, my son, are your father's only child, and you are your mother's only son. But you do not know your father and you cannot even utter his name.
> . . .
>
> If it ever comes to pass that you learn that your current father is not your real father, and if you would ever want to see the real father you have never seen, that would touch me deeply. Even though we share the same blood as father and son, if I am never able to tell you of my feelings for you, then I can only wish that heaven looks mercifully down on you and that you will grow up to be healthy and strong. Ah, pity the child, pity the father, and pity the mother. (*TRZ*, 2:702–6)

Already conscious of the newly emerging social inequities in Japanese life, the experience with Katsu, which only served to reinforce this awareness, had clearly devastated him. After his return from teaching Japanese in Shanghai for a year, he settled in Okayama for a while. Taking the job there apparently represented an effort by him to achieve some normalcy, and this is further evidenced by his willingness to accept a marriage arranged by his family. He explained that this was done in order to appease his mother in her old age, as he had never been very filial. But it was a disastrously unhappy marriage. By his own admission, he was indifferent to the point of being cruel to his wife and never gave the marriage a chance (*SD*, 623–28). The second night after the marriage he stayed away all night. He claimed that the marriage was scarcely consummated. It ended in divorce five years later, and this after Reiun had been absent from Japan for two years without his wife. This inability to lead a normal family life, on top of his earlier disastrous experience with love, is evidence of how close the whole problem of the relationship between the sexes was to him. This began to surface as a theme in his writing during the Okayama period.

While a reporter in Okayama, Reiun frequently wrote articles attacking corruption and bureaucratic meddling in education.[36] He received some unverified evidence that the prefectural governor was taking bribes from publishing companies that were working to block the adoption of new school textbooks. When he wrote an article exposing this, he was arrested and held for trial on the charge of "insulting an official." After he was detained for about two weeks, the trial was finally held, and Reiun was acquitted for lack of evidence. Following his release, he put together a series of essays recording his stay in prison along with a number of articles about the case on the way the law works and so forth. Naturally it was highly critical, and soon after it was published the prosecution appealed his original case. An Osaka court handed down a guilty verdict with a sentence of two months' imprisonment. Reiun, who was often sickly, had to enter the unheated prefectural prison in December for what was an excruciating stay.[37]

Kinoshita Naoe (1869–1937), a Christian and socialist acquaintance of Reiun's who was also very critical of modern civilization, once identified three ingredients that supported life in modern society. The first was the principle of profit or utility (*jitsuri*), which seemed to determine value. Second, there was a certain highly prized kind of knowledge, which provided the fuel that made the system operate, and this of course was scientific knowledge. Third, modern civilization took pride in its system of law, which provided the necessary social controls.[38] We have already seen that Reiun was equally suspicious of the profit motive and utilitarianism and that he was also highly critical of the scientific outlook on the universe as too narrow and constricting. After his encounter with the law, we can say that there was nothing sacred left about *bunmei* or modern civilization for Reiun. As early as June 1901, he published an article, "Kindai bunmei no kekkan" (The Shortcomings of Modern Civilization), in which he enumerated many of the achievements of modern civilization. Steamships, automobiles, railroads, cable cars, bicycles, gas lighting, electric lighting, telegraphs, telephones, wireless transmission, phonographs, typewriters, photographs, moving pictures, X-rays, theories about bacteria, blood transfusions, laws of gravitational forces, nebulae, natural selection, survival of the fittest, evolution, and probing the deepest secrets of the universe using scientific investigative techniques applied to minutiae—these were the wonders of modern civilization. So what is wrong with them? What is missing? Where are the shortcomings of such a worldview? The problem is that the progress of this so-called modern civilization is completely materialistic; it is based solely on the narrow, clever, reasoning (*chikô*, 智巧) faculty of the mind. It loves empirical knowledge and minute details, but human life is more than this. The universe cannot be reduced to the lowest common denominator. True understanding and real progress require respect for individual subjectivity, for intuition, for understanding human life from the inside.[39] It was from this standpoint that Reiun went about developing his hibunmeiron, his thoroughgoing assault on modern civilization.

Tenko: Sounding Heaven's Drum

We find Reiun's attack on modern civilization spread throughout several different publications. As we saw above, Reiun left Okayama in late 1904 and in February of the following year began publishing a new journal, *Tenko*.

In April 1905 a collection of essays written in Okayama entitled *Kochûkan* (Perceptions in a Jar) was published in Tokyo and banned instantly. Reiun removed most of what he thought to be the offensive essays from this collection, substituted some new ones, and reissued the book under a slightly different title, *Kochû Gakan* (My Perceptions in a Jar) the following year. This book was banned instantly as well.[40] Over the next three years, two more of his essay collections would be banned on publication. *Kochûkan* and *Kochû Gakan*, along with *Tenko*, provide the best material for examining Reiun's assault on modern civilization.

What was the nature of his critique? As noted in chapter 1, Reiun reflected on these years in *Sakkiden* in terms of his indebtedness to Daoist philosophy, the thought of Schopenhauer and Eduard von Hartmann, Carpenter's attack on civilization as a disease, and books such as Max Nordau's *The Conventional Lies of Our Civilization and Degeneration* (see *SD*, 670 for the full quotation). The passage below is an excerpt from what is perhaps Reiun's most vitriolic attack on modern civilization, appropriately entitled "Akumateki bunmei" (The Diabolical Civilization). The essay opens with two epigraphs: one from Nordau.

> The world of civilization is an immense hospital ward, the air is filled with groans and lamentations, and every form of suffering is to be seen twisting and turning on the beds.

The other is from Lord Byron's 1821 play *Cain: A Mystery*.

> ADAH: He is not God —nor God's: I have beheld The Cherubs and the Seraphs; he looks not Like them.
>
> CAIN: But there are spirits loftier still—The archangels.
>
> LUCIFER: And still loftier than the archangels.
>
> ADAH: Aye — but not blessed.
>
> LUCIFER: If the blessedness Consists in slavery — no.

One can only surmise that it was something about this rejection of religious dogma as a form of enslavement that spoke to Reiun. He found a parallel in the modern condition that he believed was enslaving people to a narrow, utilitarian, materialistic, instrumentalist, and reductionist view of society, knowledge, and humanity as a whole. The opening lines of his essay consist of a litany of terse indictments of modern civilization.

I am one who detests and curses contemporary civilization. Why do I detest and curse it? Because contemporary civilization is too materialistic: because it is too materialistic it stresses only the practical. Esteeming the practical so, it inevitably falls into utilitarianism and therefore becomes heartless and cruel. Contemporary civilization is too predicated on clever reasoning, and as a result it values form over content. Therefore, it is distorted and unnatural. Modern civilization is too empirical, and as a result it reifies the objective, material world. As a result, it attains only the surface of things and accordingly is too shallow. Contemporary civilization is inductive, so it esteems the facts: because of this it strives for reality but ends up with only mediocrity. It is too scientific, so it is not philosophical; it is too prosaic, so it is insufficiently poetic; it is overly logical, so it fails to be inspirational; lacking inspiration, it cannot attain the divine. Being too graphic and down to earth, it forfeits the aspect of the superb spirit, the sublime; restricting itself to the physical, it ignores the metaphysical; it is too analytic, so it is not sufficiently holistic and integrative. Being too abstract, it is never concrete. . . .

Worshipping money, it empowers the wealthy; valuing profit over everything, honor and morality mean nothing; bribery and corruption are rampant. Beholden to the letter of our laws and codes, people follow form at the expense of content and to the detriment of genuine human emotion. With such a high value placed on material things, no one pays attention to the idea of nurturing our spirit. The world has become a place where the strong prey on the weak, and it is winner take all, which is why we see the spread of imperialism. In the name of equal rights for all, we have the despotism of the rich; and in the name of charity and humanity, we have the reality of domination by the white race. These are the evils of contemporary civilization, which is why I detest and revile it.[41]

The English language may not be wholly effective in capturing all this rhythmic cursing and denunciation of modernity's failure to live up to its promises, but the rhetorical stance Reiun takes is appropriate to the relentless pounding of "Heaven's Drum." The masthead of the inaugural issue of *Tenko* depicts an oni, a demonlike figure with horns coming out his head and fangs protruding from his mouth as he pounds his drum from a standing position like a Taiko drummer.

The text beneath the image proclaims:

A drumbeat pounds; but for what reason?

It signals the attack!

It resounds to inspire and arouse people!

> Its thunder is our command to destroy all that is shallow and superficial in contemporary society, philosophy and art.
>
> It is here to denounce narrowly conceived utilitarianism, materialism, and realism.
>
> It is here to revive this world of ours, which has squandered its spirit and vitality in self-indulgence, forsaken its grandiose visions, and lost its sense of mystery, it's very soul! . . .
>
> This is no time to sit back and be silent about what is going on in the world around us. This is why we must sound the alarm and pound the drum.
>
> It is time to raise the flag in our little corner of the world of discourse,
>
> To use our writing brushes as our cudgel and let paper be our leather drumhead.
>
> We need to pound the drum ferociously, and shake people to their core!
>
> We need to encourage them, to rally them, and to command them—
>
> That is why we are calling our journal *Heaven's Drum*!
>
> *Tenko*, issue 1, February 23, 1905[42]

The rhetorical stance here is brash and confrontational. It is driven by a powerful sense of urgency that was not as evident when Reiun was writing in the early 1890s or for *Seinenbun*. He had always tried to write frankly and to tell it like it is which meant that at times his writing was abrasive and provocative. But something is new here: he is now cursing and reviling that which he cannot accept. He is relentlessly pounding the drum of righteous indignation. He is crying out that now is the time to raise the red battle flag and arouse readers so that they can see what is taking place around them. The air crackles with tension, and the sense of urgency is unmistakable. Something has to be done; there is too much at stake.

Some of this heightened sense of drama may be exaggerated, but in arguing the way he does, Reiun is actually employing a very "Chinese" method of argumentation: he reasons both by analogy and by historical example, and, employing the chain of logic technique of associative reasoning, he can claim that because of A, B must follow.[43] Certain central points are being driven home forcefully: what Reiun indubitably prefers to see is a world in which the transcendent, the "superb spirit" (神韻), has a much more central place. Let there be less selfishness and more truth. Let ideals soar; let there be more sincerity, more feeling, more heart, and less greed and pettiness.

Figure 5.1. Masthead of the inaugural issue of *Tenko*.

There is a profound need for a world in which more humane and admirable characteristics can be nurtured and allowed to flourish.

Reiun completes his opening salvo in "A Diabolical Civilization" by turning to all the likeminded people who, in their own way, have also lamented the loss of noble intentions, ideals, and a commitment to reaching the transcendent. Of course Confucius and Mencius are on this list with their call for benevolence (仁), as are Laoxi and Zhuangzi with their version of the Way; the names of the Buddha and even Christ, who suffered on the cross, are also invoked, for had they not both aimed to make the unseen world more proximate? Figures such as Socrates, Plato, Galileo, Voltaire, Rousseau, and Schopenhauer all battled against a superficial view of reality, and all had to press on in the face of opposition and ridicule. And the likes of Heine, Byron, Carlyle, Nietzsche, and Tolstoy—who also had their battles with a shallow and superficial nineteenth-century way of thinking—they, too, would have understood very well the target on which Reiun was setting his sights.

Although few articulated it with the same vehemence or vitriol, Reiun's line of argument is not at all unfamiliar. The contemporary philosopher Charles Taylor, who has been mentioned earlier on several occasions, also writes about "the conflict in our culture over the disengaged and instrumental modes of thought and action, which have steadily increased their hold on modern life," and he sees the modernist movement succeeding "Romantic expressivism both in protest against these and in search for sources which can restore depth, richness, and meaning to life."[44] To Taylor an instrumentalist society is one in which "a utilitarian value outlook is entrenched in the institutions of a commercial, capitalist, and finally a bureaucratic mode of existence" and can become what Max Weber referred to as an "iron cage." Much as Reiun did, Taylor decries the loss of passion in modern life and the way in which this instrumentalism "tends to empty life of its richness, depth, or meaning."[45] Throughout his days as a literary critic, Reiun had urged writers to come forward and funnel all their passion into uncovering the very nature of this shallow, commercialized, utilitarian society with all its supposed "realism." The problem with the narrow, scientific, rational view of human experience is that it has no place for heart, for soul, for embracing the wonders of the universe.

Taylor and Reiun agree that a spiritual and moral counterweight to the overly analytic, instrumental reason that came to be the foundation of the modern worldview was needed. As Taylor puts it, "[O]ur modern fragmented, instrumentalist society has narrowed and impoverished our lives."[46] All the wonderful new scientific inventions and instruments can amaze us and rivet our attention on the smallest particles of matter, but isn't there a cost? Won't we be missing out on something of deeper significance? If we are blind to this reality, then our lives are bound to be impoverished. This is why Reiun is so insistent, why he rails at the shortsightedness of modern civilization, and why he feels such a sense of urgency.

Love Suicides

Also in the inaugural issue of *Tenko*, Reiun published a long article ostensibly on the subject of the legendary Edo era playwright Chikamatsu Monzaemon (1653–1725) who is known for his love suicide plays, usually written for puppet theater but also performed on the Kabuki stage. The essay was entitled "Love Suicides as They Appear in Chikamatsu" with the subtitle "Sacrificial Victims of an Unnatural Society." While he did discuss some of Chikamatsu's plays, his primary purpose seems to have been another type of discussion, one that focuses on the nature of modern society. He opens by asking rhetorically:

What are love suicides? They are self-destruction; they are the joint suicides of men and women who are in love but are scorned and ridiculed by a society whose rules and morals are inflexible, a society that is quick to judge and blame the lovers, labeling them lewd and lascivious, a society whose laws are so cold, so cruel and inhuman, that we might as well call these suicides what they are: premeditated murder. Isn't this the nature of love suicides?[47]

After discussing four of Chikamatsu's plays, Reiun turns the discussion toward a flawed society that is incapable of recognizing genuine love even when it is right before its eyes; instead, it supports a marriage system that actually operates against love. It is a society that uses an artificial construct like the institution of marriage to oppress genuine feelings of love and aims to regulate natural human emotions like love by means of empty formalities. As Reiun saw it, societies have their traditions, customs, morality and laws, but these are all based on misguided premises that divide the self from others and therefore fail to see the possibilities of a higher unity. If it turns out that all the regulations, customs, morals, and legal systems only serve to restrict individual freedom, if they only cause misery and grief and deny individuals the opportunity to follow their inner natures, then something is very wrong. The idea of private possession has come to dominate the world, and marriage simply extends it to gender relations; at what point should the higher welfare of humanity be considered?

"The Coming Revolution"

The problem for Reiun is that this way of thinking comes out of a narrow and superficial way of looking at the world, a view that is promoted by *bunmei* (modern civilization). It has produced a society, an economy, and a system of laws that overlook some very basic things that should come naturally to human beings. Of course, at times, Reiun himself was not completely immune to the seductive powers of new, scientific insights if they could assist in better understanding the self. In "Gendai shisôkakumei no kizashi" (The Coming Revolution in Contemporary Thought), he argues for the possibilities latent in things like animal magnetism and hypnotism as ways to help people make the inward turn, learn more about their true natures, and develop strategies for quieting the will.[48] This essay opens with two epigraphs. The first is from Theophrastus Paracelsus (1493–1541), a Renaissance physician, alchemist, astrologer, and pursuer of occult knowledge who is believed to have traveled widely in his youth to places like India, Tibet, Constantinople, Arabia, Egypt, and the Holy Land in search of alternative healing methods. He theorized that humans are a microcosm of the planets and related the seven planets to the seven metals of the earth. The epigraph reads, "Magic is a great occult wisdom, just as Reason is a great, open folly." As usual, Reiun exhibits his distrust of the purely scientific or instrumental mode of thought (reason) and articulates his attraction to the mystical and occult. The second epigraph is from Schopenhauer's essay, "On the Will in Nature/Animal Magnetism and Magic."

> [A]nimal magnetism appears positively as *practical metaphysics*, the term which Bacon in his classification of the sciences (*Insauratio Magna* L. III) used to designate *magic*: it is empirical or experimental metaphysics. Further, since in animal magnetism, the will stands forth as thing–in–itself, we see the *principium individuationis* (space and time), which belongs to the mere phenomenon, at once annulled. Its limits that separate individuals are broken through; spaces between magnetizer and somnambulist are no separation; there ensues a community of thoughts and movements of will. The state of clairvoyance oversteps the relations that belong to mere phenomenon and are conditioned by space and time, such as proximity and distance, present and future.[49]

Empiricism and experimentalism, if applied to metaphysics, could definitely have their place. It clearly fascinated Reiun that there was so much interest in things like animal magnetism and hypnotism in western thought and that respected scientists and philosophers were pursuing these theories in his own day. Despite his inclination to distrust the modern scientific outlook for being too narrow and superficial, there is something irresistible about the hope that it might bring new technologies for better understanding the individual mind and the way the individual is situated in the universe in relation to the cosmos. He opens his essay with the argument that, whereas the early nineteenth century had witnessed, along with an expansion of individual rights in response to despotic forms of government, the emergence of gross inequities in the economy and society. By the same token, in response to the stranglehold that religious dogma held on inquiry—which had made it impossible to pursue a genuine investigation of nature—modern scientific investigative techniques had emerged. But, unfortunately, there was a compensatory overemphasis on the observable, on the objective side of experience, so that human subjectivity—the human soul—was being neglected. The result was a mechanistic view of the universe that finds no inherent meaning in the cosmos. But now, in present times, things like *socialism* had emerged to mediate between the state and the individual, and in the areas of scholarship and thought, the twentieth century could bring together experimentalism and belief in something beyond the individual in the form of such phenomena as hypnotism.

> Just as socialism today calls for a fundamental revolution in terms of social organization, in the world of academic research, hypnotism will bring about an earthshaking transformation in the way we see things. I believe that we will see a trend in the experimental sciences from looking solely at the physical side to incorporating the metaphysical, and we will see movement from the purely analytical and pluralistic models to ones that are more integrative and holistic.[50]

While Reiun may have been generally correct about the direction in which thought and academic practice were heading, obviously the study and practice of hypnotism never fulfilled the promise that many in the nineteenth century thought it would, although the argument can certainly be made that it deeply influenced Freud and the fields of psychology and psychoanalysis.[51]

Another theme that was part of the attack on modern civilization was the value of achieving a greater degree of unity in the world and among human beings by fusing and harmonizing cultures. Reiun's essay "Establishing Harmony between Old and New, East and West," ("Shinkyûsei to tôzaifû no chôwa") opens with an epigraph by Havelock Ellis (1859–1939), a well-known writer on human sexuality who was creating an imaginary dialogue about the nature of the nineteenth century. Ellis has one of his characters say:

> I have always understood that although it was the custom at that time to write letters they had no international postage, that though they were always travelling they had no international coinage, and that though nations were of more importance than we can conceive—and therefore the need of inter-communication a primary necessity—they had no international language. I do not see how you can speak of "civilization" under such conditions.[52]

Like Reiun, Ellis was clearly skeptical about many of the inflated claims that people were inclined to make for this era. Reiun clearly shares with Ellis a belief that, in order to take the next step in the advancement of humanity and for the world to become genuinely progressive, there needed to be greater integration and unification. He describes what he perceived to be a universal trend.

> There is a general trend afoot in the universe today, and it is about bringing the world closer together. As the years pass by, and one age gives way to another, the world takes another step closer to unification. Basically, progress

can be equated with ever-greater unity. The world progresses when there is a thesis followed by an antithesis and then a fusion based on the best qualities of each one, so that a new, better version is created. In other words, progress should be based on harmony; and as we reflect back on the vast sweep of time, back to the days when humanity was just beginning, in the cradle of our civilization in the high plains of the Pamir Mountains . . . even though our languages, our cultures, our customs, and our histories were different, there were also things that unified us and brought us together. . . .

Revolution is destruction and not just in terms of political structures, but cultures are destroyed, too, and cultural destruction means the destruction of ideas, and inevitably this means the end of many of our classics and traditions. That is why revolution means destruction; look at the French Revolution at the end of the eighteenth century. It destroyed the old political structure, the old ideas, the traditions, the classical literature, so that great new vistas could be opened up in the nineteenth century. In our country, of course, we had the Meiji Restoration, and this was a form of revolution, and along with the destruction of the old feudal order, all of the old ideas, the old culture and traditions were swept away, but following on the heels of all this destruction there had to be some new construction. Between the periods of destruction and construction there is always a transitional period . . . and when the new is as yet not constructed, there are elements of conflict and disharmony present. But eventually harmony will be restored, and since it will be based on a fusion of the best of the old customs and traditions and the new, it will be even stronger from the very outset.[53]

A Call for Social Revolution

In Japan's case, because the cultures of China and India were blended with indigenous traditions, a stronger culture had been generated. It was his hope for the world at large that humanity could transcend nation and race and think in truly global terms. Assimilation has always been a substantial part of Japan's historical development, and now the next step forward for Japan and the world should be to discover the harmony and fusion that is possible between East and West. But this would require a significant jolt, and it was in another essay, "The Dark Undercurrents of Contemporary Thought,"(Gendai shisô no anchô) that Reiun would make clear that sometimes the old ways had to be pushed aside or even destroyed. He argued for a connection with those who, along with him, would advocate for *hibunmei*—who would stand with him against nineteenth-century civilization—that there was a transformation taking place in the world of ideas, and there was likewise a need for *shakaiteki kakumei* (a social revolution) to bring about change in society.[54] He takes this occasion to differentiate his call for revolution from Rousseau's anti-Enlightenment stance which had its basis in individual rights.

> Today what is being demanded goes beyond the individual, beyond the nation, beyond race; it is an appeal to unite all of humanity in a universal equality, so this call inevitably incorporates *elements of socialism*.... Of course the sense of community in the coming new age that advocates of *hibunmei* envision will not involve a return to primitive forms of community; rather, while they may bear some resemblance to the values of these primitive communities, the new communities will not be small and tribal but something global in scope; they will be wider social and moral communities rooted in simplicity and closeness to nature.[55]

An important shift is now evident in both the language and the content of Reiun's critique. He has become quite explicit in his call for a social revolution, albeit a revolution that will produce communities that are founded on free individuals who can come to know both their inner and outer selves and will therefore not be limited by notions of the nation-state. It is tantamount to an appeal to think in transnational terms, to see the common history that humanity possesses.[56] The concern, evident in his earlier writings as well, with the way in which modern people were being deceived and led astray from their true natures comes to the fore in his assault on modern civilization. But when he referred in *Sakkiden*, somewhat offhandedly, to "a slight change in my stance since my younger days" (*SD*, 713–14), we understand now that it was not something that should be minimized. He is still very apprehensive about a world that is sterile, crassly utilitarian, and lacking in all manifestations of humaneness, a world devoid of natural expressions of human feeling. When he writes of modern civilization as too abstract, he is projecting his fear of a life structured around empty (external) forms and hopelessly out of touch with (inner) reality, by which he means deeper, more authentic human reality. In such a life, moral values and ideals become mere abstractions because they are severed from their natural roots in concrete reality, and this renders them meaningless. But he also knows now that narrow conceptualizations of modern nationalism and the kinds of pseudo patriotism that he is starting to observe around him cannot constitute a road map to the future. This is one reason why his supposed "slight change in stance" is actually something with profound implications.

The idea of people being able to recover their original nature, to reinstate spontaneity and a genuinely human dimension to their existence, can easily be traced to Daoist thought. Schopenhauer's influence is also still apparent.

But how do the perceptions of Carpenter and Nordau, to which he alludes in *Sakkiden*, come into play? Who are these writers and what contributions to Reiun's outlook did their ideas make? Neither Max Nordau (1849–1923) nor Edward Carpenter (1844–1929) are widely read today, although Carpenter's views on sexuality and same-sex attraction certainly can be seen as remarkably progressive for their time. It might be most accurate to say that Nordau and Carpenter provided Reiun not only with ideas but also with rich imagery and powerful metaphors around which he could construct his own critique. Moreover, it allowed him to argue that, since there are contemporary writers in Europe saying things like this about their own civilization, shouldn't Japanese people be aware of such criticisms, as well as their own issues with modernity?

Max Nordau

Max Nordau was a physician born in Pest, Austro-Hungary, and raised as an orthodox Jew who later left Judaism and married a Protestant woman only to become reenergized as a Zionist in the wake of the Dreyfus Affair in France. He was regarded as a forceful social critic, and his books went through multiple printings. To Nordau what made modern civilization so distasteful was its falsity and deceitfulness. In *The Conventional Lies of Our Civilization* (1884) he focused on the many contradictions that underlie modern life and cause it to overflow with hypocrisy. He opens the book with these lines, the first sentence of which Reiun had used as an epigraph for his "Akumateki bunmei" essay:

> The world of civilization is an immense hospital ward, the air is filled with groans and lamentations, and every form of suffering is to be seen twisting and turning on the beds. Go through the world and ask each country you come to: "Does contentment dwell here? Have you peace and happiness?" From each you will hear the same reply: "pass on, we have not that which you are seeking." Pause and listen at the borders, and the breeze will bring to your ears from each one, the same confused echoes of contention and tumult, or revolt and of oppression.[57]

Modern society, according to Nordau, is a house divided against itself. It may seem as though progress is bringing new inventions into the world almost every day, innovations that promise more comfort, but he sees more restlessness, more irritation, more discontent than ever before. Nordau was trying to show that modern human beings have been led into living out lies, seduced into a lifestyle that goes against the dictates of their innermost hearts.

Therefore, Nordau proceeds to expose these falsehoods in chapters entitled "The Lie of Religion," "The Lie of Monarchy and Aristocracy," "The Political Lie," "The Economic Lie," "The Matrimonial Lie," and so forth. He was convinced that "the form and the spirit of our life" are in direct conflict with one another.[58]

We can well imagine that Nordau's indictment of the fundamental dishonesty of modern civilization resonated well with Reiun. As a fully trained modern physician, Nordau was in a position to know something about the health of people who were caught in the midst of modernity's maelstrom, to recall Berman's term.[59] Reiun had always stressed the superficiality and sham of the so-called glorious achievements of modern civilization. Likewise, when Nordau described modern civilization in terms of degeneration in his next book (*Degeneration*, 1892), this also resonated with Reiun's beliefs, as he argued that material advancements in the West had been offset by spiritual decline. Anticipating Freud in analyzing art from an inner, psychological perspective, Nordau was part of that late-nineteenth-century turn inward that began to produce a new variety of literary criticism. One of the things that concerned Nordau was that the sheer complexity that modern civilization brings to life, the hustle and bustle of it all, was the source of many of the psychological maladies of the day.[60] On this point, there is little question that Edward Carpenter's portrayal of modern civilization through the metaphor of disease had an even greater impact on Reiun than the writings of Nordau.

Edward Carpenter

Edward Carpenter was a charismatic and dynamic personality who, although he was born to privilege, left the comforts of upper class Victorian life in order to join workers in socialist and anarchist movements. A recent biographer of Carpenter, Sheila Rowbotham, points out what a seminal thinker Carpenter was.

> Edward Carpenter possessed a knack which helped to prod the modern world into being. Rejecting his upper-middle-class upbringing, he adopted outlooks and ways of life before they crystallized into an alternative culture. In 1875, a decade ahead of the liberal middle-class "discovery" of the slums, he left his comfortable clerical fellowship at Trinity Hall, Cambridge, and went to commune with "the people" through teaching in an adult education movement, University Extension. Then, in the early 1880s, he settled at Millthorpe in the countryside outside Sheffield, where he proceeded to advocate growing your own produce and the "simple life" several years before the intelligentsia took to country cottages. He was sitting at the

feet of a holy man in Sri Lanka (then Ceylon) in the early 1890s—well in advance of the early twentieth-century bohemians who embraced Eastern mysticism. Some of his perceptions were strangely prescient; nearly a hundred years before the advent of Gay Liberation, Carpenter contemplated an organization of men who were attracted to members of their own sex.

In so far as he is known nowadays it is as a pioneer sex reformer who wrote on homosexuality, the emancipation of women and mutuality in loving. He was, however, associated with a wide swathe of other movements and causes. During the early 1880s, when the first socialist and anarchist groupings emerged in Britain, Carpenter was among the first to challenge capitalism as a social and economic system, linking external transformation with new forms of relating and desiring. Attuned to this utopian moment in radical politics, partly by the distress he had experienced in being forced to conceal his own sexual feelings towards men, Carpenter devised a flexible version of socialism with anarchist stripes which put the emphasis on changing everyday living and behavior. Stretching socialism towards environmental and humanitarian causes, he campaigned for clean air, prison reform and animal rights. He came to symbolize the possibility of a new lifestyle without the trappings of Victorian bourgeois respectability by propounding the merits of recycling wooly coats, wearing sandals and [sun] bathing nude. Resolutely resisting the fear and guilt surrounding sexuality, he found emancipation by looking backwards as well as forwards, holding forth on the most diverse topics from pagan sun worship to Plato's *Phaedrus*. Carpenter's critique of the values of his own society was strengthened by an interest in Eastern spirituality, which led him to repudiate not simply Western imperialism, but more fundamentally, Western "civilisation."[61]

This whole idea of seeking "emancipation by looking both backwards as well as forwards," and Carpenter's push to create a "flexible version of socialism with anarchist stripes which put the emphasis on changing everyday living and behavior," as well as his inclination to stretch "socialism towards environmental and humanitarian causes," were obviously all elements of his stance that coincided with Reiun's beliefs. As part of his interest in spirituality, Carpenter had also read the *Bhagavad Gita* in the early 1880s, and when A. P. Sinnett's *Esoteric Buddhism* (1883) appeared and the Theosophical movement was making a strong impression on Cambridge students and faculty Carpenter was also there, in the middle of it all, finding these ideas highly engaging.[62] For a young man like Reiun, who had also been drawn to the social research on living conditions in Japan's new urban slums, and also favored mysticism and a holistic approach to life, Carpenter's essays must have resonated profoundly. Reiun was fond of sprinkling his essays with quotes from Walt Whitman, and Carpenter had also been quite taken with Whitman's poetry as a student in

1874, so much so that he wrote to Whitman right away, meeting with him twice in the United States: once, three years later, when he visited New York; and again in 1884 when he traveled to America again.

Carpenter's take on modern civilization was that it was the outward expression of the inner disintegration of humanity, a view that fit nicely with Reiun's outlook. In *Civilization: Its Cause and Cure* (1889), Carpenter argued that, far from representing humanity's most advanced state in an upward developmental trajectory, civilization represented a condition of total degeneration and disintegration that humans must experience before they would be capable of assessing their own self-worth and living accordingly. Carpenter begins his book with the following observation.

> We find ourselves today in the midst of a somewhat peculiar state of society, which we call Civilisation, but which even to the most optimistic of us does not seem altogether desirable. Some of us, indeed, are inclined to think that it is a kind of disease which the various races of man have to pass through—as children pass through the measles or whooping cough: but if it is a disease, there is this serious consideration to be made, that while History tells us of many nations that have been attacked by it, of many that have succumbed to it, and some that are still in the throes of it, we know of no single case in which a nation has fairly recovered from and passed through it to a more normal and healthy condition. In other words the development of human society has never yet (that we know of) passed beyond a certain definite and apparently final stage in the process we call Civilisation. At that stage it has always succumbed or been arrested.[63]

In Carpenter's view, health was equivalent to a condition of unity, and disease was the result of a loss of unity. In individuals this unity was supposed to exist between the inner self (soul) and the outer self (body). The dilemma for modern people was the loss of this natural unity, which had left humans divided against themselves and unaware of their true inner selves. A parallel disintegration could be seen in the development of society. Primitive tribal communities were much more harmonious and integrated than contemporary society, in which people were divided into classes and pitted against each other in naked competition.

Carpenter's thinking was heavily influenced by the American anthropologist Henry Lewis Morgan's *Ancient Society* (1877), a study that underlined the significance of the emergence of a system of private property in the human transition from barbarism to civilization.[64] Morgan's work was on North American Native American tribes, especially the Iroquois, but he extrapolated from his fieldwork the nature of life in ancient societies. Defining a trajectory of human development from savagery to barbarism and finally to civilization, his work was very influential on both Marx and Engels. Carpenter accepted Morgan's method of identifying the origins of modern civilization, and he focused on the negative impact of the notion of property in drawing human beings away from (a) nature, (b) their true selves, and (c) their comrades.[65] He pointed to the folly of humans' retreat from nature into houses and elaborate sorts of clothing to shield them from the elements. Second, "as his power over material possessions increases, man finds the means of gratifying his senses as well." Consequently, man's instincts are no longer concentrated and functioning as a "whole" but instead are scattered here and there in the pursuit of gratification of "this or that sense or desire."[66] Third, the advent of private property, by stimulating selfishness, had drawn humans away from each other. In their anxiety to possess things for themselves, they were inevitably drawn into conflict with each other. And this is the beginning of the end.

> For the true Self of man consists in his organic relation with the whole body of his fellows: and when man abandons his true Self he abandons also his true relation to his fellows . . . then the reign of individuality begins—a false and impossible individuality, of course, but the only means of coming to the consciousness of the true individuality.[67]

It was this same "false and impossible individuality," the one based on a narrow, instrumentalist view, that elicited Reiun's ire. Perhaps taking his cue from Carpenter, the insight from Morgan's work that spoke most directly to Reiun had to do with the family becoming more complex over time, especially after the emergence of private property and the spread of material possessions that accompanied economic and scientific advances. This would have a great deal to do with his perceptions of the institution of marriage, discussed in chapter 7.

But if civilization was a stage in human history, Carpenter did not believe that it was humanity's final resting place.

> The true Democracy has yet to come. Here in this present stage is only the final denial of all outward class government, in preparation for the restoration of the inner and true authority. Here in this stage the task of civilisation comes to an end: the purport and object of all these centuries is fulfilled: the bitter experience that mankind had to pass through is completed: and out of this Death and all the torture and unrest which accompanies it, comes at last the Resurrection. Man has sounded the depths of alienation from

his own divine spirit, he has drunk the dregs of the cup of suffering, he has literally descended into Hell: henceforth he turns, both in the individual and in society, and mounts deliberately and consciously back again towards the unity which he has lost.[68]

In the optimism and religious imagery about the fall and subsequent rebirth that is so evident in this passage, Carpenter's origins as a man of the cloth in Victorian England come through clearly. In fact, as one author suggests, "His millennial visions can . . . be seen as a particularly extravagant version of the Victorian faith in progress."[69] While Reiun may have lacked this particular dimension in his own worldview, and even though he never borrowed Carpenter's metaphor of civilization as a disease outright, the latter's views were unquestionably a major source of inspiration for his critique of civilization. As Reiun himself suggested, Carpenter's and Nordau's writings brought to the surface and galvanized the beliefs and feelings that had already been taking shape in his own mind. Obviously Carpenter's overriding concern for self was also an important point of tangency. Yet, while Carpenter's writings were clearly inspirational, Reiun brought to these views his own solid grounding in Daoist thought and Schopenhauer's philosophical system, so in the end Reiun's critique of modern civilization retained its own flavor and uniqueness.

One area of fundamental agreement between Carpenter and Reiun was their distrust of what they both perceived to be at the very foundation of modern civilization: scientific knowledge. We have already seen that Reiun considered science to be highly overrated in that it offered only a one-sided, mechanical view of the universe. In his "Modern Science: A Criticism," Carpenter takes a similar stance when he takes science to task for driving a wedge between the "logical and intellectual" and "emotional and instinctive" sides of man, giving the former a *"locus standi"* of its own.[70] The failure of science in Carpenter's view is that it embarks on an impossible quest: trying "to carry out the investigation of nature from the intellectual side alone." In his view, there can be no permanently valid and purely intellectual representation of the universe.[71]

For this position, Reiun did not have to rely on Carpenter, as he had already gleaned it from Schopenhauer, if not Laozi and Zhuangzi. In Reiun's thinking, science was too empirical and analytic in that it isolates things and focuses on them as objects but neglects the realm of a holistic connection to the human experience. He accepts Schopenhauer's notion of a world separated into perceiving subjects and objects and argues that to completely ignore and deny the side of the perceiving subject was to overlook half the equation. The resulting observation suffers accordingly. Modern science claims to be deductive, but in fact it is usually inductive because all great discoveries in knowledge begin in a moment of profound insight in which there is an intuitive grasp of some axiom that is later verified.[72]

This kind of induction is strictly a matter of what Daoists understood as intellectual "discrimination" among a multitude of objects, but it is divorced from reality because the subjects of knowledge, human beings, are neglected. The end result of this discrimination among objects is the stimulation of desire, which once set in motion becomes, for Schopenhauer, the will.[73] Therefore, Reiun argues that this whole development of the faculty for "clever reasoning" in humans, which is so revered in modern times and has been the mainspring in the engine of progress, is nothing more than the refinement and development of some of our lowest instincts, our desires, our animal passions. As such, then, it expresses nothing other than spiritual decline.[74] This belief follows naturally, Reiun tells us, from the basic philosophical standpoint he has adopted. He dubs it *yuishin setsu* (唯心説) literally the theory of "mind only."[75] It expresses his belief that the human mind, the self, is the center of the universe. As a term, *yuishin* (唯心, mind only) was proposed in contrast to *yuibutsu* (唯物, the thing only), which is the standard rendition of the English word *material*, as in *materialism*. In a similar vein, he claimed to opt for the subjective (*shukan*, 主観) side of existence as opposed to the objective (*kyakkan*, 客観) side.

Reiun had learned from Schopenhauer that, although the self is the center of the universe, as it is constituted this is not the true self. But there does exist within this individual self the capacity for greater self-knowledge, by which is meant knowledge of the greater self, the self that is beyond the distinctions of the material plane of existence. This self is not of the physical world but rather of the metaphysical: it has the potential to become part of the divine. This is why Reiun tells us that he still endorses mysticism (*shimpishugi*) and why the object-oriented, overly materialistic, and insipidly analytical tendencies inherent in modern civilization hold no appeal for him.[76] Reiun wants to see the triumph of "subjectivity" (*shukan*), or human emotions, over the mechanization to which civilization subjects people.

Reiun shared with Carpenter a belief that "the truest truth is that which is the expression of the deepest feeling and if there is an absolute truth it can only be known and expressed by him who has the absolute feeling of Being within himself."[77] With his emphasis on subjectivity, Reiun also held that feelings, emotions, make up the core of one's being; they compose one's essence.[78] Emotions are really the only thing that is truly natural in human beings. An interpreter of Schopenhauer's thought makes the argument, "There are many phenomena about which people have deep feelings and intuitions, and which are not very well explained by a thoroughgoing naturalistic and scientific point of view. Moral intuitions, and aesthetic and religious feelings are chief among them. So long as these phenomena are not well explained, or explained away, by a naturalized worldview, then there is an open door to philosophers to try and determine the source of these powerful feelings."[79] Reiun conceived of the human organism as operating under the influence of three main elements: emotions, desires, and the intellect. The intellect is what receives and transmits stimuli from the environment, and in order to do this it must isolate and discriminate among stimuli. In this process, desires arise and the will is set in motion. The intellect then gives the will direction and encourages the will to work by securing for it the necessary food, objective knowledge. Over this whole tendency humans can exercise virtually no control, for this capacity to respond to stimuli is essential to the physical survival of the organism. So the intellect must continue on its merry path of discrimination.

However, as he learned from Daoism, the mind, and consequently the self, need not "attach" itself to the sensations generated by the inflow of stimuli. They can be experienced without the self adhering to them and so without desires arising. Independent ideas growing out of these desires need not be born. Using Schopenhauer's terms, Reiun argues that the will can be suppressed. If a human being can turn the will back on itself, it will be destroyed and desires will disappear. What will be left are true emotions at the center of an individual's existence. These are the natural feelings of one's *kokoro* (innermost heart), and it is the true or "sincere" heart of *makoto*.[80] This is the state that the Buddhists think of as no-self. Psychologically it is a condition of pure emotion (*junjô*, 純情), a state of self-sacrificing devotion.

A human being in this state is by no means a lifeless thing. One lives an ordinary life but does not attach to everything. If the human being is an organism that is continually responding to inputs from outside itself, it is possible for one to understand this condition and accept it. By recognizing that humans are in constant flux, a certain stasis can be achieved. This is true because by accepting change knowledge no longer confuses and divides a person. Therefore, wisdom arises in a pure and simple fashion. Above all it is natural because it arises from humans' deepest and most natural feelings (shijô, 至情).[81]

Looking Back

In Reiun's view, then, the individual who succeeds in suppressing the will, the one who ceases to attach, has become a more natural or holistic human. Clearly, therefore, the idea of a natural human being in Reiun's thought refers to a potential that exists in each individual. As we have seen, in each individual self there is the capacity for knowledge of the higher self. Rousseau, too, was interested in what a person could do and what he or she could become; he also believed that human beings were essentially good when they were in a state of nature but were corrupted by the introduction of property, agriculture, science, and commerce. In other words, they were corrupted by modern civilization. Daoism offered the same perspective, a position that was radically egalitarian for its time.[82] Reiun especially appreciated the impact that Rousseau's political and social ideas had on his era. After all, they had been the basis for a revolutionary critique of existing institutions and social practices. That is why he embraced the idea of "looking back" to a time when humanity was in a simpler state so that the best from earlier times could be brought to bear on the problems humanity faced in the present, which were global in scale. He concluded one of his important essays with these remarks.

> True, Rousseau's appeal in the late eighteenth century stood squarely against the Enlightenment, and while we can say that it did result in increasing individual rights, what we are calling for today goes beyond the individual; it goes beyond nationality and race and envisions social equality across the globe, in other words, the unification of all humanity. . . . So, even though Rousseau issued a warning for the whole world, it did not by any means result in the nineteenth century reverting to primitive times in order to restore humanity to its natural state; and, likewise, neither will the new era that we are calling for lead us back to primitive times. No, those of us who oppose certain aspects of modernity, those of us who are calling for a *hibunmeiron*, want to see new forms of community. Indeed, they may share some characteristics with those of primitive times—especially the simplicity and spontaneity of the mind—but they will be different. Yes, even though we may acknowledge that much of what Laozi and Zhuangzi talked about three thousand years ago, and of which Rousseau reminded us some one hundred years ago, retain an important validity today, what we are envisioning now is a world in which we may have to wear the outer trappings of a mechanistic civilization but on the inside we will manifest that natural simplicity and spontaneity and aspire to the universality of a global outlook that will extend to all humanity. Ah, just like at the end of the eighteenth century when Rousseau's critique of the Enlightenment provided the incendiary driving force behind the French Revolution, can't you see that

the voice of opposition to modern civilization—the *hihunmeiron*—that you hear today will likewise light the fuse and spark a social revolution?[83]

If the simplicity and spontaneity of an earlier time can be retrieved, it can be put to use in the service of humanity today. The past may have much to teach us, Reiun argues, but we can never become its prisoners. The task of the present is to construct a vision of a newly emerging global community that can carry humanity forward into the twentieth century and beyond.[84] The influence of Schopenhauer's thought remains very evident, but we cannot fail to notice that an important change has taken place in Reiun's writing, and it is not so "slight" as he would have us believe based on the passage from *Sakkiden*. Where once much attention was paid to the possibility of the individual becoming *muga* (無我, selfless), now there is a greater purpose attached to freeing oneself from restrictive attachments and desires: it is nothing less than transforming the world. It is still important to explore that inner domain and keep one's gaze focused there, but now one has to slide back toward the outside so that the inward gaze can be directed outward as well. It is a subtle shift in Reiun's critical orientation but an important one.

Rousseau had helped Reiun understand that we have to know the origins of human beings as social creatures in order to understand the course of human development. Only by seeing how humans came to be the way they are can we appreciate what they can become. Therefore, Rousseau did not share Hobbes's view that primitive human beings were fundamentally egoistic and brutish. Rather, he saw humans as essentially good, as individuals capable of living together peacefully and harmoniously. But it was the historical process by means of which society grew, and became more complex and more organized, that generated the inequalities and inequities; it was competition between individuals and groups that gave rise to the egoistic mentality. Reiun arrived at a similar awareness when he sought to understand the basic ideas underlying contemporary civilization.

Dark Undercurrents

In "Gendai shisô no Anchô" (The Dark Undercurrent in Contemporary Thought), Reiun traced the origin and development of two ideas that he deemed central to modern civilization: materialism and individualism.[85] Reiun traced the genesis of these ideas back to the Middle Ages and found that individualism developed in reaction to the political absolutism of the epoch while materialism was a response to the tyranny of religious dogma. In other words, political despotism and religious dogmatism were the characteristics of the era, so individualism and materialism were the reaction to these conditions, and what eventually replaced them. More precisely, the idea of individualism grew out of the concept of civil liberties (*jiyûkenshugi*), which emerged in opposition to the political absolutism of the Middle Ages. Likewise, materialism was the descendent of the doctrine of naturalism under which humans demanded the right to investigate nature and determine natural laws in order to be free of the restraints of an absolutist church.

How did these ideas develop? The idea of civil liberties was ultimately given political expression in the French Revolution, which then ushered in the era of constitutional government. The spirit of naturalism also undergirded the whole transformation associated with the Revolution, which would have been unthinkable if the human mind had not first been freed from the yoke of religious dogmatism and allowed to pursue its natural course. So the pursuit of civil liberties brought about liberation from the tyranny of absolute monarchies, while naturalism, by giving birth to the idea of scientific research, inaugurated a new era in scholarship and opened up new dimensions of the human mind. In Reiun's estimation, then, the results of these two paradigm shifts in intellectual and political orientation were profound.

However, drawing on a Daoist conception of change, he argued that whenever things become extreme there is bound to be a shift in the other direction.[86] There are limits to all developmental trajectories, and once those are reached, decline inevitably sets in.[87] Thus, in the West when the idea of individual freedom reached its extreme form in its exaltation of the individual, in its incitement of egoism, and in its encouragement of the idea of placing the desires of small, individualized "selves" above all other things, eventually there was bound to be a shift in the other direction. The unbalanced growth of selfishness, of narrow self-centeredness, that accompanies modern industrial civilization is tantamount to an assault on our humanity. In "Gendai shisô no Anchô," he quotes directly from one of his favorite philosophers, Zhuangzi, who, wrote in one of his best known essays from the outer chapters "Knowledge Rambling in the North," about how easy it is to become confused and not know how to become properly grounded. If one's self-knowledge takes off wandering, Zhuangzi suggests, "My will would be aimless. If it went nowhere, I should not know where it had gone; and if it went and came back again, I should not know where it had stopped. If it kept up this going and coming, I would never know when the process would end."[88] Reiun relates this passage to the idea that once desires are stirred, and the will is set in motion, the process of measuring, calculating, and thinking in terms of how beneficial this or that might be to the small willing self is also set in motion, and this is precisely why modern civilization has become so mechanical, artificial, and estranged from basic human moral and ethical values.[89]

The idea of naturalism and the framework for the instrumentalist view of society also had their natural limits, limits that were reached when human beings became so absorbed in measuring and analyzing every experience and concentrating so much on the objective side of things that they lost sight of the subjective side, the inner nature of things. In effect what began as part of a quest for greater truth and a better understanding of the world backfired and left people with an incomplete, distorted picture of reality.

Similarly, the drive for equal rights in the political sphere ironically laid the groundwork for a system featuring gross economic inequalities, for it was a system that relied on the promotion of narrow self-interest and unbridled competition among individuals. The original trend had been toward the liberation of the individual from externally imposed authority, be it church or king, thus giving people the opportunity to create their own centers of authority, their own source of value, within themselves. Yet in the end the opposite effect was achieved: humans' selfish desires were stimulated, and people became blind to their own inner natures. This failure, Reiun believes, explains why nineteenth century civilization excels at creating the trappings with which humans can adorn their society, but offers nothing concrete, nothing of substance to enrich human life.[90] Despite the brilliance of modern science's inventions, the darkness of spiritual decline cannot be dispelled. This is the reality of contemporary civilization, and the crux of the modern condition. But against this reality there is a reaction, a "dark undercurrent," which may be observed in many quarters and is most evident in Reiun's own hibunmei stance. What Reiun accomplishes in his attack on modern civilization, then, is a transformation of the discussion from one about ontology to one about social change; he has shifted his focus from seeking a better understanding of human nature to calling for both a social and an intellectual revolution in the world around him.

So, in his own eyes, Reiun's call for a social revolution was part of a general historical reaction or response to given circumstances. He freely admits that he gets inspiration from turning to the past, to ancient India and China in particular. Great thinkers before him were also discontented with the times in which they lived, and they followed the same course. Confucius, Laozi, Buddha, Jesus, Socrates, Plato, Luther, Calvin, Voltaire, Rousseau, Galileo, Schopenhauer, Byron, Carlyle, Nietzsche, Gorky, and Tolstoy—all of these people were reacting to their times and the world around them.[91] Moreover, returning to the past (*kaiko*, 回顧) does not literally mean that the past is going to be retrieved. Rather, the past offers a new way for humans to consider why things became the way they are, and it opens up new vistas for contemplating the future. After two successful wars against China and Russia, Japan was emerging on the international scene as an up-and-coming nation and was now a part of the western trajectory of modernity. But thinkers and writers were starting to question that trajectory. Was this indeed the best thing for Japan and humanity?[92]

In an essay of the same name, Reiun argues, "Philosophers always look back."[93] Rousseau, Laozi, and Zhuangzi had all done this, and the whole romantic movement in literature had done so as well. And even the Meiji Restoration, wasn't it in fact a "restoration" of the past, of course not literally but in terms of the ideas it conjured up, the image of returning things to their original and proper state? People need to draw on the past for their ideals, and these ideals must be rooted in concrete experience: they cannot be imagined or invented. Therefore, the past must be restored in the sense that its meaning can be retrieved in order to better understand what humanity can achieve in the present and the future.[94]

Reiun considered himself part of a broad response to a significant historical transformation, but he did not view his ideas as "reactionary" in the sense of being opposed to change. He was no friend of the old order. Therefore, in his autobiography he spoke disdainfully of a critic who labeled his attack on modern civilization as *chonmageshugi*, literally "topknotism."[95] By making this reference to the samurai tradition, his critic was linking Reiun's ideas to the ancien régime, and Reiun could not accept this assessment. In his interpretation, there was nothing unprogressive about reimagining the past. In fact, he argued, socialism and anarchism are basically a form of "restorationism" because they seek to restore humans to their natural state, where they lived in harmony with nature and their fellow human beings and the general welfare was elevated above that of the individual.[96]

So Reiun would find himself squarely on the side of socialism and revolution even though his relation to socialism was not uncomplicated. Although many of his friends were active in the socialist movement, Reiun never formally affiliated himself with it. As we saw, while he was living in Okayama and war clouds with Russia were gathering, he was not ambivalent about the war—he supported it wholeheartedly. He argued that in the end he was for peace and harmony in the world, but he felt that before there could be any hope of this the white imperialists would have to be expelled from East Asia.[97] Yet at the very same time that he was taking a pro-war stand in Okayama, he was also fulfilling his commitment to his friend Kôtoku Shûsui by contributing a long serialized essay to the weekly *Heimin shinbun*, the organ of the socialist antiwar group.[98] Later, in his autobiography, he publicly acknowledged his "shame" over the "shortsightedness" of his support for the war. His basic reasoning about taking a stand against western imperialism was still sound, he believed, but he had not foreseen the hardships that the Russo-Japanese War would inflict on the Japanese people.[99]

By his own admission, Reiun's socialism was "extremely simple: sympathy for the poor and nothing more."[100] He claimed that if there was anything he had absorbed from socialism it was not from Marx or Kropotkin but from Hugo and Tolstoy.[101] To him *socialism* was a very broad and flexible term, encompassing the benevolence (*ren*) of Confucius, the compassion (*ji*) of Buddha, and the love (*ai*) of Christ.[102] No doubt, this left some of his Marxist friends scratching their heads. But in socialism Reiun saw possibilities for a complete ethical transformation in humans in which selfishness would be discarded and there would be equality for all.[103] In "The Ideal New Kingdom,"("Risô no shin ôkoku") he saw socialism as the hope of a future in which the human experience in the political, economic, and ethical realms would improve. It was a commitment to completely revolutionize the existing system, which was so rooted in the human ego. Therefore, he found socialism to be against all forms of despotism, economic as well as political. It opposed unbridled competition among individuals, the notion of survival of the fittest, imperialism, militarism, and the preeminence of the state (*kokkashugi*).[104] In another essay, "Jinshuteki henken" (Racial Prejudice), Reiun addressed the natural inclination of people to think of themselves first as members of a nation or a specific race. But the coming age needed people to transcend these narrow ways of thinking, especially the pseudo patriotism and loyalty he found in Japan, and think about achieving ever greater levels of unity until all humanity was united in one whole.[105]

Reiun endorsed socialism, then, because he believed some sort of revolution was necessary to check emerging social inequities. He believed there had to be some sort of "humanist resistance" to the corrupting influence of the materialistic basis of modern civilization. In "My Version of Socialism," he explained his call for revolution primarily in terms of the need to resist the power of money.[106]

Today's civilization is a scientific civilization, a materialistic civilization, a mechanistic civilization, but the brilliance of today's culture is all a product of a certain kind of mental capacity (*chiryoku*, 智力), so contemporary civilization is really dependent on this kind of intellectual reasoning, and it wants to break everything down and compare it, make judgments on it, and then this just stimulates desires. . . . All philosophy, science, and thought contains this tendency to emphasize the intellect and neglect the emotions; this is the overarching tendency of contemporary civilization, and it is what is wrong with it. . . . What this means to me is that today's so-called progress is nothing more than the development of desires, which is to say that it is the development of intellectual capacities; and along with the development of these capacities, the idea of private possession emerges, and private possession is basically an idea for the rich. It becomes their standard for everything and is the foundation on which all modern economic thought is based.

However, individuals are really made up of three different components—the intellect, the emotions, and desires—and it depends on the harmonious operation of all three of these components. The development of the individual, as well as of society, depends on all three of these working in tandem. Today's society, relying as it does on the narrow intellectual faculty, is therefore not a whole or healthy society. In fact the major flaw of contemporary society is that it is overly reliant on this facility for clever reasoning and doesn't do enough to see emotions develop. What society should do is resist the authority of the rich and support the development of humanity. This is why there needs to be a revolution in contemporary social organization, and that is what my socialism is all about.[107]

The philosophical ideas of Schopenhauer are clearly still underpinning Reiun's thought; he continues to view the problems of modernity as the inability of people to curb the growth of the small, willing self. But being the maverick that he was, he enjoyed the "edginess" of saying that he stood for socialism or anarchism, though clearly the revolution he had in mind was a revolution in values and ethics. He wanted to see a philosophical revolution in which contemporary beliefs were turned upside down and made to stand on their heads. He had expressed similar misgivings in earlier writings about the eclipse of meaningful human values such as honor, integrity, and the brotherhood of man by the narrow selfishness engendered by modern civilization, and this was the theme of another comprehensive essay, "Gendai no byôkon" (The Roots of Contemporary Evils), which bears the subtitle "I Reject Mammonism."[108]

"The Roots of Contemporary Evils"

In "The Diabolical Civilization," Reiun repeatedly cursed modern civilization for dealing only in form or touching only on the surface of things, without providing humans with anything concrete or substantive. In "The Roots of Contemporary Evils," he traces the way in which money, as the agent of civilization, helped bring this situation about. For rhetorical effect, he opens his essay by quoting a well-known poem by British humorist, Tom Hood (1789–1845).

> Gold! Gold! Gold! Gold!
> Bright and yellow, hard and cold
> Molten, graven, hammered and rolled,
> Heavy to get and light to hold,
> Hoarded, bartered, bought and sold,
> Stolen, borrowed, squandered, doled,
> Spurned by young, but hung by old
> To the verge of a church yard mold;
> Price of many a crime untold.

This precious metal is attractive, but it can be the source of pain and unhappiness and much crime in society. Reiun finds it ironic that, while modern democracies supposedly adhere to the principle of equality, money guarantees that in fact there will always be gross inequalities in society. In fact the power of money converts democracy into a kind of despotism of the wealthy. More important, modern civilization places such a value on money that it becomes something to be prized above all else. If people are concerned only about money, and hence only about themselves, how can they entertain thoughts that go beyond the narrow individual self to encompass the community, the nation, and the world?

In effect, then, money has come to replace the function of ecclesiastical authority in the Middle Ages. That is, people are induced to worship money just as they had blindly followed the dictates of the absolute church. When humans finally realized that church dogmatism was nothing more than superstition, they protested, and this brought about the Protestant Reformation, which placed value on the individual's inner religious experience. Engaging in empty rituals to pay homage to some mysterious god was considered self-deprecating, so in place of this people opted for religion based on concrete inner experiences.

Since the time of the Reformation the drift has been against the tide of superstition; people had gone on to reject the myth of the divine right of kings, and ultimately, in the French Revolution, they had rejected the whole notion of monarchical authority. But what had transpired next? In the place of kings, yet another oppressive form of authority was substituted, the power of money. Hence monarchies were overthrown in the name of human rights, but an age of despotism by the wealthy was ushered in. What is yet to come is an era in which everybody respects not only their own persons but those of others. But in order to respect and trust themselves, people must come to know these "selves" in both their inner and outer dimensions. Moreover, they have to understand that everyone is made up of the same stuff; when they realize that everyone shares the same humanity, then it will be possible to empathize with others and show real compassion. Only then will the last of the superstitions be dispelled and humans will be able to become more fully conscious of themselves. Only then can people live a genuinely moral life. So, Reiun concludes, "It is my wish to destroy contemporary superstitions and put mankind on the path toward these ideals."[109]

One important way in which socialism could contribute to this process was through the abolition of private property. This aspect of socialism was, I believe, one of the principal elements that attracted Reiun. Carpenter's views on the notion of private property were probably an important influence on him as well. Frequently in the course of his writings on modern civilization he came back to the problem of the right to privately possess property. Drawing on Henry Lewis Morgan, much as Carpenter did, Reiun associated the emergence of private property rights with the origins of modern civilization, something that convinced him that modern civilization was founded on greed and people's selfish desires. This is why Reiun felt obliged to "look back" to an era before private property existed. In "Isei no shiyû" (Private Possession of the Opposite Sex), he traced how the whole notion of personal possession was transferred from inanimate property to include women. Monogamy is upheld by legal and moral codes, supposedly because it allows one's more bestial nature to be contained. In fact, however, it is an institution arising directly from man's lowest passions, his desires, his greed, as manifested in his selfish wish to possess everything.[110] Likewise Reiun saw most crimes, especially theft, as arising from the institution of private property.[111]

Reiun believed in his own idealized version of socialism because it seemed to be a part of a reaction to existing conditions. It held promise for him because it could bring about the abolition of differences in personal wealth by outlawing the right to possess private property. In this manner, the whole evil, corrupting influence of money could be curbed.

It was not as though Reiun was prepared to endorse any specific type of socialism, or any political platform either. To the extent that he had any image of a community of the future, it was something akin to Carpenter's vision of "True Democracy" as a community of cosmically conscious humans whose rules all come from within. No doubt Reiun's image was also modeled after the sage-king communities of ancient China. Yet even here, there could be nothing too specific, as Reiun was averse to identifying with any particular system or set of beliefs. In his autobiography, when he discussed his socialism it was under the heading "there was nothing worthy of the suffix –*ism* in my thought." This was not a source of chagrin by any means, for, as he explained, he did not wish to be "imprisoned inside a model constructed by someone else" (*SD*, 661).

One could say that Reiun's attack on modern civilization was, in the end, very much a critique of ethics. But he had altered his position significantly from the early 1890s. He is now certain that our understanding of the modern individual has to be solidly grounded in history and society; both the "times" and the social and political structures in which individuals are embedded matter. He had strong reservations about the status of morality in modern society. He found that, like Rousseau, he couldn't resist going back to the time before the right to possess private property was recognized in order to discover the true nature of humans. As long as human beings' selfishness was being unleashed, true self-knowledge would be impossible. So somehow human beings needed to reach a place where desires could be kept in check and people were no longer blinded to their true nature.

It is said of Carpenter that in the end his visions "represented a flight from the special complexities and burdens of modern history."[112] It would seem that Reiun's naive wish to turn back the clock might be open to the same charge. Yet is it fair to argue that historical actors holding alternative visions are necessarily in "flight" from existing realities? Are such people actually turning away from the "complexities and burdens" of modern life simply because they reject what they find? There may well have been a utopian tinge to Reiun's ideas and vision, but in this respect he shared much in common not only with Rousseau, as Miyake Setsurei suggested in his forward to Reiun's autobiography, but also with a small group of friends in the socialist and anarchist circles of the day.[113] These were a diverse a group of critics, activists, and writers that included people like Kôtoku Shûsui, Ogawa Usen, Ôsugi Sakae, Arishima, Takeo, Futabatei Shimei, Kinoshita Naoe, Ishikawa Sanshirô, Fukuda Hideko, Mushakôji Saneatsu, Sakai Toshihiko, Takamure

Itsue, Taoka himself, Miyazawa Kenji, and many others. One thing that distinguishes these activists and critics is that they embraced "a concept of progress toward an imagined future, [that] coexisted with and simultaneously countered the temporality of Western modernity."[114] We can see this clearly in Reiun's attack on modern civilization when he posits a future that is similar to but distinct from primitive communities: he envisions a global community, universalistic in its values, one that is open to all humanity and transcends the narrow limitations of nations, states, and races.

"My Socialism"

When Reiun wrote the essay "Chijô to tengoku" (Heaven on Earth) he claimed that his version of socialism was not based on a materialist conception of history or on scientific reasoning; nor did it arise solely out of a concern for the situation of industrial workers, although he was precocious in expressing those concerns. Rather, it was rooted in the desire to achieve a society in which humanity was writ large, one in which there was benevolence. In other words, he explained, "My socialism is an ethical socialism, a philosophical socialism."[115] This is not to say that a social revolution to address the inequities in society and the problems of labor and poverty is not necessary. But the revolution cannot be limited to politics and economics. "I am neither religious nor superstitious," he writes, "but my vision is for a society in which higher ethics and philosophy can be realized."[116] And in another short piece, "Jisei no chokka" (A Sudden Change in the Times), Reiun starts with an epigraph from Henry George's *Social Problems* (1883), "The salvation of society, the hope for the free, full development of humanity, is in the gospel of brotherhood—the gospel of Christ," and goes on to refer to Ferdinand Lasalle's (1825–64) claim that he would wait five hundred years to see socialism established if that is what it would take. But Reiun countered with a greater sense of urgency; he wanted the triumph of socialism to come much sooner.[117]

Like Rousseau, with whom he identified, Reiun was never at home in the times in which he lived. Yet wasn't it precisely because he stood outside his times that Reiun was able to look at the problems facing human beings in the way he did? Like Carpenter, Reiun was not only interested in critiquing his society and the times; he was also interested in the very nature of the way human beings perceive reality. He wanted to open the door on alternative ways of viewing and apprehending the world, ways that echoed Schopenhauer's understanding of the manner in which human beings stand in the world and how they both perceive and experience it.

In his essay "Jinrui to kishu" (The Trends in Humankind), he opens with an epigraph from Thoreau, "The morning wind forever blows, the poem of creation is uninterrupted; but few are the ears that hear it," and then proceeds to describe how humanity has progressed from tribalism to feudalism and from feudalism to the nation-state. It is from the nation-state that notions about racial identity arise, he writes, and so it is from this stage that the move to concerns about the state of all of humanity can be made.[118] Moreover, in terms of modes of political thought, we have seen the development from monarchism to individualism and from individualism to statism. From the state emerges imperialism, and, as a natural response to imperialism, we see the growth of socialism. Knowledge and education also experienced these kinds of developmental stages, so we can observe a trend or a "tendency" to seek greater unity in the growth of political and intellectual forms. But, in the end, the only outcome that makes sense to Reiun is development of a worldview based on the self, a personal philosophy, and ethics.[119]

Clearly, this is an idealistic, utopian view of a future world featuring a global community in which ethical human beings interact without regard to race or country; in fact this global community would supersede the nation, the state, and imperialism. In the end, Reiun was a literary and cultural critic, so he believed that the best way to improve our understanding of reality was by means of the free rendering of critical judgments. If they remain blind to their own true natures and operate without genuine ideals humans cannot hope to make careful or considered judgments based on reality. For that they need to be able to look deep inside themselves and learn to truly see. In February 1906, in the pages of his journal *Tenko*, Reiun returned to the topic of mysticism in an essay called "Shimpishugi o ronzu" (Theorizing Mysticism), which closely resembles some of the essays he published back in the early 1890s and even as late as 1897. Here, again, he was identifying a strong current in European intellectual life, one that had a fin-de-siècle feel to it but one that could also be considered a natural reaction to the so-called scientific worldview that had dominated the nineteenth century.[120] Reiun trots out a string of by now familiar names ranging from Nietzsche to Nordau, including artists like Ibsen, Tolstoy, Wagner, Whitman, and the symbolists, not to mention mainstays like Schopenhauer, von Hartmann, and even a new figure, Friedrich Paulsen (1846–1908), a student of Gustave Fechner, who was one of the founders of scientific psychology. His point? With all these luminaries in Europe lining up to explore and endorse the trend toward probing the inner dimensions of the human experience, the intuitive side of our beings, isn't Japan capable of generating a comparable level of interest? Shouldn't Japan be getting on this train, which is already pulling out of the station in most European capitals? The answer seemed quite obvious to Reiun.

Ostensibly, the publication of *Tenko* marks Reiun's return to the "literary world," but he did not find as much to comment on in 1905 as he had ten years earlier. However, he did identify two writers as particularly promising. The first was the young Natsume Sôseki who had just published *I Am a Cat* (1905) and the shorter works "Shield of Illusion" (Mabaroshi to tate) and "The Tower of London" (Rondon no tô). Reiun appreciated his deep learning and poetic nature, which combined to yield deep, probing works. The second writer Reiun admired was Kinoshita Naoe, a lawyer, Christian-socialist, and antiwar activist who turned his literary skills to novels such as *Pillar of Fire* (*Hi no hashira*) and *Confessions of a Husband* (*Ryôjin no jihaku*). If Sôseki was learned, deep, and sometimes dark, Naoe was clear, passionate, and soulful, though very sarcastic and ironic. *Pillar of Fire* contained a powerful antigovernment and antiwar message; consequently the government banned it in 1910. Reiun thought that together these two authors boded well for the future.[121] But clearly, for Reiun, his hopes lay less with literature than with a broader social, philosophical, and ethical critique that spoke to humanity as a whole. Yet on his way to this stance he learned the importance of reevaluating the past and reflecting on the ways in which historical thinking can shape the way we live in the present.

6

SEEKING REBELLION
TAOKA REIUN AND THE
MEIJI RESTORATION

Spirit exists only as its own product. . . . History is the process whereby the spirit discovers itself and its own concept.

Hegel, *Lectures on the Philosophy of World History*

[W]e should no longer imagine a great big Incarnate Logos called Humanity whose career is to be interpreted either as heroic struggle or as tragic decline. Instead, we should think of lots of different past human communities, each of which has willed us one or more cautionary anecdotes.

Richard Rorty, *History and the Idea of Progress*

The last years of the Meiji era were a daunting time for many Japanese. People knew that the end of an era was near, and the feeling was unnerving. The country had witnessed tremendous historical change during the prior forty years, but it was not always easy to grasp how the new society would take shape and where it was heading. There was tension in the air after Kôtoku's arrest and execution, which ushered in what is called the "winter period" (*fuyu no jidai*) of the socialist movement in Japan. It was time to pull back and contemplate the future. The young poet and critic Ishikawa Takuboku (1885–1912), who, like the painter and cartoonist Ogawa Usen, celebrated everyday life, accurately captured the spirit of the times when he referred to the era as a "period of blockade" (*jidai-heisoku*). Takuboku was fifteen years younger than Reiun, so for all practical purposes he belonged to a different generation. Yet what he had to say in 1911 at the age of twenty-five is quite close to what Reiun had expressed when he was the same age.

An Impasse: Ishikawa Takuboku and the Need to Investigate Tomorrow

In a 1910 article, "Jidai heisoku no genjô" (The Present State of Blockade in Our Era), Takuboku described the dilemma of members of his generation.[1]

Born too late, they had inherited the fait accompli of Japan as a modern nation-state, already tested and proven in the international arena. Due to historical circumstances, then, they had no cause to serve. What emerged from this was an unhealthy focus on the interests of the individual self, the swelling of one's own self-importance, something that gave rise to a wave of "selfish egoism" (*jikoshugi*). Like Reiun, Takuboku deplored the tendency to place the interests of the small willing self above all else. If people cater only to their own whims, the results will be self-destructive. How can this impasse be overcome? How can people learn to see themselves more clearly? Takuboku's answer was the "investigation of tomorrow" (*asu no kôsatsu*).[2] He writes:

> In order to escape the self-destructive situation in which we find ourselves, we have to realize that the time has come to make ourselves aware of who or what our enemy is. This is not about satisfying our own desires or needs but because it is absolutely necessary for us to do so. First, we must declare war on this impasse in which we find ourselves. We have to forget "naturalism" and quit blindly looking back nostalgically on the Genroku era. Instead we need to concentrate all our attention and energy on investigating tomorrow, that is, researching our own era in an organized and systematic manner. Investigate tomorrow! For us today, this is absolutely the one mandatory thing that we must do. In fact it is the only thing for us to do. How are we to begin this investigation and where will it take us? Of course it can only lead us toward freedom for every single individual. . . . But for now we must rigorously, boldly, and freely research "today" in order to discover for ourselves the necessity (*hitsuyô*) of "tomorrow." Necessity is our most certain ideal.[3]

Takuboku's milieu was the literary world, and he wrote this essay to critique naturalism, the most influential literary genre at the time. But it was also his way of responding to Kôtoku's execution. What he was calling for in this essay was a reawakening of the original spirit of naturalism, that is, the practice of looking critically at the world, investigating it, discovering the true facts about it, and on this basis generating what he called a genuine and meaningful literary criticism (*hiyô*).

For Takuboku, one of the few values of which one can be certain in uncertain times is that tomorrow will come; hence there is a "necessity" to investigate that tomorrow, something that would emerge naturally from a rigorous critique of today. But part of this critique, and part of the necessary investigation, was finding a way to understand the forces that would shape tomorrow. For that one needs to understand the present, and if one is looking to do so, one must also become cognizant of the nature of historical change.

As we saw in chapter 4, Reiun had arrived at this very awareness over a decade before Takuboku's essay appeared. He had also drawn on the metaphor of an impasse or "blockade" and applied it to human aspirations or the area of human talent (*jinzai-yôsoku*) that was being stymied, something he perceived as a threat that might cast Meiji society into stagnation. Like Takuboku, he expressed misgivings about the spread of a narrow, self-serving individualism that threatened to eradicate ideals, and he was very concerned about the social inequities being generated by industrialization. Takuboku had also mused in passing about "the strange power being unleashed by capital," but he took it no further than this. But these kinds of concerns clearly bothered Reiun, and they repeatedly brought him back to the question of the Meiji Restoration and the nature of the forces that it had unleashed. The men who had brought about this event were men of ideals, men of principle, but what they set in motion was now generating contradictions and social inequities.

Throughout his critique of modern civilization, Reiun had felt an increasing need to investigate the origins and development of things, to understand how the present had become what it is. This urge to dig down to the roots in order to discover the true nature of something continued to assert itself, and it brought Reiun to the doorstep of historical issues. In order to take the next step, Reiun had to go through this door and define the character of the Meiji Restoration. Accordingly, he would now start to frame questions about the past and how it shapes the present. Specifically, he was interested in the process of historical change and the nature of the Meiji Restoration. What kind of event was it? Was it an incomplete revolution? If so, what the tasks remained to be completed? He was troubled by a vision of the Japanese people floating aimlessly along, relying on imported doctrines and systems of law in lieu of drawing on their own creative capacity to develop independent visions of what the future might bring. When Reiun joined his friend Kôtoku Shûsui on the *Heimin shinbun* in late 1903 and early 1904, he was putting himself in a position to absorb a variety of new influences and perspectives from the socialist-anarchist movement.[4]

Until this time, Reiun had frequently mentioned Rousseau and had often made historical references throughout his essays. But now he began to probe history more deeply and systematically, especially during the period after he returned from two years in China in April 1907. As we saw in chapter 5, prior to that he had spent a year in Tokyo trying to make ends meet with his new journal, *Tenko*, but had moved to China out of economic necessity in September 1905. There he once again took a Japanese-language teaching position, this time in Suzhou. However, during this period his health became a problem, and it was on a return visit to Japan in August 1906 that Reiun was told at a Nagasaki hospital that he was exhibiting the early symptoms of spinal meningitis. Nevertheless, he returned to Suzhou for almost another year.

After he returned from China, though, he spent a good deal of time resting, writing, and recuperating at various resort spots in Japan. Despite the fact that by early 1908 Reiun had lost the use of his legs, he remained surprisingly active, publishing books and journals until his death in 1912. His desire to come to grips with historical change and the nature of the Meiji Restoration, in particular, is understandable: individuals raised in the shadow of such an event would naturally want to discover its meaning for themselves. As one historian notes, writers in Meiji Japan needed to be able to identify the domestic roots of "radical spiritual and cultural change" in order to make a bewildering present more understandable.[5] Reiun's way of going about this in 1908–9 was to compile the biographies of Meiji rebels in order to understand what prompted them to risk their lives by resisting the state in early 1880s Japan.

"At Nagatamura"

Reiun's most systematic and comprehensive treatment of the problem of the Meiji Restoration can be found in the introductory essay to his book *Meiji hanshinden* (Biographies of Meiji Rebels, 1909), a study of the leaders of five major radical political uprisings that took place during the most radical and violent phase of the popular rights movement in the early 1880s. The choice to single out these individuals and celebrate their lives—individuals who at the time had posed a serious threat to the social and political order—was courageous and underscores a sense of urgency Reiun felt as his illness began to cripple him. The year before *Meiji hanshinden* appeared, however, while Reiun was resting and recuperating at his brother's second home overlooking the Nagata Shrine near Kobe, he wrote a wide-ranging essay titled "Nagatamura ni te" (At Nagatamura), which offers a preliminary look at what he was thinking at the time.[6]

The essay is divided into ten sections, opening with a surprisingly eco-sensitive appeal. Although water, air, and land are all essential to human existence, access to them, which should be every human being's right, was being restricted because of capitalism and industrialization. Land is necessary to produce the food we eat, he wrote, and streams and lakes are needed to

Figure 6.1. The Nagata Shrine today. (Photo by the author)

provide people with clean water. But with the growth of the market, the price of land is steadily being driven up, and people now have to pay for access to water; in fact, due to industrial pollution, clean air and water are becoming increasingly difficult to find. As cities expand into the countryside, pristine nature is on the run. Is this the way it has to be? Shouldn't everyone, regardless of how much money they have, still be able to acquire these basic building blocks of life? Is it necessary to have a system whereby some people are privileged and others have to starve and suffer? Reiun is starting to see the environment as a potential point of contestation in Japan's path to modernity. A decade before, in 1897, he had written about the Ashio Mine Pollution Incident, and here it is clear that he is thinking about potential long-run conflicts between society and the environment.

Seeing the problem as not just economic and social but philosophical, environmental, and ethical, Reiun is able to take on some of the disturbing trends he observes in modern Japan and relate them to his critique of modern civilization or to the fundamental questions he raises about humans and their relationship with nature. What he saw was that, as the consciousness of the individual self expands, so, too, does selfishness and egoism. There was a time when people were not so focused on their own self-interest and acquisitiveness was not so all consuming. He points his readers to one of his favorite texts, the *Daodejing*, specifically chapter 18, where he finds:

> When the great Way is forgotten,
> the doctrines of humanity (仁) and morality (義) arise.
> When knowledge (智) and cleverness (慧) appear,
> there emerges great hypocrisy.
> When family relationships are not in harmony,
> filial piety and parental love are advocated.
> When a country falls into chaos and disorder,
> there is praise of loyal patriots.[7]

The point of this passage is that laws and regulations only become necessary after people lose touch with the original Way, or "Great Way," of nature. Humans tend to live their lives trying to achieve specific goals, always busy, always planning and striving. But Daoists want to see human activity freed from this artificial drive to accomplish things, freed from restrictive social rituals and societal norms that restrict personal freedom. True freedom comes naturally from within individuals—the same kind of freedom to which Takuboku referred—when they are appropriately attuned to the inner truths of the universe or the Dao.[8] With that awareness, the individual can render decisive judgments and undertake meaningful human action. That is why the *Daodejing* continues, in the next stanza, to urge rulers to forget about sageliness and abandon narrow conceptions of "wisdom."

> Let people discover their own way naturally:
> Abandon wisdom and discard cleverness,
> and people will benefit a hundredfold.
> Abandon humanity (*ren*, 仁) and discard morality,
> and people will rediscover love and duty.
> Abandon skill and discard profit,
> and there will be no thieves or robbers.
> These three things relate to externals and are inadequate.
> People need what they can *depend* on:
> reveal simplicity; embrace the natural;
> control selfishness; reduce desires.[9]

Controlling desires and selfishness is the key; all the regulations aimed at governing individual conduct only get in the way. The best hope for manifesting "humanity" (*ren*) among human beings is to eliminate all the artificial constructs and simply allow harmonious interactions to emerge among individuals naturally. Humans need to free themselves from vanity and "the impulse to determine what is right and wrong."[10] Once they do this, they will have something "they can *depend* on." In that way, they will "rediscover" things like obligation and duty naturally and will therefore do the right thing. It is not necessary to artificially impose solutions on them.

While Reiun does not advocate a return to past, he understands that in order to comprehend how things came to be the way they are we have an urgent need to look at the past, to investigate it. This was part and parcel of the inward or "expressivist turn" to which Reiun was committed, and it brings with it a conception of history "which saw it resembling a spiral, from primitive undifferentiated unity, to a conflictual division between reason and sensibility, human and human, to a third and higher reconciliation, in which the gains of the second period, reason and freedom, were fully retained."[11] While this rupture between reason and intuition is recognized by many writers as part of becoming modern, Bruno Latour is not convinced. In *We Have Never Been Modern*, he argues that this notion of a "conflictual division" is not persuasive because he sees revolution as a "modality of historical action" rather than a distinct process. If we had never become modern, he argues, these sorts of divisions or ruptures would make little sense.[12] But to Reiun it seemed patently obvious that Japan's economic transformation was responsible for increasing social inequities and class differentiation, so he could certainly appreciate a model that sees history spiraling toward increasing conflict before eventually arriving at a greater reconciliation.

In the third section of "At Nagatamura," Reiun brings up the economy and laments the fact that "value" in modern times is exclusively conceived of in economic terms; everything comes down to the law of supply and demand. But what has become of intrinsic value? Modern civilization, he concedes, has done a great job of offering the opportunity to create wealth, but the problem is that huge differences in economic well-being have emerged and ostentation flourishes everywhere. Goods are the measure of the person, acquisitiveness is equated with success, and the whole system is biased in favor of the rich. Society has become a plutocracy, and the true, intrinsic value of people and things has been lost.

In section 4 of "At Nagatamura," Reiun writes about political rights and responsibilities. While he concedes that western liberalism has much to recommend it, politics also has a way of increasing the awareness of the smaller self in people, causing them to focus only on the rights that are best for them, the rights that will allow them to operate most effectively in society. By being less aware of their higher or transcendent selves, they run the risk of becoming little more than parasites. In sections 5 and 6, he addresses the emergence of the modern family, noting that, although everyone calls attention to and wants to celebrate it, in reality the family in Japan is little more than a vehicle for oppression, especially of women.

In section 7, Reiun broaches the topic of citizenship and the state, and he wants to make the point that individuals are not just members of nation-states; they also belong to a global community. We may be born in Japan, he writes, and this makes us Japanese citizens, but that does not mean that we should refrain from building transnational connections with people in other countries. We are also citizens of the world, he writes, and that should mean something. In section 8, he takes up the subject of the state and its relationship with its people, observing that despotism seems to be a natural trend among those who hold and monopolize power. This is exactly how individualism developed, he suggests, as a response to the exercise of despotic power by absolute monarchs. He recalls sadly that when he was serving time in prison for violating press laws, he saw what happened to a young man, a teenager, who had gotten drunk and thrown rocks at a train. The courts sentenced him to six years at hard labor. He was just a young boy and could not handle prison. He became angry, got in fights, his sentence was lengthened, and eventually he suffered a complete mental breakdown and literally went insane. His sentence became, in effect, a death sentence. Is this the best way for society to treat its youth?

In section 9, he touches on the Meiji Restoration. What made it a great historical moment was that the old four-class system was eliminated. But then Itô Hirobumi betrayed the whole spirit of the Restoration by creating a peerage in the 1880s. The time had come in the 1860s for an old, decadent political structure to be dismantled, but was reinstating a privileged aristocracy so soon after the Restoration the right thing to do? True, it was incumbent on Japan to resist the naked aggression of imperial powers on the people of Asia, but now Japan, too, was sending troops into China to deal with the Boxer Rebellion. Is this really consistent with what the Meiji Restoration was all about? He wrote about the city of Kobe, where he was living, and how the foreign presence had made its impact felt in the community with increases in prostitution, violent crimes, and rape. This is a serious problem but it seems to be what naturally accompanies industrialization, economic growth, trade, imperialism, and so forth. These are things that should be carefully and vigorously scrutinized.

Finally, in section 10, Reiun concludes his essay with the following curious yet audacious statement.

> If I had been born in Russia, no doubt I would have been a bomb-throwing nihilist. If I had been born in Qing China, I probably would have become like Xu Xilin (1873–1907)—a participant in the Anying Rebellion in Anhui Province—who murdered the Chinese official, Eng Ming. If I had been born a Korean, I would like to have been like Yi Jun (1859–1907), the attorney who tried to bring Korea's case against Japan's forcible takeover of the Korean Peninsula to the International Court of Arbitration at The Hague. But, alas, I was born in Japan, with all the benefits of a rich and glorious past, where I am free to lie on my sickbed and leisurely cultivate my illness. To me this is the greatest joy and happiness.[13]

While these final lines are obviously steeped in irony, we need to consider the distance Reiun has traversed, and we are reminded, once again, that the "slight change in his stance" was really something quite substantial. He is now willingly and forcefully advocating radical social transformation and calling for a social revolution. In "At Nagatamura," after outlining the way in which modernity has brought challenges and problems to the doorstep of the modern individual, he proceeds to allude to three instances in which people outside Japan—but subject to the pressures of imperialism or the forces of revolutionary change—made the decision to become involved and act. The fact that Reiun chooses to identify himself with individuals who exhibited historical agency and carried out radical acts in order to bring about political change tells us something about his mind-set. Reiun himself, of course, had never done anything like this, although he did talk about going to Cuba in 1898 and joining the revolution. But he clearly admired those individuals who were willing to stand up and be counted. By singling them out, he acknowledges that there are times when armed resistance to the state by its citizens is justified, and he clearly registers his lack of enthusiasm for Japan's annexation of Korea and its utter lack of sympathy for the aspirations of the Korean people. Because it takes courage to stand up to the state, he wanted to recognize the sacrifices of martyrs such as Xu Xilin and Yi Jun—the latter having been found dead in his hotel room at The Hague a few days after protesting the decision to bar Korean delegates from the conference—as well as the Meiji Rebels of the 1880s.[14]

That is why now, he wants to bring the focus back home and compile the biographies of the young popular rights activists who attempted to resist the power of the new Meiji state and discuss them in the context of "rebellion." In

1909 young historical actors who had organized protests and revolts against the Meiji government in the early 1880s were starting to look like heroes to Reiun. That he would turn his eyes in this essay to locales and actors outside Japan and imagine himself in their circumstances, and would think about the impact of imperialism and colonialism, underscores his capacity to think transhistorically and push his vision beyond the limitations of the nation and nation-states.

Uncovering Rebellion

There was an important historical context for these acts of resistance against the Meiji state, or the *gekka-jiken*, as they are called by Japanese historians. Finance Minister Matsukata Masayoshi's deflationary policies of 1881—which incidentally sparked central government retrenchment and contributed to the *kansei-kaikaku*, the bureaucratic reforms that had affected Reiun at the Osaka Middle School—hit rural areas very hard, especially small-scale farmers and silk producers. For example, in Fukushima members of the Liberal Party led by Kôno Hironaka protested the "despotic rule" of Governor Mishima Michitsune (1835–88) who had been dispatched by the central government to deal with the situation. Mishima responded by rounding up Liberal Party members after thousands marched on government buildings. Justice was swift; trials were held, and Kôno and others were found guilty and sentenced to long prison terms. When Liberal Party protests turned violent in the neighboring prefectures of Tochigi and Saitama, the government sent in troops and arrested hundreds, even thousands.[15] At times police stations were attacked, rifles were fired, and even bombs were thrown. But most of these popular rights movement incidents ended in fierce government repression with widespread arrests and stiff sentences, including executions, handed down for the leaders.[16]

This was one of those rare moments in modern Japanese history when citizens directly contested the state's authority over their political and economic lives. In *Meiji hanshinden*, Reiun wanted to tell the story of a few individual leaders whose courageous acts of resistance were noteworthy even though officials would have preferred to see their actions erased from history. So he took up, in the following order, the stories of Kôno Hironaka and the Fukushima Incident, Kôno Hiroshi and the Kabasan Incident, Kawazu Tokujirô and the Iida Incident, Okumiya Kenshi and the Nagoya Incident, and Nakano Jirôsaburô and the Shizuoka Incident. These *gekka-jiken* indicate how deeply embedded and widespread ideas that originated in the popular rights movement had become by the early 1880s. As Roger Bowen notes, *rebellion* can mean that "the traditional grounds of obedience upon which the state rests are being challenged," and states do not ordinarily appreciate having their citizens contest their authority.[17] By providing a sympathetic treatment of these radical political leaders who had risked everything and were either killed or imprisoned for their efforts, Reiun was underlining the importance of the popular rights movement as a vehicle for the transmission of the spirit of the Meiji Restoration to the "children of the revolution."[18] In a word—affirming the point made earlier—he was arguing that the popular rights movement provided an important link between the Meiji Restoration and the generation born just after it, for the young people of Reiun's generation had been deeply inspired by the movement as children and had thoroughly embraced and internalized its ideals. But now what were they facing? How should these violent political incidents of the 1880s be viewed in the early twentieth century?

On The Character of the Meiji Restoration

In the introduction to *Meiji hanshinden*, Reiun clarifies why, in 1909, he was interested in reexamining the events surrounding the radical political uprisings of the mid-1880s.[19] There were a number of reasons. In the first place, it was an important but jarring statement about the times in which his narrative appeared, in the wake of the Russo-Japanese War, when political leaders were exultant but many ordinary citizens were harboring doubts. At that time, much attention and reverence were being heaped on the dead who had fallen in Japan's two foreign wars in the space of a single decade; it was a time when the government was promoting the "heroism" of those who had sacrificed their lives for the state. Reiun wanted to make the point that those who had struggled on behalf of "populism" (*heiminshugi*) at home during the 1880s should also be regarded as heroes and that their contribution to the development of modern Japan should not be overlooked.[20] At the very moment when his countrymen were basking in the glory of the victory over China in 1895, Reiun had felt uneasy. He urged caution and introspection because it had been too easy. Again, in 1909, he shifts the focus away from the present and the international arena and asks, in effect, what about the battles that were fought on native soil? The historical record was ignoring both the narratives of these individuals and their actions. Someone must tell their story.

The leaders of the Fukushima, Kabasan, Iida, Nagoya, and Shizuoka incidents, were people who courageously responded to the spirit of the times with passion and sincerity. They were literally self-sacrificing people who were willing to struggle, resist, and contest. Their lives contained more than a touch of tragedy and grief, and for this reason their stories are instructive. Just as the pursuit of individual gain is inconsistent with the approach of an upright and sincere man, so someone who responds to the higher call of duty must be prepared to accept the worst. Such a person's contribution might not be recognized in his or her own time. Who was more aware of this fact than Reiun himself, who was already coming to view his life as a tale of misfortune? Therefore, he wanted to convey, for everyone to see, the bitter fate that had been the lot of these ardent supporters of popular rights.

Perhaps the most important reason for revisiting these events at this time, however, was to provide a framework in which Reiun could work out his interpretation of the Meiji Restoration and to project the image of social change that this event embodied for him. At the time when the biographies were compiled, because Reiun had already lost the use of his legs, he had to rely on the assistance of a young friend and admirer, Tanaka Kotarô, to actually compile and draft the biographies. Therefore, other than the original concept, the introductory essay is Reiun's main creative contribution to the book.[21] Also, when we examine this essay in conjunction with a corresponding section of Reiun's autobiography, composed a few years later, we have a fairly systematic treatment of what was an important theme throughout Reiun's life: the value of history in understanding the character of the Meiji Restoration.

Reiun opens his discussion with the observation that Japan had experienced two major cultural transformations as a result of contacts with foreign civilizations.[22] The first instance, known as the Taika reforms, had occurred in the seventh century. At that time, intensified contact with China and Korea spiritually and materially enriched Japanese culture. Contact with the civilization on the continent brought many new things to Japan, and in effect this exposure placed Japan squarely in the mainstream of Asian civilization. That is, key elements of the two great Asian centers of civilization, India and China, were introduced to and assimilated by Japan, so Reiun could link the Taika reforms to the "Asianization" of Japan. This experience represented Japan's initial step into the outside world.

The second instance of widespread cultural interaction with a foreign civilization came over a millennium later when Japan was brought into contact with the West. If the Taika changes had awakened Japan's Asian consciousness, then the Meiji Restoration and the inflow of western culture that it sparked brought Japan a step farther into the world. The Restoration, then, symbolizes Japan's awakening to world culture. As such, it is a principle dividing line in Japanese history, at least as meaningful as the Taika reforms.

In fact, however, the Meiji Restoration was in one crucial respect profoundly different from the Taika reforms, and in this regard it was vastly more significant. By all accounts, in introducing the benefits of a more advanced civilization to Japan, the Taika reforms had restricted their diffusion to a limited number of people at the very highest levels of society. In contrast, the single most important aspect of the Restoration was that by proclaiming the equality of the four classes it held out the promise of making the benefits of modern western civilization available to all people on an equal basis. In this regard, the Restoration was, in Reiun's eyes, a victory for the people and the ideal of the common person (*heiminteki risô no shôri*).[23]

This was part of what Reiun identified as the "dual significance" of the Restoration.[24] That is, he saw the Restoration as simultaneously accomplishing two things: it unified the nation under the banner of *ôsei-fukko*; and in doing so, it overcame the narrow limitations of a semifeudal system of shogunal rule. But also the Restoration gave expression to the ideal of expanding popular rights. He recognized that this unity was forged at the time out of necessity, in the face of a pressing external threat. Nevertheless, by the very act of recognizing only a single locus of authority in the emperor, there was a framework to support the notion that all people were equal beneath the sovereign.

By stressing the twin themes of unity and equality, Reiun established the foundation for an image of a national and popular Restoration, an image found later in the writings of Nakano Seigô.[25] As was the case with Nakano, these two features of the Restoration convinced Reiun that it was indisputably "progressive." Not only did it unify the country in order to successfully open the nation's doors to the inflow of world culture, but the it also represented the culmination of an internal drive to establish equality among members of this new national community. Reiun referred to this internal drive as an ikioi (勢い, a dynamic historical force). He considered the ikioi that rose to the surface of events with the collapse of the bakufu to be a truly "eye-opening experience."[26]

What Reiun is trying to point to here is the presence of a force, a spirit, which had been gathering considerable strength well before the Restoration and was now given expression in many events after the Restoration. The post-Restoration leadership proclaimed equality among the four classes and articulated the notion of *kôgi-yôron*, the idea that issues should be widely discussed among the people. He found in the language of the Charter Oath, issued by the new government in 1868, where it declared that "all matters of state shall be decided by open discussion" and "the high and low shall unite in carrying out the affairs of state," an explicit endorsement of the idea of a participatory political system. When this same spirit surfaced again later in the popular rights movement, and in the drive to create a system of constitutional government, however, it was considered a challenge to state authority and deemed dangerous. It was too destabilizing and contestatory.

Reiun was anxious to show that this *ikioi*, which had been welling up in Japan, was far more potent than any of the external forces shaping the historical moment. His confidence in the existence of this spirit can be seen in his remarks about the popular rights movement in *Sakkiden*.

> So when Itagaki voiced his call for popular rights, although the particular phrase that was adopted, *jiyûminken* [liberty and people's rights], may have been a newly coined rendition of a foreign concept, in substance it was not at all a case of importing a western idea. Likewise, it is inaccurate to view the call for peoples' rights as a retaliatory move in connection with the cabinet debate over the invasion of Korea. Even if there had been no Itagaki, and no cabinet debate, the call for the spread of peoples' rights is something that would have burst forth on its own accord. (*SD*, 505)

In other words, it was the energy manifested by ordinary people in Edo times, the *heimin*, that had generated the circumstances that made the Restoration possible. Reiun continues:

> But now forty years have passed since the Restoration; a constitution has been promulgated that was largely the product of people joining together in the popular rights movement to resist despotic authority. However, the rebels whose blood flowed back in those days are now in danger of being forgotten; those who survived are old now, and that is why we need to get their experiences into the record. That is why, if we do not listen to the stories of the people who participated in these events, they will be dead and buried, and with this the opportunity to write the history of the Meiji rebels (明治謀叛史) will be lost. That is precisely my motivation for compiling *Meiji hanshinden* at this time. It is true that we have fought and won two wars against China and Russia, but officials of the current government would have you believe that it was all due to their endeavors; but we must never forget that this was something accomplished by the efforts of all the people. The constitution that we have and all the good fortune that our

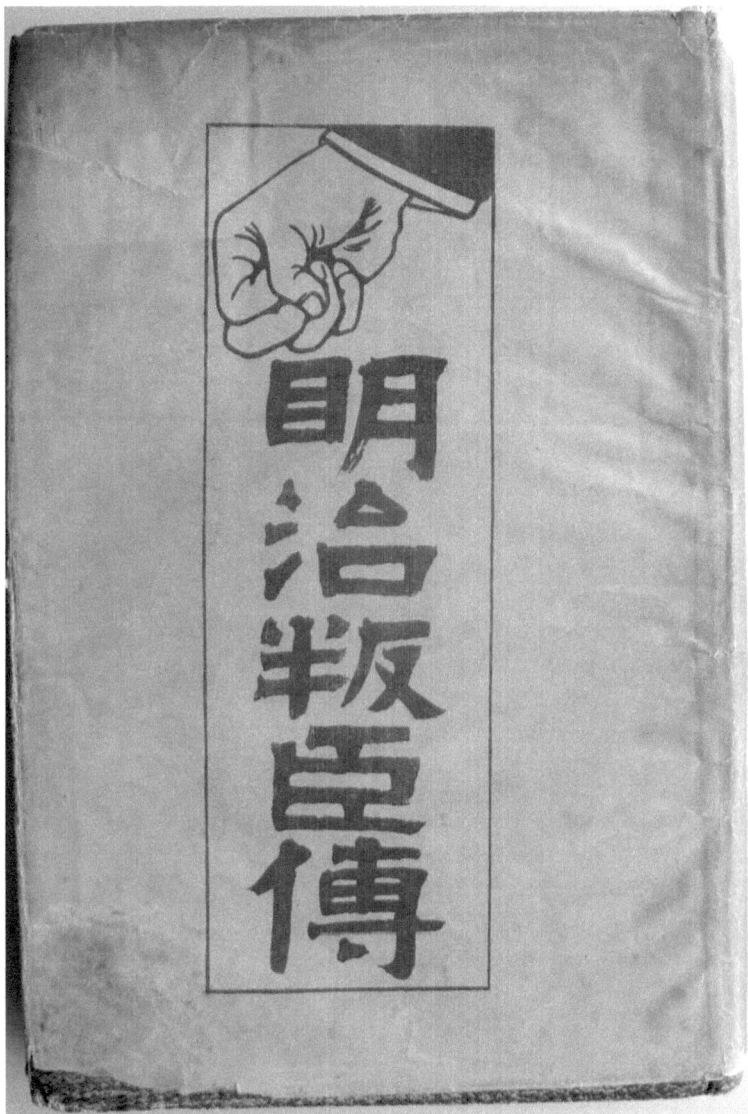

Figure 6.2. Inside cover of *Meiji hanshinden*. Courtesy of Nishida Masaru.

nation has enjoyed are not due just to prime ministers like Itô or Katsura. . . . I believe it is only natural that we look back to the incredible energy and sacrifices made by these "Meiji rebels," who helped bring about our current constitutional system. (*MHD*, 274–75)

In spite of Reiun's insistence on the importance of internal dynamic forces, he also recognized that there was such a thing as larger "world trends" (*sekai no taisei*, 世界の大勢), which may have originated outside national borders but were still capable of penetrating those borders and interacting with indigenous forces to produce change.[27] This is one significant aspect of his treatment of *ikioi*. Another is his focus on the inevitability of change when these dynamic forces are at work. This was Reiun's version of Takuboku's "necessity of tomorrow"—the inevitability of change—and the way he characterized the *ikioi* operating in Japan prior to the Restoration.

First, he pointed to the indigenous roots of a natural trend toward populism (*heiminshugi*) as far back as the period of transition from aristocratic rule by the Fujiwara regents to the simpler—and in Reiun's eyes more popular—rule by the warrior (*bushi*) class under the Genji (*SD*, 504–5). This does not mean that Reiun equated the supremacy of the warrior class with popular or "commoner" government. At this stage, the trend toward populism was a latent tendency only just beginning to be felt. In its early stages of development, it had to struggle to become manifest. However, it was very definitely the trend of the times as documented by the fact that the Kemmu Restoration, an attempt in the fourteenth century to reinstate the power of the court, was a complete failure. It was doomed to failure, Reiun would argue, because it was trying to move in opposition to this trend of the times.

The trend is also quite apparent in the Ashikaga period. To be sure, under the Ashikaga the warrior class itself displayed aristocratic tendencies, and of course the people were not at all free. But even if the trend was not an overpowering force, its presence could be distinctly felt. The spirit of the times found expression in the Zen-inspired art of the age, with its simplicity and universality. Likewise, on the stage, the *kyôgen* emerged as the voice of the common people. The situations and themes of the *kyôgen* were taken directly from their daily lives. When the country was plunged into the Warring States period, the tendency toward populism advanced even further because out of the turmoil came the reality that a peasant today could be lord of the realm tomorrow. With the source of leadership widened in this fashion, access to power was considerably more open than it had been under the narrowly based aristocratic rule.

Second, Reiun noted that when the Tokugawa finally restored order, and for the first time brought Japan under the rule of a single military leader, they saw to it that this spirit was contained in the interest of prolonging their control. But that the spirit remained in evidence is testimony to the blossoming of the *chônin* (merchant culture) of the mid-Edo period. In the literature and art of the period the voice of the common people (平民, *heimin*) could be heard. Later, when early contacts with foreigners occurred, and when the *bakufu*'s inability to handle the situation became apparent, this same spirit resurfaced and found expression in the cries of *sonnô-jôi* (revere the emperor, expel the barbarians) and *tôbaku* (topple the *bakufu*). In other words, these slogans were the culmination of popular aspirations that had been building within Japan for centuries. "It was nothing less than the ideas and beliefs of the ordinary people, the *heimin*, who were resisting the authority of aristocratic and privileged families," Reiun wrote (*MHD*, 278). That they became focused on the *bakufu* and ultimately were responsible for bringing down the entire feudal system was because the Tokugawa had intervened and tampered with natural trends. The Tokugawa severed members of the *bushi* class from their natural roots in the countryside and made their existence dependent on the continuity of their own personal rule. In other words, they tried to adjust the flow of *ikioi* to satisfy their own personal ends.

Third, Reiun pointed out that this internal drive directed toward the equalization of the classes, though extremely important, was not the sole factor responsible for bringing about the Restoration. There was also operating at this time a world ikioi (勢) with origins outside Japan. This *taisei* (大勢) had surfaced in France with the French Revolution, and its impact had been sweeping through Europe ever since, even reaching the shores of Japan. Even if only subconsciously, Reiun argued, the *bakumatsu shishi* were touched and moved by this great revolutionary tide, making the case in favor of a universal yearning among humans for individual freedoms. Of course some countries directly absorbed the stress on national unity exemplified by late unifiers like Italy and Germany, but even this was part of the revolutionary current that had been unleashed by the French Revolution.

The proof supporting the contention that it was the revolutionary aspect that was most significant can be located in the course the Restoration ultimately took. That is, it abolished feudalism, established a constitution and a Diet, and aligned itself with the idea of returning rights to the people. Therefore, despite the fact that on the surface the Restoration appeared to have been a struggle between the *bakufu* and the court, there was more to it than met the eye. As a restoration of imperial power, it may have seemed to be of an entirely different order from the revolutions in Europe that overthrew monarchical structures. But because the Meiji Restoration brought down the *bakufu*, which had been standing between the people and the emperor, and thus made it possible for all people to stand equal in relation to that sovereign, it could be construed as an extension of the general trend (*sûsei*, 趨勢, an *ikioi* with wide-ranging tendencies) that had first emerged in Europe.

The Restoration, then, was the product of an interaction between this world (*ikioi*) and the internal momentum that had gradually been moving the Japanese toward a society in which popular forces were ascendant. These forces were, for Reiun, what gave the Restoration its character. But he understood that this impetus toward radical change, the sudden destructive impact of a revolutionary force, does not last indefinitely: "This is why after only four or five years, the revolutionary spirit began to wane" (*MHD*, 282). And this is why it was necessary for the Meiji rebels to do what they did in the early 1880s.

Progress as "Rebellion": An Image of Historical Change

The implication of Reiun's understanding of the Meiji Restoration was that it was as a progressive force because it emanated from the fundamental human desire for liberation. But what had been its final outcome? As we saw, in his 1908 essay "At Nagatamura," he argued:

> What made the Meiji Restoration great was that it destroyed the classes, and proclaimed the just and righteous cause of equality for all. Mr. Itô, who created a peerage anew, and gave to this aristocracy a variety of special privileges, cannot escape being labeled as the one who destroyed the great achievement of the *isshin-kakumei* (restoration-revolution). In this regard, he is a criminal who has left a stain on the history of the Meiji enlightenment.[28]

This interpretation of history strongly contests the legitimacy of the modern state structure created by the Meiji oligarchs. But "rebellion" is clearly a force that moves history. This may explain why the collection of essays in which "At Nagatamura" appeared, *Wanderings from the Sickbed* (*Byôchû-Hôrô*), was banned on publication. The implications of the remarks quoted above are clear: the natural movement of the forces for greater freedom and increased human rights is subject to manipulation, diversion, and dissipation by those whose aim is obstruction.

Therefore, the moral of this story was clear, and this was the fourth and final reason for compiling *Biographies of Meiji Rebels*: to issue a call for rebellion (muhonron, 謀反論). "Rebellion, rebellion," Reiun writes, "There are people for whom this word has a most unfortunate ring, but to my ears there is no more thrilling sound"(*MHD*, 267) . And at the conclusion of this section, he writes:

> Ah, rebellion, rebellion. Those who shudder when they hear your name are the ones who block the road; they are the enemies of progress. Rebellion is always the driving force behind progress, nurturing it and giving it life. (270)

Reiun has defiantly and resolutely placed his cards on the table. History teaches us that natural tendencies toward popular rights and freedom are real and significant, but there are enemies who would obstruct the flow of these natural tendencies. It is the presence of these forces that resist progressive change, and this is what calls forth rebellion.

How does this work? Just as evolution is the rule governing development in the material realm, in the human realm it is the animating force, the *taisei* (大勢), that pushes history forward. That is to say, the *taisei* is a force that is always moving in the direction of progress. Whatever stands in the way of this development, then, is the enemy of progress, and humanity. Rebellion, then, becomes the act of overcoming these obstacles so that there can be a natural, unobstructed flow to history. Rebellion is the catalyst that stimulates the *taisei* and gives it life. It naturally opposes existing conditions—the status quo—which represents a state of arrest.

We saw in chapter 5 that Reiun believed historical change or "development" was something slow and natural that operated within set limits. When these inherent limits are reached, decline sets in, or, in his terms, "when extremes are reached, change is inevitable." In the context of the Meiji Restoration, Reiun adapts this Daoist perspective and converts it into a "dynamic principle" of history. In establishing this principle, Reiun relied on a distinction between the material realm and the world of human beings. By the former he meant the outward, physical manifestations of the inner forces, and it was here, he held, that the laws of evolution apply. The human realm, the domain of the human spirit, is where natural tendencies, like the trend toward freedom and progress, are manifested. History, then, is nothing but a succession of rebellions. As a force, rebellion has its own natural limits, and when these are reached, stagnation sets in. Therefore, as soon as existing changes are altered by rebellion, the evil influence of stagnation and decay can be felt. Two types of people play a role in shaping history: *yin* and *yang*. It is the former, the yin types, who are conservative and constructive. But the basic element in *yin* is negative. Although the *yang* types are destructive and progressive, they are the positive force because they are on the side of progress. The yang types cannot sit idly by, content with existing conditions. So they resist and ultimately try to destroy the present. They carry out rebellions.

A decade earlier, in "Seinen to shimpô" (Youth and Progress), the 1897 essay aimed at encouraging Meiji youth to act, Reiun had observed:

> Progress means destruction, and destruction brings improvement. Stagnation is the enemy of progress. In other words, revolution means progress. Because revolution wants to bring about improvements, it must first destroy. If you do not have revolution, then you will inevitably experience stagnation. With stagnation comes decay. Revolution brings regeneration. When things reach extremes, change must follow. Revolution is nothing more than the transformation of things that have reached their natural limits. Revolution, revolution, revolution. Revolution is dynamic: politics must undergo revolution; the state must undergo revolution; society, religion, literature, even human nature—all of these need to experience a revolution from time to time. Look at the situation here in the late Meiji. The years are rushing by, politics has become stagnant, society is in decay, and what about religion? What about literature? Isn't it time to swing the mighty hammer of revolution?[29]

Reiun added a little flourish to his "dynamic principle" of history by representing it graphically and sprinkling it with Hegelian terminology. If A represents the present state (thesis) and B the reaction to it (antithesis), then A1 is the new condition (synthesis) brought about by rebellion. But if in response to this (thesis A^1) there emerges a reaction (antithesis B), then rebellion will create a new synthesis between B and A^1, which is B^1. Since each new thesis represents an advance over the previous one, there is a progressive development until an endpoint (or final goal) is reached. And so it goes ad infinitum. The process of change is continuous.[30]

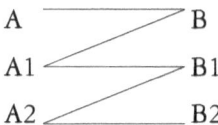

In this view, of course, the Restoration was part of a progressive force, a push for rebellion. But not long after its basic principles had been declared in the Charter Oath, with its call for equality, the elites began to acquire power and develop a system to monopolize it. They became the forces of stagnation, and they placed great obstacles in the path of the *taisei*. A strong current of reaction arose against this, and it was known as the popular rights movement.

That today Japan has a constitutional system at all can be attributed to the call for rebellion voiced by popular rights advocates against the forces of stagnation. But in forging the new synthesis, the elites were able to divert and distort the *taisei*. Like the Tokugawa, the oligarchs took things into their own hands and tried to use the *taisei* for their own ends. That is why a "call for rebellion" was issued, and those who answered this call were the five young men whose lives were being celebrated in *Meiji hanshinden*. If Japanese people were going to pay tribute to the many soldiers who gave their lives on foreign soil in the Sino-Japanese and Russo-Japanese wars, then they should also learn something about and be able to express their appreciation for the people whose blood was shed on Japanese soil, and whose lives were taken because they rebelled against the Meiji government in the hope of obtaining genuine popular rights and freedoms in the 1880s (*MHD*, 280–81). By issuing a "call" for rebellion, Reiun was asserting that Meiji history had slipped and gone in the wrong direction, which is why its course needed to be corrected. It is moments like these that shape historical consciousness, and after the Russo-Japanese War there was reason to wonder whether the current path was the correct one for Japan.[31] While the government was able to forge political unity and support for the war, it was not universal. Kôtoku and his friends who rallied around the *Heimin shinbun* saw the war as little more than a transparent effort to enhance the power of the state and to launch Japanese imperialism.

Each section of *Meiji hanshinden* provides a thorough account of events as they unfolded. There were moments of high drama in each story, such as when Kôno Hiroshi is quoted as saying, "When we stood atop Mt. Kaba, it felt as though we were truly part of a force (*ikioi*) destined to carry out a sacred mission" (*MHD*, 331). Though poorly armed, the Kabasan activists had homemade bombs and planned to use them on government officials. So the stakes were high, and when arrests followed, seven of the participants received the death penalty; because Kôno was under twenty years of age at the time, his sentence was ten years at hard labor. After he was released he traveled to the United States and later immigrated to Mexico. His uncle, Kôno Hironaka, had been similarly sentenced in the Fukushima Incident. By the time of the Shizuoka Incident, with government military suppression eliminating the possibility of raising a viable military force to challenge the government, armed robbery and assassination had become part of the rebels' plans. Reiun's point was that activists who were dedicated to realizing the ideals of the popular rights movement had been driven to these kinds of desperate acts by an oppressive Meiji government.

The Problem of Progress in Japanese Historical Consciousness

In Reiun's view, rebellion was the agent of historical change. Rebellion frees the *taisei* so that it can flow in its natural course toward progress. In his concern with discovering natural tendencies and getting back to one's roots and tracing growth and development in things, Reiun sounds much like writers in nineteenth-century Europe and later who believed that progress was a natural condition.[32] As Robert Nisbet explains it, there was a vision in European history "in which Progress is held to be the natural and normal trend of mankind, but which for its free and uninterrupted flow, requires from time to time the obliteration of obstructing institutions and beliefs."[33]

Reiun's interpretation of the Restoration as encompassing a deeply rooted tendency toward popular participation attributable to the "commoner spirit," which was diverted first by the Tokugawa and again by the oligarchs in the 1880s, meant that the promise of freedom and social equality inherent in the Restoration had not been realized. In "Rekishi isshiki no 'kôsô'" (On the Deepest Layer of Historical Consciousness), Maruyama Masao points out that in the West, with its indebtedness to theology and the notion of Providence, it was natural to have a focus on some ideal state of being, or some perfect society, as an unchanging goal toward which mankind is moving.[34] But he wonders if it makes sense for Japanese to see history same way. While Maruyama may be quite correct when pointing to something lodged at the deepest level of Japanese historical consciousness, one would be hard pressed to find people in Meiji Japan who did not subscribe to some version of the western idea of progress, especially during the early years when Fukuzawa Yukichi and the Meiji Six Society were busy introducing western interpretations of history, progress, and government to Japanese readers. Even though Reiun was more inclined toward a nonteleological approach to modernity, he obviously made use of the term *progress*, as we just saw. In fact, in "Ki-itsuteki sûsei" (Trends toward Greater Unity) he posited that humanity does experience improvements, and we think of them as "development," and therefore the ideal for humankind is greater unity. He goes on to chart the progression from primitive village communities to the modern nation-state to racial and ethnic identification and finally to complete unity at the global level, which means transcending nation and race. Imperialism builds on this unification on the national level, but if we really want to achieve genuine human and global unification, it cannot be based on members of national communities or racial/ethnic groups but must be based on humans as members of a social community. In other words, global unity must bring unification among all societies so that for the first time we will be able to achieve the ideal of socialism and peace on a global scale and see to the welfare of all human beings. Real socialism means pursuing the ideal of equality among all humans.[35] But to imagine these transnational, nonethnically, or racially based social communities coexisting on a global scale is not the same as embracing the generally accepted pattern of development envisioned by the West.

Reiun was clearly drawn to history because he wanted to fill in the spaces left by those "fragmented inner narratives," but he also turned to it out of concern for problems in the world around him and, therefore, in order to better see how things came to be the way they are so that he might imagine what they might become. In this regard we might say that he had a bias toward the present because he was dissatisfied with existing conditions. In his foreword to *Meiji hanshinden*, Reiun expressed his disillusionment with the prevailing attitudes among young people, just as he had a decade earlier. In his view, they were becoming increasingly self-centered and servile (*MHD*, 253–54). They were "hollow men," to anticipate T. S. Eliot's term, much too callow and self-aggrandizing, as Ishikawa Takuboku would point out the following year. Their main concerns, he argued, were to find a job after graduation and to build a solid career. Consequently, they embraced no grandiose ideas and entertained no daring visions; nor were they driven by lofty ideals. The youths who carried out the Restoration, and those who struggled on behalf of popular rights, had acted in the public interest without a thought for themselves or even their families. Reiun was hopeful that his biographies of such men would inspire the young of the post war era and rekindle a spirit of engagement and determination in them.

This was not to say, and Reiun was explicit on this point, that he was urging young people to rush out and take part in the administration of the nation's affairs. He knew the impracticality of this from his own experience. What he was talking about was a way to conceptualize the self and ground one's existence in the present. Reiun was committed to understanding "present conditions in terms of past changes," something that emerged naturally out of the "reflectiveness" and concern for the self that he had absorbed from Rousseau and other romantics.[36] This "seeking of origins," this tendency to view nature historically, has been called "the single most revolutionary aspect of romanticism" in Europe, and it was a significant part of Reiun's motivation to go back and uncover the stories of the Meiji rebels.[37] For Reiun, and many other Japanese in the postwar years, there was an urgent need to look to the past in order to construct a vision of a more palatable future, a future that did not necessarily consider a strong nation-state to be the only viable option.

On what for Reiun was a rare occasion to write in a simple, conversational style, in 1910 he published an essay called "The Future of the Concepts of Loyalty and Filial Piety," two loaded terms that would be put to unfortunate use by the state in the 1930s but which he handled very adroitly in this essay. He begins by noting that his views are a bit extreme, writing that since "the freedom of expression is severely curtailed in this day and age, in the end, I cannot write as frankly as I would like."[38] He finds filial piety to be a natural emotion, which stems from parents' love of their children, so he does not anticipate any need for this emotion to fundamentally change. However, with the rise of a thoroughly materialistic civilization and the growing importance of the individual, it is only logical that something like the bonds of loyalty to one's lord or master will weaken. Since the individual in this setting does not really recognize the significance of the self, it is easy for this to turn into blind obedience and submission to authority. In this context, values like loyalty and filial piety require submissiveness on the part of human beings (*ningen no fukujû*, 人間の服従). That is why contemporary times have to be called the age of submissiveness. However, this age will pass, and an era will arrive in which individuals will realize that they have their own lives to sacrifice as they see fit. Then they can transcend the era of meaningless submissiveness and enter into one in which they can make genuinely noble sacrifices for the sake of others.

> True sacrifice comes about when individuals appreciate that there is something greater than their small individual selves, something greater than their family or the state, and this would be humanity (*jinrui*, 人類). There is no value in blindly following others without self-awareness; but becoming aware of the value of sacrifice for a greater good, this would be a genuine human virtue. As long as individuals live in society, sacrifices need to be made for the greater good of the community (*kyôzonteki*, 共存的), and when this sacrifice is for all humanity and means leaving the smaller self behind, then we have achieved the very essence of sacrifice.[39]

Although Reiun has told his readers that he is not at liberty to express himself as freely as he would like, the future trend that he envisions is one that rejects individuals mindlessly following the dictates of the state; instead, he favors communities of self-aware or self-conscious (自覚して) individuals who willingly make sacrifices for the greater good. In other words, without being able to come out and say so directly, he implies that he would demolish the narrowly conceived state-centered version of history, with its interpretation of concepts like loyalty and filial piety, and infuse it with real meaning and value. A reconsideration of the past would make a new, more appealing future possible.

Interestingly enough, Maruyama notes that, with a few exceptions, the idea behind *ikioi*, which originated on the continent, had not played a major role in Chinese thought. One exception, where the concept of *ikioi* appears frequently, is in the *Yijing* (Book of Changes), whose underlying principle can be succinctly stated as "Change: that is the unchangeable."[40] Reiun was fond of the *Yijing*, and in one of his short essays in *Tenko* he referred to it as a kind of dictionary for people in modern times. The old Chinese characters identified with each trigram and hexagram are images rooted in the distant past; not only do they provide definitions and meanings, but "through the eight trigrams and the sixty-four hexagrams, they offer readers insights into a mystical worldview; you could even say that they show us how to follow the Way."[41] Deeply rooted in this ancient way of thinking, Reiun found in it something that helped shape his understanding of history and enabled him to ground a modern sense of global community in a vision of the past. It is what underpins his image of historical change. It is from this premise of the inevitability of change, every bit as much as from Hegel, that Reiun derived his scheme of revolution-stagnation-regeneration, although by drawing on some of Europe's most recent thinking about the nature of historical change he was able to find collateral support for his arguments.

Moreover, the concept of "change" that we find in the *Yijing* is hardly the same thing as the notion of progress or development in western thought. As Helmut Wilhelm notes, "change" in the *Yijing* "is not an external, normative principle that imprints itself upon phenomena: it is an inner tendency according to which development takes place naturally and spontaneously. . . . To stand in the stream of this development is the datum of nature: to recognize and follow it is responsibility and free choice.[42]

This is a very important distinction because, above all, Reiun wants his readers to confront the currents of historical change and exercise freedom of choice, for therein lies the possibility of meaningful human action. In the end, Reiun's whole quest to understand the self can be seen as a search for a framework in which meaningful and responsible human activity is possible. However, without a realistic picture of the world in which we live, people can neither act responsibly nor build a meaningful future. The fact that Reiun was always preoccupied with ideals underscores how concerned he was with responsibility in human activity. Why? Because ideals set the standards on which humans can base their judgments and actions. Ishikawa Takuboku had argued that "necessity" should be youth's most cherished ideal, and Reiun would add to this the notion that responsible action in pursuit of this necessity requires human judgment as a prerequisite.

A clear link is discernible between Reiun's early interest in national essence (*kokusui-hozon*) and his interest in history, which emerged later. To grasp national essence is to engage in historical understanding, and insofar as Japanese nationalism in the late 1880s and early 1890s was a quest to understand something "Japanese" (a spirit? an essence?) that was constant over time, it was fundamentally historical in nature.[43] It stimulated a kind of reflective thinking, a going back to search for origins, which, as we have seen, was very much what motivated Reiun's concern for history. It is interesting, then, that Reiun's image of historical change stressed rebellion because he was, in the words of Maruyama Masao, among the last bearers of the standard of resistance to the establishment of complete hegemony by the emperor system in the late Meiji period.[44] According to Maruyama's argument, in his essay on "Loyalty and Treason," people like Reiun, Miyake Setsurei, Tokutomi Rôka, and Yamaji Aizan shared a certain spirit: each in his own way opposed the imposition of orthodoxy. But among them, there was also a qualitative distinction to be made, for, while Miyake and Yamaji had expressed themselves primarily in terms of personal or individual resistance to younger people like Reiun and Rôka, writing some twenty years later, it had come to be a question of rebellion, and Reiun is singled out by Maruyama as one of the first to conceive of "rebellion" as a source of motivation for a modern sense of self.[45]

There is an interesting anecdote about the novelist Tokutomi Rôka that bears repeating. When Rôka first learned of the arrest of Kôtoku and the other anarchists, he was dismayed at first and then stunned when he learned that they had been executed without an open trial or any right of appeal. It was completely arbitrary and despotic. Around that time, he was invited to speak to students at Ichikô, or the First Higher School, an elite educational institution. When asked what his topic would be, he simply wrote the characters for *muhon* (謀反, rebellion) in the charcoal brazier around which they were seated. Deemed too controversial a topic to announce in advance, the publicity flyers went out with the words "Not Yet Decided" on them. When he spoke, though, he engaged the topic and "deplored the total lack of protest by civil and religious leaders at the arbitrary action taken by the government," comments that sparked great controversy in the days that followed.[46] For Reiun rebellion was ordinarily something that originated within the self, and this was an autonomous self that could be detached from the system and even from history itself.[47] However, as *MHD* suggests, there are times when acts of political rebellion are necessary.

While Latour may be skeptical of the notion of a significant rupture between modernity and the past, he does acknowledge something he calls the "second enlightenment, that of the nineteenth century," when the emerging social sciences allowed critics to take on phenomena like ideology, the economy, language, and the unconscious and subject them to scrutiny.[48] Reiun no doubt would have accepted the idea that he was, indeed, a member of that coterie of "second enlightenment" critics who believed that it was their responsibility to apply whatever analytical tools were at hand in order to look at the world around them and discern what was going on beneath the surface. Coming to better understand the present by exploring the past is one of the tools Reiun had at his disposal to help him develop a more serviceable vision of the future. It also explains why he would have agreed with his younger colleague Ishikawa Takuboku in his assessment that what all people *can* do—indeed, what they *must* do—is "research today" in order to discover for themselves the "necessity of tomorrow." How to make that discovery was no easy matter; but it was likely to involve struggle and contestation: a grappling with ideas to be sure; but it might also involve coming to terms with the harsh realities of "rebellion."

Reiun's choice to publish the biographies of five popular rights leaders, men who sparked five bloody confrontations with the state, was not only courageous but confrontational as well. He believed that sometimes the cudgel of revolutionary change needed to be wielded. If at times he seemed circumspect about being an anarchist or socialist, there can be little doubt that he was inclined toward radical transformations, and he supported the development of a strong, autonomous self in twentieth-century Japan. And part of being autonomous was to be freed from narrow conceptions of history that posit a dynamic, industrializing, modernizing "West" imposing its conception of historical change on the rest of the world. Reiun's hopes for the future were more along the lines of a transnational, cosmopolitan, universal vision that was not beholden to old binaries like East-West, white-nonwhite, or traditional-modern. These were old constructs that were now blocking the path forward; by the early 1900s, critics like Reiun were thinking in these kinds of broader terms.

It would not be long before a very narrow conception of the nation, and the state, embodied in the term *kokutai*, would be developed by Japanese conservatives and put to unfortunate use by militarists. This practice would put enormous pressure on that discursive space in which it was possible to imagine and long for a different world, a world in which humanity could realize its destiny. This was not something that countries or cultures could do, and it was definitely not something nation-states would undertake. Rather, this was a task for all humanity. But somewhere, inside of nations and cultures, there needed to be a space where autonomous, self-aware individuals could thrive and grow. But where could such a discursive space be located in late Meiji Japan? After Kôtoku's execution in 1911, and the murder by police of the anarchist Ôsugi Sakae in 1923, progressive thinkers on the left were under duress. By 1925 the revised Peace Preservation Ordinance had made it illegal to advocate any change in the *kokutai*—the national polity—and this meant that voicing utopian visions or talking about changes in the status of the monarchy or the private property system was prohibited. Taoka Reiun would never have sanctioned this kind of narrowing of options for the individual.

7

THE FINAL YEARS
TOWARD A NEW VISION FOR WOMEN, SOCIETY, AND THE INDIVIDUAL

> Regardless of the question whether woman is oppressed as a proletarian, we must recognize that in this world of private property she is oppressed as a sex being. On all sides she is hemmed in by restrictions and obstacles unknown to the man. Many things a man may do she is prohibited from doing; many social rights and privileges enjoyed by him, are considered a fault or a crime in her case. She suffers both socially and as a sex being. It is hard to say in which respect she suffers more, and therefore it only seems natural that many women wish they had been born men instead of having been born women.
>
> August Bebel, *Women and Socialism*

> The storm of progress has left nothing untouched, including our understanding of gender. "Gender" refers to the social construction of identities on the basis of biological difference. . . . As an analytic tool, gender is deployed to distinguish between sexuality or biology, on the one hand, and that which is understood as the imposition on a sexual being of a particular identity from the outside, as it were. Gender has to do with that species of imposition. All feminist analyses, in one way or another, to one degree or another, hold that gender is not given as a natural category but is socially and politically determined.
>
> Jean Bethke Elshtain, *History and the Idea of Progress*

To Reiun, existing conceptions of the individual, society, history, the nation-state, progress, gender, and even modernity itself were all things to be investigated, destabilized, and contested. This is why he maintained his commitment to "research today" in order to be able to accept the "necessity of tomorrow." Behind such a commitment lay a conviction that something concrete, something worth investigating and defending, does indeed exist. On what did Reiun base this conviction? The answer is deceptively simple: it is the individual, the "self." In the end, it is individuals who go through life, discover what there is to discover, and try to have as full an experience as a human being as possible. How should one live? What should one do? These are choices that individuals have to make. At times Reiun echoes Rousseau, the "romantic empiricist," who insisted that, while humans can and must discover the facts, facts by themselves are worthless without reference to the inner self.[1] Engels once noted that Rousseau and the other "great French philosophers of the eighteenth century .... recognized no external authority of any kind whatever. Religion, natural science, society, political institutions—everything was subjected to the most unsparing criticism."[2] Reiun, too, found it "against my nature to recognize any authority above or outside myself."[3] Instead, he placed his hopes in beliefs that were rooted in things that he could investigate for himself. So, no doubt, he aspired to this same kind of unsparing criticism as well. It is what he had asked of writers back in the 1890s: pay attention to what you see around you but never lose sight of the ideal of deeply penetrating the human heart in order to uncover a complete picture of reality. Realism is good for providing the stuff of your novels, the raw materials, but you need to bring something else: the passion of your inner vision, the cauldron of your ideals, in order to make what is "real" become truly alive and meaningful.

This is a tall order, and that is why he was rarely satisfied as a literary critic. It is also, perhaps, why he earned the reputation of being exceedingly *surudoi* (pointed) in his critical essays, and this was probably a generous way of putting it. He was not merely critical but often confrontational and contentious. He took this kind of stance because he believed in the value of examining, studying, and questioning, and he was certain that within each individual there was something concrete, something real, that could be uncovered, perhaps fused with a higher spirit, in order to achieve a deeper understanding. Mysticism, esoteric thinking, Daoism, Schopenhauer, the Vedas and Upanishads, Buddhism, Swedenborg, Böhme, Mme. Guyon, Carpenter—they all convinced Reiun that this was not only a real possibility but the only thing that was worth pursuing. He never backed down from this conviction.

Reiun died relatively young, so we have no way of knowing how he might have interpreted the world in his more mature years. However, in view of the strict censorship to which his writings were subjected, there is no basis for believing that he would ever have been allowed to say what he really wanted to. That is why he commented wryly that if he had been born elsewhere, such as in Russia, China or Korea, he probably would have joined some terrorist or revolutionary group, but since he was fortunate enough to have been "born in Japan, with all the benefits of a glorious past," he was free to "lie on my sickbed and leisurely cultivate my illness. To me, this is the greatest joy and happiness."[4] These are the words of someone all too familiar with feelings of frustration and helplessness over having his writings arbitrarily censored or banned, which is precisely what Takahashi Tadashi meant when he alluded to the difficult fate that lay ahead of Reiun when he left the world of literary criticism in 1897.

Yet we do know something about what was on Reiun's mind during his last years because in his final collection of essays there is a revealing letter to a friend that articulates precisely the tasks in which Reiun hoped to become engaged if time permitted. Originally published in 1909, "In Reply to [Masaoka] Geiyô" was written with the awareness that his illness was terminal. Therefore, much of the essay was taken up with the question of death.[5] When death is near, one's sense of time changes. How many years remain? Is it time to think in terms of days, hours, and minutes? Reiun reasoned that people experience the most meaning in their lives when they are active and engaged; to turn away from this engagement is the same as choosing death. Despite losing the use of his legs, he wanted to stay active during his final years. He was not about to seek solace in organized religion as he never had done so during his life. He remarked on Takayama Chogyû's embrace of Nichiren Buddhism, [Tsunashima] Hayakawa's earnest belief in a beatific vision of God, and writer Kunikida Doppo's Christianity—but none of these suited him, he proclaimed: "That I could not believe in organized religion at all, was definitely a source of unhappiness for me, yet I did not feel any sense of loss that my faith was not like Doppo's. All I really desire is to be able to face death like a man, to die as the Stoics of old would have."[6] "Like Tolstoy," he wrote, "I am an anarchist, but unlike Tolstoy I am an atheist."[7] A profound admirer of Tolstoy, to whom he claimed he was indebted for his understanding of socialism and anarchism, he did not share the writer's embrace of Christianity late in his life, even though it was an unorthodox and radical version of Christianity. Reiun expected little more from the end of his life than to pass away quietly in his futon exhibiting some modicum of courage and manifesting at least some small amount of dignity.

The reflective tone of this essay found expression in another way, too. Looking back over his years as a critic in the literary world, Reiun concluded that he was a straggler (*rakugosha*), someone out of step with the times.[8] But, while other people in the literary world might be content to endorse some foreign doctrine or "ism" (at that particular time it was naturalism) and declare that they did not want to be "enslaved," Reiun put the matter differently.

> Doesn't being enslaved mean that you do not have anything to defend? Yet the people today ridicule those who have something to defend, calling them enslaved, never realizing that in their hatred of enslavement it is they themselves who become enslaved by the vicissitudes of their imported western ideas. People who wish for freedom from enslavement should defend their individual selves more strongly (最も強く自己を守るものならざる可からず).[9]

In other words, people without their own set of core beliefs are the ones who lack a solid foundation. They do not know their inner selves, so they do not have anything concrete within them that they can call their own. In the same vein, people who stand by their beliefs, and remain unflinching and unchanging because of them, should not be called prisoners. Herein lies the irony: today, if one has something to which one can be true, one is in danger of being dismissed as a conservative or an anomaly, an intellectual straggler, someone who lags hopelessly behind the times. Reiun reflected on the way in which he had become an outsider to a movement of which he was once very much a part.

> When I first began to write for my journal *Seinenbun* fifteen years ago, I pursued my vocation full of youthful vigor and with great confidence in myself and in the value of literature. To this latter end I devoted my total being with complete and utter sincerity, so it was inevitable that at times my thoughts were crudely expressed, not unlike those of a child. Nevertheless, beneath this childlike quality there was a profound earnestness, a deathly seriousness that at times took on the proportions of a mania. Since that time I've been around a bit and tasted my share of this world's hardships. Once my fever subsided and my head cooled, my vision grew increasingly clear. But along with this, my thirst for pleasure and excitement withered and the flame of my imagination grew dim. Eventually . . . I came to view literature solely as something with which to pleasurably pass the time.
>
> Instead, what came to stir my passions were the problems of social inequality and humanity's seemingly wretched fate. In other words, I became involved with the shortcomings of this world. As a critic, what I want to see is not another volume of prose but a means whereby the person who weeps out of cold and starvation can at least be provided with a bowl of gruel. Rather than arguing philosophy and investigating the vast expanse of truth, I believe we must urgently seek out a complete cure for contemporary problems. Since this is the area where my attention is turning, isn't it conceivable that

my present distance from the literary world is not the product of boredom alone?[10]

Indeed it is. His distance from the literary world is not at all the result of boredom alone. Quite the contrary: it has more to do with the course of his thought, that "slight change in his stance" to which he alluded in his memoir. Nearly fifteen years earlier, he had set great store by the power of literature to change the world, but now he is feeling that one more work of fiction is not going to help the people who need it most. For that something more along the lines of a radical social transformation was going to be required.

Finding Projects: Narrativizing the Self

Late in his life, a drive toward praxis was challenging Reiun's commitment to a philosophical exploration of the world. The significance of this can be seen in his discussion of the themes to which he wanted to devote his attention during the remaining years of his life.[11] In all he listed four projects in his "Reply to Geiyô" essay. Little needs to be said about two of them, except that one was accomplished and one was not. The former was the task of writing an autobiography, one that would be a spiritual and psychological record of the times. In contrast to Rousseau, who asserted in his autobiography, *Confessions*, "I am made unlike anyone that I have ever met: I will even venture to say that I am like no one in the whole world," Reiun wanted *Sakkiden* to be read as the story of an ordinary person's life.[12] The dominant impression one gets from reading this work is just the reverse of course; Reiun comes off as sui generis, a unique individual who resists facile categorization. Professor Nishida is correct in his assertion that, although Reiun did complete *Sakkiden*, it turned out to be a less ambitious project than he originally intended and therefore, we may presume, less successful in achieving the desired results.[13]

Translating Schopenhauer

The second project, one that was not accomplished, was perhaps even more ambitious. Reiun wanted to attempt a complete and systematic translation of Arthur Schopenhauer's works so that Japanese could become better acquainted with his ideas. Although there is no evidence that this project was even begun, the fact that he wanted to do it is interesting; it reminds us of how important Schopenhauer's ideas were to Reiun throughout his life. He writes:

> The philosophy of Arthur Schopenhauer thoroughly dominated the second half of the nineteenth century. It influenced the likes of Tolstoy, Gorky,

> Ibsen, Nietzsche, and even Wagner. And his influence was not just limited to such individuals; he had the much wider impact of being a pioneer in the quest for a synthesis of eastern and western ideas. For me, as someone from the East, I am convinced that this makes his philosophy worth studying. But so far only a few fragments of his work have been translated into Japanese: the late Nakae Chômin included Schopenhauer in his 1894 reference work on logic, and in 1907 Kakuta Kanichirô translated some of Schopenhauer's essays in his *Ren'ai to Geijustu to Tensai* [Love, Art, and Genius]. It seems odd, though, that these days in the literary world there is so much fascination with western writers and we have so many translations of short works by Maupassant, Gorky, and Turgenev—but aren't names like these just being thrown out there because there is money to be made by hawking them? Avoiding the translation of the longer, more substantial works—is this really the best way to introduce western ideas to Japanese readers? Given the lack of depth in my academic training, I may not be the best person to grasp all the nuances of a serious philosopher's writing, but I would really like to see this translation project move forward. I may not claim any single ideology as my own, but if there is a cornerstone to my outlook, it is this man's philosophical teachings, and if I am granted time to do it, and can rouse myself from my sickbed, this is the prize on which I would set my sights.[14]

For many people, a fascination with Schopenhauer seems to be a phase in their lives that is eventually left behind. But for Reiun it is clear both from this essay and from everything else he wrote, that he remained engaged with Schopenhauer's thought throughout his life. No doubt he followed Schopenhauer's admonition in the preface to the first edition of *The World as Will and Representation* that "the only way to completely fathom the thought presented here is to read the book twice, and in fact with considerable patience the first time, the sort of patience that comes from a voluntary conviction that the beginning presupposes the end almost as much as the end presupposes the beginning."[15] This was in part because Schopenhauer believed that "a system of thought must always have an architectonic coherence, i.e. a coherence in which one part always supports another."[16] Reiun understood that Schopenhauer's work needed to be read carefully and in its entirety, and he wanted to provide Japanese readers with a full and accurate translation if at all possible. Unfortunately, time did not permit this.

An Allegory for Humanity

The other two pieces that Reiun hoped to write merit somewhat closer attention. In both instances, some effort was made to launch these projects, but the results were only partial at best. He said that he wanted to keep writing on the theme of what it means to become modern, giving special attention to the distinctions between precivilized and civilized society. As such, it was an extension of his quest to understand human nature, for Reiun believed that in turning away from nature humans were opting for "formalism" over freedom. He observed, "Contemporary people might say that their primitive ancestors were barbaric, but they were inferior only in terms of material achievements and in matters of technical skill. As far as matters of the spirit and morals are concerned, primitive humans far surpassed their so-called civilized counterparts."[17]

Reiun declared that he wanted to write an essay reminding humans that "they were born naked," and by this he meant both spiritually and morally. That is, humans are born with a certain nature, a potential. It was up to each individual to realize that potential. An interesting essay along these lines was found among an assortment of unpublished papers that Professor Nishida received from Reiun's son, Taoka Ryôichi.[18] It was an earlier version, dating from the Okayama period, so it was probably there that the concept first emerged. Written in a tongue-in-cheek style, the essay is an allegory set in an African desert. The leading characters are animals and representatives of the insect world. The situation is that an angel has been sent from above to inform these creatures that God has taken pity on their plight, their maltreatment at the hands of humans, and He is willing to alleviate their condition by elevating them to the status of humans. A humorous debate ensues in which the various flaws of humans are dissected and ultimately the Lord's offer is respectfully declined. One thing that makes this essay noteworthy is its style. It shows that Reiun was prepared to take a less direct route in expressing his opinions if necessary. After many unfortunate experiences at the hands of the censors, it seems that he was willing to resort to avenues other than the straightforward critical essay. Probably he envisioned doing something in this vein on a substantial scale, but he was never able to complete the project.

A Call for Women's Liberation (*joshi-kaihôron*, 女子解放論)

The fourth and final area in which Reiun wanted to develop his ideas is perhaps the most interesting. He wanted to write a *joshi-kaihôron* (treatise on women's liberation).[19] In this work he intended to systematically discuss the nature of the relationship between the sexes. In order to grasp the nature of this relationship Reiun was convinced that it was necessary to go back to the roots of existing social conditions and discover what had brought about changes. But Reiun was looking back with a definite premise in mind. In "Geiyô ni fukusu" (In Reply to Geiyô) he expressed it like this.

> The present status of women is completely unnatural.... In biological and anthropological terms the relationship between men and women is a factor of the reproductive function. But from the standpoint of reproduction, it is the woman who is the principal and the man who is the agent. So, if we are going to speak of a natural relationship between men and women, then it is women who should be placed above men. In fact, however, the reason why the present relationship between men and women appears to be reversed has to do with something entirely different from the reproductive function. The reason is that women, trapped in the stultifying bonds of marriage, have been made into economic parasites dependent on men. Therefore, in order to liberate women from their present condition, the prison of the family system as it is currently organized must be razed, the chains of the husband-wife relationship must be severed, and men and women must be set free to establish relationships based on love (*ren'ai*).
>
> You might say that such an argument is excessive, that it is vulnerable to becoming lost in extremes. But consider this: it took a religious revolution to bring about intellectual liberation for human beings and the French Revolution to bring about political liberation for individuals. The coming revolution will surely be one aimed at sexual liberation.[20]

To the two great revolutions, the French and the Industrial, Reiun proposed to add a third: the sexual revolution.

Two elements in Reiun's thought had converged to persuade him that women's current status was unnatural. In the first place, he was not at all convinced that monogamy was natural. He had raised this issue in a 1904 essay entitled "Is Monogamy Really a Natural Law?"[21] The two most fundamental human drives, he began, are hunger and sex. The former emerges from a concern for the survival of the individual, however, while the latter is based on the natural urge to ensure the continuity of the species. Therefore, the two are of a different order, as the first is rooted in individual needs while the second is concerned with the greater interests of all humanity. What is a monogamous marriage founded on? We have seen that in "Isei no shiyû" (Private Possession of the Opposite Sex) Reiun argued that the institution of marriage was nothing more than the extension of humans' selfish desire to possess things, and as such an outgrowth of the notion of private possession of property.[22]

In this way the second element in Reiun's thought was brought to bear on the problem. That is, he saw the same selfishness that had been unleashed by the recognition of the right to possess private property as a major corrupting influence on the relationship between the sexes. In arriving at this opinion, Reiun may have been influenced by Max Nordau. In *The Conventional Lies of our Civilization*, Nordau held:

> The falseness of the economic, social and political conditions of our civilization has also poisoned the intercourse between the sexes—all the natural instincts that should ensure the perpetuation and perfection of the race are distorted and diverted into wrong channels, and the future generations . . . are sacrificed without hesitation to the prevailing selfishness and hypocrisy.[23]

And elsewhere, on the economic organization found in modern civilization, he posed a question: "What does it matter to a society organized in this way that the reproduction of the species occurs under the most unfavorable conditions?"[24]

This was Reiun's basic point of departure, then, when he returned from Suzhou in 1907 and was recuperating at Awaji Jima. There he drafted an outline of his *Treatise on Women's Liberation*. He had only just begun to develop his ideas, however, when his friend Sasagawa Rimpû cabled him from Tokyo requesting assistance in launching a new journal, *Tôa Shimpô* (East Asian Progress).[25] During the next year in Tokyo, Reiun launched another journal with his friends, *Koku-Byaku* (The Dark and the Bright) in which he serialized what he had composed so far on the liberation of women, along with excerpts from *MHD*.[26] The magazine folded and his series was never completed, but in *Sakkiden* Reiun indicated that he had wanted to do a three-part study to focus on (1) the natural state of relations between the sexes, (2) how this natural state was altered, and (3) what must be done to bring about the liberation of women and why it is necessary (SD, 700-701).

The general drift of the essays serialized in *Koku-Byaku* is that primitive humans lived without the notion of private possessions, so everything was held communally. It was only after people began to individually possess things that the old harmony gave way to individual units centered on their own plots of land. This meant that a man singled out one or more women and took possession of them, just as he did with land and tools. Therefore, Reiun dismissed notions that tried to account for the status of women in terms of inherent female characteristics. As noted above, Reiun felt that if we followed this logic we would be forced to conclude that women should be dominant because of their principal role in the reproduction process. Therefore, he could not agree with Schopenhauer's assessment that women were naturally

Figure 7.1. Cover of the journal *Koku-Byaku*. Courtesy of Nishida Masaru.

deceitful, or innately this or that, and therefore unfit for higher tasks. Rather, any such qualities found in women were social constructs; they were the product of their subjugation, not the cause.[27]

Engels, Morgan, and Bebel

In addition to Carpenter and Nordau, Reiun drew on the works of three writers who addressed the position of women in contemporary society. In *The Origin of the Family, Private Property, and the State*, Engels had noted that monogamy:

> was not in any way the fruit of individual sex-love, with which it had nothing whatever to do; marriage remained as before marriages of convenience. . . .

Thus, when monogamous marriage first makes its appearance in history, it is not as the reconciliation of man and woman, still less as the highest form of such reconciliation. Monogamous marriage comes on the scene as the subjugation of the one sex by the other; it announces a struggle between the sexes unknown throughout the whole prehistoric period.[28]

Engels was heavily indebted to the work of anthropologist Henry Lewis Morgan, whom Reiun had read, and between Morgan, Engels, Nordau, and Carpenter, Reiun found grounding for his perception of the institution of marriage. He also referred to the writings of a third person, August Bebel (1840–1913). In the introduction to his 1879 book *Women and Socialism*, Bebel sounds not unlike Carpenter when he writes:

We are living in an age of great social transformations that are steadily progressing. In all strata of society we perceive an unsettled state of mind and an increasing restlessness, denoting a marked tendency toward profound and radical changes. Many questions have arisen and are being discussed with growing interest in ever widening circles. One of the most important of these questions and one that is constantly coming into greater prominence is the woman question.

The woman question deals with the position that woman should hold in our social organism, and seeks to determine how she can best develop her powers and her abilities, in order to become a useful member of human society, endowed with equal rights and serving society according to her best capacity. From our point of view this question coincides with that other question: In what manner should society be organized to abolish oppression, exploitation, misery and need, and to bring about the physical and mental welfare of individuals and of society as a whole? To us then, the woman question is only one phase of the general social question that at present occupies all intelligent minds, its final solution can only be attained by removing social extremes and the evils which are a result of such extremes.[29]

Bebel also saw the modern institution of marriage as ineffective and unsuited to meet society's needs.

"Marriage and the family are the foundations of the state. Whoever, therefore, attacks marriage and the family, is attacking society and the state and undermining both." Thus exclaim the defenders of the present order. Monogamic marriage as has been sufficiently shown, is the outcome of the system of gain and property that has been established by bourgeois society, and therefore undoubtedly forms one of its basic principles. But whether it is adapted to natural needs and to a healthy development of human society is a different question. We will show that this marriage, which depends upon the bourgeois system of property, is a more or less forced relation, having many disadvantages, and frequently fulfilling its purpose only insufficiently or not at all.[30]

One of Reiun's longer and more developed articles on the "woman problem" bore the title "Jôshikaihô wa danshikaihô nari" (Women's Liberation Means Men's Liberation).In it he argued that women's liberation would benefit men every bit as much as it would benefit women. He begins the essay by admitting that men are probably not very interested when they hear talk about women's liberation, and they probably associate it with the emergence of a modern, less feminine, and submissive type of woman. But, he writes, it is really men who will benefit most from women's liberation: "The liberation of women is a major issue for humanity as a whole, but it should never be misunderstood as simply a means of encouraging women to become masculine."[31]

Of course, Reiun's interest in the problems of women was also a logical outgrowth of his concern with ideals, and the ideal of liberated human beings is one he held particularly strongly. In his basically Daoist view, Reiun treated all the laws, customs and conventions of society, and its morality, as artificial impositions from without that have nothing to do with the inner self. In fact, because they are imposed strictures, their effect is to burden individuals and obstruct the ideal of human liberation. By focusing on the problem of the subjugation of women, Reiun was recognizing, as Nordau had, that women were only the most "immediate victims," in that they experienced bondage directly and in its most extreme forms, but that the problem of bondage is one that extends to all humanity.[32] As we have seen, to Reiun the problem is one of bondage to the Schopenhauerian will, of enslavement to one's selfish desires. These desires had been awakened by the acceptance of the right to private possession that provided the foundation for the institution of marriage. Therefore, in Reiun's view, along with the property system, marriage and the family as currently construed would have to be eradicated.

In addition to Reiun's intellectual path to the problem of women's liberation, there was also an emotional factor rooted in his own life experience that must not be ignored. While it may be unusual to find such a radical critique of marriage and the existing family system in late Meiji Japan, it is all the more remarkable that it came from Taoka Reiun, a rather unlikely source. After all, he was remarkably unsuccessful in establishing enduring relationships with women. His acceptance of an arranged match and cruel treatment of a wife he did not love or respect hardly qualified Reiun as a person with enlightened views on women. But this is rather beside the point, for Reiun's experiences in his life, his disastrous love affair at Tsûyama, his painful marriage, and the experience of seeing his child raised by others while he remained without a family, all convinced him of the "unnaturalness" and meaninglessness of existing codes of morality. They were unnatural because they were artificial and built on false premises and selfish illusions. Most important, they were part of an environment that blinded individuals to their true natures and so prevented them from attaining natural emotional states. This was demonstrated for him by the fact that the truest and most loving emotions were often experienced outside the bonds of marriage.[33]

Chikamatsu, Carpenter, and the Institution of Marriage

The bitterness and anger generated by his personal experiences set the tone for Reiun's attack on marriage and the subjugation of women. They also provided the central theme that ran through his essays on the position of women in society; his conception of marriage; and, by extension, by means of a unique essay carried in the first issue of *Tenko*, the theme of love suicide in Chikamatsu's plays, which he utilized as a means of uncovering the customs and conventions of society that interfere with and distort human's natural emotions. This was captured in the subtitle of the essay that described those who commit love suicides as "victims of an unnatural society."[34]

In Reiun's interpretation, the principals in Chikamatsu's best-known works were trying to realize their love in a realm beyond the physical world where the fetters of confining customs and sham morality conspired with administrative codes to oppress the most natural human feelings. One such feeling is the urge to reproduce, a deeply rooted instinctual drive. The feeling of love is the mechanism whereby the two sexes are drawn together in a union so that reproduction will be accomplished. It is, therefore, clearly a part of an individual's essential nature. Also, because it ensures that mankind will have a future, it is a sacred instinct, the basis for all hopes and dreams, the source of all ideals.

The sexual instinct is also sacred because to be involved in reproduction is to take part in an act of creation. When two people come together for this purpose, the totality of their separate beings is merged into a single focal point: they embrace the One. Love, then, is the fire that fuses the sexes, its intense heat forging the union. Love suicides abandon the lives the characters cherish out of desperation because society will not allow their true feelings to develop. In his treatment of the urge to reproduce as a sacred instinct, Reiun was influenced by Carpenter. In the article "The Sex Passion" in Carpenter's collection of essays entitled *Love's Coming of Age*, the author confronts the difficulty of writing about sex.

> The subject of Sex is difficult to deal with. There is no doubt a natural reticence is connected with it. There is also a great deal of prudery. The passion occupies, without being spoken of, a large part of human thought; and words on the subject being so few and inadequate, everything that is said is liable to be misunderstood. Violent inferences are made and equivocations surmised, from the simplest remarks; qualified admissions of liberty are interpreted into recommendations of unbridled license; and generally the perspective of literary expression is turned upside down.[35]

And in "Woman in Freedom" Carpenter asserts:

> It is clear enough, from what has been said, that what Woman most needs today, and is mostly seeking for, is a basis of independence for her life. Nor is her position likely to be improved until she is able to face man on an equality; to find, self-balanced, her natural relation to him; and to dispose of herself and of her sex perfectly freely, and not as a thrall must do.
>
> Doubtless if man were an ideal creature his mate might be secure of equal and considerate treatment from him without having to insist upon an absolute economic independence but as that is only too obviously not the case there is nothing left for her to-day but to unfold the war-flag of her "rights," and (dull and tiresome as it may be) to go through a whole weary round of battles till peace is concluded again upon a better understanding.
>
> Yet it must never be forgotten that nothing short of large social changes, stretching beyond the sphere of women only, can bring about the complete emancipation of the latter. Not till our whole commercial system, with its barter and sale of human labor and human love for gain, is done away, and not till a whole new code of ideals and customs of life has come in, will women really be free. They must remember that their cause is also the cause of the oppressed laborer over the whole earth, and the laborer has to remember that his cause is theirs.[36]

It would not be long before Japanese women were talking explicitly about their need for independence, especially financial independence from the *ie* (family system).[37] What is unique about Reiun's critique is his overriding interest in the ways in which society interferes with and distorts natural human instincts and prevents people from experiencing this most natural and sacred of all human feelings. Therefore, Reiun can sympathize with victims who elect to take their own lives in Chikamatsu's works because they are willing to sacrifice their bodies and lives in order to resist the oppression of a deceit-filled, artificial society. How does society oppress natural human instincts and feelings? By senselessly decreeing that reproduction can only take place legitimately within the confines of marriage.

But what is marriage? Is it undertaken as a response to the surfacing of love's emotions? Does the marital state come about because of loving feelings rooted in the noble aim of perpetuating the species? No. Marriage is undertaken to preserve some individual family line or improve its material fortunes. Usually it comes about without reference to the feelings of the principals. If such feelings do exist at the outset, they are soon constricted in the bonds of marriage. At the same time, any natural expression of these sacred feelings is viewed with scorn and reproach by society because they occur outside its laws. But what are laws other than artificial codes that have nothing to do with feelings but are imposed on people in order to mold their behavior? Besides, what determines how something becomes a law or custom? It is simply what becomes accepted practice and fixed into morality over time. It has no sacred or divine origins.

Therefore, Reiun is pointing to the classic struggle between human instincts and the customs and conventions of society. In his eyes, though, those who adhere to convention encounter an inertia that cannot be overcome. Conventions are just the dregs of history, morals the skin that covers the essence, and laws the superficial and empty husks of propriety. Just as in the case of private possession of property, marriage is an institution that thrives on selfishness, and, as it distorts and misshapes people, it generates "deceitful" or hollow men because it legitimizes the possession of a member of the opposite sex under the rubric of man and wife. Therefore, the urge to propagate and the natural expression of this, what we call love, are natural principles that live within people. Marriage is a superficial external code imposed on people, and it attacks and eradicates these feelings.

In *Love's Coming of Age*, Carpenter argues that love is capable of overcoming the lies and falsity on which private possession insists. "Love," he writes, "burns this falsity away.... That is why love—even rude and rampant and outrageous love—does more for the moralising of poor humanity than a hundred thousand Sunday schools. It cleans the little human souls from the clustered lies in which it has rested itself—from the petty conceits and deceits and cowardice and covert meanness."[38] For someone like Reiun, who was looking for radical transformation in the world around him, the entire

210 : THE TURN AGAINST THE MODERN

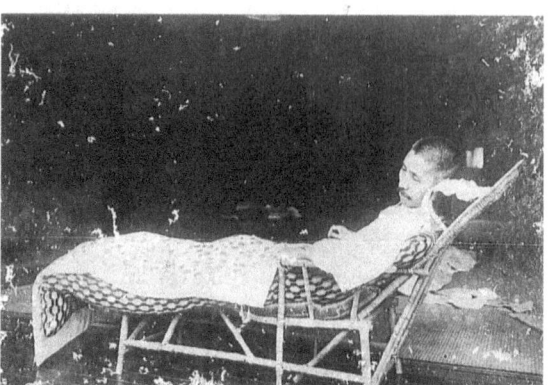

晩年、藤椅子に横たわる嶺雲

Figure 7.2. Taoka Reiun at Nikkô near the end of his life.
Courtesy of Nishida Masaru.

system of gender relations needed to be reconfigured. That is precisely what he called for and what he meant when the claimed that "women's liberation means men's liberation" (*joshikaihô wa danshikaihô nari*). In a 1909 essay, "Uzô muzô," he stated the case bluntly to the effect that as long as women's only options are to marry and become a slave to a man or to live as an "Old Miss" and be looked down on by society, they do not have a fighting chance. But the time may be upon us when women have to struggle, and experience all the pain and discomfort this entails, in order to bring about the era when women can function equally not only in the workplace but as spiritual equals with men.[39] This was, no doubt, a bitter pill for Japanese to swallow prior to 1910. After all, it preceded by a couple of years the moment when Japanese feminists came together to create their literary journal, *Seitô*, in 1911, and it was well before the Russian Revolution and World War I, after which many of these issues were much more widely discussed. Nevertheless, these ideas helped define the kind of future on which Reiun was setting his sights.

Final Days

It was an ambitious agenda that Reiun set for himself, and one that he was unable to complete. He continued to physically deteriorate, although he managed to write and engage with the issues that most attracted his attention. The young man Tanaka Kotarô, who assisted Reiun in completing the manuscript of *Meiji hanshinden*, visited Reiun frequently. He noted how

Figure 7.3. Taoka Reiun grave marker (the marker on the left is for Shirakawa; the one on the right is Taoka's). Photo by the author.

frail he looked and that he needed to be taken to the bathroom. Two of his older brothers were making sure that he was comfortable and had what he needed, including two maids who looked after him. But he was prone to fevers, and his paralysis was getting worse. One day he said to Tanaka, with a wry smile, "I know I don't have much time left."[40]

At the time Taoka Reiun became infected with spinal meningitis, the disease was fatal for 75 to 80 percent of the patients who contracted it. The year after his death, the American pathologist, Simon Flexner (1863–1946), developed an antimeningococcal serum that decreased the rate of mortality significantly. Unfortunately, this development came much too late for Reiun. On September 7, 1912, at 4:30 a.m. on a cool, drizzly morning, Reiun died in the historic resort town of Nikkô. He was forty-one years and nine months old. Two days later, on the ninth, friends and family gathered at the Jôkoji temple where an inscribed wooden pillar honoring his name was installed. Today, one can see two stone pillars in the cemetery at Jôkoji that were erected by his friend Shirakawa Riyô to commemorate their deep friendship, a bond that was likened to one between two siblings.

On the following day, September 10, a memorial ceremony was conducted at the Yanaka Funeral Hall in Tokyo, to which, in a gesture of solidarity, some three hundred fellow writers and critics came and paid their respects to a fallen comrade, including the likes of Miyake Setsurei, Anezaki Chôfû, Shiga Nagoya, Natsume Sôseki, Izumi Kyôka and Sakai Toshiko, to name a few.[41]

8

Last Thoughts
On Defending the Modern Self

> There is a mode of vital experience—experience of space and time, of the self and others, of life's possibilities and perils—that is shared by men and women all over the world today. I will call this body of experience "modernity." . . . Modern environments and experiences cut across all boundaries of geography and ethnicity, of class and nationality, of religion and ideology: in this sense, modernity can be said to unite all mankind. But it is a paradoxical unity, a unity of disunity: it pours us all into a maelstrom of perpetual disintegration and renewal, of struggle and contradiction, of ambiguity and anguish.
>
> Marshall Berman, *All That Is Solid Melts into Air*

As a determined and independent-minded critic, Reiun has few parallels. His concern was not only for his own country's fate but for that of the entire planet. It seemed to him that the world had taken a wrong turn and it was time to reassess. But the first step in any reassessment would have to be grounded in a strong sense of self. As noted previously, Maruyama Masao, writing in the 1940s and 1950s, was also deeply concerned that the Japanese people had lacked a sufficiently strong sense of self in the prewar years and that was why they had been so easily overwhelmed by militarism and the state. Was a greater sense of individual agency and subjectivity not possible? He liked to recall a scene from Charlie Chaplin's film *The Great Dictator* in which the Chaplin character is flying upside down in an airplane with a wounded pilot but the airplane is in a cloudbank so they are not aware that they are flying upside down. When asked what time it is, he reaches for his watch and it falls *upward*, out of his pocket, and dances around in front of his face, surprising him. He keeps trying to stuff the watch back in his pocket, but, unable to defy gravity, it keeps popping up again. Maruyama's point is that the film is asking what kind of an age this modern one is. His answer is that it is "an upside down age."[1] The problem is that "people have come to regard the 'upside-down world' they live in as a normal state of affairs"; instead, they need to understand individuals "in their otherness," and "while remaining 'inside'" they must extend their vision back "to the 'outside.'"² This question of how to retain an "inside" focus while extending one's vision to the "outside" is precisely what engaged Taoka Reiun throughout his career as a literary and cultural critic and the reason why he merits our attention.

In the debates over subjectivity, Maruyama called for the development of an "autonomous self" (*jishuteki jinkaku*, 自主的人格), by which he meant an individual with the capacity to achieve "psychological independence from the surrounding environment . . . [from] political society, or the state."³ He believed that the modern individual should live "by the fundamental ethical belief that the individual is always prior to society and stands as an 'end in himself.'"⁴ Reiun spent his entire career urging his readers to pursue the development of this very same kind of independent self, one capable of developing and "defending" the higher ideals to which humans could and should aspire. Moreover, he understood "otherness" and cultural differences, and ever since his *kokusui-hozon* days, he had advocated "preserving" and attending to them. He appreciated the need to move back and forth between the inside and the outside. But he also envisioned a pluralistic world order and global culture in which both eastern and western societies could achieve a synthesis and work toward a broader, more inclusive definition of humanity. Although they lived in very different times and historical circumstances, Reiun and Maruyama were in agreement on this fundamental point. Moreover, they shared an important experience: they had both been arrested and interrogated by the prewar police.

Reiun, of course, was not only detained in 1910 when his friend Kôtoku was arrested, but he had also been imprisoned for his writings earlier, so he was very familiar with the intrusive power of the state. When Maruyama was in high school at Ichikô—the First Higher School—in Tokyo, his father, Maruyama Kanji's good friend and fellow liberal journalist, Hasegawa Nyozekan, had been invited to speak at the school in 1933 by a student group with an interest in Marxism. When Masao went to hear the talk, the police interrupted the lecture and ordered the meeting dissolved. Suspected of being one of the ringleaders, Masao was arrested and interrogated by the Special Higher Police. He was roughed up and detained for a few days, and while his life may never have been in danger, he was sufficiently exposed to state power and its abuses to have come away with an enduring negative impression.⁵

Reiun, too, was marked by his two-month-long imprisonment and having so many of his writings banned or censored. One might say that it simply reinforced his inclination to approach the problem of the self as a contrarian, to see the world in which he lived as something that needed to be contested. Like many other modernists, Reiun was troubled by modernism's "betrayal of its own human promise."[6] As iconoclasts, modernists were intent on assaulting modern civilization's traditions whenever they could. But at times this meant that they might be engaging in what Gabriel Josipovici calls "the daily struggle of a dialogue with the world, without any assurance that what one will produce will have value," a sentiment with which Reiun was all too familiar.[7] For had he not engaged with important issues and pushed his readers to see reality through a new lens only to have many of his most important writings banned? It made him wonder at times whether what he was doing was making a difference. As he reflected in *Sakkiden*, trying to make a living "by reading books and writing may end up being meaningless" (*SD*, 688).

By the early twentieth century, though, the stakes were getting higher in Japan. Reiun noted in his autobiography that after his return from Suzhou in 1907 he had to readjust to his native country, which he described as a "police state" (*keisatsu no kuni*) (*SD*, 685–87). Almost as though he were anticipating Maruyama's observation that prewar ultranationalism was a "many-layered, though invisible net over the Japanese people," Reiun was becoming increasingly aware of how widely that net was being cast into the fabric of society, especially after the High Treason Incident and Kôtoku's execution.[8] That is why he so strongly encouraged individuals to come up with something with its own intrinsic value, something that could be "defended" in the face of the powerful currents unleashed by the "maelstrom" of modernity.

Even though Reiun felt the sting of censorship and admitted later in life that he was unable to express himself as frankly as he would have preferred, he believed in the value of struggle and grappling with ideas. Contestation was an essential part of all the reading and writing that he did throughout his life. That is why Reiun may be considered a classic outsider, what he referred to as a "straggler." But, as Josipovici points out, this kind of marginalized status may also have offered him an all-important "vantage point" from which to "see things which might otherwise remain hidden."[9] If there is one thing we can assert with confidence about Reiun's life and work it is that he was always willing to dig deeper and try to uncover that which was not immediately visible. In his estimation, this was the critic's job. If he believed in the value of looking into the past and learning about history, it wasn't because he revered the past or wanted to return to it. All the great teachers and philosophers he admired had looked back in order to better understand how the present came to be as it was. But still he could not help feeling like a straggler at times, or, as he put it, a "country bumpkin" in the big city world of ideas.[10] But this may just have been ironic self-deprecation. We now understand that when he addressed in *Sakkiden* the "slight change in my stance [that has] emerged since my younger days," he was not only being ironic but actually pointing his readers to something profound: it was the genesis of his determination to resist "the oppressive nature of the pseudo patriotism" that he saw steadily growing around him. That was precisely why, he explained, he could not help "going against the grain and being a contrarian" (SD, 713–14).

Struggles and Contradictions

For Taoka Reiun, writing was serious business. That is why he sounded alarm bells and pounded ferociously on drums in order to awaken his readers to what was at stake. When Ienaga Saburô tried to understand Reiun's ideas, he came to the conclusion that he was a "contradictory thinker" (*mujin seru shisôka*). Fair enough. Marshall Berman also appreciates that "struggle and contradiction," and "ambiguity and anguish" are hallmarks of the modern experience.[11] But was Reiun really so contradictory? If Anthony Giddens is correct and the modern self is much less a matter of "a distinctive trait, or even a collection of traits, possessed by the individual" but rather something that is *"reflexively understood by the person in terms of her or his biography,"* then Reiun's self-reflexivity, and his urge to narrativize his life in *Sakkiden*—his conscious attempt to structure an account of his life in order to impose meaning on what he experienced—situates him squarely in the mainstream of the modern experience.[12] Moreover, it lent gravitas to his enterprise and a consistency that belies any notion that he was contradictory. Schopenhauer had opened up new vistas for conceiving of the self as something independent of reason and understanding, and Reiun applied that insight to his own experiences of looking inward and observing the self simultaneously from first- and third-person stances. But searching for a self that could stand on its own and defend itself took other forms as well.

For example, like many before him, Reiun believed for a time in the power of literature to help human beings anchor themselves in the world. He especially appreciated literature composed by writers who were aware of what was real in the world around them. In the case of Japan in the 1890s, this meant understanding how industrialization was transforming society and creating disturbing gaps between the wealthy and the poor. In the years after 1905, he came to believe that Japan was at a point where it needed a radical social transformation. He valued the study of history, too, because he believed that it could help us understand the human experience as it had actually unfolded. He also appreciated the role philosophy could play in providing individuals with the internal strength and ballast needed to see things as they are. Reiun found some of this ballast first in the world of ancient Chinese and Indian thought, supplemented, of course, with generous doses of Schopenhauer, Tolstoy, Engels, Carpenter, von Hartmann, Nordau, and the rest. In this he was extremely consistent. From his essays we know how aware he was of the tension between the environment and the inner self; he wanted writers to embrace that tension and put it to good use. He urged writers, as well as his readers, to probe, explore, and ultimately transcend this tension.

Movement of Thought

Reiun eventually expanded his critique from literature to the broader subject of modernity itself, calling for revolutions in both social and gender relations. He wanted his revolution to encompass philosophy and ethics so that the stance that he assumed could be defended. His ideas had both breadth and depth. Perhaps something that Tadashi Karube wrote about Maruyama is applicable to Reiun as well: it is not only the nature of the ideas he explored that was significant but also "the *movement* of his thought" that energized it and "gave it life."[13] Reiun's exploration of ideas was also energized by this kind of *movement*. The sweep of what interested him ranged from Europe to Asia, from the precivilized world to contemporary times, and from the self and individual rights to women's liberation. He delved deeply into literature, philosophy, religion, history, and mysticism. Perhaps the very breadth of his interests, and the way he moved from one cluster of ideas to another, made him appear contradictory. But in reality he was much less concerned about contradictions at the horizontal level, such as might be manifest between different ideas or thought systems, than he was focused on the vertical relationships between ideas. What mattered to him were the contradictions between appearance and reality, between what is on the outside or surface of things as opposed to what resides within. He wanted his readers to appreciate the worth of moving along that continuum from inside to outside and back again. We saw in his essay "At Nagatamura" how Reiun was troubled by the way modernity—with the advent of industrialization and capitalism—let market forces determine the "value" not only of objects and people but also of the very air we breathe and the water we drink. The notion of individuals and goods having intrinsic value seemed to be lost on members of contemporary society, and this bothered Reiun.

But Reiun was never indifferent to the goings on in society around him, and he was without question among the most forceful and adamant literary critics who advocated that contemporary problems, especially "social problems," should be made the stuff of fiction. In fact the most lasting impression he left on the literary world was his appeal to writers to more successfully integrate these social issues—*shakai-mondai*—into their narratives. More than any other critic he pointed to the data on social problems that reporters were compiling, and he wanted Japanese writers to be more cognizant of the picture painted by this information. But at the same time he had little use for perceptions that ignored the inner life of the individual because only individuals who were capable of transcending selfishness and egotism could truly empathize with other human beings and connect with them via the mechanism of what he called *dôjô* (同情, compassion), Schopenhauer's *Mitleid*.

Finding Meaning through Engagement

In all of these insights, Reiun was reacting profoundly to the world around him. It was a world in which the ideas, the cultural patterns, and the whole way of life of the Japanese people were undergoing a substantial transformation. It was a modern world, an "upside-down" world, one that drew Reiun to philosophers and thinkers who were intent on discovering the ways in which social and cosmic realities are constituted. Perhaps Reiun was drawn to what J. L. Talmon calls a "total and foolproof explanation of social, not to say cosmic, reality," but this did not mean that he was unrealistic about what was going on around him.[14] Writing to his friend Masaoka Geiyô near the end of his life, he observed that "people experience the most meaning in their lives when they are active and engaged" (*jinsei wa katsudô no ue ni igi ari*), and he knew that to turn away from his beliefs now would be the same as choosing death.[15] Even though he was bedridden, he was opting to remain engaged, and this is why he wanted to undertake all the projects that he outlined while he was still capable of gripping his writing brush. He was unwilling to simply languish on his deathbed until his demise.

Perhaps there is no better indication of the movement of his ideas than the list of projects that he hoped to complete before he died, but we can also locate the energy and movement of his ideas in his fascination with *rebellion*. He wanted to infuse the spirit of the times, the *ikioi*, with energy and dynamism. He wanted to further individual liberties because he understood that "being enslaved [is] when you do not have anything to defend," advising his readers that, "People who wish for freedom from enslavement should defend their individual selves more strongly" (*SD*, 194). You cannot defend a self unless you commit to developing one, something Maruyama also came to appreciate fully. Oddly enough, it is also something that Sigmund Freud alluded to in one of his last works, *Civilization and Its Discontents*, where we find a brief statement: "The liberty of the individual is no gift of civilization. It was greatest before there was any civilization, though then, it is true, it had for the most part no value since the individual was scarcely in a position to defend it."[16]

In one sense, before the advent of modernity, humans had experienced a kind of freedom, but since they were not particularly aware of themselves and not in a position to defend their freedom, it did not matter much. Perhaps this is why Reiun so admired the voices from India and China that had emerged before a rational, empirical worldview had drawn a line in the sand between objective and subjective experience. In the Vedas, the *Upanishads*, the *Laozi*, and Zhuangzi, Reiun discovered a certain kind of freshness, an immediacy in the way the human experience was perceived. Schopenhauer had also observed that "in the early ages," when people "stood considerably nearer to the beginning of the human race and to the original source of organic nature than we do, [they] also possessed both greater energy of the intuitive faculty of knowledge, and a more genuine disposition of mind. They were thus capable of a purer and more direct comprehension of the inner essence of nature, and were thus in a position to satisfy the need for metaphysics in a more estimable manner."[17] A more estimable manner, indeed: to be more intuitive, to possess a "more genuine disposition of mind," and to be able to directly comprehend "the inner essence" of things"—these were among the principal aims of Reiun's attack on modern civilization. He wanted to recapture some of that immediacy that early human beings experienced in order to better understand how the individual self can relate to society, history, and the world.

Rousseau, one of Reiun's heroes, had held up a simpler, more holistic version of humanity (the "noble savage") so that people could learn about the present from the past. But, like Rousseau (and Carpenter, who followed Rousseau closely on this point), Reiun never really believed that the primitive state was an ideal toward which contemporary people should strive or that primitive people somehow represented more highly evolved human beings than did their modern descendants. To understand the condition of precivilized people, however, was to become more aware of the potential that human beings possessed to live an engaged and meaningful existence. Reiun would seek to inject into modern life, alongside the scientific or instrumentalist view of the world, a framework for understanding the impulses that drive individual human beings and the historical forces that operate on them. Without this kind of inner awareness, without self-exploration, there could be no true appreciation of human freedom.[18]

Becoming a Subject of Modernity

When it came to examining human nature, Reiun staunchly maintained that the process must begin with the individual self. It is only from this vantage point that individuals are able to construct something that is worth preserving, a viable, autonomous self. While this "inward turn" may bear a strong resemblance to the interiority explored by the romantics in the nineteenth century, it was different. By the twentieth, the self was a much less unified and integrated entity, and Reiun understood this. He appreciated that the self was something multifaceted and complex; it was a loose construct within which there is a timeless and mystical depth, to be sure, but also tensions, contradictions, struggles, and disruptions. Schopenhauer had made it clear that "the intellect is neither the sole nor necessarily the main factor of the self," so the person who looks within must come to terms with this reality.[19] But the self offered tremendous possibilities as well.[20] It was the repository of "the psychological facts of our self-experience" as Sophia Vasalou notes, but in order to access those facts one needed self-reflexivity; one needed that double awareness that enables a person to stand back and view the self simultaneously from both the first- and third-person stances.

As Berman reminds us, the modern experience has offered "an amazing variety of visions and ideas that aim to make men and women the subjects as well as objects of modernization, to give them the power to change the world that is changing them," and whenever Reiun availed himself of these kinds of visions and ideas, he was being quintessentially modern.[21] He had a method for probing the self: look, study, reflect, struggle, and write. When he felt his efforts yielded insights that were singular and new, he tried to direct his readers' attention to what he had discovered. If the times required him to be a contrarian and to grapple with forces that were xenophobic, undemocratic, and hostile to personal liberties, he was prepared to meet that challenge.

For Reiun, then, to become modern meant to plumb the depths of the individual self from the inside out. That he still believed this at the end of his life, and the fact that he placed such a high value on the idea of contestation and struggle as a means of achieving this end, is testimony to the solidity of his grounding, not the contradictory nature of his thought. He wrote in

Sakkiden not only about the value of having "something to defend" as the key to achieving freedom from "enslavement," but also that, "even when in the eyes of others someone's words or deeds may seem contradictory or foolish, from that person's own vantage point *it may represent an appropriate psychological path from which he is capable of adequately protecting or defending himself*" (SD, 477, italics mine). That he could identify the capacity of modern individuals to find their own "appropriate psychological path" as a way to defend themselves simply underscores his belief that in order for there to be individual freedom there had to be something concrete within the individual, something to defend, something in which freedom could be anchored. And his attempts to become self-reflexive and narrativize his experiences of finding his own path to these insights further tethered him to the modern experience.

In Reiun's own words, "All I ever wanted to do was to keep the self at the center of all I did" (SD, 662). Maruyama expressed his aspirations for the modern individual in terms of being able to take "a stance of independence in relation to potentially deterministic, external forces"; Reiun anticipated him by writing that if modern individuals wanted freedom, they must start with the self and create something there worth defending.[22] This echoes Charles Altieri's observation—noted at the outset of this study—that the essence of subjectivity may not reside in "*the content of the beliefs*, or in the history that formed them, *but in something specific to the way they are held*."[23] In other words, it is not just about the nature of the ideas in which one believes but about the stance one adopts in relation to society and the world. In coming to terms with his own sense of self, with the identity he forged as a writer and critic, Reiun understood that the *manner* in which he held his beliefs mattered. On this subject, he was quite transparent. After all, he knew that he was someone born in Japan who had been swept up in the popular rights movement in his youth, and when this movement's promises were betrayed, he became determined to seek the kinds of freedoms that it had offered in other arenas. So he took the "inward turn," and explored life through literature, philosophy, and history—those discursive spaces he needed to inhabit in order to create that "stance of independence" on which he placed so much value. From this vantage point, he was able to discover an "appropriate psychological path" that would lead him to the kind of insights and awareness about the self and its place in the modern world that he believed would be worth defending. There were times when he struggled, even times when he despaired. But the stance he assumed remained remarkably consistent: he wanted to see the world as it really was and convey what he saw to his readers. Perhaps, working together, they could make it a better place.

Notes

Preface

[1] See Bernard Bailyn's presidential address to the American Historical Association in 1981, "The Challenge of Modern Historiography," in which he notes, "The drama of people struggling with the conditions that confine them through the cycles of limited life spans is the heart of all living history," accessed June 2016, https://www.historians.org/about-aha-and-membership/aha-history-and-archives/presidential-addresses/bernard-bailyn.

[2] Karl J. Weintraub was among the first scholars to theorize autobiography. See his book *The Value of the Individual: Self and Circumstance in Autobiography* (Chicago: University of Chicago Press, 1978). Ideally, one wants to balance the story of an individual's life with an account of the times and environment in which the person lived so that readers can see the connections between his or her life experiences and the context in which they occurred. When he arrived at the end of his long "essay" dealing with the autobiographies of two luminaries, Rousseau and Goethe, Weintraub concluded that generating a sense of self and narrativizing it are intimately connected: "The growth of an individuality is possible only in this *coexistence with a world*. And individuality forms itself only by *the active process of making the continuous encounter with the world an individualized experience*. Only by continually accepting and forming one's world can one be forming oneself" (376, italics mine). See also See Karl J. Weintraub, "Autobiography and Historical Consciousness, *Critical Inquiry* 1:4 (June 1975), 821–48, where he states, "Real autobiography is a weave in which self-consciousness is delicately threaded throughout interrelated experience" (824).

[3] See Gabrielle M. Spiegel's presidential address to the American Historical Association in 2009, "The Task of the Historian," http://www.historians.org/about-aha-and-membership/aha-history-and-archives/presidential-addresses/gabrielle-m-spiegel#fn51. Accessed February 2, 2015. Wrestling with the influence of the linguistic turn, Spiegel also points out in this address, "We live in a moment of great cultural instability and uncertainty. As historians, we struggle to know the absent and the other, to affirm a right to words and to speech. . . . Precisely what instruments we will deploy in the pursuit of our historical labors is not entirely clear. But I persist in believing that there is one thing that deconstruction has taught us, more powerfully than any other strategy of reading that I know of, and that is to listen to silence."

[4] Nick Mansfield, *Subjectivity: Theories of the Self from Freud to Haraway* (New York: New York University Press, 2000), 1. Mansfield goes on to identify four types of subject: "the *subject of grammar*," "the *politico-legal subject*," "the *philosophical subject*," and "the *subject as a human person*" (3–4). It will become evident that Taoka Reiun was interested in all four of these varieties of subjectivity but none more than the philosophical subject.

[5] I wish to undertake this discussion of Reiun's interest in the "self" and subjectivity even though, as Lydia Liu makes clear in *Translingual Practice: Literature, National Culture, and Translated Modernity in China, 1900–1937* (Palo Alto, CA: Stanford University Press, 1995), it can be fraught with difficulties and can force us to contend with "pseudo-universals." The question she raises is whether terms such as *self* and *individual* can have exact equivalencies in other languages, especially if we are dealing with languages and cultures as different from each other as English, Chinese, and Japanese. As she correctly points out, we can neither "assume hegemony" nor "blot out the history of each word" in its respective culture when dealing with concepts like these (6–10). Liu even quotes Charles Taylor's important book *Sources of the Self: The Making of Modern Identity* (Cambridge, MA: Harvard University Press, 1989), on which I have relied a great deal in this study. Aware of these pitfalls, however, because Reiun dug deep into western philosophy, especially that of Schopenhauer, as well as Chinese, Indian, and Buddhist understandings of the self, I am going to proceed with the idea that, since Reiun himself was dedicated to grasping these equivalencies, it is worthwhile for us to make the effort as well. He tried very hard, over a long period of time, to situate an understanding of the self in the nexus between eastern and western philosophy and to address the question of how modernity was reconfiguring this understanding, so I believe that the argument in favor of keeping this issue at the forefront of this study remains viable, although we would all do well to keep Liu's cautionary advice in mind.

[6] Charles Altieri, *Painterly Abstraction in Modernist Poetry: The Contemporaneity of Modernism* (Cambridge: Cambridge University Press, 1989), 375 (italics mine).

[7] David Hall and Roger Ames captured this spirit very well when they gave their translation the title *Daodejing, Making This Life Significant*. As they put it, "[T]he defining purpose of the *Daodejing* is bringing into focus and sustaining a productive disposition that allows for the fullest appreciation of those specific things and events that constitute one's field of experience." See David Hall and Roger Ames, trans., *Daodejing, "Making This Life Significant": A Philosophical Translation* (New York: Ballantine Books, 2003), 11.

[8] See Akira Iriye, *Global and Transnational History: The Past, Present, and Future* (London: Palgrave Macmillan, 2013), 30.

[9] Rana Mitter, "Modernity," in *The Palgrave Dictionary of Transnational History*, ed. Akira Iriye and Pierre-Yves Saunier (London: Macmillan, 2009), 720–22.

[10] These facts are taken from Reiun's memoir, *Sakkiden* [A record of misfortune] (hereafter cited as *SD*), in Nishida Masaru, comp., *Taoka Reiun zenshû* (hereafter cited as *TRZ*), 5:415–743 (Tokyo: Hôsei daigaku shuppankyoku, 1969–2013; see the reference to Japan as a police state on pp. 685–87.

[11] See Maruyama Masao, "Chûsei to hangyaku," in *Kindai Nihon shisôshi kôza*[Lectures on Modern Japanese Intellectual History](Tokyo: Chikuma shobô, 1951), 377–471. A recent book on Maruyama by Tsuzuki Tsutomu, *Maruyama Masao e no michi annai* (Tokyo: Yoshida shoten, 2013), devotes considerable space to a discussion of this important essay. See especially pp. 171–89. While Tsuzuki does an excellent job of contextualizing the essay, he does not mention Maruyama's "take" on the role of late Meiji intellectuals like Reiun and Tokutomi Rôka.

[12] See Ienaga Saburô, *Sûkinaru shisôka no shôgai: Taoka Reiun no hito to shisô* (The Career of an Unfortunate Thinker: Taoka Reiun, the Person and His Ideas) (Tokyo: Iwanami shoten, 1955.

[13] See especially Nishida Masaru, "Taoka Reiun no tennôseikan" [Taoka Reiun's View of the Emperor System] in *Kindai bungaku no senseiryoku* [The Latent Power of Modern Literature] (Tokyo: Yagi shoten, 1973), 39–51. Takahashi Tadashi summarizes the gist of the Ienaga-Nishida debate in his short biography *Taoka Reiun,* Pamphlet no. 3 (Kôchi: Kôchishiritsu jiyûminken kinenkan tomo no kai, 1994), 46–52.

[14] See Nishida Masaru, *Kindai wa hitei dekiru ka?* [Can we deny the modern?] (Tokyo: Orijin shuppan sentaa, 1993), 26–46. See especially pp. 38–42 for the material on Reiun.

[15] See Mitsuhiro Yoshimoto, *Kurosawa* (Durham, NC: Duke University Press, 2000), 114

[16] Joseph Levenson, *Liang Ch'i-ch'ao and the Mind of Modern China* (Berkeley: University of California Press, 1967), 1.

[17] Ibid., 205.

[18] Ibid., 3.

[19] Marshall Berman, *All That Is Solid Melts into Air: The Experience of Modernity* (New York: Simon and Schuster, 1982), 15.

[20] Anthony Giddens, *Modernity and Self-Identity: Self and Society in the Late Modern Age* (Stanford, CA: Stanford University Press, 1991), 53. *Careering* here means "moving at full speed, especially with an uncontrolled or unsteady motion," and when Giddens returns to elaborate on this metaphor some eighty-five pages later, he offers a definition of *juggernaut* as

> a runaway engine of enormous power which, collectively as human beings, we can drive to some extent but which also threatens to rush out of our control and which could rend itself asunder. The juggernaut crushes those who resist it, and while it

sometimes seems to have a steady path, there are times when it veers away erratically in directions we cannot foresee. The ride is by no means wholly unpleasant or unrewarding; it can often be exhilarating and charged with hopeful anticipation. But so long as the institutions of modernity endure, we shall never be able to control completely either the path or the pace of the journey. In turn, we shall never be able to feel entirely secure, because the terrain across which it runs is fraught with risks of high consequence. Feelings of ontological security and existential anxiety will coexist in ambivalence." (139)

We will see subsequently that many other critics who write on the subject of modernity point to the feelings of ambivalence and uncertainty that accompany it, while Berman writes in terms of the "struggle and contradiction" and "ambiguity and anguish" that modernity elicits. (Berman, *All That is Solid*)

[21] Berman, *All That Is Solid*. Notice how Berman also points to the risks that becoming modern entails, and how in his eyes modernity promises so much on the one hand, but then, with the other hand, threatens to withdraw all that is promised. Indeed, modernity may destroy "all that we have, and all that we are," according to Berman. This is not at all unlike Gidden's metaphor of the juggernaut that may offer a pleasant, even exhilarating ride for part of the time, but ultimately leaves us anxious and ambivalent. In the next chapter, we will see how Berman elaborates on the way modernity betrays so many of its own promises.

Chapter One

[1] Pankaj Mishra, *From the Ruins of Empire: The Revolt against the West and the Remaking of Asia* (London and New York: Penguin Books, 2013), 9.

[2] Both of these adjectives were employed by Ienaga Saburô in his biography of Taoka Reiun, *Sûkinaru shisôka no shôgai: Taoka Reiun no hito to shisô* [The Career of an unfortunate thinker: Taoka Reiun, the person and his ideas] (Tokyo: Iwanami shoten, 1955).

[3] See Sho Konishi, *Anarchist Modernity: Cooperatism and Japanese-Russian Intellectual Relations in Modern Japan* (Cambridge, MA: Harvard University Press, 2013), 3–4.

[4] Ibid., 5–6.

[5] See Cemil Aydin, "Japanese Pan-Asianism through the Mirror of Pan-Islamism," in *Tumultuous Decade: Empire, Society, and Diplomacy in 1930s Japan*, ed. Masato Kimura and Tosh Minohara, eds. (Toronto: University of Toronto Press, 2013), 44.

[6] As F. G. Notehelfer points out, there remains considerable "mystery" surrounding the trial that sentenced Kôtoku to be hanged, compounded by the fact that certain court records have never been made public. But it is clear even from Kôtoku's own testimony that he had been interested in "direct action," in creating confusion through acts of violence, in bombing the homes of the wealthy, and in setting fire to downtown Tokyo in the vicinity of the Imperial Palace. Indeed, he even admitted

having discussed harming the emperor himself. But his contention was that by the end of 1909 he had distanced himself from the plot and the plotters and was only interested in pursuing his program of research and writing. Therefore, his affiliation with the plot at the time it was carried out was not direct. Since there was a provision in the Criminal Code (article 43) that allowed for "mitigation" if preparations for a crime were voluntarily abandoned before the crime was carried out, apparently many assumed that Kôtoku would not receive a death sentence. However, as far as it is known, the article 43 provision was never brought up at trial. See F. G. Notehelfer, *Kôtoku Shûsui: Portrait of a Japanese Radical* (Cambridge: Cambridge University Press, 1971), 184.

[7] Quoted from one of nineteen forewards published in the bound version of *SD*, which was originally serialized in the journal *Chûô kôron*. Tokuda's preface is *TRZ* 5: 423.

[8] See the vignette in Kano Masanao, *Kindai kokka o kôsôshita shisôka-tachi* [The intellectuals who shaped the conception of the modern state] (Tokyo: Iwanami Junia shinsho, 2005), 146–51.

[9] Quoted in George Elison, "Kôtoku Shûsui: The Change in Thought," *Monumenta Nipponica* 22:3–4 (1967): 441. For Reiun reading Henry George would come later, sometime in the early 1900s.

[10] *SD*, 662.

[11] See *TRZ 2*, where Reiun writes:

> I loathe these people who manipulate the word *sonnô*—reverence for the emperor—but do their best to implement despotism; I detest those who grab the nation's precious resources and make a mockery out of military heroism in order to further imperialism; I hate these people who would kill others and steal their country just so they can expand their empires. So now my hatred for these enemies of freedom, these enemies of peace, and these enemies of humanity is matched by Kôtoku's; but if there is any slight difference between his views and mine it is that my lamentation of the current popularity of imperialism is not even as great as his!" (204–5)

A recent translation and analysis of Kôtoku's *Imperialism* by Robert Thomas Tierney, *Monster of the Twentieth Century: Kôtoku Shûsui and Japan›s First Anti-imperialist Movement* (Berkeley: University of California Press, 2015), provides excellent background and context for Kôtoku's book. As he notes in his introduction:

> Kôtoku's book was among the first general studies of imperialism to be published anywhere in the world, preceding J.A. Hobson's *Imperialism: A Study* by one year. Unlike Hobson's study and Vladimir Ilyich Lenin's *Imperialism: The Highest Stage of Capitalism* (1916), Kôtoku treats imperialism primarily as a pathology of the nation-state, a 'plague' caused by patriotism and exacerbated by militarism. He also offers the contemporary reader a fresh view of imperialism from the perspective of an observer situated in a peripheral nation then emerging from semicolonial dependency to imperialist world power. (1)

[12] *TRZ*, 2:334–35.

[13] Konishi, *Anarchist Modernity*, 6–12. Konishi's term for this community of likeminded individuals is "cooperatist anarchists."

[14] George Elison notes with regard to Kôtoku, "[H]e had watched the 'Fighting Jiyûtô [Liberal Party]' lose all its combative character and continue in transmogrification to a point of mutual embrace with the oligarchic government. He now turned to socialism in his quest for an energetic, pure force to save society—specifically the society of Japan in the Sino-Japanese War's aftermath—from corruption." Elison, "Kôtoku Shûsui, 442. It was with similar feelings, and in precisely this environment of the postwar period, that Reiun launched his career as a literary critic.

[15] Jason Adams, "Non-western Anarchisms: Rethinking the Global Context," accessed March 2015, http://theanarchistlibrary.org/library/jason-adams-non-western-anarchisms, 4.

[16] Hasan Baku, "Anarchism in Turkey," quoted in ibid., 7.

[17] *SD*, 725. Hereafter quotations from Reiun's autobiography are cited in this form in the text. The formal term for *anarchism* is 無政府主義, or "absence of government"; 無秩序 refers literally to the "absence of order" (秩序), hence notions of confusion, disorder, and anarchy are usually associated with this term.

[18] Adams, "Non-western Anarchisms," 7.

[19] See Sho Konishi, *Anarchist Modernity*, 142–67, where he uses the term *anarchist transnationalism* in relation to Kôtoku's thought.

[20] Bailyn, "The Challenge of Modern Historiography."

[21] Philip Lopate, *To Show and to Tell: The Craft of Literary Nonfiction* (New York and London: Free Press, 2013), 6. Konishi also makes a very important observation when he notes:

> Historians have tended to focus on such prominent academics as representative of "Japanese thought." I suggest, on the contrary, that their writings were relatively isolated within the restricted spaces of the university and upper echelons of the government and had little to do with the thought and knowledge circulating throughout the larger populace. Historians' understanding of "modern Japanese thought" in Euro-America has been based primarily on the writing of academics employed by imperial institutions of higher education for their articulation of political ideologies for the nation-state. Other, much more widely influential voices outside these ideologies have been ignored in the historiography. (*Anarchist Modernity*, 121)

[22] "Reply to [Masaoka] Geiyô," in *TRZ*, 4:457–66. The term he uses is *kyûshiki* (旧式), literally "old-fashioned" or "outdated."

[23] See Kajima Ôkan's foreword to *SD*, 440.

[24] See the reference in Ienaga, *Sûkinaru shisôka no shôgai*, ii–iii. Other historians, such as Irokawa Daikichi and Kano Masanao, also included a few pages on Reiun in their books on Meiji intellectual history, considering him an antimodernist. In the lead essay in a recent volume celebrating the hundredth anniversary of Ienaga's birth, Professor Kano discussed how important Kant's notion of a moral imperative was to Ienaga during his formative years, from ages nineteen to thirty-three, during which the state dictated the concept of the *kokutai* (national polity) to the populace. Ienaga appreciated the gift that philosophy offered him, allowing him to realize how unacceptable the normalization of this abnormality was. See Kano Masanao, "Ienaga Saburô no gakumon to rekishiksi ninshiki [Ienaga Saburô's scholarship and historical awareness] in *Ienaga Saburô tanjô hyakunen* [On the 100th anniversary of Ienaga Saburô's birth], ed. Jikkô-iinkai (Tokyo: Nihon Hyôronsha, 2014), 3–23. Kano noted in his concluding remarks that in the years since Ienaga's death in 2002, the very things he stood for, such as exercising one's conscience and having the capacity to express one's ideas freely, were under a great deal of pressure once again as the conservative revisionists were clamoring to have Japan return to being a state capable of waging war (23).

[25] Marshall Berman, "Why Modernism Still Matters," in *Modernity and Identity*, ed. Scott Lash and Jonathan Friedman (Cambridge, MA: Blackwell, 1992), 33.

[26] It is interesting to note that Reiun was not the only person drawn to the writing of the Daoists. Around the same time that he was undertaking his studies and working with Miyake Setsurei, who was also interested in Daoism and its congruence with Schopenhauer's philosophy, a twenty-six-year-old Russian Orthodox novitiate, Konishi Matsutarô, addressed a rapt audience in Moscow at a meeting of the Moscow Psychological Society on the subject of Laozi's philosophy, which eventually led to a translation of the *Daodejing* into Russian on which he worked closely with Tolstoy. According to Sho Konishi, "The anarchist theology in *Tao te ching* provided for the deconstruction of hierarchies through a moral system that radically overturned conventional notions of virtue and social worth." Konishi Matsutarô told his Russian colleagues that the *Daodejing* "preserved the freedom of individual judgment and responsibility for action, not within a theory of rational existence, but within a theology of universally shared virtue. According to this theology, conscience, the voice of divine Truth, comes naturally from within each individual and gives decisive judgment on every human action. Free human action without unnecessary and restrictive ritual and societal norms thus formed the foundation of the thought in *Tao te ching*." Konishi, *Anarchist Modernity*, 110–11.

[27] See T. J. Jackson Lears, *No Place of Grace: Antimodernism and the Transformation of American Culture, 1880–1920* (New York: Pantheon, 1981), xiii, 7.

[28] Interestingly, antimodernism in America incorporated a fascination with Asian culture, so there is room to think about some overlap with the ideas that Reiun was exploring. However, Reiun was clearly responding to a different set of historical and

230 : THE TURN AGAINST THE MODERN

intellectual circumstances in Japan in the 1890s, so we must be careful to situate his critique appropriately. For one thing, as Lears points out, the United States and Europe were experiencing a second, deeper stage of the Industrial Revolution, but Japan was still in the early stages of the process. In the second stage of industrial growth, it was clear that people were being affected differently: some were advantaged, while others were disadvantaged. Reiun, too, was struck by the spread of economic inequality as a result of industrialization, but one consequence in the West was that the older, powerful Victorian equation of moral and material progress was becoming more difficult to sustain, which partially accounts for the deep-seated doubts and concerns about modernization. Also taking a blow in the West was the myth of the autonomous individual. For it appeared that, as economic rationalism spread throughout society, individuals were less moral thinking people than they were machinelike in their economic response to incentives. See ibid., 8–26. Lears also notes, "The image of the Promethean self-made man was mythic in a double sense: it was part of a world view that provided many Americans with meaning and purpose; and it was false" (18).

[29] Taylor, *Sources of the Self,* 462. Another well-known authority on modernism, Peter Gay, emphasizes how important it was for modernist writers and critics to go against the grain and contest existing social norms and inherited values. He refers to this as "the lure of the heretical," which, along with "a fresh way of valuing works of culture and their makers…[and a] commitment to a principled self-scrutiny," constituted the "two defining attributes" of the process of becoming modern. Peter Gay, *Modernism: The Lure of Heresy from Baudelaire to Beckett and Beyond* (New York: Norton, 2007), 3–4.

[30] In *No Place of Grace*, Lears extends this thought by pointing out, "The older conception of the self had been the foundation of the bourgeois world view; the newer one undermined that foundation at every point. The older conception was solid, the new one insubstantial" (38).

[31] Taylor, *Sources of the Self,* 389 (italics mine). For Taylor the postexpressivist era means the late nineteenth century, after the work of Schopenhauer and others had emptied interiority of the idealized content provided by the romantics.

Chapter Two

[1] Actually, Reiun wrote (*SD*, 491) that he was past his third birthday before he began walking, but this statement was apparently based on a method of age computation that assumes the child is at least nine months old when born. However, Reiun was probably beyond his second birthday when he finally began walking.

[2] Ibid.

[3] For example, it seems that Reiun often wore a kimono made by his aunt from fine material she had obtained during her tenure as an attendant to a court lady

in Kyoto. As a result, he was often better dressed than his older brothers, and this generated some degree of envy. See ibid., 732–33.

⁴ These terms are explained in Marius Jansen, *Sakamoto Ryôma and the Meiji Restoration* (Palo Alto, CA: Stanford University Press, 1971), 25–27.

⁵ *SD*, 485.

⁶ Reiun goes on to explain that this, "sympathy" is what drove him to adopt "a kind of socialism (though organizationally, I was never a part of any socialist group, nor was I formally affiliated with the movement)."(*SD*, 490). The term *sympathy* derives from Schopenhauer's notion of *Mitleid,* which might best be translated as "compassion" or "empathy." It stems from a recognition that every individual has the same inner nature as oneself. Once this truth is acknowledged, it is possible to experience the suffering of others as though it were one's own; in this way, the good, just person intuitively grasps the oneness of everything in the world and will act magnanimously toward others.

⁷ Hirao Michio, *Jiyûminken no keifu* (Kôchi: Kôchi shimin toshokan, 1970), 28.

⁸ Ibid., 31.

⁹ See, for example, Takahashi, *Taoka Reiun,* 2–16.

¹⁰ See also Nishida Masaru, comp., *Taoka Reiun senshû* [Selected works of Taoka Reiun] (hereafter cited as *TRS*) (Tokyo: Aoki Bunko, 1956). For the official statement of this group, see Itagaki Taisuke, comp., *Jiyûtôshi* (Tokyo: Aoki bunko, 1958), 1:250–52.

¹¹ See Nishida's explanatory notes on *Sakkiden* in *TRZ,* 5:807–8.

¹² Quoted in Kenneth Strong's introductory essay to his translation of Christian socialist Kinoshita Naoe's *Pillar of Fire,* UNESCO Collection of Representative Works (London: Allen and Unwin, 1972), 11 (Japanese title *Hi no hashira*See also Itagaki comp.,*Jiyûtôshi,* 2:207. In Nakae Chômin's *Sansuikeirinmondô* (A Discourse by Three Drunkards on Government), which was widely read, the author stakes out various political positions that were found in the political party movements of the day. The position usually associated most closely with Nakae, that of "Master Nankai," incorporates some of the notions that Reiun endorsed, such as rejecting westernization as the sole path available to Japanese, recommending a synthesis between western and ancient Chinese ideas, and believing "in a future in which Japan becomes more democratic while maintaining peace with its neighbors." Tierney, *Monster of the Twentieth Century,* 28–30.

¹³ For more on the Meiji rebels and Reiun's book, see chapter 6.

¹⁴ Reiun encountered Yamagata Isô again when they were both students at Tokyo Bunka Daigaku, and after graduation they cooperated in putting out the literary magazine *Seinenbun,* for which Reiun was the chief critic. See the interview with Yamagata in the appendix to Ienaga, *Sûkinaru shisôka no shôgai,* 195–201.

[15] On Futabatei Shimei, see Marleigh Ryan, *Japan's First Modern Novel: Ukigumo of Futabatei Shimei* (New York: Columbia University Press, 1967), 34–35. For further details on the *kansei-kaikaku*, see Asukai Masamichi, "Hirotsu Ryûrô no shoki," *Jinbungakuhô* 10 (March 1959): 115–32.

[16] On this subject, see Konishi, *Anarchist Modernity*, 73–77. The quotations appear on pp. 74–75.

[17] For a thorough study of Mori Arinori, see Ivan Hall, *Mori Arinori* (Cambridge, MA: Harvard University Press, 1973), especially chapters 9 and 10, 324–466.

[18] See Okuma Shigenobu, comp., *Fifty Years of New Japan*, edited and translated by M. B. Huish, 2 vols. (London: Smith Elder, 1909), 2:94. This scene is also cited in part in Hane Mikiso, "Early Meiji Liberalism: An Assessment," *Monumenta Nipponica* 24:4 (1969): 363.

[19] On Tokutomi Sohô, see Kenneth B. Pyle, *The New Generation in Meiji Japan* (Palo Alto, CA: Stanford University Press, 1969); and John D. Pierson, "The Early Liberal Thought of Tokutomi Sohô," *Monumenta Nipponica* 29:2 (Summer 1974): 199–224.

[20] About nine years later, in 1895, the Min'yûsha would publish a translation of Edward Carpenter's *Civilization: Its Cause and Cure* (London: Swan Sonnenschein, 1891), a book that would have a significant impact on Reiun. It is most likely that Reiun worked with the original English version.

[21] Irokawa Daikichi, *Shimpen Meiji Seishinshi* (Tokyo: Chûô kôronsha, 1973), 481.

Chapter Three

[1] Reiun claimed that the most significant event of his tenure at the school was a brief encounter with Uchimura Kanzô, who was moonlighting at the School of Fisheries teaching a course on anatomy. Reiun recollected being admonished by Uchimura, "Don't be hypocritical!" (*SD*, 550).

[2] For a photograph of the monuments, see figure 7.3.

[3] Pyle, *New Generation,* 188.

[4] Yanagida Izumi, *Nihon kakumei no yogensha: Kinoshita Naoe* (Tokyo: Shinshû, 1961), 9.

[5] Ibid., 10.

[6] Miyake Setsurei, "Yohai-dôshi wa ikanaru shugi o toite ka undô subeki?," *Nihonjin* (September 1888), quoted in Motoyama Yukihiko, "Meiji nijû-nendai no seiron ni arawareta nashionarizumu," in *Meiji zenhanki no nashionarizumu,* ed. Sakata Yoshio (Tokyo; Miraisha, 1958), 58.

[7] See Kano Masanao, "Kokusuika-tachi no kindaika no kôsô: Jiritsuteki henkaku e no mosaku" [The approach of *kokusui* thinkers to modernization: Groping for self-reliant change], in *Nihon kindaika no shisô* (Tokyo: Kenkyûsha, 1972), 73–78.

⁸ Matsuda Michio, "Nihon no chishikijin," in *Kindai Nihon shisôshi kôza*, vol. IV.) Tokyo: Chikuma shobô, 1950), 20–21.

⁹ There is another aspect of the *kokusuishugi* movement that makes Reiun's attraction to it revealing. As Pyle points out, the nationalist group never had the ideological unity or popular reception enjoyed by Tokutomi Sohô's Min'yûsha, the rival group that was so focused on western ideas. Basically the two groups had different constituencies. While Tokutomi was primarily interested in reaching members of the progressive landed gentry class (*inaka-shinshi*), Miyake and Kuga Katsunan of the newspaper *Nihon* often found themselves addressing the less fortunate residents of the more backward economic areas, sometimes referred to *ura Nihon* (backwater Japan). So nationalist publications like *Nihonjin* came to be seen as a voice for those who were being forgotten or ignored by Japan's economic transition, for example, the tea growers and silkworm cultivators of northern Japan who were being adversely affected by economic modernization. For details, see Kano, "Kokusuikatachi no kindaika no kôsô, 76.

¹⁰ For a discussion of the coal-mining situation with particular reference to the problems at the Takashima mine, see Morisue Yoshiaki, Hôgetsu Keigo, and Konishi, Shirô eds. *Seikatsushi* III Vol. 17 of *Taikei Nihonshi sôsho* (Tokyo: Yamakawa shuppansha, 1969), 48–68. For the coverage in *Nihonjin*, see issue 9, August 3, 1887.

¹¹ This article, "Hintenchi Ôkikankutsu tankenki," is reprinted in Nishida Takeyoshi, ed., *Meiji zenki no toshi kasô shakai* [The lower strata of urban society in the early Meiji period] (Tokyo: Kôseikan, 1970), 65–121.

¹² This sort of publicity certainly contributed to Miyake's image as a strong and independent-minded critic who was not afraid to attack the government. It earned him the label among Japanese historians of "out-of-power nationalist" (*zaiya no nashionarisuto*) or "member of the loyal opposition." See Matsumoto Sannosuke, "*Nihon* oyobi *Nihonjin*," *Bungaku* 24:4 (1956): 513–19. Also revealing is Uete Michinari, "*Kokumin no Tomo/Nihonjin*," *Shisô*, no. 453 (March 1962): 112–22, which compares *Nihonjin* to Tokutomi Sohô's *Kokumin no Tomo*. For further treatment, see Waizumi Aki, "*Nihonjin*," *Bungaku* 23:4 (1955): 91–97.

¹³ It is interesting that Maruyama Masao also noted Miyake's staunch opposition to subservience on an individual, personal level, as well as his contempt for what he called *jidaishugi* (lusting after power and office), which endured through the 1920s. Maruyama points out that Miyake urged the youth of the Taishô period to resist and "not submit to the trends of the times" (*jidai shuchô ni kutsuji suru nakare*). Maruyama, "Chûsei to hangyaku,"(455–456).

¹⁴ It is not certain when Reiun first came into contact with Miyake, nor what the precise circumstances surrounding their relationship may have been. However, we can be certain that a personal relationship did exist. See Miyake's foreword in *SD*, 419–20. Until 1888 Miyake had held out hope for the Daidôdanketsu, the coalition

among political parties representing the aspirations of the popular rights movement. But once hopes for this "Grand Alliance" faded and the first Peace Preservation Ordinance (Chian jôrei) went into effect, curtailing freedom of speech and assembly, Miyake began to concentrate more on his writing.

[15] This work is reprinted in Yamamoto Sanehiko, ed., *Miyake Setsurei shû, Kindai Nihon shisôtaikei,* vol. 5 (Tokyo: Chikuma shobô, 1975), 3–56. Here the drive to establish equivalence with the West finds expression in two ways. First, Miyake argued persuasively in the introduction to *Gakan shokei* that while attainment of economic and military parity with the West would require a vast expenditure of energy and resources, scholarship aimed at reasserting the great ideas of the ancient East, equal in value to the West in the realm of thought, could be accomplished with relatively little cost. Second, we might note that the title of Miyake's *Gakan shokei* distinctly conveys the author's intention to express his *own* thoughts about the act of bringing together the two systems of thought of Daoism and Schopenhauer. In particular, the idea behind joining *ga* (我, "self") and *kan* (観, "perception, outlook") points to a new view of the self in relation to the world, as well as the cosmos. In the language of the day, this was a rather unorthodox form of self-assertiveness, something we can presume Reiun admired.

[16] See ibid., 22-30.

[17] Reiun's contributions to this journal are reprinted in *TRZ,* vol. 1. Four issues of *Tôa Zeirin*, probably all that were published, are available at the library of Kyoto Imperial University. Miyake's contribution was on the Han and Wei forms of pronunciation in the ancient Chinese language. See *Tôa Zeirin* 1 (November 1894): 5-7. For a brief description of Miyake's *Tôhô kyôkai,* see Pyle, *New Generation,* 156.

[18] For a brief introduction to the figure and a selection of Reiun's works in translation, see Burton Watson, *Su T'ung-po* (New York: Columbia University Press, 1965). Reiun's essay, "Sotôba," is found in *TRZ,* 1:50–118.

[19] A *kanbun* essay in this context means that the word order and sentence structure are virtually the same as in Chinese. While this essay may well have been the first submitted manuscript for which Reiun was compensated, he had published two articles the previous year in the journal *Ajia* (Asia) and one in the rival of Miyake's *Nihonjin, Kokumin no Tomo,* which were critical of Yamaji Aizan's three-part essay in *Kokumin no Tomo* arguing that the haiku poetry of the Edo era fell short of achieving the "sublime." Reiun strongly disagreed and argued forcefully that in its simplicity and purity haiku poetry by the likes of Bashô, Yuson, and Issa definitely rose to the level of genius found in Shakespeare, and he cited Carlyle in reference to the "sacred mysteries" that could be uncovered in the sublime portrayal of nature. Since Aizan was a Christian, Reiun chided him to the effect that perhaps his "jealous God" did not permit him to see the beauty in works that started from the premise that life is sometimes bleak, often tinged with sadness, and always transitory (*TRZ,* 1:1–16). Nishida points out in his commentary on these earliest essays that Reiun's

debate with Yamaji Aizan preceded by some four months the more famous debate between Aizan and Kitamura Tôkoku in which Tôkoku challenged Yamaji's narrow, utilitarian view of literature and his argument that if literature could not be "useful" to people it was of little value. See chapter 4, note 15, for more details.

[20] "Sôshi no shôyôyû" [Zhuangzi's 'Free and Easy Wandering'] in *TRZ*, 1:191–215.

[21] See Livia Kohn, *Early Chinese Mysticism: Philosophy and Soteriology in the Taoist Tradition* (Princeton, NJ: Princeton University Press, 1991), 77–80. Kohn suggests that for Guo "the world as it was meant to be, as it would be if we let it go naturally, is entirely perfect. . . . In order to get there, every individual has to forget his or her artificial and culturally defined self" (13). In other words, Guo Xiang, perhaps more than Zhuangzi, was able to posit the realization of a true, authentic self not in isolation from humanity but through immersion in it. One accomplishes everything simply by doing naturally that which one is supposed to do. Kohn notes, "Zhuangzi thus reaches for a mastery over the cosmos, for oneness with the creative forces behind the manifest world. Guo Xiang limits his ideal to a perfect going-along. . . . '[F]ree and easy wandering' is, for Guo Xiang, not freedom without restraint. Rather, he identifies it with 'spontaneous realization,' the perfection of one's nature in the fulfillment of one's duty to society. Guo Xiang, therefore, postulates that freedom is found in doing fully what one has to do" (80).

[22] See Ames and Hall, *Daodejing*, 77. For many translations from the *Daodejing*, I have relied on John C. H. Wu's older but familiar translation, in John C. H. Wu, trans., and Paul Sih, ed., *Lao Tzu/Tao Teh Ching* (New York: St. John's University Press, 1961). This was one of the first versions to print the Chinese characters on the left-hand page and the English rendering on the right. But the newer, more philosophical translations by authors such as Roger Ames and David Hall, Hans Georg-Moeller, Michael LaFargue, and Robert Hendricks often offer richer and more nuanced language. For example, Ames and Hall add something significant when they discuss the etymology of the character for *Dao* (道) as it is used in the text for it is not really a noun meaning "the Way" as much as it is a "gerundive, processional, dynamic" word that they render as "way-making." As they put it, "At its most fundamental level, *dao*, seems to denote the active project of 'moving ahead in the world,' of 'forging a way forward,' of 'road building.' Hence, our neologism: 'way-making'" (56). Therefore, they render the opening lines of the text as "Way-making (*dao*) that can be put into words is not really way-making. / And naming (*ming*) that can assign fixed reference to things is not really naming" (77). They suggest that there is something more at stake here, and it is beyond the reach of language. They write, "We will argue that the defining purpose of the *Daodejing* is bringing into focus and sustaining a productive disposition that allows for the fullest appreciation of those specific things and events that constitute one's field of experience. The project, simply put, is to get the most out of what each of us is: a quantum of unique experiences. It is making this life significant" (11).

236 : THE TURN AGAINST THE MODERN

²³ The "mysteries of all things" is how Ames and Hall render 妙 in *Daodejing* (77). They also point to the three *wu* forms as very important in Daoism: *wuwei* (無為), *wuzhi* (無知), and *wuyu* (無欲), meaning, "respectively, noncoercive actions in accordance with the *de* of things; a sort of knowing without resort to rules or principles; and desiring which does not seek to possess or control its 'object'" (38).

²⁴ In *Daodejing,* Ames and Hall provide this notion of the "swinging gateway" in order to capture the idea that in Daoism "there is no appeal to a static vision of a reality or a mind that passively mirrors it. It offers a wholly transactional relationship between a world-making heart-and-mind and a heart-and-mind-shaping world. In this process, we tap the indeterminate aspect of our experience to think and speak a novel world into being" (78–79). The *Encyclopedia of Chinese Philosophy* has a very succinct way of explaining the qualities of the Dao: "*Dao* is thus the process in which the whole of nature manifests itself and the process in which and by which things are created or procreated and nature is manifested. The process is the way, and the way is the process." Chung-ying Cheng, "Dao (Tao): The Way," in *Encyclopedia of Chinese Philosophy,* ed. Antonio S. Cua (New York: Routledge, 2003), 203. Process is very central to Ames and Hall's interpretation as well. They note that in the *Daodejing*: "Experience is processual, and thus always provisional. Process requires that the formational and functional aspects of our experience are correlative and mutually entailing. Our new thoughts shape how we think and act. And how we are presently disposed to think and act disciplines our novel thoughts. While the fluid immediacy of experience precludes the possibility of exhaustive conceptualization and explanation, enduring formal structures lend the flow of experience a degree of determinacy that can be expressed productively in conceptual language. The relative persistence of formal structures permits us to parse and punctuate the ceaseless flow of experience into consummate yet never really discrete things and events." That is why "The Dao that can be talked about is not the true Dao" or the Dao that can be named is never quite the complete or true Dao; a "fixed reference to things" can never be firmly established. Ames and Hall, *Daodejing,* 77–78.

²⁵ As Michael LaFargue expresses it, the first verse of the *Daodejing* needs to be read as an argument against overreliance on the "naming" of things because events and concepts need to be "understood in direct experience rather than grasped through concepts ('names')." Michael LaFargue, *The Tao of the Tao Te Ching: A Translation and Commentary* (New York: State University of New York Press, 1992), 95.

²⁶ Kohn, *Early Chinese Mysticism,* 55.

²⁷ Ames and Hall, *Daodejing,* 78. .The authors take full advantage of recent archaeological and textual discoveries at Mawangdui and Guodian to offer fresh insights. At the end of chapter 10 they render 玄德 as "the profoundest efficacy" because, beyond the notions of "virtue" and "power" that are usually associated with the word *de,* it also has to do with process and efficacy. As they note in their

glossary, "Recognizing the meaning-creating and meaning-disclosing power of the cultivated human being, the *Daodejing* emphasizes the way in which this personal articulation extends beyond the human community into appreciating the cosmos itself. Those of 'highest efficacy' (*shangde*, 上德) as paragons of achieved excellence have cosmological significance in maximizing the symbiotic relationship between the human experience and the context within which that drama unfolds" (61).

[28] See Ames and Hall, *Daodejing*, 94–95. LaFargue, in *The Tao of the Tao Te Ching*, includes for this passage the following gloss: "What is the source of the great damage done to me? It is because I have a self" (40). He believes that chapter 13 should be grouped with other chapters "that speak of the desire for fame or wealth as mentally agitating and so 'damaging' to our being" (41).

[29] Wu and Sih, *Lao Tzu/Tao Teh Ching*, 7.

[30] Ames and Hall, *Daodejing*, 83.

[31] Wu and Sih, *Lao Tzu/Tao Teh Ching*, 9.

[32] Ibid., 13. "Virtue," of course, is the *de* (德) of the *Daodejing*, which Ames and Hall prefer to think of as "efficacy" rather than the standard translation of "virtue" because "*De* encompasses both participating agency and its effects." They note, "It is this process of focusing *de* that, for the human being, generates cognitive, moral, aesthetic, and spiritual meaning." Ames and Hall, *Daodejing*, 60.

[33] Wu and Sih, *Lao Tzu/Tao Teh Ching*, 17–19.

[34] Ibid., 81. As a further example of how the Ames and Hall translation in *Daodejing* offers deeper philosophical insights, note their comment in this chapter, "While maintaining one's particular integrity, one comes together with other things in relationships that have no sharp edges or tangles. In this equilibrium between integrity and integration, between insistent particularity and the coordination of the shared creative opportunities that emerge, the optimization of the process of experience, like a most elegant dance or like the most remarkable bronze, precludes the possibility of adding or taking away from it. It is simply right" (165).

[35] For more on the Taiji diagram, see Joseph A. Adler, "On Translating *Taiji*," in David Jones and Jinli He, eds., *Rethinking Zhu Xi: Emerging Patterns within the Supreme Polarity* (Albany: State University of New York Press, 2015), 51–81.

[36] *TRZ*, 1:231–32.

[37] Also Descartes makes the comment in his *Meditations* II that "I have fallen unexpectedly into a deep *whirlpool* which tumbles me around so that I can neither stand on the bottom nor swim to the top," which points to the recurrent nature of this feeling of being in a storm or maelstrom that accompanies the modern condition. John Cottingham, Robert Stoothoff, and Douglas Murdoch, trans., *The Philosophical Works of Descartes*, (Cambridge: Cambridge University Press, 1984), 16, italics mine. The quote is also found in Anthony J. Cascardi, *The Subject of*

Modernity (Cambridge: Cambridge University Press, 1992), 58. It is certainly a fair point to note that the individual subject was thought about differently in classical Chinese philosophy than in modern (post-Descartian) western philosophy. Most ancient Chinese texts would not be thinking first about a fully independent, autonomous individual; rather, they would be more likely to conceive of personhood as developing in an individual who is integrated into the forces that surround and structure life, including family, community, society, rulers, war, the cosmos, and so on. Individuals are definitely granted the freedom to make decisions for themselves in classical Chinese thought and to shape the course of their own lives to the degree to which they are capable. But the ideal would be a picture of someone realizing his or her authentic, genuine nature within the context of a larger, more complex environment.

[38] *TRZ*, 1:209–10.

[39] See Reiun's "Zhuangzi's Free and Easy Wandering," in *TRZ*, 1:208–10. Later, in 1904, Reiun would write a very brief piece about the relationship between Shingon—the Japanese esoteric sect of Buddhism—and the Brahmanical tradition ("Shingon to Baramon," in TRZ, 3:139–40), which opens with an epigraph from the *Bhagavad Gita* ("to become centered and to still the mind is to unite individual consciousness with the ultimate self, the Absolute"), and he goes on to stress the significance of the fact that when the Chinese monk Huanzang (Genjô in Japanese) (602–64) traveled extensively in India and brought back the texts of many sutras, it enabled him to develop the Yogācāra school of Buddhism and also to generate the definitive version of the Heart Sutra. In doing so, he inevitably incorporated some of the great wisdom from the Brahmanical tradition in India, namely, the "Prajna-Paramita" doctrine—"the point where subject and object no longer exist"—cited by Schopenhauer in the final lines of his *The World as Will and Representation,* ed. Judith Norman, Alistair Welchman, and Christopher Janaway (Cambridge: Cambridge University Press), 2010 (hereafter cited as *WWR/2010*): "[T]o those in whom the will has turned and denied itself, this very real world of ours with all its suns and galaxies, is—nothing" (1:412).

[40] See chapter 31 (the penultimate verse) of Red Pine, *The Diamond Sutra: The Perfection of Wisdom*, text and commentaries translated from Sanskrit and Chinese by Red Pine (Washington, DC: Counterpoint, 2001), 419–27. I have relied on an online version called "The Diamond Sutra: A New Translation," accessed June 2015, http://www.diamond-sutra.com/index.html.

[41] *TRZ*, 1:210.

[42] Ibid., 215.

[43] Ibid., 212–13 (至人無己，神人無功，聖人無名). Liezi is thought to have been a historical figure from the fourth century BCE, although it is also the name of an early Daoist text that offers interpretations of Zhuangzi.

44 See Kohn, *Early Chinese Mysticism*, 54–58.

45 As Sophia Vasalou expresses it, the legacy Schopenhauer claimed from Kant was his understanding that "contrary to traditional philosophical understanding, it was not our knowledge that conformed to objects, but objects to our knowledge. Properties that had formerly been ascribed to things themselves and to realities outside our minds—such as time and space—in fact constituted nothing but the forms of our knowledge and the conditions of our experience." Sophia Vasalou, *Schopenhauer and the Aesthetic Standpoint: Philosophy as a Practice of the Sublime* (Cambridge: Cambridge University Press, 2013), 9.

46 See *WWR/1969*, 1:404–5. As he says at the end of this passage, "Behind our existence lies something else that becomes accessible to us only by our shaking off of the world" (405).

47 Stephen Cross, *Schopenhauer's Encounter with Indian Thought: Representation and Will and Their Indian Parallels* (Honolulu: University of Hawai'i Press, 2013), 222–23.

48 See Urs App, "Schopenhauer and China: A Sino-Platonic Love Affair," *Sino-Platonic Papers*, no. 200 (April 2010): 1–160. Available in .pdf format.

49 Iriye, *Global and Transnational History*, 31.

50 "Haikaikaneken," and "Bashô," TRZ 1:124-128; and 175-190 respectively

51 *TRZ*, 1:184–85.

52 Quoted in *TRZ*, 1:180. See also *WWR/1969*, 1:251, where the same quote appears. This kind of declaration, of course, is a classic expression of the romantic outlook that, as John B. Halstead notes, "tended to distrust calculation and stressed the limitations of scientific knowledge. It was held that the rational counters of scientific abstraction fail to apprehend the variety and fullness of reality, and the process of rational analysis destroys the integrity of naïve experience of the stress of sensation and in this violation misleads the knower into error." Also it is pointed out that romantics believed that "men could learn not just through experiment and induction, or by logical processes, but in intuitive flashes, by trusting their instincts." John B. Halstead, ed., *Romanticism* (New York: Harper and Row, 1969), 13.

53 *TRZ*, 1:185. The translation is from Yuasa Nobuyuki, *Bashô: "The Narrow Road to the Deep North" and Other Travel Sketches* (Middlesex: Penguin, 1966), 33.

54 *TRZ*, 1:177–78.

55 This is the precise argument that Reiun made to Yamaji Aizan, who did not believe that haiku could achieve the "sublime." See note 19.

56 *TRZ*, 1:124–28.

57 *WWR/1969*, 1:185–86.

58 See ibid., 375–78, where we find: "[W]hat can move [people] to good deeds

and to works of affection is always only *knowledge of the suffering of others*, directly intelligible from one's own suffering, and put on a level therewith." (375). As he talked about what he meant by the word *compassion* or *Mitleid*, Schopenhauer explained in *On the Basis of Morality*, "It is, what we see every day, the phenomenon of Compassion (*Mitleid*) in other words, the direct participation, independent of all ulterior considerations, in the sufferings of another, leading to sympathetic assistance in the effort to prevent or remove them; whereon in the last resort all satisfaction and all well-being and happiness depend. It is this Compassion alone which is the real basis of all voluntary justice and all genuine loving-kindness. Only so far as an action springs therefrom, has it moral value; and all conduct that proceeds from any other motive whatever has none. When once compassion is stirred within me, by another's pain, then his weal and woe go straight to my heart, exactly in the same way, if not always to the same degree, as otherwise I feel only my own. Consequently the difference between myself and him is no longer an absolute one." Arthur Schopenhauer, *On the Basis of the Morality* translated by E. F. J. Payne (Indianapolis: Bobbs-Merrill, 1965), 144 (hereafter cited as *OBM*). The language is slightly different here as I prefer Arthur Broderick Bullock's translation, accessed June 2015, http://www.monsalvat.no/mitleid.htm.

[59] *TRZ*, 1:216–36.

[60] *WWR/1969*, 2:613.

[61] Ibid., 1:332.

[62] *TRZ*, 1:219–20.

[63] Ibid., 220.

[64] Ibid., 221–22.

[65] Wu and Sih, *Lao Tzu/Tao Teh Ching*, 17–18. Ames and Hall render the final lines in a more literal and direct fashion: "Hold tightly onto way-making in the present / To manage what is happening right now / And to understand where it began in the distant past. / That is what is called the drawstring of way-making" (*Daodejing*, 96).

[66] Wu and Sih, *Lao Tzu/Tao Teh Ching*, 29. Ames and Hall render the last lines as "Though nebulous and dark / There are seminal concentrations of *qi* within it / These concentrations of *qi* are authentic / And have within them true credibility" (*Daodejing*, 107). It is interesting that the romanized term *qi* is used, for the character 精 is usually read as *jing*.

[67] *TRZ*, 1:226. See Milton K. Munitz, *Cosmic Understanding: Philosophy and Science of the Universe* (Princeton, NJ: Princeton University Press, 1986), where, like Daoists, he sees two dimensions to reality: one is knowable but the other, much like the Dao, is beyond intelligibility. Munitz refers to this unknowable entity as "Boundless Existence" and sees it, like the Dao, as "not anything that rational thought can comprehend, for it has no internal structure of its own" and is not reducible, so it "cannot be analyzed into anything more simple or fundamental. He adds, "To

become aware of Boundless Existence is a level of human experience unlike any other" (274–75). While there is no indication that Munitz read any Daoists texts, if he had he certainly would have experienced a deep resonance.

[68] Emanuel Swedenborg (1688–1772) was a quintessential man of science, an engineer, working mineralogist, and student of human physiology. However, he had a religious experience midway through his life and became a mystic. D. T. Suzuki dubbed him "The Buddha of the North." See Devin Zuber, "The Buddha of the North: Swedenborg and Transpacific Zen," *Religion and the Arts* 14 (2010): 1–33. Jakob Böhme (1575–1624) was a German Christian mystic influenced by neo-Platonism and the Greek philosopher Paracelsus.

[69] *TRZ*, 1:226–27.

[70] Quoted in Ibid., 223.

[71] Ibid., 233–34.

[72] Ibid., 232–33. Ames and Hall translate this line from chapter 28 as "As a river gorge to the world, / You will not lose your real potency (*dé*), / And not losing your real potency, / You return to the state of a newborn babe" (120).

[73] See Bryan Magee, *The Philosophy of Schopenhauer* (Oxford: Oxford University Press, 1983), quoted in David E. Cartwright, "Compassion and Solidarity with Sufferers: The Metaphysics of *Mitleid*," in *Better Consciousness: Schopenhauer's Philosophy of Value*, ed. Alex Neil and Christopher Janaway (London: Wiley-Blackwell, 2009), 147.

[74] See Cartwright, "Compassion and Solidarity," 151. The Janaway reference is to his *Self and World in Schopenhauer* (Oxford: Clarendon Press, 1989).

[75] *TRZ*, 1:231. Hans-Georg Moeller uses the term *impulses* in his interpretation of Daoism in *The Philosophy of the Daodejing* (New York: Columbia University Press, 2006), 134–36. He believes that the notion of making distinctions, of having likes and dislikes, is what makes us human but the Daoist sage is not governed by these impulses. "The Daoist sage is," he writes, "the only human who is free from human vanity, free from the impulse to determine what is right and what is wrong—and this can be understood in any sense: aesthetically, morally, emotionally, 'scientifically.' The sage is the only human who has no desire to prefer, for instance, the beautiful over the ugly, to label this as good and that as evil, to find dying emotionally more disturbing than living, to deem one opinion correct and another as incorrect. This does not mean that Daoist sages would deny these human distinctions, but they do not 'inwardly wound their persons' with them" (135–36).

[76] *TRZ*, 1:129–74.

[77] See Odagiri Hideo, "Taoka Reiun: Meiji shakai to no tairitsu," in *Nihon no shisôka*, ed. Asahi Jyanaru, 2:127–44. Tokyo: Asahi Shinbunsha, 1963.

[78] *TRZ*, 1:129–30. The quote from Schopenhauer, in German, is from *WWR/1969*, vol. 1, book 4, paragraph 56, 310.

⁷⁹ The reference is to Eduard von Hartmann (1842–1906). See Dennis N. Kenedy Darnoi, *The Unconscious and Eduard von Hartmann* (The Hague: Martinus Nijhoff, 1967). Lears notes, "As early as the 1880s, the unconscious mind had become a common topic of conversation among educated Europeans and Americans. The lay public was fascinated by hypnotic trances and multiple personalities, by any psychiatric experiments revealing a state of mind outside normal waking consciousness. By 1908, a *North American Review* contributor, citing experiments in hypnotism . . . could assert that 'the human self is a much more complex and unstable affair than has generally been supposed . . . Indeed, the self of which man is normally conscious is but a self within a larger self, of which he comes aware only in moments of inspiration, exultation, and crisis.'" Lears, *No Place of Grace*, 38. Von Hartmann's book was extraordinarily popular in Europe and America, and the desire of readers to learn more about the unconscious was one of the trends in European thought that Reiun pronounced profound and significant.

⁸⁰ Some of the German giants of the age, for example, Hegel and Goethe, died in 1831 and 1832. Heine moved to France in 1831 after the July Revolution, where he lived as an expatriate for the next twenty-five years. No doubt, he appealed to Reiun not only because of his deeply romantic disposition but also because he was a misfit and a wanderer, too, someone who never felt at home in his times.

⁸¹ *TRZ*, 1:171.

⁸² Ibid., 172–73.

⁸³ *TRZ,* 1:259-70. See also my essay, "Discovering the Other: The East through the Eyes of the Nineteenth Century West," in *Three Rs: Reading as the aRt of Rumination,* ed. William Duvall, Supplemental Series, no. 2 (Salem, OR: Willamette Journal of the Liberal Arts, 1988), 1–20.

⁸⁴ *TRZ*, 1: 259

⁸⁵ *TRZ*, 1:269–70.

⁸⁶ Ibid., 261.

⁸⁷ It is not exactly clear to which "scholarly conference" Reiun is referring, although it may be to the First International Congress of Psychology, which happened to feature a number of special sessions on mental telepathy and hypnotism. The World's Fair, or Exposition Universelle, at which the Eiffel Tower was unveiled, was also held in Paris in 1889. There were exhibitions of indigenous cultures in European colonies, but this does not seem likely to be the conference to which Reiun was referring, although it is possible that meetings held in conjunction with the Exposition dealt with the themes that most interested him. An International Congress of Orientalists also took place in 1889, but that meeting was held in Stockholm. Another possibility is the well-known 1893 World's Parliament of Religions, which was held in Chicago on the shore of Lake Michigan and occurred very close to the time in which Reiun was writing his essay. It was the largest

and most spectacular event of its kind, marking the first time that representatives of eastern and western spiritual traditions had gathered to conduct a serious interreligious dialogue on a global scale. Reportedly the Hindu monk Swami Vivekananda mesmerized the five thousand assembled delegates and left a lasting impact. For details, see the website "Parliament of the World's Religions" at http://people.bu.edu/wwildman/bce/worldparliamentofreligions1893.htm.(Acessed April 12, 2016)

[88] The Letourneau reference is likely to the French anthropologist and physician who authored such books as *Property: Its Origin and Development* (1892), and *Evolution of Marriage and Family* (1900). I was unable to locate the original for either this quotation or the one from Zola, so these are my retranslations from the Japanese.

[89] Sheila Rowbotham, the biographer of Edward Carpenter, writes, "Despite the efforts of A. P. Sinnett to elevate their profile, the Theosophists retained many of the features of a sect, sporadically blighted by bitter internal feuds over who held the truth and embarrassing sexual scandals." Sheila Rowbotham, *Edward Carpenter: A Life of Liberty and Love* (London: Verso, 2008), 150.

[90] Stephen Batchelor, *The Awakening of the West: The Encounter of Buddhism and Western Culture* (Berkeley, CA: Parallax Press, 1994), 270.

[91] Ibid., 270–71.

[92] Ibid.

[93] With regard to Steiner, there are further interesting connections to topics that engaged Reiun. He was an Austrian philosopher and educator—and the founder of the Waldorf Schools, still thriving today—who was also very interested in spiritualism and esoteric teachings. Believing that science and spiritualism could work effectively together, he founded an esoteric spiritual movement called anthrosophy. After studying science and mathematics at the Vienna Institute of Technology, he worked as an editor on Goethe's archives in Weimar, as well as on compilations of Schopenhauer's complete works, and eventually earned a PhD in philosophy, writing his dissertation on Fichte's concept of the ego. When his dissertation was published as a book, he dedicated it to Eduard von Hartmann, whose work influenced Reiun. Due to space limitations in this study, I have not been able to include an extensive discussion of von Hartmann's work, *The Philosophy of the Unconscious*, although Reiun had clearly read it and quoted it frequently. Steiner was an active member of the Theosophical Society, was appointed by Annie Besant to lead the German branch in 1902, and adapted many of their ideas to his own evolving thought system. He is also known for practicing biodynamic agriculture and organic farming. He was a social and political progressive who was later attacked by Hitler and the Nazi party and accused of being Jewish, probably because he had supported Émile Zola's stance in the Dreyfus Affair. For biographical data on Steiner, see http://www.rsarchive.org/RSBio.php. Accessed June 2016.

94 Quoted in Terence Brown, *The Life of W. B. Yeats: A Critical Biography* (Malden, MA: Blackwell, 1999), 32–33. In what is often considered the classic poetic statement about the modern condition, Yeats wrote in "The Second Coming," the following oft-quoted lines: "Turning and turning in the widening gyre / The falcon cannot hear the falconer; / Things fall apart; the centre cannot hold," alluding to the turmoil, the "maelstrom," the nightmare that confronts modern humanity. Richard Ellmann, another Yeats biographer, notes that Theosophy gave Yeats "a system of arcane correspondences and symbols, establishing interrelationships between parts of the body, the seasons, colours, elements, and the like, giving the naked universe a garment at once mystical and personal. It inspired him, too, to go to [Jakob] Böhme and [Emanuel] Swedenborg for further study." Richard Ellmann, *Yeats: The Man and The Masks* (London: Faber and Faber, 1961), 67.Of course, as we have seen, Reiun, too, was drawn to the writings of Böhme and Swedenborg.

95 A. P. Sinnett, *Esoteric Buddhism* (London: Trübner, 1883), 44. We will see in chapter 5 that when one of the most influential figures on Reiun, Edward Carpenter, was at Cambridge, *Esoteric Buddhism* was being widely read and discussed.

96 A. P. Sinnett, *The Occult World* (London: Trübner, 1883), 8.

97 Note how Yeats expressed his fascination: "The mysteries never were, never can be, put within the reach of the general public . . . [for] the adept is the rare efflorescence of a generation of enquiries; and to become one, he must obey the inward impulses of his soul, irrespective of the prudential considerations of worldly science or sagacity." Quoted in Brown, *Life of W. B. Yeats,* 34.

98 Edwin Arnold, *The Light of Asia,* 149–55, PDF downloaded from http://www.buddhanet.net/pdf_file/lightasia.pdfFebruary 2012.,

99 See Urs App, *Schopenhauer's Compass: An Introduction to Schopenhauer's Philosophy and Its Origins* (Wil, Switzerland: University Media, 2014), 238.

100 See Eduard von Hartmann, *Philosophy of the Unconscious* (London: Routledge and Kegan Paul, 1950), 1:251–57. See also Darnoi, *The Unconscious and Eduard von Hartmann*, especially 46–51. Von Hartmann set for himself a most difficult task. As Darnoi points out, "In his natural proclivities, in his innermost self, he is an idealist, but, at the same time, he cannot detach himself completely from the taints of materialism which played a decisive role in the formation of the culture of the nineteenth and early twentieth centuries." He saw it as "his historically appointed task to bridge the chasm between idealism with its neglect of reality, and the empirical sciences, with their scorn for any immaterial absolute. In the sublimated unity of the two lay the foundation of a new philosophy of culture" (166). Most critics feel that this "sublimated unity" never worked, but it certainly exemplifies the point Charles Taylor makes about the legacy of the conflict between the instrumentalist view of the world or society and the idealist one. He sees that "the idea of the creative imagination, as it sprang up in the Romantic era, is still central to modern culture." We still look to art, literature, and poetry to

be "epiphantic," by which Taylor means that "this notion of a work of art as the locus of a manifestation which brings us into the presence of something which is otherwise inaccessible, and which is of the highest moral or spiritual significance; a manifestation, moreover, which also defines or completes something, even as it reveals." Taylor, *Sources of the Self*, 419. It is not only that great art may make us feel a certain way: it reveals truth to us, it initiates us into truth so that, as Taylor expresses it, it "completes something, even as it reveals." On Taylor's use of the term *epiphany*, see Nicholas Smith, *Charles Taylor: Meaning, Morals, and Modernity* (Cambridge: Polity Press, 2002), where he explains, "The epiphany articulates a sense of reality which at once makes the reality more intensely or more concretely manifest. . . . [A]nd in this sense there is something ineradicably 'subjective' about an epiphany. Inwardness or interiority is not an object of scientific discovery: on the contrary, the scientific attitude of disengagement and objectification denatures this realm" (230). This seems to be precisely the point that Reiun tries to bring to his readers' attention throughout his critical project: the gaze of the instrumentalist worldview, of the disengaged scientific observer, will not suffice if literature or art is to expose us and bring us into contact with the higher and deeper realms of the human experience. Reiun consistently spoke up for literature's need to make that which is inaccessible to ordinary perception more real, more manifest, more concrete, and that is why he constantly sounded the refrain that the twentieth century was the time to transcend the limitations of a narrow, objective, instrumentalist view based on "reason" and proceed to embrace a more subjective view, one that grows directly from the individual's subjectivity.

[101] The classic accounts of Schopenhauer as a pessimist can be found in earlier works such as V. J. McGill's *Schopenhauer: Pessimist and Pagan,* published in 1931 and reprinted by Haskell House in 1971; and Frederick Copleston, *Arthur Schopenhauer, Philosopher of Pessimism* (London: Burns, Oaks and Washburne, 1947). In the 1960s, writers such as Patrick Gardiner tried to get away from this restrictive approach. See his *Schopenhauer* (Middlesex, UK: Penguin Books, 1968). Also Dorthea Dauer did a very credible job in her *Schopenhauer as a Transmitter of Buddhist Ideas* (Berne: Lang, 1969), although it was not widely distributed. However, it has really been in the last twenty-five years that many new and much more nuanced studies of Schopenhauer's philosophy have become available. These include Eric von der Luft, ed., *Schopenhauer: New Essays in Honor of His 200th Birthday* (Lewiston, NY: Edwin Mellen Press, 1988); Janaway, *Self and World*; Arthur Hübscher, *The Philosophy of Schopenhauer in Its Intellectual Context: Thinker against the Tide*, trans. Joachim T. Baer and David E. Humphrey (Lewiston, NY: Edwin Mellen Press, 1989); Rüdiger Safranski's classic biography, translated from the German, *Schopenhauer and the Wild Years of Philosophy* (Cambridge, MA: Harvard University Press, 1990); Dale Jacquette, ed., *Schopenhauer, Philosophy, and the Arts* (Cambridge, UK: Cambridge University Press, 1996. Dale Jacquette, *The Philosophy of Schopenhauer* (Chesham, UK: Acumen, 2005); Christopher Janaway, ed., *The Cambridge Companion to Schopenhauer* (Cambridge: Cambridge University

Press, 1999); Paul F. H. Lauxtermann, *Schopenhauer's Broken World-View: Colours and Ethics between Kant and Goethe* (Dordrecht: Kluwer Academic, 2000); R. B. Marcine, *In Search of Schopenhauer's Cat: Arthur Schopenhauer's Quantum-Mystical Theory of Justice* (Washington, DC: Catholic University of America Press, 2006); Gerard Mannion, *Schopenhauer, Religion, and Morality: The Humble Path to Ethics* (Farnham, UK: Ashgate, 2003); Steven Neeley, *Schopenhauer: A Consistent Reading* (Lewiston, NY: Edwin Mellen Press, 2004); Alex Neil and Christopher Janaway, eds., *Better Consciousness: Schopenhauer's Philosophy of Value* (London: Wiley-Blackwell, 2009); Neil Jordan, *Schopenhauer's Ethics of Patience: Virtue, Salvation, and Value* (New York: Edwin Mellen Press, 2010); David E. Cartwright, *Schopenhauer: A Biography* (Cambridge: Cambridge University Press, 2010); Robert Wicks, *Schopenhauer's "The World as Will and Representation": A Reader's Guide* (London: Continuum, 2011); and Bart Vandenabeele, ed., *A Companion to Schopenhauer* (Malden, MA.: Wiley-Blackwell, 2012). Three quite recent and very impressive studies of Schopenhauer are Cross, *Schopenhauer's Encounter*; Vasalou, *Schopenhauer and the Aesthetic Standpoint*; and App, *Schopenhauer's Compass*. I did not encounter Cross's book until rather late in the process of preparing this book, but I found his work extremely thorough and helpful, especially given the fact that he can work with original texts in both German and Sanskrit.

[102] Arthur Schopenhauer, *The World as Will and Representation,* edited by Judith Norman, Alistair Welchman, and Christopher Janaway (Cambridge: Cambridge University Press, 2010), 1:viii (hereafter cited as *WWR/2010*). It is interesting to note what Schopenhauer biographer, Rüdiger Safranski, said in an interview about the timelessness of some of Schopenhauer's ideas: "Schopenhauer came to maturity at a time that I have described as the 'wild years of philosophy'; an intoxicating kaleidoscope of philosophy involving the discovery of the ego and logos that penetrates right through nature. Schopenhauer takes a stand against this high-flying idealism of Fichte, Hegel and the Romantics—reminding us right up to the present day not to overestimate reason. For him, redemption can only be achieved by aesthetically distancing oneself from tumult; a mysticism of negation that follows on from Buddhist teachings. In this timeless sense Schopenhauer is still topical." See Thomas Koster, "'Schopenhauer is Always Topical' An Interview with Rüdiger Safranski" http://cafephilosophy.co.nz/articles/schopenhauer-is-always-topical-an-interview-with-ruediger-safranski/. Accessed on June 26, 2016, Safranski closes the interview with the following comment on Schopenhauer's appeal: "For me, one reason his philosophy is so alluring is that, in literary terms, it is so perfectly presented. Reading Schopenhauer is a great pleasure, an enormously enriching experience. In my view, the beginning part of the second volume of *The World as Will and Representation* is linguistically one of the best pieces of work ever produced by a western philosopher."

[103] See John Gray, *Straw Dogs: Thoughts on Humans and Other Animals* (New York: Farrar, Straus and Giroux, 2003), 42.

[104] See David Cooper, "Schopenhauer and Indian Philosophy," in *A Companion to Schopenhauer*, ed. Bart Vandenabeele (UK: Wiley Blackwell, 2012), 266–79. See especially pp. 268–271 for a discussion of the correspondence between the Four Noble Truths and Schopenhauer's philosophy.

[105] *WWR/1969*, 1:8–9.

[106] Schopenhauer was no doubt familiar with the very serviceable Latin translation of the *Yijing* completed by three Jesuit scholars, which actually circulated in manuscript form for over a century before being published in two volumes in Germany in 1834 and 1839, respectively. See John Minford, *I Ching (Yijing): The Book of Changes*, trans. with an introduction and ,ommentary by John Minford (New York: Viking, 2014), xxi–xxii.

[107] *WWR/1969*, 1:444 (italics in the original).

[108] Ibid. 445–46. Although Schopenhauer was not necessarily aware of this, there is ample reason to believe in some degree of contact with and influence on Greek philosophy from ancient Indian and Buddhist teachings. Alexander the Great (356–323 BCE) did not invade India until the fourth century BCE, but, since both Socrates and Plato were born shortly after the Buddha's death, there is no reason to think that ideas associated with his and other Indian teachings (the Vedas and Upanishads) had not come to the attention of Greek philosophers.

[109] Stephen Cross makes an excellent point in *Schopenhauer's Encounter with Indian Thought* when he observes that as a conceptual philosopher Schopenhauer had different ideas from those of many Indian writers about what philosophy could and should do: "It can endeavor to tell us *what* the world is in its inner nature—and that is the task that Schopenhauer set for himself—but it cannot go further than this; it cannot tell us *why* the world is or what lies beyond it" (16).

[110] See Urs App, "Schopenhauer's Initial Encounter with Indian Thought," in *Schopenhauer and Indian Philosophy: A Dialogue between India and Germany*, ed. Arati Baruna (New Delhi: Northern Book Centre, 2008), 7–57. See also App, *Schopenhauer's Compass*, where the author writes that Schopenhauer borrowed two volumes of *Asiatiches Magazin* from the Weimar ducal library on Dec. 4, 1813. Though he usually resituated books expeditiously, he kept these volumes for almost four months . . . [and] on March 26 of 1814 Schopenhauer went to the ducal library in Weimar and borrowed Anquetil's two large volumes along with Colonel Polier's *Mythologie des Indous*. He returned both books on May 18, 1814 prior to his departure for Dresden. Two weeks later, on June 8, the *Oupnek'hat* is listed as Schopenhauer's first book borrowing from the Dresden library and we can assume that around the return date (July 21) Schopenhauer had purchased his copy that has fortunately been preserved with all of his markup." (176–81)

[111] See Cartwright, *Schopenhauer*, 266–67. Cartwright relies on the pioneering archival research of App's "Schopenhauer's Initial Encounter.".

[112] See Urs App, "Arthur Schopenhauer and China: A Sino-Platonic Love Affair," ed. Victor Mair, Sino-Platonic Papers, no. 200, http://www.sino-platonic.org/complete/spp200_schopenhauer.pdf, 35. Accessed August 2011. Appendix 2 of this article includes all of Schopenhauer's notes on volumes 1–9 of *Asiatick Researches* (see pp. 81–101). Since the 1820s, Asia-related journals had been proliferating, and the volume of information about Asia's religions was exploding. Schopenhauer was an avid reader of such publications and learned, for example, to identify the cardinal virtues of the Chinese. In volume 22 (1826) of the *Asiatic Journal and Monthly Register for British India and Its Dependencies,* one of the most important sources of orientalist information, he found an unsigned article entitled "Chinese Theory of the Creation" from which he jotted down two excerpts in his 1828 notebook.

[113] Quoted in App, *Schopenhauer's Compass*, 4. It is fascinating to me that when I began to study Reiun's writing in the 1970s and needed to educate myself on the place of Arthur Schopenhauer in the history of philosophy, there was no more than a handful of works in English on Schopenhauer and several were from the 1930s. Today, as noted above, there is a burgeoning interest in Schopenhauer with over a dozen monographs having appeared in just the last decade or so.

[114] See Arthur Schopenhauer, *Parerga and Paralipomena: Short Philosophical Essays*, trans. E. F. J. Payne, 2 vols. (Oxford: Clarendon, 1974), 2:396–97. This quotation can also be found in J. J. Clarke, *Oriental Enlightenment: The Encounter between Asian and Western Thought* (London: Routledge, 1997), 68. It is an interesting sidenote that apparently neither Anquetil-Duperron nor Schopenhauer was aware that Prince Dara Shukoh (1615–59), who oversaw the translation of the Upanishads from Sanskrit to Persian, was not providing a direct translation from Sanskrit but rather an overview with a commentary that he added, mixing it in with the actual translations from the original so that the reader would not know where the translation left off and the commentary, by eighth-century theologian Śamkara, for example, began. It is now clear that Prince Dara's deep engagement with Sufism provided an interpretive overlay to his version of the Upanishads. Given this, Stephen Cross poses the very legitimate question of how reliable Anquetil-Duperron's translation is. He draws on the work of Indian scholar B. J. Hasrat, who, "after comparing the Sanskrit texts of the major Upanishads," declares them "faithful to the original, 'simple and unaffected' in style, and nowhere [trying] to take liberties with the texts it translates." Perhaps more to the point, drawing on the German scholar Paul Deussen's work on the Upanishads, Cross maintains that Deussen's cannot "quarrel with Schopenhauer's own assessment that in spite of being a double translation, Anquetil-Duperron's text provided him with a source for philosophical and religious thought of Hindu India that was much superior to any other available during his lifetime." Cross, *Schopenhauer's Encounter*, 34–38. So it is safe to say that, despite the peculiarities of the text with which Anquetil-Duperron

worked, it did provide a solid and reliable introduction to the ideas contained in the Upanishads.

[115] See *Schopenhauer's Compass*. Oddly enough, no scholar until Urs App's recent work has actually looked at Schopenhauer's copy of the Duperron translation where one can see his underlines and margin notes, something that convinces App that the influence from Anquetil's work on Schopenhauer was decisive.

[116] App, *Schopenhauer's Compass*, 181. App also elaborates on Dara's understanding: "Since his youth, Prince Dara had been in search of this all-oneness. He had, under the guidance of Sufi masters and with the help of various techniques of meditation and breath control, attempted to understand it not just intellectually but to realize it essentially. . . . Everything turns around the overcoming of illusory multiplicity and the awakening of all-oneness" (131). In England, too, in the circles frequented by Carpenter at Cambridge and in the back-to-the-land movement, Plotinus was much discussed as he "provided a route between Plato and Hindu mysticism." Rowbotham, *Edward Carpenter*, 98.

[117] WWR/1969: 428. For the impact of the idea of a "mystical awakening " on Schopenhauer's thought, see App, *Schopenhauer's Compass*, 257. App notes that in 1815 Schopenhauer wrote, "What was and what is? *The will* whose mirror is life, and the *will-free pure subject of knowing* which contemplates the will in this mirror, and in doing so attains salvation." (See Hubscher, ed., *Manuscript Remains* Volume I, 337)

[118] *WWR/1969*, 2:169. It would now appear, thanks to the work of Urs App, that the influence of both the Upanishads and the *Bhagavad Gita* came even earlier and was more important than previously thought. App, *Schopenhauer's Compass*, 178.

[119] App, "Arthur Schopenhauer and China." As App notes, this article gives an account of the Buddha's life, provides the gist of his message, and includes a number of translations from an unidentified Chinese source. The author's full name was Michel-Ange-André le Roux Deshauterayes (1724–95). He was an Arabist and Sinologist who had probably attempted his translations in the 1780s, but they languished until they were published in *Journal Asiatiques* in 1825 under the title "Rescherches sur la religion de Fo." The particular Chinese text on which he based his translation remained a mystery until recently, when App identified the text as a Song dynasty work with a strong Zen flavor called *Dazang yilan* (大藏一览, *The Buddhist Canon at a Glance*). In this essay, as Cross points out, "The Buddha's life is movingly described, and into his mouth Ch'an teachings—and consequently the ideas of the Mahāyāna, from which they are developed—are placed. Here Schopenhauer was able to discover concepts distinctly similar to his doctrine of *representation*." Cross, *Schopenhauer's Encounter*, 41.

[120] Braid garnered attention because he linked hypnotic phenomena to brain physiology, and he introduced terminology that was more acceptable to the medical

and scientific establishment, helping prepare the way for the eventual use of hypnosis in psychological research.

[121] Braid also published a book on the meditation techniques used in ancient yoga, *The Power of the Mind over the Body* (1846).

[122] *TRZ*, 1:274–85. Jean Martin-Charcot (1825–93), considered the founder of modern neurology (and through his student, Sigmund Freud, seen as an important figure in the development of the discipline of psychology as well), was also a dedicated practitioner of hypnotism. In 1878 he began to employ hypnosis in the study of hysteria and discovered that in doing so he could reproduce many of its symptoms.

[123] Eugene Melchior de Vogüé, "The Neo-Christian Movement in France," *Harper's Monthly,* January 1892, 241. Monod is quoted in *TRZ,* 1:266 from his 1893 essay on "The Political Situation in France," *The Contemporary Review*, 613-28. In "The Neo-Christian Movement," de Vogüé expressed concern about some emerging trends among French youths, who were finding science and material progress wanting by themselves. He refers to "the masters of contemporary thought, a Schopenhauer, a Taine, a Tolstoi," with their interest in such things as "Buddhist nirvana" and "mystic asceticism." He proceeds with a long quotation from Tolstoy, which includes the remark, "I lost faith early in life. I lived for a while like all the world on the vanities of life. I practiced literature, and, like the others, taught that which I did not know. Then the Sphinx set to pursuing me, crueler than ever. 'Guess my riddle or I will devour you.' Human science explained nothing to me. To my eternal; question—the only question of importance—'Why do I live'? science replied by teaching me other things of which I take no heed. With science the only thing to be done was to join the time-honored chorus of the sages, Solomon, Socrates, Çyaka-Mouni, and Schopenhauer, and repeat after them, Life is an absurd Evil" (238). Of course, "Çyaka-Mouni" is a reference to Shakyamuni, the Buddha.

[124] Interestingly, Reiun did not offer any comments on the similar process of cultural transmission that had already taken place in America when Emerson and Thoreau were devouring whatever Asian texts they could find in the 1850s. Much like Schopenhauer and the later German romantic philosophers, the American transcendentalists discovered in the Vedas and Upanishads a great deal to admire, and they were quite taken with the rich and contemplative nature of the ancient Indian writings that had found their way into their possession. There is an interesting essay on this topic in by Todd Lewis and Kent Bickness, "The Asian Soul of Transcendentalism," *Education About Asia* 16:2 (Fall 2011): 12–19. As for Rousseau, Reiun very much appreciated the role he had played in revolutionizing European thought, as he turned Descartes on his head to reverse the classic "I think therefore I am" statement and make it something more like "I am therefore I think." Rousseau understood the importance of turning inward in order to gain direct experience of the sensation of the self. For more on this, see Safranski, *Schopenhauer and the Wild Years,* 110. Reiun constantly quoted Rousseau in his essays and even

quoted Schiller's ode to Rousseau's grave in one of his earliest essays, "On Freedom Part 1," where we find, in German, the lines "Rousseau's grave, how dear thou art to me. Calm repose be to thy ashes blest! In thy life thou vainly sought'st for rest, But at length 'twas here obtained by thee!" *TRZ*, 1:33–34.

[125] When I first read this essay on the place of eastern thought in the nineteenth-century West in the early 1970s, it was well before the appearance of the Internet and before it was possible to conduct Google searches on individual's names, for example, or to access online textual archives on Asian philosophy and religion. Therefore, looking up the unfamiliar names rendered in *katakana* of people like Anquetil-Duperron, Sinnett, Colebrooke, Arnold, and Braid was not as easy as it is today, especially since Reiun often omitted book titles when referring to these authors. In fact it was usually a challenge just to correctly decipher the spelling of a name from the phonetic *katakana* script used in the original.

[126] When I first discovered Schwab's book, more than a decade had passed since I read Reiun's 1894 essayOn the Place of Eastern Thought in the Nineteenth-century West" I was elated to find mention in one place of so many of the same people that Reiun had discussed and about whom I knew very little. I also discovered that an English translation was in the works and would be appearing in 1984, which it did. See Raymond Schwab, *The Oriental Renaissance: Europe's Rediscovery of India and the East, 1680–1880*, trans. Gene Patterson-Black and Victor Reinking (New York: Columbia University Press, 1984). In a review of this book, J. B. Katz notes that after its initial appearance in French in 1950 it "may have been more often skimmed than thoroughly read" by English speakers, but he reiterates Schwab's argument that "we shall never be able to understand European Romanticism, 19th century thought, and the 'modern soul' without 'recording the consequences of the Oriental Renaissance in all provinces on the mind.'" J. B. Katz, Review of Raymond Schwab, *La Renaissance Orientale, Journal of Indian Philosophy* 18 (1990): 341–46.

[127] Edward Said, *Orientalism* (New York: Random House, 1978), 19–20 and 73.

[128] Batchelor, *Awakening of the West*, 234.

[129] See the author's introduction in Yuasa, *Bashô*, 33.

[130] Said, *Orientalism*, 20-21 As Said notes later, acknowledging the "fruitful Eastern discoveries of Anquetil and Jones during the latter third of the century,…all such widening horizons had Europe firmly in the privileged center, as main observer… For even as Europe moved itself outwards, its sense of cultural strength was fortified. From trevelers' tales, and not only from great institutions like the various India companies, colonies were created and ethnocentric perspectives secure." (117)

[131] Quoted in Urs App, *The Birth of Orientalism* (Philadelphia, Pennsylvania: University of Pennsylvania Press, 2010), 363.

[132] See Cross, *Schopenhauer's Encounter*, 26. On the same page, Cross also quotes from W. Halbfass, *India and Europe: An Essay in Philosophical Understanding* (Delhi:

Motilal Banarsidass, 1990) to the effect that one of Anquetil's main interests was "to demonstrate that the sages of all countries and all times had basically 'always said the same' or at least meant the same." (115)

[133] App, *Birth of Orientalism*, xiv (italics mine). Of course, App sees that Anquetil-Duperron had an agenda, as did many Europeans who were seeking greater knowledge about Asia. He was looking for evidence of a monotheistic Asian religion whose antecedents were much older than Judaism. He looked to Zoroastrianism and really believed he had found what he was looking for in the *Zend-Avesta* and the Upanishads. According to App, this process of transformation was aided and expressed by the research of early British Sanskritists in Calcutta and their articles in the *Asiatick Researches* journal, and he notes that 1795 was the year in which Europe's first secular institution for the study of oriental languages was established, the École Speciale des Langues Orientales Vivantes in Paris, which sought to separate the study of Asia and its languages from the realm of theology and biblical studies (xii).

[134] *TRZ I:*, 271–73.

[135] Ibid., 271–72.

[136] See Gay, *Modernism,* where he notes the enduring legacy of Freud and the moderns, who placed "the mind in its natural world . . . making contradictory feelings—ambivalence—central to [their] picture of the world"(xxi–xxii). See also p. 5.

[137] See Pericles Lewis, *The Cambridge Introduction to Modernism* (Cambridge: Cambridge University Press, 2007), 7–10.

[138] See Altieri, *Painterly Abstraction*; and Taylor, *Sources of the Self.* Altieri had to admit that, although he "love[d] Kant's work as art too much to want to defend it as philosophy," at times it seemed that Kant's principles were "haunted by the empiricism they attempt to resist." These were the very limitations that Schopenhauer sought to overcome. Taylor credits Kant with establishing the conception of a "noumenal rational agent" (367), but long before Taylor took up this topic Mead attempted to uncover the origins and character of the modern self, a process that ultimately forced him back to nineteenth-century thought, and the impact of romanticism, in order to understand how a new self-consciousness, a new way of thinking and feeling about the world and experience, evolved. See George Herbert Mead, *Mind, Self, and Society* edited with an introduction by Charles W. Morris (Chicago: University of Chicago Press, 1962), especially chapter 1, 1–24 (originally published in 1934). In both this book and his other major work, *Movements of Thought in the Nineteenth Century*, Mead argues that what distinguishes nineteenth-century thought from all that had gone before was a move away from the "subject-attribute" approach to knowledge in favor of one that focuses on the subject-object relationship. Instrumental in this shift, of course, was the contribution of Kant, the "philosopher of the revolution." That is, Kant provided

the metaphysical tools with which to demonstrate that the human mind creates our categories of understanding, like space and time, so that the mind does not so much *learn* the laws of nature as *legislate* them, the very point that Taylor echoes today. Obviously, this interpretation of reality opened up a whole new role for the self, or the subject in the subject-object equation, and Schopenhauer took one of the first and most important steps toward probing how to better understand the thing-in-itself. See George Herbert Mead, *Movements of Thought in the Nineteenth Century*, edited with an introduction by M. H. Moore (University of Chicago Press, 1972) (originally published in 1936).

[139] See the "Criticism of the Kantian Philosophy" in the appendix to *WWR/1969*, 1:413–534. For a newer translation in the Cambridge edition, see WWR/2010, pp.441–565. Critic John Gray put it this way in *Straw Dogs*:

> Like most philosophers, Kant worked to shore up the conventional beliefs of his time. Schopenhauer did the opposite. Accepting the arguments of Hume and Kant that the world is unknowable, he concluded that both the world and the individual subject that imagines it are *māyā*, dreamlike constructions with no basis in reality. Morality is not a set of laws or principles. It is a feeling—the feeling of compassion for the suffering of others which is made possible by the fact that separate individuals are finally figments. Here Schopenhauer's thought converges with the Vedanta and Buddhism, which despite their differences share the central insight that individual selfhood is an illusion. (42–43)

[140] Quoted in Cross, *Schopenhauer's Encounter*, 107.

[141] Safranski, *Schopenhauer and the Wild Years of Philosophy*, 118-19.

[142] Cross, *Schopenhauer's Encounter*, 31.

[143] *WWR/1969*, 1:404.

[144] Quoted in Vasalou, *Schopenhauer and the Aesthetic Standpoint*, 207. She also refers to John Atwell's quotation from Schopenhauer claiming that his philosophy represented "a new philosophical system, but new in the complete sense of the word—not a new presentation of what is already on hand, but a series of thoughts hanging together in the highest degree that up to now has never come into any human head." John Atwell, *Schopenhauer on the Character of the World* (Berkeley: University of California Press, 1995), 1. Vasalou offers a unique take on Schopenhauer, suggesting that rather than quibbling over whether this part or that part of his work is consistent or logical, we should locate his theorizing in the realm of aesthetics, and especially its relationship with the sublime and the sense of wonder that it stimulates. She believes that "the aesthetics of the sublime . . . offers itself as the most illuminating context in which to locate the 'cosmic' (*Schopenhauer and the Aesthetic Standpoint*, 83) and that by placing Schopenhauer's ideas in this context, we permit ourselves to wonder; and to "wonder" may simply mean: to entertain possibility; to be prepared to ask. And if we do, if we have this will to

wonder, we can allow ourselves to see in this standpoint one that we may want to continue to cultivate as a location for self-knowledge—as a location that tells us who we are, and that reattunes us to what we desire, thus enabling us to seek it; namely, an understanding of ourselves and the world that might respond to this identity and to what we dare to hope or believe of its grandeur, and to reveal to us how it could find its truest flourishing and fulfillment. (226)

In other words, she urges readers to embrace Schopenhauer's work for what it is—for the sense of wonder it contains and the cosmic standpoint it encourages—and to put these to good use. Let his philosophy help us understand where we are, how we live, and how we can live better, a perspective that I believe Reiun would have wholeheartedly endorsed.

[145] See Christopher Janaway, "Schopenhauer's Philosophy of Value," in *Better Consciousness: Schopenhauer's Philosophy of Value,* ed. Alex Neil and Christopher Janaway (London: Wiley-Blackwell, 2009), 2. Janaway also puts the matter very succinctly in another short book, *Schopenhauer,*(New York: Oxford University Press, 1994), where he writes, "Adapting the thought of both Plato and Kant, he had become convinced that there was a split between ordinary consciousness and a higher or 'better' state in which the human mind could pierce beyond mere appearances to a knowledge of something more real. The thought had aesthetic and religious overtones: Schopenhauer wrote of both the artist and the 'saint' as possessing this 'better consciousness'—though it should be said straightaway that his philosophical system was atheist through and through" (5). As Schopenhauer himself wrote, "The philosopher theoretically presents *the better consciousness* in all purity by separating it accurately and entirely from the empirical. The saint does the same practically." Arthur Schopenhauer, *Manuscript Remains,* ed. Arthur Hübscher, trans. E. F. J. Payne, 4 vols. (Oxford: Berg, 1988), 162n249. Finally, John Atwell, in *Schopenhauer on the Character of the World,* explains the different forms consciousness can take: "The human consciousness, Schopenhauer supposes, has a choice between two forms: the empirical (temporal) or the better (free, even atemporal). From the empirical consciousness, nothing of genuine value can be discovered; no true knowledge, no real virtue, no pure aesthetic contemplation." (78) He also quotes Schopenhauer directly from his *Manuscript Remains* about the way "liberation from the temporal consciousness leaves the better, eternal consciousness behind" (79).

Urs App explains that what would later take the place of the term *better consciousness* is the notion of the denial or "the turning of the will," that is, "The will can want to abolish its concrete phenomenal appearance, whereby it overcomes itself; and this is the freedom, the possibility of deliverance" (*Schopenhauer's Compass*, 206). Or, as Cross states it, "[F]or Schopenhauer salvation lies in a transformation of identity from the relentlessly willing empirical consciousness to the *denial of the will* and its replacement by *better consciousness* (*Schopenhauer's Encounter*, 228). App makes a very convincing case for the decisive influence of Anquetil-Duperron's Latin translation of the *Oupnek'hat* in helping Schopenhauer see how "pure knowledge or insight" could make an "overcoming of the will" possible was not only the Sufi influences on Prince Dara but also the writings of neo-Platonists like Plotinus and mystics like Böhme and Mme. Guyon, which Schopenhauer so cherished, that helped him arrive at this understanding. App writes, "In order to be true to that better consciousness 'we must renounce empirical consciousness' and 'wrest ourselves from it'; and such liberation can only be achieved through 'death of the ego' in the sense of Jakob Böhme and Madame Guyon" (184). In particular, App finds entry 213 in Schopenhauer's *Manuscript Remains* to be the compelling moment (in 1814) when he quotes the *Oupnek'hat* for the first time to the effect that "Just when insight arrives, desire leaves the scene," for now he comes to see *māyā* as the source of "the love (for the object) whose objectification or manifestation is the world" (202; see also *Manuscript Remains*, 130–31). Willing is now understood as the "fundamental error and the world its manifestation" (201), which provides Schopenhauer with the scaffolding he needs for his metaphysics of will and is the source of the insight that gives rise to the title of his major work, *The World as Will and Representation*.

[146] Mannion, *Schopenhauer, Religion, and Morality*, 48. Schopenhauer also included in his notes the following observation: "All philosophy and all the consolation it affords go to show that there is a spiritual world and that in it we are separated from all the phenomena of the external world and from an exalted seat can view these with the greatest calm and unconcern, although that part of us, belonging to the corporeal world, is still pulled and swung around so much in it." Schopenhauer, *Manuscript Remains*, 1:8. Mannion believes that Janaway overlooks "Schopenhauer's 'humble path' method and the link between the mystical, better consciousness and nothingness" (*Schopenhauer, Religion, and Morality*, 277). Recognizing the limitations of the capacity of humans to perceive reality does not necessarily mean pessimism, he argues; rather, it can bring the seeker a sense of humility. Moreover, by understanding that the "I" can become conscious of itself, we become aware that freedom can also exist as a possibility. The fact that the nature of the thing-in-itself can never fully be defined bothers many philosophers because it makes the distinction between religion and morality difficult to draw. Just as religion ends in mystery, so, too, does Schopenhauer's thought, which is why Mannion sees him "as a thinker 'on the boundary' of theology" (289). While Reiun professed that organized religion never offered him anything he could rely on, I do not think he would have been bothered by the fact that Schopenhauer's thought sometimes approached the religious, even using terms like *salvation*, because, like any good Daoist, he accepted that the deepest mysteries of life must lie beyond the reach of cognitive understanding.

[147] App, *Schopenhauer's Compass*, 89. App demonstrates convincingly Schopenhauer's familiarity with the writings of Jakob Böhme and that he could detect their influence on Schelling (116).

[148] Janaway believes that Schopenhauer did think of himself as a "system-building metaphysician," although he has not necessarily been taken seriously as such. (See

Christopher Janaway, *Schopenhauer*, 6-10. However, as Atwell points out, many critics believe that "Schopenhauer's 'philosophical system' cannot be regarded as a genuine system, for it is riddled with inconsistencies, contradictions, and irresolvable paradoxes. This judgment has not persuaded all critics to dismiss Schopenhauer's philosophy entirely—for many individual aspects have been lauded and appreciated—but it has convinced most of them that as a whole, his philosophy cannot withstand critical scrutiny." Atwell, *Schopenhauer on the Character of the World*, 1. However, when we read editor Arthur Hübscher's preface to Schopenhauer's *Manuscript Remains*, we get a completely different picture. He writes, "We know that Schopenhauer saw a great merit of his philosophy in the fact that its truths fitted freely and easily into an organic structure of ideas which was complete in itself. The manuscripts show how this early conceived unity was built up in detail and out of many parts. They make us look back to the original experiences and reflections out of which the system was gradually brought to maturity and perfection." Schopenhauer, *Manuscript Remains*, I, vii.

[149] Lauxtermann, *Schopenhauer's Broken World-View*, 3.

[150] Initially, Schopenhauer's principal work appeared in English under the title *The World as Will and Idea*, the Haldane and Kemp (London: Routledge & Kegan Paul, 1883) translation being the most widely used for three-quarters of a century (See R.B. Haldane and J. Kemp, *The World as Will and Idea*. Volumes I and II. London: Routledge & Kegan Paul, 1948). Perhaps because of Plato's influence on Schopenhauer, the term *idea* was chosen for the title. I have relied primarily on the translation by E. F. J. Payne, who explains his reasons for adopting *representation* as the best rendition of the German *Vorstellung* in his translator's introduction to *WWR/1969*.

> One of the difficulties in rendering a German philosophical work into English comes from the inability of the English language to reproduce adequately and accurately some of the philosophical terms and expressions of which there are so many in German. . . . *Anschauung* is used by Schopenhauer to describe what occurs when the eye perceives an external object as the cause of the sensation on the retina. "Perception" has been selected as the nearest English equivalent, although it may also be translated "intuition" in the sense of an immediate apprehension. . . . *Vorstellung* is important, for it occurs in the German title of this work. Its primary meaning is that of "placing before," and it is used by Schopenhauer to express what he himself describes as an "exceedingly complicated physiological process in the brain of an animal, the result of which is the consciousness of a picture *there*." In the present translation "representation" has been selected as the best English word to convey the German meaning, a selection that is confirmed by the French and Italian versions of *Die Welt als Wille und Vorstellung.* (viii–x)

To this Cross adds the explanation that *Vorstellung* points to "the inner mental picture made up of objects related to one another in space that at each successive moment our cognitive faculty places before our consciousness. The continuous flow of such mental images, when derived from sensory perception rather than dream or thought, is what we think of as the external world. However, it is only the mental representation that we experience with immediacy and certainty; we do not know whether these correspond to an external reality existing in its own right and outside our consciousness" (*Schopenhauer's Encounter*, 51). In 2010, for the first time in forty years, a new translation from Cambridge University Press became available, which I have quoted from time to time. See *WWR/2010*. In explaining the need for a new translation, Janaway writes in the general editor's preface,

Almost all the English translations of Schopenhauer in use until now, published though they are by several different publishers, stem from a single translator, the remarkable E.F.J. Payne. These translations, which were done in the 1950s and 1960s, have stood the test of time quite well and performed a fine service in transmitting Schopenhauer to an English-speaking audience. Payne's single-handed achievement is all the greater given that he was not a philosopher or an academic, but a former military man who became a dedicated enthusiast. His translations are readable and lively and convey a distinct authorial voice. However, the case for new translations rests partly on the fact that Payne has a tendency toward circumlocution rather than directness and is often not as scrupulous as we might wish in translating philosophical vocabulary, partly on the fact that recent scholarship has probed many parts of Schopenhauer's thought with far greater precision than was known in Payne's day, and partly on the simple thought that after half a century of reading Schopenhauer almost solely through one translator, and with a wider and more demanding audience established, a change of voice is in order. (viii–ix)

[151] *WWR/1969*, 3.

[152] Cross, *Schopenhauer's Encounter*, 65.

[153] Ibid., 30–33.

[154] *WWR/1969*, 24.

[155] Vasalou, *Schopenhauer and the Aesthetic Standpoint*, 8 (italics mine).

[156] Günter Zöller, "Schopenhauer on the Self," in T*he Cambridge Companion to Schopenhauer,* ed. Christopher Janaway (Cambridge: Cambridge University Press, 1999), 18–43 (italics mine).

[157] *WWR/1969*, 1:99. Thomas Mann writes in the introduction to his little selection of highlights from Schopenhauer's philosophical writings, "Schopenhauer—all his misanthropy notwithstanding and all that he says about the corrupt condition of life in general and the distortion of the spirit of man in particular; notwithstanding his despair over the wretched social state one is born into as a human being—Schopenhauer is humanly full of pride and reverence as he contemplates the 'crown of creation.' To him the words mean, just as they did to the author of *Genesis*, man, the highest and most developed objectification of the will. . . . Man, according to

him, is to be reverenced because he is the *knowing* creature." Thomas Mann, *The Living Thoughts of Schopenhauer Presented by Thomas Mann* (London: Cassell, 1939), 19.

[158] *WWR/1969*, 1:103.

[159] Consider, for example, the following passage, which clearly reveals Schopenhauer's view of human nature:

> Therefore, in this sense, the old philosophical argument about the freedom of the will, constantly contested and constantly maintained, is not without ground, and the Church dogma of the effect of grace and the new birth is also not without meaning and significance. . . . For just what the Christian mystics call the *effect of grace* and the *new birth*, is for us the only direct expression of the *freedom of the will*. It appears only when the will, after arriving at the knowledge of its own inner nature, obtains from this a *quieter*, and is thus removed from the effect of the motives which lie in the province of a different kind of knowledge, whose objects are only phenomena. The possibility of the freedom that thus manifests itself is man's greatest prerogative, which is forever wanting in the animal, because the condition for it is the deliberation of the faculty of reason, enabling him to survey the whole of life independently of the impression of the present moment. The animal is without any possibility of freedom, as indeed it is without the possibility of a real, hence deliberate, elective decision after a previous complete conflict of motives, which for the purpose would have to abstract representations. Therefore, the hungry wolf buries its teeth in the flesh of the deer with the same necessity with which the stone falls to the ground, without the possibility of the knowledge that it is the mauled as well as the mauler. *Necessity is the kingdom of nature: freedom is the kingdom of grace*. (ibid., 403–4)

Reiun quotes this last phrase verbatim in his essay "Zhuangzi's Free and Easy Wandering," and, as we have seen, App singled out the language in the Anquetil-Duperron translation of the *Oupnek'hat* (note 213 of Schopenhauer's *Manuscript Remains*) that grabbed Schopenhauer's attention: "Just when insight arrives, desire leaves the scene" (*Schopenhauer's Compass*, 187–89). This seems to be a corollary of the notion found in the *Daodejing* that when we lose touch with the "Great Way," or true understanding, that is precisely when the need for laws and regulations arises. (See verse 18, "When the great Way is forgotten, the doctrines of humanity and morality arise. When knowledge and cleverness appear, there emerges great hypocrisy.") It is only after individuals lose touch with the Way that they need external controls to protect them from their incessant desires. On the other hand, once the individual becomes aware that the world as representation is an illusion, once the individual understands that the self can be at once the subject and the object of knowing, true freedom is possible, and it comes by means of renouncing or overcoming ("turning") the will, which is the key to arriving at "a better consciousness."

[160] Charles Muses, *East-West: Schopenhauer's Optimism and the Lankavatara Sutra* (London: John W. Watkins, 1955), 41.

[161] Mannion, *Schopenhauer, Religion, and Morality*, 87 (italics mine).

[162] David Cartwright makes the point that Schopenhauer "argued that compassion is the source for all actions possessing moral worth, that all love is compassion, and that compassion is the Leitmotiv for individuals who possess a morally good character." Such individuals "live in a world essentially different than that experienced by egoistic and malicious characters, who live in a world they find to be indifferent, if not hostile, to their welfare. Everything and everyone are viewed as other, as 'Not I', and they live in moral isolation from others. Conversely, compassionate people live in a world they perceive as homogeneous to their nature, and they view others as an I once more." David Cartwright, "Schopenhauer on the Value of Compassion," in, *A Companion to Schopenhauer*, ed. Bart Vandenabeele (Malden, MA: Wiley-Blackwell, 2012), 249. Note also Schopenhauer's remarks in *On the Basis of Morality*, quoted in an epigraph in chapter 4, where he observes that people imbued with compassion "will assuredly injure no one, will wrong no one, will encroach on no one's rights; on the contrary, he will be lenient and patient with everyone, will forgive everyone, will help everyone as much as he can, and all his actions will bear the stamp of justice, philanthropy, and loving-kindness." *OBM*, 172.

[163] The phrase is Gerard Mannion's in *Schopenhauer, Religion, and Morality* Schopenhauer did put great stock in the power of art to still the operations of the will, at least temporarily. He writes:

> Raised up by the power of the mind, we relinquish the ordinary way of considering things . . . and let our whole consciousness be filled by the calm contemplation of a natural object actually present, whether it be a landscape, a tree, a rock, a crag, a building or anything else. We lose ourselves entirely in this object, to use a pregnant expression; in other words, we forget our individuality, our will, and continue to exist only as pure subject, as clear mirror of the object, so that it is as though the object alone existed without anyone to perceive it, and thus we are no longer able to separate the perceiver from the perception, but the two have become one, since the entire consciousness is filled and occupied by a single image of perception. (*WWR*, 1:178–79)

[164] Kitamura Tôkoku, is discussed in more detail inchapter 4.

[165] Halstead, *Romanticism*, 38.

[166] Notehelfer shows that Kôtoku couldn't shake the conviction that he was destined to serve the nation somehow. See his *Kôtoku Shûsui*, especially chapter 2.

[167] Konishi, *Anarchist Modernity*, 210.

Chapter Four

[1] *SD*, 568.

[2] See Yamagata Isô's recollections in the appendix to Ienaga, *Sûki naru shisôka*, 195–201. For a general description of *Seinenbun*, see Nishida Masaru, "Seinenbun," *Bungaku* 24:8 (1956): 105–10.

[3] Taoka Reiun, "Tônan no kakusha yori Geiyô ni fukusu," in *TRZ*, 4:457–66. See also Nishida Masaru, ed., *Taoka Reiun senshû* [Selected works of Taoka Reiun] (Tokyo: Aoki bunko, 1965), 195.

[4] For the importance of Usen as an artist who represented expressed anarchist ideas in his paintings and drawings, see Sho Konishi, "The People at Rest: The Anarchist Origins of Ogawa Usen's 'Nihonga,'" *World Art* 1:2 (2011): 235–56. For more on Ogawa and Reiun's relationship, see chapter 5.

[5] See Reiun's two companion pieces expressing anguish over leaving the literary world, "Fude o yaku no ki" and "Kyô o saru no ji," both of which are included in Odagiri Hideo, ed., *Meiji shakaishugi-bungaku shû* (1), *Meiji Bungaku Zenshû*, vol. 83 (Tokyo: Chikuma shobô, 1965), 41–43. "Fude o yaku no ki" is also included in TRZ, 1:589–91, and and "Kyô o saru no ji" in *TRZ*, 2:111–13.

[6] "Shinshun no dai-ikkatsu," *TRZ*, 2:,301-305.

[7] See, for example, Donald Keene, "The Sino-Japanese War of 1894–5 and Its Cultural Effects on Japan," in *Tradition and Modernization in Japanese Culture,* ed. Donald Shively (Princeton, NJ: Princeton University Press, 1971), 121–75.

[8] This is based on a quote from Watsuji Tetsujirô, *Jiden no kokoromi*, quoted in Sumiya Mikio, *Nihon teikoku no keiren, Nihon no rekishi* ,vol. 22 (Tokyo: Chûô kôron, 1971), 64.

[9] For more on the significance of this period, see David Ambaras, "Social Knowledge, Cultural Capital, and the New Middle Class in Modern Japan, 1895–1912," *Journal of Japanese Studies* 24:1 (1998): 1–33.

[10] For a discussion along these lines, see Asukai Masamichi, "Kokuminteki bunka no keisei 1," in *Iwanami kôza Nihon rekishi, Gendai 1* (Tokyo: Iwanami shôten, 1963), 1:287–311.

[11] For a general description of this magazine, see Senuma Shigeki, "*Taiyô*," *Bungaku* 23:7 (1955): 70–78.

[12] Kano Masanao, *Shihonshugi keiseiki no chitsujo isshiki* (Tokyo: Chikuma shobô, 1969), 449.

[13] Quoted in ibid.

[14] Francis Mathy, "Kitamura Tôkoku, the Early Years," *Monumenta Nipponica* 18:1–4 (1963), 1. Among the critics who have focused attention on Tôkoku as the precursor of modernism in Japanese literature, two stand out. The historian Tôyama

Shigeki made his case in "Nihon kindaika to Tôkoku no kokumin bungaku ron," *Bungaku* 20:5 (1952): 1–8. Karaki Junzô stressed Tôkoku's search for a modern self in his *Gendaishi e no kokoromi* (Tokyo: Chikuma shobô, 1963). Two other important contributors to the popularization of Tôkoku's role in modern Japanese history are Odagiri Hideo and Irokawa Daikichi. Many of Odagiri's essays on Tôkoku were assembled in one volume, *Kitamura Tôkoku ron* (Tokyo: Yagi shoten, 1970). Tôkoku also occupies a prominent place in Irokawa's *Shimpen Meiji seishinshi*, and he published a 1994 biography, *Kitamura Tôkoku* (Tokyo: Tokyodaigaku Shuppankai, 1994), in which he notes, "Kitamura Tôkoku was also one of those late-nineteenth-century figures who succumbed to the spell of the supremacy of the state as the modern nation was being founded in Japan. However, not infrequently he was able to free himself from this straightjacket and move outside the boundaries of 'the modern' in order to immerse [himself] in a more abstract world of universal human [dignity] where he was free to explore the mysteries of the cosmos and the inner self" (iii).

[15] Tôkoku first came to the attention of the literary world for his incisive literary criticism. He was the first Japanese writer to define a concern with the inner life (*naibu seimei*). Tôkoku founded a new journal in early 1893, *Bungakkai* (Literary World), and he published there an article titled "What Does It Mean to Be 'Beneficial to Humanity'?" (Jinsei ni aiwatarazumba to wa nan no ii zo), challenging another critic, Yamaji Aizan, to clarify what he meant when he said that literature should be considered a form of enterprise (*jitsugyô*), a serious undertaking and consequently somehow directly beneficial to humans; otherwise, he declared, it is empty and meaningless (*jinsei ni aiwatarazumba kû no kû nari*). Tôkoku responded that, while literature should serve human beings in their struggle with life, it also had to be much more. Literature, according to Tôkoku, expresses the author's own search, and it has to come from the writer's awareness of the higher realms of consciousness, where battles are fought but there are no victories. Literature, then, must flow from the highest level of human experience and should never be constricted by specific narrow, pragmatic objectives in the service of society. On this basis, Tôkoku glorified the inner life, creating for himself a proposition he would spend the rest of his career trying to define. See Katsumoto Seiichirô, comp., *Tôkoku zenshû* (Tokyo: Iwanami shoten, 1970–73), 1:254–64. See also Sasabuchi Yûichi, *Romanshugi bungaku no tanjô* (Tokyo: Meiji shôin, 1958), 311–63, for a standard treatment of the founding of the journal *Bungakkai*.

Obviously, Reiun felt very much the same as Tôkoku about literature's need to be connected to the author's inner experiences and the need for an awareness of higher realms of consciousness. As noted in chapter 3, note 19, Reiun also had issues with Aizan's position and argued that his utilitarian Christian outlook prevented him from perceiving the sublimity and human centeredness of a view of nature like that of Bashô, whereby his oneness with the universe could impart life to even the most desolate manifestations of nature. Thus, to construe the Japanese sense of *wabi* (desolate loneliness) as pessimistic or amoral is to fail to appreciate the fact that the poet has transcended the world of duality and distinction so that such judgments are meaningless. Moreover, to reject the shallow world of wealth and fame does not denote pessimism and world-weariness but rather an awakening to reality. He cautioned Aizan against confusing morality with aesthetics and concluded with the barb that his Christian God is a "jealous God." When Reiun wrote this essay, he was still very young, only beginning to formulate his ideas, and it did not contain as systematic a statement on the "inner life" as Tôkoku's did. However, it illustrates the affinity between Reiun and Tôkoku and shows that they were approaching related problems in literature at around the same time from their respective individual viewpoints. There is a 1996 article in English by Graham Squires and Itô Yushi, "How Can Literature Be Beneficial to Life? The Yamaji-Kitamura Controversy Reconsidered," 1996, Nichibunkan, accessed April 2016, http://publications.nichibun.ac.jp/en/item/kosh/1996-03-25-3/pub, in which the authors argue that Yamaji and Kitamura both opposed political conservatism and so had much in common. But Yamaji was clearly more oriented toward the state than was either Tôkoku or Reiun.

[16] For a discussion of *iki*, see Hisamatsu Ken'ichi, *The Vocabulary of Japanese Aesthetics* (Tokyo: Center for East Asian Cultural Studies, 1963), 63–66.

[17] See Ryan, *Japan's First Modern Novel*, 54–56.

[18] Katsumoto, *Tôkoku zenshû*, 2:277–78. *Ninjô* refers to the classic tension between natural human feelings and the obligations imposed on people by the feudal system.

[19] Ibid., 278.

[20] Ibid., 279.

[21] Ibid.

[22] Gay, *Modernism*, 3.

[23] Tôkoku's position on this was expressed clearly in an essay published in July 1892, "Tokugawa jidai no heiminteki risô," (in Katsumoto, comp., *Tôkoku Zenshû* vol 1: 353-372) in which, in the words of one writer, he skillfully used history to treat the problems of the present and in so doing successfully created a new view of the past. The literature of Genroku had been celebrated as representing the voice of the *heimin* (commoners) breaking through the barriers of feudalism and finding expression. Tôkoku was aware of this aspect of the literature, and he, too, felt "unlimited joy" at the sight of the *heimin* spirit finally emerging after so many years. But he insisted that it was also prudent to remember the fate of this spirit. Unable to evolve freely and escape the restraints of feudalism, its vitality was sapped as it was plunged into dissipating eroticism. As a result, the themes of chivalry and purity became perverted and stunted, and their ideals gave way to self-deprecation. See Senuma Shigeki, "Tôkoku no rekishi isshiki," *Bungaku* 24:2 (1956): 20–25. Accordingly, he was forced to state boldly, "The history of our nation's *heimin* is

from beginning to end a record of darkness and obstruction." Katsumoto, *Tôkoku zenshû*, 2:365–69. Note also that, as Reiun would observe later on, Tôkoku felt "great pity" for the fate of the *heimin*, but he did not want the same mistake to be repeated in the Meiji period. The Meiji Restoration, however, had presented a great opportunity to the Japanese people. In "Meiji bungaku kanken" (My View of Meiji Literature), which was never completed, Tôkoku explains why he believed this was true. While one could see a degree of individual freedom being recognized after the Restoration, a broader freedom for all the people to realize their self-potential in the outer world was denied. But with the Meiji Restoration, and the union of the *bushi* and the *heimin* into an organic whole, the *kokumin* (citizenry), this traditional grip was loosened, and Tôkoku could see an unprecedented opportunity for change, for spiritual growth, at the popular level. See Katsumoto, *Tôkoku zenshû*, 2:166–67.

[24] Yoshida Seiichi, *Shizenshugi no kenkyû* Vol 1 (Tokyo: Tôkyôdôshuppan, 1955), 1:24.

[25] *TRZ*, 1:248. The complete quote reads, "The mystic is opposed to the philosopher by the fact that he begins from within, whereas the philosopher begins from without. The mystic starts from his inner, positive, individual experience, in which he finds himself as an eternal and only being, and so on." *WWR*, 2:611.

[26] *WWR*, 2:611–12. Scotus Erigena was to a ninth-century mystic, later revived by the neo-Platonists, who argued that a transcendent and "unknown" God, beyond being and nonbeing, could actually be brought into being and consciousness by means of a trajectory of going out and coming back into the self. Likewise, Mme. Guyon (1648–1717) was a French Roman Catholic mystic who left a lengthy autobiographical narrative of her journey to mystical oneness with God.

[27] Quoted in App, *Schopenhauer's Compass*, 25.

[28] This is from Vasalou, *Schopenhauer and the Aesthetic Standpoint*, 18.

[29] *TRZ*, 1:274–85.

[30] Ibid., 281.

[31] See ibid., 419–29. The first essay was a review of Motora Yûjirô's recent book on Zen practice, and the second followed up with an essay on Zen's recent popularity.

[32] "Bungaku no fuyu," in *TRZ*, 1:298.

[33] "Gunka no ryûkô," in *TRZ*, 1:303–4.

[34] "Meiji dainijû-hachi nen no hekitô ni oite seinen no tabônaru unmei o omou," in *TRZ*, 1:305–7.

[35] Ibid., 306.

[36] "Tokutomi Sohô," in *TRZ*, 2:22–24. The essay is also reprinted in Odagiri, *Meiji shakaishugi-bungaku shû* (1), 75.

37 "Kôyô," in *TRZ*, 2:1–3.

38 "Ijin o dete yo," in *TRZ*, 2:156–58.

39 "Shajitsu to risô," in *TRZ*, 1:528–30.

40 "Shinrai to kyônetsu," in *TRZ*, 1:523–25. Note the similarity between Reiun's idea of *kyônetsu* and Tôkoku's notions of *jônetsu* and *netsu-i*, as explained in Katsumoto, *Tôkoku zenshû*, 2:297–302 and 255–59 respectively.

41 "Tensai to kyônetsu," in *TRZ*, 1:448–49.

42 "Bungaku to Shûkyô," in *TRZ*, 2:194–95.

43 See "Dai fuhei nare!," in *TRZ*, 1:332.

44 Ibid.

45 See, for example, Reiun's review of a collection of short stories by Ken'yûsha writers edited by Kôyô. In the review Reiun claimed that with a little effort the younger writers in the group could surpass their teacher. "Gochôshi' o hyôsu," in *TRZ*, 1:579–88.

46 See Odagiri Hideo, *Bungakushi* (Tôyôkeizai shimpô sha, 1961), 207–25.

47 For more on Kyôka's work, see Yoshida, *Shizenshugi no kenkyû*, 59–73.

48 See, for example Hirota Masaki, "Nihon kindai shakai no sabetsu kôzô" [The structure of discrimination in modern Japanese society], in *Sabetsu no shosô* [Aspects of discrimination](Tokyo: Iwanami shoten, 1990). Hirota's work is also discussed in Narita Ryûichi, *Kingendai Nihonshi to Rekishigaku: Kakikaerarete-kita kako* (Tokyo: Chûô kôronsha, 2012), 92–94. Narita points out that as historians refine their thinking about the Meiji period, and especially things like the popular rights movement, there seems to be a drift away from just being critical of what it means to become modern and toward expressions of profound doubt about the way historians regard the process (126).

49 Nishida M., "Taoka Reiun to hisan shôsetsu," *Meiji-Taishô bungaku kenkyû*, no. 15 (February 1955): 46–59.

50 See, for example, "Ryûrô," in which Reiun compares Kyôka and Ryûrô in this light, in *TRZ*, 1:410–11. See also Odagiri, *Bungakushi*, 72–73.

51 "Shijin to dôjô," in *TRZ*, 1:406.

52 Ibid.

53 See "Ryûrô," in *TRZ*, 1:410–11; and "Izumi Kyôka," in *TRZ*, 1:371–72.

54 This widely used periodization is reviewed critically by Daikichi Irokawa in his article "*Bungakkai*," *Shisô*, April 1962, 123–35.

55 Sasagawa Rimpû, "Reiun shûenki," *Chûô kôron*, October 1912, 81–88.

56 Odagiri, *Bungakushi*, 217.

[57] See Reiun's "Ichiyô-joshi" and "Ichiyô-joshi no 'Nigorie,'" in *TRZ*, 1:310–11 and 493–504 respectively. English translations exist for these works by Ichiyô, with which Reiun was particularly taken. See Higuchi Ichiyô, "Growing Up" [Takekurabe], trans. E. Seidensticker, in *Modern Japanese Literature*, ed. Donald Keene (Tokyo: Tuttle, 1957), 70–110; and Higuchi Ichiyô, "Muddy Bay" [Nigorie], trans. H. Tanaka, *Monumenta Nipponica* 14:1–2 (1958): 173–204.

[58] See "Ichiyô-joshi no 'Nigorie,'" in *TRZ*, 1:494.

[59] "Kyôgû to reisei," in *TRZ*, 1:521–23.

[60] Ibid.

[61] This is very close to Schopenhauer's understanding of what the artist and the saint bring to their respective tasks. Stephen Cross also draws on the metaphor of lightning flashes when he writes, "The inspiration of both artist and saint results from transient appearances of the better consciousness. It is like lightning flashing in the darkness, and once it has passed, the everyday empirical consciousness again prevails. Genius and saint stand, as it were, at the threshold of the better consciousness; as they move back and forth between it and the empirical consciousness, their actions in the world reflect its presence." Cross, *Schopenhauer's Encounter*, 196.

[62] This tendency to view human beings in terms of two different levels of existence was, of course, a key feature of Kitamura Tôkoku's thought as well. Growing out of his attack on the one-dimensional utilitarianism of Yamaji Aizan, Tôkoku developed his conception of the inner life (*naibu-seimei*). Even several months prior to this, he had distinguished between the inner and outer *kokoro*. The latter is the realm of everyday life as we know it, equivalent to Reiun's external self, while the former is a secret and sacred chamber to which entry is most difficult. But nevertheless, he concludes, it is the latter that is the most important realm of human existence, and it is incumbent on writers to explore it, to "shed light on it, rectify it, purify it, and make it public." See Tôkoku's "Kakujin shinkyû-nai no hikyû," in Katsumoto, *Tôkoku zenshû*, 2:3–14. This exhortation closely corresponds to Reiun's appeal to writers not only to treat the outward, environment-oriented side of humanity but to strive for truth and to reveal the essential, true inner mind.

Another point of similarity between Tôkoku and Reiun is instructive. In his long essay on Meiji literature, Tôkoku stressed the importance of "freedom of spirit" (*seishin no jiyû*) and argued that truly noble undertakings (*jigyô*) do not arise from one's environment or immediate surroundings but from the movement of this inner spirit. This is in contrast to the actions in everyday life that emanate from the self (*ga*) whose sole aim is to promote the cause of this self in the context of the struggle for survival. Such a view of the self is quite similar to the Schopenhauer-inspired version that Reiun set forth in "Bi to Zen." For Tôkoku the human spirit, which is presumably another way of describing what is encountered in the inner *kokoro*, was all important in releasing human beings from the grip of the small, "willing" self and making possible a union with the universal self. In later essays, however, Tôkoku seemed to be questioning the impact of the growth of materialism on that spirit. In *Mamba* he stated, "The spirit of the present age is being plundered by the materialistic revolution. This revolution doesn't grow out of an internal collision of irreconcilable elements. It arises from an external stimulus. It is not a revolution; it is transition." See part 2 of Tôkoku's essay, , "Meiji bungaku kanken," which carries the subheading "Seishin no jiyû" (Freedom of the Spirit) in Katsumoto, comp., *Tôkoku zenshû* vol II 159-167

[63] Unknown to Reiun, a rough contemporary was also formulating teachings about the internal divisions within humans—such as intellectual, emotional, and instinctive—and their inability to do other than respond mechanically to the stimuli they encounter in everyday life. George Ivanovich Gurdjieff (1866–1949), a Russian Armenian, was an influential spiritual teacher first in Russia and later in Europe and America. As a part of that trend of questioning the values underlying the materialistic civilization of the West, Gurdjieff developed an understanding of the self that was very similar to Reiun's notion of the difference between an inner, spiritual side and an external, social side more subject to the influence of the environment. Gurdjieff offered his followers a set of esoteric teachings that stressed what human beings could do to alter their level of consciousness or awareness. Gurdjieff believed that all esoteric traditions speak in terms of a division between higher and lower levels of consciousness, and he taught that of the seven possible levels of consciousness humans tend to occupy only the two lowest levels, what he called "sleep" and "waking sleep." He called on his students to awaken from their sleep state and discover that other, higher levels of awareness were possible.

The struggle to awaken and be "present" in everyday life, then, was at the heart of Gurdjieff's teaching; it is a struggle that leads to a full engagement with the here and now. "It may surprise you," he told. P. D. Ouspensky, "if I say that the chief feature of modern man's being which explains *everything else that is lacking in him is sleep*. A modern man lives in sleep, in sleep he is born and in sleep he dies. . . . And if you think about it and at the same time remember that sleep is the chief feature of our being, it will at once become clear to you that if man really wants knowledge, he first of all must think about how to wake, that is, about how to change his *being*." Quoted in P. D. Ouspensky, *In Search of the Miraculous* (New York: Harcourt, Brace and World, 1949), 66. (It is worth noting in passing, given Reiun's deep appreciation for Edward Carpenter's writings, that Ouspensky, too, before he met Mr. Gurdjieff, was quite impressed by Carpenter and had translated several of his works into Russian. Moreover, Ouspensky traveled to Millthorpe in 1913 to meet with Carpenter. See Sheila Rowbotham, *Edward Carpenter*, 347-48, for details).

Regarding the distinction among the self, the spirit, the soul, and the environment that Reiun was writing about, Gurdjieff taught that in each human being there is an "essence," which is a permanent and unchanging feature, and a "personality," which develops over time from external influences. Essence is what you are born with; personality is what you acquire during the course of your life. Obviously, this bears a close relation to what Reiun wrote about when he was trying to distinguish between the "environment" and "spirituality" in the fiction of Higuchi Ichiyô. For more on the Gurdjieff system, see Antoine Faivre and Jacob Needleman, eds., *Modern Esoteric Spirituality* (New York: Crossroad, 1992); Kathleen Riordan Speeth, *The Gurdjieff Work* (Berkeley, CA: And/Or Press, 1976); and J. G. Bennett, *Gurdjieff: Making a New World* (New York: Harper Colophon, 1973). On personality and essence, see P. D. Ouspensky, *The Fourth Way* (New York: Vintage, 1957), 78–80. Most of the key works by or about Gurdjieff are available in Japanese, but this was a post-WWII phenomenon; I have not uncovered any evidence that his teachings were known to Japanese people in the prewar years, although it is quite possible that they were.

[64] Munitz, *Cosmic Understanding*, 276.

[65] See Cartwright, "Compassion," 150–51.

[66] "Busshitsuteki kaika to jindô," in *TRZ*, 2:389.

[67] "Shijin to enseikan," in *TRZ*, 1:384–87.

[68] "Sôkosha no fuhai," in *TRZ*, 2:96–97.

[69] Ibid.

[70] As Brett Walker puts it in *Toxic Archipelago: A History of Industrial Disease in Japan* (Seattle: University of Washington Press, 2010), events like the Ashio mine disaster were making "such celebrated figures as Fukuzawa Yukichi, who was intellectually complicit in saturating the toxic archipelago, look like idiots, with their pedantic preaching about modernity, conquering nature, and promoting enterprise" (107).

[71] "Shôsetsu to shakai imbi," in *TRZ*, 1:402–3.

[72] "Karyû no saimin to bunshi," in *TRZ*, 1:403–5.

[73] "Shakai mondai" is the title of an essay by Reiun that can be found in *TRZ*, 2:519.

[74] Jacob L. Talmon, *Romanticism and Revolt* (New York: Harcourt, Brace and World, 1967), 20.

[75] Ibid.

[76] For what biographical data there are available, see Nishida Taketoshi, "Yokoyama Gennosuke chaku 'Nihon kasô shakai' no seiritsu," *Rekishigaku kenkyû*, no. 161 (January 1953): 36–47.

[77] Yokoyama Gennosuke, *Nihon no kasô shakai* (Tokyo: Aoki bunko, 1949).

[78] Ibid., 19–38. See also the treatment in Sumiya, *Nihon teikoku no keiren*, 80.

[79] Yokoyama Gennosuke, *Naichi zakkyo ato no Nihon* (Tokyo: Iwanami shoten, 1954).

[80] Yokoyama, *Naichi zakkyo ato no Nihon,* quoted in Morisue Yoshiaki, Hôgetsu Keigo, and Konishi, Shirô eds.,*Seikatsushi III,* 119.

[81] See Konishi, *Anarchist Modernity,* 85–88.

[82] Yokoyama, *Naichi zakkyo ato no Nihon,* quoted in Morisue Yoshiaki, Hôgetsu Keigo, and Konishi, Shirô eds. *Seikatsushi III,* 120.

[83] "Ankokumen to sôkosha" [Writers and the dark side], in *TRZ,* 2:26–28. originally published in *Seinenbun* 3:2 (March 10, 1896): 3–4.

[84] Reiun took this position in "Bungaku to minshin," in *TRZ,* 2:117–19, also reprinted in Odagiri, ed. *Meiji shakaishugi bungakushû* (Tokyo: Chikuma shobô, 1965), 61.

[85] This general theme is reiterated in literally scores of Chogyû's essays. Among the best known are "Nihonshugi," "Nihonshugi to tetsugaku," "Nihonshugi ni taisuru yohyô o gaisu," "Sedaishugi to kokkashugi," "Kokumin seishin no tôitsu o ronzu," "Kokku-ijôshugi ni taisuru gojin no kenkai," and "Kokusui-hozonshugi to Nihonshugi." See Takayama Chogyû, *Chogyû zenshû,* 6 vols. (Tokyo: Hakubunkan, 1914–15), vol. 4. The use of the term *particularism* here is in line with Robert Bellah's observations about the "crystallization" of the emperor system around 1890, when he remarked in reference to the Imperial Rescript on Education (drafted by Inoue Tetsujirô, its most ardent defender) and the imperial constitution, "No clearer assertion of Japanese particularism was possible." Robert Bellah, "Japan's Cultural Identity," *Journal of Asian Studies* 24:4 (August 1965), 369-423. Reprinted in John A. Harrison, ed. *Enduring Scholarship,* 2:47–68. Tuscon, AZ: University of Arizona Press, 1972.

[86] This approach is taken in an essay by Hashimoto Bunzô, "Takayama Chogyû: Zassetsu shita Meiji no seishin," in *Nihon no shisôka,* ed. Asahi Jyanaru (Tokyo: Asahi Shinbunsha, 1963), 2:162–78. There is also an interesting discussion that compares and contrasts three Meiji figures that were at *Tôdai* during roughly the same period: Chogyû, Reiun, and Nishida Kitarô. See Miyajima Hajime, *Meijiteki shisôka no keisei* (Tokyo: Miraisha, 1960), 271–33. For a straight comparison of Reiun and Chogyû, see the classic treatment by Hijegata Teiichi, "Takayama Chogyû to shihai suru kenkyû no romanshugi Taoka Reiun," in the author's *Kindai Nihon bungaku hyôronshi* (Tokyo: Hôsei University Press, 1973), 22–26.

[87] The best source for biographical data on Chogyû is Akiyama Seikô, *Takayama Chogyû: Sono shôgai to shisô* (Tokyo: Sekibunkan,, 1957). See also Hashimoto, "Takayama Chogyû."

[88] See "Waga kuni genkon no bungeikai hihyôka no honmu," in Chogyû, *Chogyû zenshû,* 2:403–16.

[89] Ibid., 403.

[90] Ibid., 404–5.

[91] Takayama Chogyû, "Meiji no shôsetsu," in *Chogyû zenshû*, 2:417–76.

[92] Takayama Chogyû, "Iwayuru shakai shôsetsu o ronzu," in *Chogyû zenshû*, 2:477–84.

[93] Ibid., 477.

[94] Ibid., 479–80.

[95] Ibid., 479.

[96] In a way, this rehashes some of the issues raised in one of the most celebrated debates in modern Japanese literature, the argument between the romantic writer Kitamura Tôkoku and the more pragmatic Yamaji Aizan about where meaning in literature resides (see note 15 above). Was literature supposed to provide a practical service or perform a valuable social function? Or was its purpose more to inspire in readers a higher or deeper moral understanding? There are numerous interpretations of the debate, but one of Tôkoku's leading chroniclers, Katsumoto Seiichirô, offers a most interesting one. He believes that the two men, Aizan and Tôkoku, both Christians, were essentially having an intrafaith squabble. Aizan's depiction of literature as an enterprise mirrors the influence of Calvinism, while Tôkoku's affinity for the internal religious experience reflects the impact of Quaker ideas. Tôkoku was actively involved with a Quaker group at the time and editing a magazine called *Heiwa* (Peace) for it. See Katsumoto Seiichirô, "Tôkoku no shûkyô shisô," *Bungaku* 24:2 (1956): 8–19. In Chogyû's case, the contrast is apparent. In his "Kokka-ijôshugi ni taisuru gojin no kenkai" (*Chogyû zenshû*, 4:350–64), he claimed that if individualism was such that each person understood and carried out his obligations properly, he would have no grounds for disapproval. But in reality the only way to realize human ideals was through the state, and so the only thing loyal citizens should put their faith in (he was arguing against Christianity here) was the state (*kokkashugi*) and Japanism (Nihonshugi). See Takayama Chogyû, "Shûkyô to kokka," in *Chogyû zenshû*, 4:285–95.

[97] Chogyû, "Iwayuru shakai shôsetsu oronzu," 477–84.

[98] Ibid., 478–79.

[99] *Ibid.,* 480–83.

[100] "Seinen to kinji no tokuiku," in *TRZ*, 1:520–21, also reprinted in Odagiri, *Meiji shakaishugi bungakushû (1)*, 26–27.

[101] "Seinen ni oyoboseru kôriteki bunmei no hei," in *TRZ*, 2:314–16.

[102] Ibid.

[103] "Seinen to shimpô" [Youth and progress], in *TRZ*, 2:347, originally published in *Kôkô Bungaku*, no. 3 (January 1897): 81–82.

[104] Ibid., 347.

105 "Jinzai yôsoku," in *TRZ*, 2:182–85, also reprinted in Odagiri, *Meiji shakaishugi bungakushû (1)*, 4–5.

106 Ibid., 182–83.

107 Ibid., 184.

108 Taoka Reiun, "Hyûmanichii," in *TRZ*, 1:571–72.

109 See "Shimpi setsu kanken," in *TRZ*, 2:320–46, originally published in *Kôkô Bungaku*, nos. 3, 5, and 6 (January, April, and May 1897).

110 Ibid., 330. This language is very reminiscent of Schopenhauer, who wrote, "The subject is the seat of all cognition, but itself is not cognitized by anything. Accordingly it is the support for the world and always presupposed as the general condition of all appearances, of all objects: whatever exists, exists only for the subject." *WWR*, 1:25.

111 "Shimpi setsu kanken," in *TRZ*, 2:341.

112 "Indo no shimpisetsu," *Taiyô* 3:10 (May 1897): 170–78

113 "Seinen ni gekisu," in *TRZ*, 2:508–10, also reprinted in Odagiri, *Meiji shakaishugi bungakushû (1)*, 39–40.

114 "Shakai mondai," in *TRZ*, 2:519, also reprinted in Odagiri, *Meiji shakaishugi bungakushû (1)*, 25–26.

115 Two articles by Reiun on the benefit concert for Korean students were published in *Yorozuchô*, March 19 and 22, 1898.

116 Tatsuo Arima, *The Failure of Freedom* (Cambridge, MA: Harvard University Press, 1969), 3.

117 Ibid., 5–6.

118 Arima, Ibid., 6.

119 See Schopenhauer, *Manuscript Remains*, 437n583. This passage is also quoted in App, *Schopenhauer's Compass*, 250–51. See also the lines from Schopenhauer's *On the Basis of Morality* in one of the epigraphs that open this chapter.

> Boundless compassion for all living things is the firmest and surest guarantee of pure moral conduct, and needs no causitry. Whoever is inspired with it will assuredly injure no one, will wrong no one, will encroach on no one's rights; on the contrary, he will be lenient and patient with everyone, will forgive everyone, will help everyone as much as he can, and all his actions will bear the stamp of justice, philanthropy, and loving-kindness. (*OBM*, 172)

120 Takahashi, *Taoka Reiun*, 34.

Chapter Five

[1] Morse Peckham, *Beyond the Tragic Vision: The Quest for Identity in the Nineteenth Century* (New York: George Braziller, 1962), 84. For an earlier treatment of the material in this chapter, see my article "The Inversion of Progress: Taoka Reiun's *Hibunmeiron*," *Monumenta Nipponica* 40:2 (1985): 191–208.

[2] Ibid.

[3] Lears, *No Place of Grace*, 58.

[4] Taylor, *Sources of the Self*, 481.

[5] Ruth Abbey comments on Taylor's use of the term "radical reflexivity" to talk about the way thinkers have conceptualzed the self.. She writes: "This term refers to a focus on the self *qua* self, the turning of attention toward what sort of self it is that has experiences of knowing, feeling and so on. In this process, the inquiry's concern moves from objects of experience to the subject of experience." Ruth Abbey, ed., *Charles Taylor* (Cambridge: Cambridge University Press, 2004), 83. Although Taylor may feel that this kind of movement is particular to the western sense of self, going back as far as Saint Augustine, it seems evident that Reiun also viewed the self in precisely this way for he constantly argued for the need to take the subjective point of view over the purely objective focus that the nineteenth-century scientific worldview seemed to demand.

[6] Ames and Hall, *Daodejing*, 40.

[7] See Thomas Nagel, *Mortal Questions* (London: Cambridge University Press, 1979), 213. The context for this remark is Nagel's final chapter, "Subjective and Objective," where he writes, "There is a problem that emerges in several areas of philosophy whose connection with one another is not obvious. . . . The problem is one of opposition between subjective and objective points of view. There is a tendency to seek an objective account of everything before admitting its reality. But often what appears to a more subjective point of view cannot be accounted for in this way. So either the objective conception of the world is incomplete, or the subjective involves illusions that should be rejected" (196). To Reiun, the latter course would be highly inappropriate, for he believed strongly that the "objective conception of the world" was incomplete and needed to be supplemented with a healthy dose of the subjective point of view.

[8] Konishi, *Anarchist Modernity*, 140–41.

[9] Ibid., 10–11.

[10] Ibid., 5.

[11] Berman, *All That Is Solid*, 15.

[12] For background information on this journal, see Nishida Masaru, "Tenko," *Bungaku* 24:9 (1956): 125–28. As with *Seinenbun*, Reiun supplied a monthly column

entitled "Hekirekiben" (Thunder Rod). A collection of his essays from this column was published in a single volume, *Hekirekiben,* in 1907.

[13] Both quotations are from Konishi, "The People at Rest," 243.

[14] For details on the relationship between Reiun and Usen, see Nishida Masaru's brief essay, "Kaisetsu" (Explanatory Notes) in a reprint of *Yûzo Muzo* (Tokyo: Takayamabô, 2000), 1–8.

[15] *Sempô Yojin,* in *TRZ,* 5:4–121.

[16] *SD,* 607–8.

[17] See Keping Wang, "Wang Guowei: Philosophy of Aesthetic Criticism," in *Contemporary Chinese Philosophy*, ed. Chung-Ying Cheng and Nicholas Bunnin (New York: Wiley, 2008), 37–56. There is also an interesting article by Takemura Noriyuki, "Wang Guowei (王國維) no kyôkaisetsu (境界説) to Taoka Reiun (田岡嶺雲) no kyôkaisetsu [Wang Guowei's theory of "boundaries" and Taoka Reiun's theory of "boundaries"], in *Studies in Chinese Literature,* December 31, 1986, 127–48, JAIRO (Japanese Institutional Repositories Online), accessed June 2015, http://catalog.lib.kyushu-u.ac.jp/handle/2324/9731/p127.

[18] See Joey Bonner, *Wang Kuo-wei: An Intellectual Biography* (Cambridge, MA: Harvard University Press, 1986), 19, 30, 46. Toward the end of her book, Bonner seems to have confused Reiun with someone else when she refers to his having "sacrificed his life after the death of the MeiJi Emperor to protest the demise of traditional Japanese culture" (213). Perhaps she was thinking of the character Sensei in Sôseki's novel *Kokoro* (1914).

[19] See Nishida Masaru, "Nihon kindai bungaku to kyûba kakumei," in *Kindai bungaku no sensei ryoku* [The latent power in modern literature] (Yagi shoten, 1973), 52–54.

[20] *SD,* 608–10. See also Nishida's Masaru, "Taoka Reiun no daigaku jiyûron," in *Kindai bungaku no sensei ryoku* [The latent power in modern literature] (Yagi shoten, 1973, 29–38. Reiun apparently met and was most impressed with Tang Caichang during this period. See the tribute to Tang he wrote on hearing of his death, "Tang Caichang o itamu," in *TRZ,* 2:707–8. See also Nishida, "Nihon kindai bungaku to kyûba kakumei," in *Kindai bungaku no sensei ryoku,* 52–54.

[21] See *SD,* 608–10. According to Nishida, Reiun's experience in Shanghai was a turning point that signaled his complete alienation from the emperor system and the Japanese state. See Nishida Masaru, "Taoka Reiun no tennôseikan," in *Kindai bungaku no sensei ryoku* [The latent power in modern literature] (Yagi shoten, 1973), 39–51.

[22] "Tang Caichang o itamu" [Grieving over Tang Caichang], in *TRZ,* 2:707–8.

[23] See Hung-yok Ip, "The Power of Interconnectivity: Tan Sitong's Invention of Historical Agency in Late Qing China," *Journal of Global Buddhism* 10 (2009): 323–74.

²⁴ Richard Wilhelm (Cary F. Baynes, trans.), *The I Ching or Book of Changes* (Princeton, NJ: Princeton University Press, 1967), 48. The 2014 translation by Minford, *I Ching (Yijing)*, summarizes the judgment as "The Small Depart, the Great Arrive. This is Auspicious. Fortune" (108).

²⁵ Tan Sitong, quoted in Ip, "Power of Interconnectivity," 337–38.

²⁶ John Makeham, ed., *Transforming Consciousness: Yogācāra Thought in Modern China* (New York: Oxford University Press, 2014), 13–19.

²⁷ *Sempô Yojin*, in *TRZ*, 5:4–121.

²⁸ Ibid., 69.

²⁹ "Tôa Dômei," in *TRZ*, 2:430–35.

³⁰ Ibid., 434–35. China had ceded the Liadong Peninsula to Japan but the Triple Intervention by Germany, France, and Russia forced Japan to retrocede the peninsula to China in return for financial compensation. But two years later Germany seized the Jiaozhou Bay and obtained the lease of a naval base for ninety-nine years from the Qing government while Russia also received a twenty-five-year lease in Dalian. Many Japanese considered this a difficult lesson in international realpolitik.

³¹ *SD*, 571–92.

³² In his autobiography, Reiun describes his first platonic love from afar of a lady whose name he never learned. Ibid., 551–59.

³³ Reiun's treatment of the whole affair can be found in ibid., 572–92.

³⁴ This is mentioned briefly in Notehelfer, *Kôtoku Shûsui*. For more on the Risôdan, see Asukai Masamichi, "Shiryô Meiji sanjû nendai minshûshugi no ichimen," *Jinbungakuhô*, no. 17 (November 1962): 89–146.

³⁵ "Awarenaru wagako" (My pitiable child], in *TRZ*, 2:702–6. Written in the form of a letter to a son he does not know who thinks another man is his father, Reiun laments the situation with which all three of them must live and longs for the day when he might see his son. His son eventually did meet his father and took his last name, becoming Taoka Ryôichi. He had a distinguished career as a jurist and a Kyoto University professor of international law.

³⁶ One article in particular, "Gakuri ni taisuru seiken no hakugai," published in *Chôgoku Minpô* in 1903, contained Reiun's reaction to the "Tetsugakkan jiken," an incident involving the firing of a teacher from the Tetsugakkan school for introducing dangerous ideas. The teacher quoted philosopher Alfred Muirhead to the effect that right and wrong are merely relative concepts, citing the example of justifiable regicide. Not only was the teacher dismissed, but the whole school was punished when the Ministry of Education rescinded its special status. Reiun considered the action unwarranted and a dangerous infringement on academic

freedom. See Nishida Masaru, "Taoka Reiun no daigaku jiyûron," in *Kindai bungaku no senseiryoku*, 29-38. Reiun's article also appears in Shimizu Yoshi, comp., *Tetsugakkan jiken to rinri mondai* (Tokyo: Bunmeidô, 1903).

[37] See *Gegokki*, in *TRZ*, 5:123–248. Nishida's extended comments on the background and events surrounding Reiun's imprisonment were most helpful in unraveling this complicated story. See *TRZ*, 5:780–95.

[38] This is noted in a classic article on antimodernism in Japan, Ienaga Saburô, "Hankindaishugi no rekishiteki seisatsu," in *Nihon kindai shisôshi kenkyû* (Tokyo: Tokyo daigaku shuppankai, 1953), 236.

[39] "Kindai bunmei no kekkan," *TRZ*, 3:218–23.

[40] In late 1904 and early 1905, the government was cracking down on left-wing activities. The *Heimin shinbun* had been targeted, and socialists Kôtoku Shûsui and Nishikawa Kojirô were on their way to prison for violating press laws. Sakai Toshihiko would be added to the list after a translation of the *Communist Manifesto* was published to commemorate the paper's one-year anniversary. While it may have been Reiun's frequent use of the word *revolution* in his writings at this time that drew the ire of the government, it could also simply have been a case of guilt by association that brought the heavy hand of censorship down on him. He was a known friend and associate of the Heiminsha founders, frequented their offices and, as we have seen, actively lending his support to the group.

[41] Taoka Reiun's essay "Akumateki bunmei" was published in *Kochûkan* in 1905. *Kochûkan* is reprinted in its entirety in *TRZ*, 3:1–186. "Akumateki bunmei" can be found on pp. 21–31.

[42] From the inaugural issue of *Tenko*; reproduced in *TRZ* IV: 5–6.

[43] See Xing Lu, *Rhetoric in Ancient China, Fifth to Third Century B.C.E.: A Comparison with Classical Greek Rhetoric* (Columbia: University of South Carolina Press, 1998), 27–28.

[44] Taylor, *Sources of the Self*, 495. To be quite clear, while he clearly would applaud the restoration of "depth, richness, and meaning to life," Taylor is describing this critique of an overly utilitarian or instrumentalist view of society as a significant phenomenon in European intellectual history, not endorsing the position.
As Terry Pinkard puts it, Taylor is neither a harsh critic nor a "booster" of modernity, although he does identify "malaises" in the world such as "an excessive individualism flattening the meaning of the world, its granting overarching normative authority to instrumental reason, and its social atomism undoing our deeper connections to our communities and histories." Terry Pinkard, "Taylor, 'History,' and the History of Philosophy," in *Charles Taylor*, ed. Ruth Abbey (Cambridge: Cambridge University Press, 2004), 187–213. While Reiun may not have believed that the utilitarian or scientific outlook was going away anytime

soon, he clearly felt compelled to point out the limitations of such a shallow way of perceiving the world and structuring our lives accordingly.

[45] Taylor, *Sources of the Self*, 500.

[46] Ibid., 490.

[47] "Chikamatsu ni arawaretaru shinjû," in *TRZ*, 4:25–43. The quotation is from p. 25.

[48] "Gendai shisôkakumei no kizashi" [The coming revolution in contemporary thought], in *TRZ*, 3:32–42.

[49] Arthur Schopenhauer, "On the Will in Nature/Animal Magnetism and Magic," in *On the Will in Nature*, trans. E. F. J. Payne, ed. David E. Cartwright (Oxford: Berg, 1992), 106–7. A version is also available at Wikisource, accessed March 2016. http://en.wikisource.org/wiki/On_the_Will_in_Nature/Animal_Magnetism_and_Magic.

[50] *TRZ*, 3:32–33.

[51] Thomas Mann notes, "Schopenhauer, as psychologist of the will, is the father of all modern psychology. From him the line runs, by way of the psychological radicalism of Nietzsche, straight to Freud and the men who built up psychology of the unconscious and applied it to the mental sciences." Mann, *Living Thoughts*, 24.

[52] Havelock Ellis, *The Nineteenth Century: An Utopian Retrospect* (Boston and London: Small, Maynard, 1901), 3.

[53] Taoka Reiun, "Shinkyûsei to tôzaifû no chôwa," in *TRZ*, 3:52–59.

[54] Gendai shisô no anchô in *TRZ*, 2:427–36 The call for a social revolution is on p. 435.

[55] Ibid., 434–35.

[56] For an overview of the concepts underlying transnational history, see Simon Macdonald, "Transnational History: A Review of Past and Present Scholarship," accessed April 2016. https://www.ucl.ac.uk/cth/objectives/simon_macdonald_tns_review. See also Mae Ngai, "Promises and Perils of Transnational History," in *Perspectives on History*, American Historical Association, October 2012, accessed April 2016, https://www.historians.org/publications-and-directories/perspectives-on-history/december-2012/the-future-of-the-discipline/promises-and-perils-of-transnational-history. Also see a conversation among scholars C. A. Bayly, Sven Beckert, Matthew Connelly, Isabel Hofmeyer, Wendy Kozol, and Patricia Seed, where Bayly points out, "The problem with the modernization theorists of the 1960s and 1970s, as with more recent historians of the 'rise of the West,' is not that they misidentified the process, but that they reified it overmuch, that they identified only one model of 'modernization' and failed to note this building of capacity away from the Western core." "On Transnational History," *American Historical Review*

(2006). The article is also available at the Graduate Institute website, accessed May 15, 2016, http://graduateinstitute.ch/files/live/sites/iheid/files/sites/international_history_politics/users/stratto9/public/intro_ahr111.5.. This seems to be precisely the point that Taoka Reiun is driving home.

[57] Max Nordau, *The Conventional Lies of Our Civilization* (Chicago: L. Schick, 1884), 1.

[58] Ibid., 28.

[59] Berman, *All That Is Solid*, 15.

[60] Nordau's rant against so many things in *Degeneration*, however, would probably not have appealed to Reiun. As a firm believer in science, Nordau could not abide the likes of Tolstoy, mysticism, idealism, or socialism—many of the things for which Reiun held high hopes.

[61] Rowbotham, *Edward Carpenter*, 1–2.

[62] Ibid., 70. Rowbotham notes, "The book resonated equally with Carpenter. Through the Bhagavad-Gita the former Anglican curate cold find in another spiritual idiom an endorsement of the selfless endeavor to serve others which he, like so many of his contemporaries, still valued after discarding the Christian faith. Through the Gita he could conceive another kind of redemption" (70).

[63] Carpenter, *Civilization*, 1. Carpenter's book is currently available as a reprint from the University of Michigan Libraries collection; the page numbers are the same as in the original. The Min'yûsha published a Japanese translation by Fukai Eigo in 1895 under the title *Bunmei no hei oyobi sono kyûji* [文明の弊およびその救治], Volume 5 in the Heimin sōsho series (Tokyo: Min'yûsha, 1895). This occurrence is also reported by Sheila Rowbotham in her biography, *Edward Carpenter* (348). It is not known whether Taoka read this translation or relied on the original English version. It can be noted, however, that in late 1898, perhaps echoing Carpenter's title, Kôtoku Shûsui published an article, "The Degeneration of Society: Its Causes and Cure," in which, like Reiun, he lashed out at the signs of corruption and degeneration in society but claimed that they were "not so much the fault of the corrupt or degenerate individual as they are the crime of the system or organization that prevails in society today and forces them to fall into these against their will." Quoted in Notehelfer, *Kôtoku Shûsui*, 45. This is a position to which Reiun was gradually coming around.

[64] See Carpenter, *Civilization*, 5.

[65] Ibid., 27–29.

[66] Ibid., 28.

[67] Ibid., 28–29.

[68] Ibid., 33–34.

[69] Stanley Pierson, "Edward Carpenter, Prophet of a Socialist Millennium," *Victorian Studies* 13:3 (March 1970): 301–18.

[70] Carpenter, *Civilization,* 51–52.

[71] Ibid., 64.

[72] See Taoka Reiun, "Shajitsushugi no konpenteki byûsô," in *TRZ,* 3:268–73.

[73] "Akumateki bunmei," in *TRZ,* 3:5–7.

[74] Ibid. See also "Daraku no bunmei," in *TRZ,* 3:128–129; and "Bunmei to jinrui no daraku," *TRZ,* 4: 69-77.

[75] "Akumateki bunmei," in *TRZ,* 3:24–25. The "mind only" doctrine is a feature of Yogācāra Buddhism to which Reiun was exposed in Shanghai (if not before) when he met Tang Caichang, Wang Kangnian, and the other refugees from Kang Youwei's 100 Days Reform movement. The expression "mind only," or sometimes "consciousness only," captures the idea that "the empirical world, and its phenomena are, on close investigation, found to be nothing but representations arising in mind. It is mind that is the source and substance of the world" a statement that is very close to Schopenhauer's understanding. Cross, *Schopenhauer's Encounter,* 152. Cross points out that Yogācāra teachings would not have been available to Schopenhauer but were widely known in Japan in Taoka's time (149).

[76] "Akumateki bunmei," in *TRZ,* 3:22–24.

[77] Carpenter, *Civilization,* 83–84.

[78] "Akumateki bunmei," *TRZ* 3: 21–31. See also "Gendai shisô no anchô," in *TRZ,* 3:427–36.

[79] Sandra Shapshay, "Poetic Intuition and the Bounds of Sense: Metaphor and Metonymy in Schopenhauer's Philosophy," in *Better Consciousness: Schopenhauer's Philosophy of Value,* ed. Alex Neil and Christopher Janaway (London: Wiley-Blackwell, 2009), 71.

[80] "Akumateki bunmei," in *TRZ,* 3:27.

[81] Ibid.

[82] See Donald J. Munro, *The Concept of Man in Early China* (Palo Alto, CA: Stanford University Press, 1969), especially chapter 5, 117–39. In *Daodejing,* Hall and Ames describe the world as "a myriad of spontaneous transactions" and warn that individuals must be wary of tendencies to "institutionalize and enforce an overly static vision of the world, and in so doing, deprive both language and life of their creative possibilities" (44–45).

[83] "Gendai shisô no anchô," in *TRZ,* 3:434–36.

[84] Nishida Masaru makes a very similar point in *Kindai wa hitei dekiruka,* 41–42. The context is an essay on the nature of responsibility borne by science for the

development and deployment of nuclear weapons. Nishida is responding to a 1980 essay by Karaki Junzô, who, like 1949 Nobel prize winner in physics Yukawa Hideki, looked back to the thought of Laozi and Zhuangzi and the notion of *wu-wei* (noncoercive action) in order to fully appreciate how natural science operates. But Nishida sees Reiun's grasp of Daoism as more subtle and convincing than Karaki's.

[85] *TRZ*, 3:427.

[86] Ibid., 432–36.

[87] D. C. Lau points out, "Development and decline are totally different in nature. Development is slow and gradual: decline is quick and abrupt. Development can only be achieved by deliberate effort: decline comes about naturally and inexorably." D. C. Lau, *Lao-tzu/Tao Te Ching* (London and new York: Penguin Books, 1963), 27.

[88] See "Knowledge Rambling in the North," paragraph 6, as found at http://nothingistic.org/library/chuangtzu/chuang64.html. Accessed Feb. 2, 2015. Also found in this section is a notion that is very basic to Daoism: "That which makes things what they are has not the limit which belongs to things, and when we speak of things being limited, we mean that they are so in themselves."

[89] "Gendai shisô no anchô," in *TRZ*, 3:432–34. The Zhuangzi quotation is on p. 432.

[90] This is very similar to the point made by Taylor as well: that the utilitarian, commercial, scientific and instrumentalist worldview had the unfortunate consequence of degrading life and depriving it of its "richness, depth and meaning" (*Sources of the Self*, 500). As Nicholas Smith notes in *Charles Taylor*, Taylor sees "the exploration of sources that lie 'outside the subject' but which 'resonate within him or her' as the central aspiration of modernism" (226). It can be convincingly argued that Reiun spent much of his life and career trying to find that connection between the individual self and the surrounding world, and therefore he made the question of the self and the nature of subjectivity his "central aspiration."

[91] "Akumateki bunmei," in *TRZ*, 3:13–14.

[92] This is precisely the point made by Konishi in his chapter "The History Slide," in *Anarchist Modernity*, 224–36.

[93] "Tetsujin wa kaikô su," in *TRZ*, 3:129–30.

[94] Ibid. See also "Gendai shisô no anchô," in *TRZ*, 3:434–36.

[95] *SD*, 670–71.

[96] "Fukkoteki shakaishugi," in *Kochûkan*, *TRZ*, 3:112–13.

[97] See Reiun's fifth collection of essays, *Urokuun* (Tokyo: Takayamabô, 1905), especially 1–42.

⁹⁸ The essay, "Boze-kô totsu-totsu go," was published in fourteen installments in *Heimin shinbun* beginning on November 29, 1903. The last installment was published on May 8, 1904. It is reprinted in *TRZ*, 3:384–420.

⁹⁹ *SD*, 659–60.

¹⁰⁰ Ibid., 661–62.

¹⁰¹ Ibid.

¹⁰² "Jin, ji, ai," in *Kochûkan*, *TRZ*, 3:117–18.

¹⁰³ "Chijô no tengoku," in *TRZ*, 3:118–19.

¹⁰⁴ "Risô no shin ôkoku," in *TRZ*, 3:114.

¹⁰⁵ "Jinshuteki henken," in *TRZ*, 3:356–57.

¹⁰⁶ "Yoga shakaishugi," in *TRZ* 3:63–65.

¹⁰⁷ Ibid. Although it is slightly different, *chiryoku* (智力), which refers to a mental or intellectual faculty, is very similar to Reiun's preferred term, *chikô* (智巧), which he regularly used to mean "clever reasoning."

¹⁰⁸ The following discussion draws on "Gendai no byôkon—Mamomizumu o haisu," [The Roots of Contemporary Evils—Worshipping Mammonism] in *TRZ*, 3:73–90.

¹⁰⁹ Ibid., 90.

¹¹⁰ "Isei no shiyû," in *TRZ*, 3:109–10.

¹¹¹ "Tôshin wa shizen nari," in *TRZ*, 3:119–20.

¹¹² Pierson, "Edward Carpenter," 318.

¹¹³ *SD*, 419–20.

¹¹⁴ Konishi, *Anarchist Modernity*, 8.

¹¹⁵ "Chijô to tengoku," in *TRZ*, 3:118–19.

¹¹⁶ Ibid.

¹¹⁷ "Jisei no chokka," in *TRZ*, 3:119. For the quote from Henry George, see his *Social Problems* (New York: Schalkenback Foundation, 1953), 9 (originally published in 1883). It can also be found online accessed March 2, 2015, http://www.wealthandwant.com/themes/underpop/gospel_of_brotherhood.htm. According to Professor Nishida's explanatory notes, George's main work, *Progress and Poverty: An Inquiry into the Cause of Industrial Depressions and of Increase of Want with Increase of Wealth; The Remedy* (1879), was extremely influential in Japan (*TRZ*, 3:792). In the United States it was also a best seller, with several million copies to its credit. Tolstoy was also influenced by the economic thinking of Henry George and incorporated some of his ideas into later works such as *Resurrection*.

[118] "Jinrui to kishu," in *TRZ*, 3:127–28. Carpenter quotes the same lines from Thoreau, after which he asks, "And how can we, gulfed as we are in this present whirlpool, conceive rightly the glory which awaits us?" (*Civilization*, 35).

[119] Ibid.

[120] "Shimpishugi o ronzu," in *TRZ*, 4:275–79.

[121] "Sakkanarazaru ni shôsetsuka," in *TRZ*, 4:113–16.

Chapter Six

[1] Ishikawa Takuboku, *Takuboku zenzhû*, ed. Kindaichi Kyôsuke et al., 8 vols. (Tokyo: Chikuma Shobô, 1967–68), 4:256–65. "Jidai heisoku no genjô" can also be found in Odagiri Hideo, ed., *Ishikawa Takuboku shû*. Meiji Bungaku zenshû, vol. 52 (Tokyo: Chikuma shobô, 1970): 259–64. An interesting translation of the title of this essay, "The State of Alienation and Spiritual Stagnation," appears in Nobuya Bamba and John Howes, ed., *Pacifism in Japan: The Christian and Socialist Tradition* (Vancouver: University of British Columbia Press, 1978). See also Donald Keene's recent biography of Takuboku, *The First Modern Japanese: The Life of Ishikawa Takuboku* (New York: Columbia University Press, 2016), where he states that "Although it is difficult to name the qualities that make a poet appear modern, Takuboku's poems make their modernity clear without needing further explanation." (3) While it amy be the case that no explanation of what constitutes being or becoming modern is necessary, it is worth noting that Reiun, fifteen years Takuboku's senior, did work very diligently to explain what he thought the nature of becoming modern was all about. Interestingly, even though his subject matter and his similes were steeped in the many feelings that we associate with being modern, Takuboku never deviated from composing his 31-syllable *tanka* in classical Japanese, something that might have lent them a somewhat archaic feel. But one cannot disagree with Keene that Takuboku's poems never feel other than completely modern. Reiun did not compose poetry, nor did he write in the classical language though his admiration for Chinese thought was often apparent in his syntax. Takuboku may well be Japan's first modern poet but it is not clear that this gives validity to the claim that he is "the first modern Japanese."

[2] *Takuboku zenshû*, 4:264.

[3] Ibid., 263–65.

[4] We should also remember that Reiun had reviewed Kôtoku's books *Imperialism* and *Essence of Imperialism* very favorably. Likewise, during his *Seinenbun* years, Reiun had grappled with the contradictions and corruption that seemed to be pervasive in Japan in the wake of the Sino-Japanese War, much as Kôtoku had. Ienaga recounts a story related by Reiun's young assistant, Fujisawa Morihiko, when he was publishing his small journal *Koku-Byaku*. One day Fujisawa was visiting Taoka at his residence, where the journal was being published. It seems that Kôtoku Shûsui

barged into the house as though he was being pursued. He had a package with him that he wanted Reiun to hold for him, but Reiun declined, saying there was no safe place there to store anything. His journal *Tenko* had been censored, as had many of his books, so whatever Kôtoku wanted him to hide, Reiun was not interested. When Fujisawa spoke up and said that he would take care of the package, Reiun abruptly disabused him of that notion. Only a matter of minutes after Kôtoku left, the police came, asking about him and any items he might have had in his possession. Ienaga hints that this story may tell us something about the philosophical differences between Reiun and Kôtoku, but I think it is more likely that Reiun was just being smart. Kôtoku was his friend, and he sympathized with his views, but he could not put his journal, operating on a shoestring as it was, at risk. But the very fact that Kôtoku would come to him suggests that they were kindred spirits, definitely members of a community with similar values and a shared vision. See Ienaga's explanatory notes to the reprint of some early issues of *Koku-Byaku* published in 1966 by the Meichaku kankôkai, 3, "Taoka Reiun no '*Koku-Byaku*.'" *Bungaku* 24:6 (1956): 104–6.

[5] Peter Duus, "Whig History Japanese Style: The Min'yûsha Historians and the Meiji Restoration," *Journal of Asian Studies* 33:3 (May 1974): 415–36.

[6] "Nagatamura ni te," in *TRZ*, 4:311–27.

[7] See Sanderson Beck, *The Dao De Jing Way Power Book* by Lao-zi. Accessed January 27, 2015, http://www.san.beck.org/Laotzu.html#18.

[8] In this sense, the lines from chapter 18 are a corollary to the lines from Anquetil-Duperron's translation of the *Oupnek'hat*, "Just when insight arrives, desire leaves the scene," which may well have been a turning point in the development of Schopenhauer's metaphysics.(See Urs App, *Schopenhauer's Compass*, 202) Once understanding is arrived at, the will is quieted and desires lose their grip on the human psyche. The *Daodejing* is simply pointing out that this is how things were before people lost touch with the original Way.

[9] See Beck, *The Dao De Jing*, chapter 19, accessed February 6, 2015, http://www.san.beck.org/Laotzu.html#19 (italics mine).

[10] Hans-Georg Moeller takes the position that while Daoist sages recognize human characteristics they are "untouched" by them. They remain "truly and universally affirmative . . . by not siding with any specific affirmation at the expense of others." That is how they can "affirm *everything*," which means that Daoists are not especially "humane . . . and not particularly concerned with human beings." Moeller, *Philosophy of the Daodejing*, 134–36. Reiun seemed to think that the individual who knows the Way, as the Daoists see it, is in a better position to be aware of a fuller and deeper reality and hence in a better position to serve others.

[11] Quoted in Taylor, *Sources of the Self*, 386.

282 : THE TURN AGAINST THE MODERN

[12] Bruno Latour, *We Never Have Been Modern* (Cambridge, MA: Harvard University Press, 1993).

[13] *TRZg*, 4:327. The first convention on the settlement of international disputes was held at The Hague in 1899, the second in 1907. At the second convention, which included the United States, Great Britain, Austria-Hungary, Germany, France, Italy, Spain, Russia, Japan, and China, a Korean delegation tried to participate in order to argue that Japan's use of force to annex Korea was illegal, but the delegation was denied entrance by Japanese and British troops. Yi Jun died during the convention under mysterious circumstances.

[14] See the entry on Yi Jun, http://www.revolvy.com/main/index.php?s=Yi%20Jun&uid=1575. Accessed June 2016. While one interpretation of Yi Jun's death was that it was suicide, there were rumors that Japanese spies may have had a hand in his demise.

[15] See James McClain, *A Modern History of Japan* (New York: Norton, 2002), 191–97.

[16] For details on these incidents, see Roger Bowen, *Rebellion and Democracy in Meiji Japan: A Study of the Commoners in the Popular Rights Movement* (Berkeley: University of California Press, 1980).

[17] Ibid., 67–69. Much later, in 1909, this same Okumiya Kenshi (or Tateyuki), who had some exposure to bomb making during these *gekka-jiken* days, would meet with Kôtoku and help him get in touch with someone who actually could produce plans for making a bomb. Apparently Kôtoku relayed this information to Miyashita Daikichi, a factory worker and socialist, who actually managed to explode a bomb made with this formula in November 1909. See Notehelfer, *Kôtoku Shûsui*, 176–77.

[18] Taoka Reiun, "Seinen to shimpô," [Youth and progress], in *TRZ*, 2:347.

[19] *Meiji hanshinden* is reprinted in *TRZ*, 5:251–413 (hereafter cited as *MHD*). The introduction is on pp. 267–85.

[20] Ibid., 271–75.

[21] See Tanaka Kotarô, "Taoka Reiun, Kôtoku Shûsui, Okumiya Kenshi no tsuikairoku," *Chûô Kôron*, December 1914, 1–26.

[22] This discussion draws on two very similar treatments of the Restoration: in *MHD*, 275–85; and *SD*, 503–6.

[23] *MHD*, 270.

[24] *SD*, 503.

[25] See Tetsuo Najita, "Nakano Seigô and the Spirit of the Meiji Restoration in Twentieth Century Japan," in *Dilemmas of Growth in Prewar Japan*, ed. James Morely (Princeton, NJ: Princeton University Press 1971), 375–421. Note that Nakano's *Meiji minkenshi ron* (1913) was written around the same time that Reiun was compiling *Sakkiden* and that the two men shared a common link to Miyake Setsurei.

[26] *MHD*, 281.

[27] *Taisei* (大勢) literally means "large *ikioi*."

[28] *TRZ*, 4:311–27. The same essay can also be found in a nice facsimile reproduction of Reiun's book, Nishida Masaru, comp., *Byôchû Hôrô* [Wanderings from the Sickbed], 166–98.

[29] *TRZ*, 2:347.

[30] The figure appears on *TRZ* 5: 269. It should be noted that, while attributing the thesis-antithesis-synthesis model to Hegel is common, he never seems to have actually used it himself. His primary interest is in how the "spirit" evolves historically over time and eventually achieves the reflexivity or self-consciousness that allows it to become aware of itself as a subject for which something distinct from itself, an object, is presented.

[31] Konishi refers to this change in historical consciousness as "the history slide," which, he argues, brought about a "reconceived subjectivity of the present as a point of moral action" (*Anarchist Modernity*, 226). Whether it was the antiwar movement centered on Kôtoku and the *Heimin shinbun* or the high cost and misery that the war created for many Japanese citizens, the war provided an occasion for people like Reiun and others to question Japan's trajectory. "History was narrated into the future," Konishi writes, "and the present became the backward past. The present as a product of Western human progress and civilization was now perceived as behind and no longer morally justifiable" (ibid.).

[32] If there was a belief in a deep current of historical change that was progressive in nature, to use Robert Nisbet's phrase in *Social Change and History* (London: Oxford University Press, 1969), it would be

> the idea that beneath the crimes and follies of history, actual history, there is a deep current of natural progress, needing only to be aided in its flow, only to be freed of the earthworks of superstition and tyranny, could not help but prove an attractive and valuable one to the French *philosophes* at the end of the eighteenth century. To their hatred of church, aristocracy, guild, and feudal tradition on political grounds, on grounds of utopian dream there could be added a vision of human development in which all these institutions were to be deemed not simply moral evils, but obstacles to the natural course of progress of civilization that would prevail if only these groups and institutions could be extirpated. (116–17)

[33] Ibid., 117.

[34] See Maruyama Masao, "Rekishi isshiki no 'kôsô'" [On the deepest layer of historical consciousness] (Tokyo: Chikuma shobô, 1972), 1:3–46. Drawing heavily on the language of the *Kojiki* and other early Japanese historical writings, Maruyama singles out a *basso ostinato*, a rhythmically repeated refrain that he believed shaped the way Japanese look at historical change: *tsugi-tsugi ni nariyuku ikioi* (つぎつぎになりゆく勢い), "a dynamic force (*ikioi*) that is in a perpetual state of becoming."

Tsugi-tsugi ni means "continually," and *nariyuku* means "to become." According to Maruyama, Japanese historical consciousness, then, would actually be concerned not with the past as such, or with the future, but only with a present that is eternally unfolding, which might make it sound as though Japanese are largely ahistorical. Moreover, Maruyama contrasted the use of a word like *naru* in Japanese creation myths to describe coming-into-being with the frequent use in biblical texts of the words *make* and *do* (*suru* in Japanese) in corresponding situations. The inference is clearly that the Japanese attitude toward change is intrinsically passive. See especially pp. 6–14.

[35] Taoka Reiun, "Ki-itsuteki sûsei," in *TRZ*, 3:43–51.

[36] Mead, *Movements of Thought*, 145.

[37] Halstead, *Romanticism*, 12.

[38] Taoka Reiun, "Chûkô kannen no zento," in *TRZ*, 4:676–78; the quote in from p. 676

[39] Ibid., 677.

[40] See Maruyama, "Rekishi isshiki no 'kôsô'," 29. The translation is by Hellmut Wilhelm in *Eight Lectures on the I Ching* (Princeton, NJ: Princeton University Press, 1973), 23.

[41] Taoka Reiun, "Eki wa jishonari," in *TRZ*, 3:143.

[42] Wilhelm, *Eight Lectures*, 17.

[43] See Motoyama, "Meiji nijû-nendai no seiron ni arawareta nashionarizumu," in *Meiji zenhanki no nashionarizumu*, edited by Sakata Yoshio, (Tokyo: Miraisha, 1958), 37-87. The quotation is from pp. 65–66.

[44] Maruyama, "Chûsei to hangyaku." Nearly one hundred pages in length, this essay is wide ranging. See especially the section "Teikô no seishin to muhon no tetsugaku" [The spirit of resistance and the philosophy of rebellion], 455–71.

[45] Ibid., 463.

[46] The principal of Ichikô, who was none other than Nitobe Inazô at the time, was a Ministry of Education appointee, so he resigned in embarrassment. See Kenneth Strong's introduction to his translation of Tokutomi Rôka's novel, *Footprints in the Snow* (London: Allen and Unwin, 1970), 36–38.

[47] See Maruyama, "Chûsei to hangyaku," 463, where the author quotes the passage from *Sakkiden* where Reiun discusses wanting the self to be at the center of everything he does and his unwillingness to accept any ideology not rooted in the self. To Maruyama this represents a rare opportunity to forge connections between the inner self and a sense of individual autonomy (*jishusei*, 自主性) in the outer world. For an argument as to why *Sakkiden* should be considered among Japan's first genuinely self-reflexive autobiographies, see Ronald Loftus, "In Search of Japan's First Modern Autobiography," *biography* 6:3 (1983): 256–72.

⁴⁸ Latour, *We Never Have Been Modern*, 35–36. Latour notes, somewhat sarcastically, when describing these second Enlightenment critics, "The traps of naturalization and scientific ideology were finally dispelled. No one who has not waited for that dawn and thrilled to its promises is modern. . . . The critical power of the moderns lies in this double language: they can mobilize Nature at the heart of social relationships, even as they leave Nature infinitely remote from human beings; they are free to make and unmake their society, even as they render its laws ineluctable, necessary and absolute" (36–37). So the modern condition is paradoxical and contradictory; it insists on dividing the human experience into opposing camps and decreeing that they are absolute categories even though this supposition can never be convincingly demonstrated.

Chapter Seven

¹ J. Bronowski and B. Mazlish, eds., *The Western Intellectual Tradition* (Harper and Row, 1960), takes this approach to Rousseau. See 293–94 especially.

² Lewis S. Feuer, ed., *Marx and Engels: Basic Writings on Politics and Philosophy* (Anchor Books, 1959), 68. The quote is from Engels's "Socialism: Scientific and Utopian."

³ *TRZ*, 4:458.

⁴ "Nagatamura ni te," in *TRZ*, 4:327. The essay is also reprinted in Nishida, *Byôchû Hôrô*, 166–98 (see especially pp. 197–98).

⁵ Taoka Reiun, "Tônan no kakusha yori Geiyô ni fukusu," in *TRZ*, 4:457–66. The essay is also reprinted in Nishida, *Byôchû Hôrô*, 101–21. The quote is from pp. 108–9.

⁶ The reference in the text was to a "Mr. Yanagawa" (梁川) and his *kenshinsetsu* (見神説), literally "having a vision of God" (*TRZ*, 4:458-59). Yanagawa was a Waseda University philosophy graduate, Tsunashima Sakunichirô, who adopted the Yanagawa (梁川) name; his ideas were discussed in a 1907 book by Usami Eitarô, which included an essay by one of Reiun's friends, Ômachi Keigetsu.

⁷ *TRZ*, 4:458.

⁸ Ibid., 458–59.

⁹ Ibid., 460–61.

¹⁰ Ibid., 461–62.

¹¹ Ibid., 462–66.

¹² See the sections in *SD* entitled "Bonjin no tenka" and "Bonjin no kachi," 473–78. Rousseau is quoted in Bronowski and Mazlish, *Western Intellectual Tradition*, 281.

¹³ See Nishida Masaru, "Taoka Reiun no ibun" [Posthumous writings of Taoka Reiun], in *Kindai bungaku no sensei ryoku* [The latent power in modern literature]

(Tokyo: Yagi shoten, 1973), 16–28.

14. *TRZ*, 4:464–64.

15. *WWR/2010*, 1:6.

16. Ibid., 5.

17. *TRZ*, 4:463–64.

18. These papers were published in Nishida Masaru, "Taoka Reiun mihappyô ikyô (I)," *Bungakuteki tachiba* 1 (July–August 1965): 91–96. It was the inaugural issue of this journal.

19. All the materials associated with Reiun's *joshi-kaihôron* were collected by Professor Nishida in a single volume, Nishida Masaru,*Taoka Reiun joshikaihôron* [Taoka Reiun's essays on women's liberation] (Tokyo: Hôsei daigaku shuppankyoku, 1987) (hereafter *JKR*). See Nishida's own essay on pp. 173–90.

20. *TRZ*, 4:462–63.

21. Taoka Reiun, "Ippu-ippu wa hatashite tensoku nariya," *Shinsei* 11:4 (March 1904): 87–90.

22. *TRZ*, 3:109–10.

23. Nordau, *Conventional Lies*, 272.

24. Ibid., 287.

25. *SD*, 700–701.

26. See Ienaga Saburô's discussion of this journal in "Taoka Reiun no 'Koku-Byaku,'" *Bungaku* 24:6 (1956): 104–6. His essay was updated when spme issues of *Koku-Byaku* were reprinted in 1996. See his *kaisetsu* (explanatory notes) to issues 2, 3, and 6, published in *Bungaku* 24:6 (1956):,1–4.

27. Taoka Reiun, "Joshikaihôron," *Koku Byaku*, no. 2 (March 20, 1909): 1–2. Reprinted in *JKR*, 1–26.

28. Frederick Engels, *The Origins of the Family, Private Property, and the State: In Light of the Research by Lewis H. Morgan* (New York International Publishers, 1942), 57–58.

29. Bebel's work is available in an online archive, accessed January 2015, http://www.marxists.org/archive/bebel/1879/woman-socialism/introduction.htm.

30. Ibid.

31. See an excerpted version of "Jôshikaihô wa danshikaihô nari" in *JKR*, 111–15. The quote is from p. 115.

32. Nordau, *Conventional Lies*, 289.

33. Taoka Reiun, "Kekkon to kantsû,"in *TRZ*, 3:110.

34. Taoka Reiun, "Chikamatsu mono ni arawaretaru shinjû: Fushizen naru shakai no

gisei," in *TRS*, 124–25; reprinted in *JKR*, 63–84.

[35] Edward Carpenter, *Love's Coming of Age* (George, Allen and Unwin, 1896), 1–2.

[36] Ibid., 53–54.

[37] See the memoirs by Japanese women compiled in Ronald Loftus, *Telling Lives: Women's Self-Writing in Modern Japan* (Honolulu: University of Hawai'i Press, 2004).

[38] Carpenter, *Love's Coming of Age*, 53–54.

[39] Reiun Taoka, "Uzô muzô," in Nishida, *Byôchû hôrô*, 215–25. An abridged version may be found in *JKR*, 99–101.

[40] Tanaka, "Taoka Reiun,' 1–26.

[41] The list of the 16 contributors plus the 3 special forewards are listed in *TRZ* 5:417. Detailed explanatory notes (*kaisetsu*) accompanying *Sakkiden* are found in *TRZ*, 5:800–20.

Chapter Eight

[1] See Tadashi Karube, *Maruyama Masao and the Fate of Liberalism in Twentieth-Century Japan*, trans. David Noble (Tokyo: International House of Japan, 2008), 158–59. See also Maruyama Masao, "Politics and Man in the Contemporary World," in *Thought and Behavior in Modern Japanese Politics*, ed. Ivan Morris (London: Oxford University Press, 1969), 321–22.

[2] Karube, *Maruyama Masao*, 158–59. It is also noteworthy that Nick Mansfield makes a similar point when he writes that "the subject is always linked to something outside of it—an idea or principle or the society of other subjects." Mansfield, *Subjectivity*, 3.

[3] Karube, *Maruyama Masao*, 71.

[4] J. Victor Koschmann, "The Debate on Subjectivity in Postwar Japan: Foundations of Modernism as a Political Critique," *Pacific Affairs* 54:4 (Winter 1981–82): 626.

[5] This account is based on Karube, *Maruyama Masao*, 35–45, where the author observes, "These experiences gave the young Maruyama Masao a painful lesson in 'the character of Japanese state power as infinitely invasive of one's innermost spirit.'" As Karube points out, after his release, Maruyama received twice-yearly visits from the Tokkô (the Spevial Higher Police) and the Kenpeitai (the military police who joined the Higher Police in suppressing dissent) and when he reported for his "annual inspection of draft-age men conducted by the army, he alone would be pulled from the ranks and subjected to questioning by the Kenpeitai." (45)

[6] Berman, "Why Modernism Matters," 33.

[7] Gabriel Josipovici, *What Ever Happened to Modernism?* New Haven: Yale University Press, 2010), 185.

[8] Maruyama Masao, "Theory and Psychology of Ultra-Nationalism," in *Thought and Behavior in Modern Japanese Politics,* ed. Ivan Morris (London: Oxford University Press, 1969), 1.

[9] Josipovici, *What Ever Happened to Modernism?*, 187.

[10] See *SD*, 668, where he refers to himself as a "*shisôjô no inaka mono*" (country bumpkin).

[11] Ienaga, *Sûki naru shisôka*, 162; Berman, *All That Is Sold*, 15.

[12] Giddens, *Modernity and Self-Identity*, 53 (italics in the original). In one of Giddens's other major works, *The Consequences of Modernity* (Stanford, CA: Stanford University Press, 1990), he writes about the "discontinuities which separate modern social institutions from the traditional social order" and focuses on three things: (1) "the sheer *pace of change*; . . . the rapidity of change in conditions of modernity is extreme"; (2) "the *scope of change*"; and (3) the "intrinsic *nature of modern institutions*." He goes on to say, "The development of modern social institutions and their worldwide spread have created vastly greater opportunities for human beings to enjoy a secure and rewarding existence than any type of pre-modern system. But modernity also has a somber side, which has become very apparent in the present century" (6–7). As this study has made clear, this aspect of the "somber side" of modernity also became very apparent to Taoka Reiun in the late nineteenth and early twentieth centuries.

[13] Karube, *Maruyama Masao*, 9 (italics mine).

[14] Talmon, *Romanticism and Revolt*, 12.

[15] Taoka Reiun, "Geiyô ni fukusu," in *TRZ*, 4:457.

[16] Sigmund Freud, *Civilization and Its Discontents* (New York: Norton, 1961), 42.

[17] *WWR*, 2:162. Interestingly, a contemporary admirer of the *Daodejing* wrote in the foreword to Wu and Sih, *Lao Tzu/Tao Teh Ching*:

> The *Tao Teh Ching* was written in the morning of the human race, and still bears the freshness of the morning upon it. It exhibits a rush of language, a boldness and exuberance of expression for which paradox is the only adequate form. Hence one who expects to find in it a reasoned, chain-like sequence of thought will be disappointed. Let him not, however, turn away from it on this account. For the Taoists, Reality was beyond measurement, but not beyond the apprehension by a mind that is still. The Book's greatest gift, in my view, is its mind-stretching quality; it challenges us at every turn to expand our view of life's possibilities. (x)

These are Arthur Hummel's words, and I note the way that he, too, is struck by the "freshness of the morning" of the human race that can be felt in the text, something that Schopenhauer clearly found when he read the Vedas and Upanishads.

[18] For details on Rousseau's position, see Taylor *Sources of the Self*, 360–63. As Ruth Abbey notes in her study of Taylor's ideas, "In fact, Rousseau is troubled by the

whole bundle of goods bequeathed by the scientific revolution of the seventeenth century, and fears that the hegemony of instrumental reason has had deleterious consequences, partly because it obscures humans' natural feelings, which are typically benevolent. For all these reasons, Rousseau's thought was a great sense of inspiration to the whole Romantic movement and its reaction against the Enlightenment." Ruth Abbey, Charles Taylor (Princeton, NJ: Princeton University Press, 2000), 86. Obviously, Reiun shared Rousseau's (and Taylor's) concerns about "the hegemony of instrumental reason" and its impact on contemporary life.

[19] Zöller, "Schopenhauer on the Self," 19.

[20] Taylor, *Sources of the Self*, 495–521. Taylor shares with Reiun a concern about so-called "scientific rationality," which Reiun found to be so shallow and narrow in its focus. Reiun believed that an individual's identity is closely tied to the commitments one makes, the stances one takes, and the values one embraces. Taylor underscores the importance of realizing that our selfhood is not externally defined but something attained through turning inward, taking a reflexive stance, and exploring our inner structures, very much what Reiun called for in the 1890s and early 1900s. It has to be said, though, that Taylor is also quite wary of unbridled subjectivism and probably would not concur fully with Reiun's passionate denunciation of the modern scientific outlook, although he would understand exactly where these concerns came from. It is probably accurate to say that neither Taylor nor Reiun can be considered fully successful in resolving the dilemmas of becoming modern. But they both are hopeful about the possibility of a new synthesis, even though this was not something whose fruition either of them was able to witness.

[21] Berman, *All That Is Solid*, 17.

[22] Koschmann, "Debate on Subjectivity, 610, 625–26. The modern, autonomous individual needs to be "equipped with internalized constraints—a conscience" and must always be an "end in himself." What it came down to for many was the ability to "negotiate the distance between public and private realms of life" (626). Koschmann also recounts the moment in a 1948 roundtable discussion on "Materialism and Subjectivity" when the Marxist critic Miyagi Otoya spoke of the need for Marxists to add a dose of Freud to their Marx, to which Maruyama responded, "You should rather say Marx plus Freud plus ethos" (624). In other words, to a thoroughly materialistic worldview one had better add some character and values—that independent vantage point that is the necessary corollary of freedom. See also Andrew Barshay, "Imagining Democracy in Postwar Japan: Maruyama Masao as a Political Thinker," in *The Social Sciences in Modern Japan* (Berkeley: University of California Press, 2004), 197–239.

[23] Altieri, *Painterly Abstraction*, 375 (italics mine). Altieri mentions being indebted to Thomas Nagel's *Moral Questions* for this insight.

BIBLIOGRAPHY

Primary Materials

Works by Taoka Reiun

MHD *Meiji Hanshinden* [Biographies of Meiji Rebels], reprinted in *TRZ*, 5:251–413.

JKR Nishida Masaru, comp. *Taoka Reiun joshi-kaihôron* [Taoka Reiun's essays on women's liberation]. Tokyo: Hôsei daigaku shuppankyoku, 1987

SD *Sakkiden* [A record of misfortune]. In Nishida Masaru, comp., *Taoka Reiun zenshû*, 5 vols. to date, 5:415–743. Tokyo: Hôsei daigaku shuppankyoku, 1969–2013.

TRS Nishida Masaru, comp. *Taoka Reiun senshû* [Selected works of Taoka Reiun]. Tokyo: Aoki bunko, 1956.

TRZ Nishida Masaru, comp. *Taoka Reiun zenshû.* 5 vols. to date Tokyo: Hôsei daigaku shuppankyoku, 1969–2013.

Works by Arthur Schopenhauer

OBM Schopenhauer, Arthur. *On the Basis of Morality.* Translated by E. F. J. Payne. Indianapolis: Bobbs-Merrill, 1965. See also Arthur Broderick Bullock's translation. Accessed June 2015. http://www.monsalvat.no/mitleid.htm.

WWR/ 1969 Schopenhauer, Arthur. *The World as Will and Representation.* Translated by E. F. J. Payne. 2 vols. New York. Dover, 1969.

WWR/ 2010 Schopenhauer, Arthur. *The World as Will and Representation.* Edited by Judith Norman, Alistair Welchman, and Christopher Janaway. Cambridge: Cambridge University Press, 2010.

Schopenhauer, Arthur. *Essays and Aphorisms.* Translated with an introduction by R. J. Hollingdale. London: Penguin Classics, 1970.

———. *Manuscript Remains.* Edited by Arthur Hübscher. Translated by E. F. J. Payne. 4 vols. Oxford: Berg, 1988.

———. *On the Will in Nature.* Translated by E. F. J. Payne, edited with an introduction by David E. Cartwright. Oxford: Berg, 1992.

———. "On the Will in Nature/Animal Magnetism and Magic." In *On the Will in Nature.* Translated by E. F. J. Payne, edited by David E. Cartwright.

Oxford: Berg, 1992. A version is also available on the Wikisource website. Accessed. Jan. 2016. http://en.wikisource.org/wiki/On_the_Will_in_Nature/Animal_Magnetism_and_Magic.

———. *Parerga and Paralipomena: Short Philosophical Essays*. Translated by E. F. J. Payne. 2 vols. Oxford: Clarendon, 1974.

———. *The World as Will and Idea*. Volumes I and II. Translated by R. Haldane and J. Kemp. London: Routledge & Kegan Paul, 1948. First published in 1883.

Secondary Works on Schopenhauer

App, Urs. "Arthur Schopenhauer and China: A Sino-Platonic Love Affair." Edited by Victor Mair. Sino-Platonic Papers, no. 200. PDF. Downloaded August 2011). http://www.sino-platonic.org/complete/spp200_schopenhauer.pdf.

———. *Schopenhauer's Compass: An Introduction to Schopenhauer's Philosophy and Its Origins*. Wil, Switzerland: University Media, 2014.———. "Schopenhauer's Initial Encounter with Indian Thought." In *Schopenhauer and Indian Philosophy: A Dialogue between India and Germany*, edited by Arati Baruna, 7–57. New Delhi: Northern Book Centre, 2008.

Atwell, John E. *Schopenhauer: The Human Character*. Philadelphia: Temple University Press, 1990.

———. *Schopenhauer on the Character of the World: The Metaphysics of Will*. Berkeley: University of California Press, 1995.

Berger, D. L. *The Veil of Maya: Schopenhauer's System and Early Indian Thought*. Binghamton, NY: Global Academic Publishing, 2004.

Cartwright, David E. "Compassion and Solidarity with Sufferers: The Metaphysics of *Mitleid*." In *Better Consciousness: Schopenhauer's Philosophy of Value*, edited by Alex Neil and Christopher Janaway, 138-156. London: Wiley-Blackwell, 2009.

———. *Historical Dictionary of Schopenhauer's Philosophy*. Lanham, MD: Scarecrow Press, 2005.

———. *Schopenhauer: A Biography*. Cambridge: Cambridge University Press, 2010.

———. "Schopenhauer on the Value of Compassion." in *A Companion to Schopenhauer*, edited by Bart Vandenabeele, 249–65. London: Wiley-Blackwell, 2012.

Cooper, David. "Schopenhauer and Indian Philosophy." In *A Companion to Schopenhauer*, edited by Bart Vandenabeele, 266–79. London: Wiley-Blackwell, 2012.

Copleston, Frederick. *Arthur Schopenhauer, Philosopher of Pessimism*. London: Barnes and Noble, 1975.

Cross, Stephen. *Schopenhauer's Encounter with Indian Thought: Representation and Will and Their Indian Parallels.* Honolulu: University of Hawai'i Press, 2013.

Dauer, Dorthea. *Schopenhauer as a Transmitter of Buddhist Ideas.* Berne: Peter Lang, 1969.

Gardiner, Patrick. *Schopenhauer.* Middlesex, UK: Penguin Books, 1968.

Halbfass, W. *India and Europe: An Essay in Philosophical Understanding* (Delhi: Motilal Banarsidass, 1990

Hamlyn, D. W. *Schopenhauer.* London: Routledge and Kegan Paul, 1980.

Hübscher, Arthur. *The Philosophy of Schopenhauer in Its Intellectual Context: Thinker against the Tide.* Translated by Joachim T. Baer and David E. Cartwright. Lewiston, NY: Edwin Mellen Press, 1989.

Jacquette, Dale, ed. *Schopenhauer, Philosophy, and the Arts.* Cambridge: Cambridge University Press, 1996.

———. *The Philosophy of Schopenhauer.* Chesham, UK: Acumen, 2005.

Janaway, Christopher, ed. *The Cambridge Companion to Schopenhauer.* Cambridge: Cambridge University Press, 1999.

———. *Schopenhauer.* Past Masters. New York: Oxford University Press, 1994.

———. *Schopenhauer: A Very Short Introduction.* New York: Oxford University Press, 2002.

———. "Schopenhauer's Philosophy of Value." In *Better Consciousness: Schopenhauer's Philosophy of Value,* edited by Alex Neil and Christopher Janaway. London: Wiley-Blackwell, 2009, 1-10.

———. *Self and World in Schopenhauer.* Oxford: Clarendon, 1989.

———, ed. *Willing and Nothingness: Schopenhauer as Nietzsche's Educator.* Oxford: Clarendon Press, 1998.

Jordan, Neil. *Schopenhauer's Ethics of Patience: Virtue, Salvation, and Value.* Lewiston, NY: Edwin Mellen Press, 2010.

Jordan, Neil, and Christopher Janaway, eds. *Better Consciousness: Schopenhauer's Philosophy of Value.* London: Wiley-Blackwell, 2009.

Koster, Thomas. "'Schopenhauer is Always Topical' An Interview with Rüdiger Safranski" http://cafephilosophy.co.nz/articles/schopenhauer-is-always-topical-an-interview-with-ruediger-safranski/. Accessed on June 26, 2016.

Lauxtermann, P. F. H. *Schopenhauer's Broken World View: Colours and Ethics between Kant and Goethe.* Dordrecht: Kluwer Academic, 2000.

Magee, Bryan. *The Philosophy of Schopenhauer.* Oxford: Oxford University Press, 1983.

Mannion, Gerard. *Schopenhauer, Religion, and Morality: The Humble Path to Ethics.* Farnham, UK: Ashgate, 2003.

Mann, Thomas. *The Living Thoughts of Schopenhauer Presented by Thomas Mann.* London: Cassell, 1939.

Marcine, R. B. *In Search of Schopenhauer's Cat: Arthur Schopenhauer's Quantum-Mystical Theory of Justice.* Washington, DC: Catholic University of America Press, 2006.

McGill, V. J. *Schopenhauer: Pessimist and Pagan.* New York: Haskell House, 1971. Originally published in 1931.

Neeley, Steven. *Schopenhauer: A Consistent Reading.* Lewiston, NY: Edwin Mellen Press, 2004.

Neil, Alex, and Christopher Janaway, eds. *Better Consciousness: Schopenhauer's Philosophy of Value.* London: Wiley-Blackwell, 2009.

Nicholls, Moira. "The Influences of Eastern Thought on Schopenhauer's Doctrine on the Thing-in-Itself." In *The Cambridge Companion to Schopenhauer*, edited by Christopher Janaway, 171–212. Oxford: Oxford University Press, 1999.

Ryan, Vincent T. *Schopenhauer's Philosophy of Religion: The Death of God and the Oriental Renaissance.* Leuven: Peeters, 2010.

Safranski, Rüdiger, *Schopenhauer and the Wild Years of Philosophy.* Translated by Ewald Osers. Cambridge, MA: Harvard University Press, 1990.

Shapshay, Sandra. "Poetic Intuition and the Bounds of Sense: Metaphor and Metonymy in Schopenhauer's Philosophy." In *Better Consciousness: Schopenhauer's Philosophy of Value*, edited by Alex Neil and Christopher Janaway, 58–76. Chichester, UK: Wiley-Blackwell, 2009.

Vandenbeele, Bart, ed. *A Companion to Schopenhauer.* Malden, MA.: Wiley-Blackwell, 2012.

Vasalou, Sophia. *Schopenhauer and the Aesthetic Standpoint: Philosophy as a Practice of the Sublime.* Cambridge: Cambridge University Press, 2013.

Von der Luft, Eric, ed. *Schopenhauer: New Essays in Honor of His 200th Birthday.* Lewiston, NY: Edwin Mellen Press, 1988.

Wicks, Robert. *Schopenhauer's "The World as Will and Representation": A Reader's Guide.* London: Continuum, 2011.

Young, Julian. *Schopenhauer.* London: Routledge, 2005.

———. *Willing and Unwilling: A Study in the Philosophy of Arthur Schopenhauer.* Dordrecht: Martinus Nijhoff, 2013. Originally published in 1987.

Zöller, Gunter. "Schopenhauer on the Self." In *The Cambridge Companion to Schopenhauer*, edited by Christopher Janaway, 18-43. Cambridge: Cambridge University Press, 1999.

Other Works Consulted

Abbey, Ruth. *Charles Taylor.* Princeton, NJ: Princeton University Press, 2000.

———, ed. *Charles Taylor.* Cambridge: Cambridge University Press, 2004.

Adams, Jason. "Non-western Anarchisms: Rethinking the Global Context." Accessed March 2015. http://theanarchistlibrary.org/library/jason-adams-non-western-anarchisms.

Adler, Joseph A. "On Translating Taiji." In *Returning to Zhu Xi: Emerging Patterns within the Supreme Polarity,* edited by David Jones and He Jinli. Albany: State University of New York Press, 2015, 51-81.

Akiyama, Seikô. *Takayama Chogyû: Sono shôgai to shisô.* Tokyo: Sekibunkan, 1957.

Altieri, Charles. *Painterly Abstraction in Modernist Poetry: The Contemporaneity of Modernism.* Cambridge: Cambridge University Press, 1989.

Ambaras, David. "Social Knowledge, Cultural Capital, and the New Middle Class in Modern Japan, 1895–1912." *Journal of Japanese Studies* 24:1 (1998): 1–33.

Ames, Roger, and David L. Hall, trans. *Daodejing, "Making Life Significant": A Philosophical Translation.* New York: Ballantine, 2003.

App, Urs. *The Birth of Orientalism.* Philadelphia, Pennsylvania: University of Pennsylvania Press, 2010.

———. "Schopenhauer and China: A Sino-Platonic Love Affair." *Sino-Platonic Papers,* no. 200 (April 2010): 1–160. http://www.sino-platonic.org/complete/spp200_schopenhauer.pdf. Dowloaded August 8, 2011.

Arima, Tatsuo. *The Failure of Freedom.* Cambridge, MA: Harvard University Press, 1963.

Asahi Jyanaru, ed. *Nihon no shisôka.* 3 vols. Tokyo: Asahi shinbunsha, 1963.

Asukai, Masamichi. "Hirotsu Ryûrô no shoki." *Jinbungakuhô* 10 (March 1959): 115–32.

———."Kokuminteki bunka no keisei 1." In *Iwanami kôza Nihon rekishi, Gendai,* vol. 1, 287-311. Tokyo: Iwanami shoten, 1963.

———. "Shiryô Meiji sanjû nendai minshushugi no ichimen." *Jinbungakuhô* 17 (November 1962): 89–146.

Aydin, Cemil. "Japanese Pan-Asianism through the Mirror of Pan-Islamism." In *Tumultuous Decade: Empire, Society, and Diplomacy in 1930s Japan,* edited by Masato Kimura and Tosh Minohara, 44–68. Toronto: University of Toronto Press, 2013.

Bailyn, Bernard. "The Challenge of Modern Historiography." Accessed June 2016. https://www.historians.org/about-aha-and-membership/aha-history-and-archives/presidential-addresses/bernard-bailyn.

Bayly, C.A., Sven Beckert, Matthew Connelly, Isabel Hofmeyer, Wendy Kozol, and Patricia Seed, "On Transnational History." *American Historical Review* (2006). Accessed May 15, 2016, from the Graduate Institute website, http://graduateinstitute.ch/files/live/sites/iheid/files/sites/international_history_politics/users/stratto9/public/intro_ahr111.5.

Bamba, Nobuya, and John Howes, eds. *Pacifism in Japan: The Christian and Socialist Tradition.* Vancouver: University of British Columbia Press, 1978.

Barshay, Andrew. "Imagining Democracy in Postwar Japan: Maruyama Masao as a Political Thinker." In *The Social Sciences in Modern Japan*, 197–39. Berkeley: University of California Press, 2004.

Batchelor, Stephen. *The Awakening of the West: The Encounter of Buddhism and Western Culture.* Berkeley, CA: Parallax, 1994.

Bellah, Robert. "Ienaga Saburô and the Search for Meaning in Modern Japan." In *Changing Japanese Attitudes towards Modernization,* edited by J. Hall and M. Jansen. 369-423. Princeton, NJ: Princeton University Press, 1965.

———. "Japan's Cultural Identity." *Journal of Asian Studies* 24:4 (August 1965), 573- 594. Reprinted in John A. Harrison, ed. *Enduring Scholarship*, 2:47–68. Tuscon, AZ: University of Arizona Press, 1972.

Bennett, J. G. *Gurdjieff: Making a New World.* New York: Harper Colophon, 1973.

Berman, Marshall. *All That Is Solid Melts into Air: The Experience of Modernity.* New York: Simon and Schuster, 1982.

———. "Why Modernism Matters." In *Modernity and Identity*, edited by Scott Lash and Jonathan Friedman. Cambridge, MA: Blackwell, 1992, 33-58.

Bickness, Kent, and Todd Lewis. "The Asian Soul of Transcendentalism." *Education About Asia* 16:2 (Fall 2011): 12–19.

Bonner, Joey. *Wang Kuo-wei: An Intellectual Biography.* Cambridge, MA: Harvard University Press, 1986.

Bowen, Roger. *Rebellion and Democracy in Meiji Japan: A Study of the Commoners in the Popular Rights Movement.* Berkeley: University of California Press, 1980.

Bronowski, J., and B. Mazlish, eds. *The Western Intellectual Tradition.* New York: Harper and Row, 1960.

Brown, Terence. *The Life of W. B. Yeats: A Critical Biography.* Malden, MA: Blackwell, 1999.

Carpenter, Edward. *Civilization: Its Cause and Cure.* London: Swan Sonnenschein, 1891.

———. *Love's Coming of Age.* London: George Allen and Unwin, 1896

Cascardi, Anthony J. *The Subject of Modernity.* Cambridge: Cambridge University Press, 1992.

Cheng, Chung-ying. "Dao (Tao): The Way." In *Encyclopedia of Chinese Philosophy*, edited by Antonio S. Cua. New York: Routledge, 2003, 202-206..

Clarke, J. J. *Oriental Enlightenment: The Encounter between Asian and Western Thought*. London: Routledge, 1997.

Coates, Wilson H., and Hayden V. White. *The Ordeal of Liberal Humanism: An Intellectual History of Western Europe*. Vol. 2. New York: McGraw-Hill, 1970.

Copleston, Frederick. *Arthur Schopenhauer, Philosopher of Pessimism*. London: Burns, Oaks and Washburne, 1947.

Cottingham, John, Robert Stoothoff, and Douglas Murdoch, trans. *The Philosophical Works of Descartes*. Cambridge: Cambridge University Press, 1984.

Cua, Antonio S. *Encyclopedia of Chinese Philosophy*. New York: Routledge, 2003.

Darnoi, Dennis N. Kenedy. *The Unconscious and Eduard von Hartmann*. The Hague: Martinus Nijhoff, 1967.

De Vogüé, Eugene Melchior. "The Neo-Christian Movement in France." *Harper's Monthly*, January 1892, 234–42.

"The Diamond Sutra: A New Translation." Accessed June 2015. http://www.diamond-sutra.com/index.html.

Duus, Peter. "Whig History Japanese Style: The Minyûsha Historians and the Meiji Restoration." *Journal of Asian Studies* 33:3 (May 1974): 415–36.

Ellis, Havelock. *The Nineteenth Century: An Utopian Retrospect*. Boston: Small, Maynard, 1901.

Elison, George. "Kôtoku Shûsui: The Change in Thought." *Monumenta Nipponica* 22:3–4 (1967): 437–67.

Engels, Frederick. *The Origin of the Family, Private Property, and the State: In Light of the Researches of Lewis H. Morgan*. New York: International Publishers, 1942.

Ellmann, Richard. *Yeats: The Man and the Masks*. London: Faber and Faber, 1961.

Faivre, Antoine, and Jacob Needleman, eds. Modern Esoteric Spirituality. New York: Crossroad, 1992.

Feuer, Lewis S., ed. *Marx and Engels: Basic Writings on Politics and Philosophy*. New York: Anchor Books, 1959.

Freud, Sigmund. *Civilization and Its Discontents*. New York: Norton, 1961.

Fukai, Eigo. *Bunmei no hei oyobi sono kyûji* [文明の弊およびその救治], a translation of Edward Carpenter's *Civilizations: Its Cause and Cure*, Volume 5 in the Heimin sōsho series. Tokyo: Min'yûsha, 1895.

Gay, Peter. *Modernism: The Lure of Heresy from Baudelaire to Beckett and Beyond.* New York: Norton, 2008.

Giddens, Anthony. *The Consequences of Modernity.* Stanford, CA: Stanford University Press, 1990.

———. *Modernity and Self-Identity: Self and Society in the Late Modern Age.* Stanford, CA: Stanford University Press, 1991.

George, Henry. *Progress and Poverty: An Inquiry into the Cause of Industrial Depressions and of Increase of Want with Increase of Wealth; The Remedy.* New York: Schalkenback Foundation. 1879.

———. *Social Problems.* New York: Schalkenback Foundation, 1953. Originally published in 1883.

Gray, John. *Straw Dogs: Thoughts on Humans and Other Animals.* New York: Farrar, Straus and Gioux, 2003.

Hall, Ivan P. *Mori Arinori.* Cambridge, MA: Harvard University Press, 1973.

Hall, J., and M. Jansen, eds. *Changing Japanese Attitudes towards Modernization.* Princeton, NJ: Princeton University Press, 1965.

Halstead, John B., ed. *Romanticism.* New York: Harper and Row, 1969.

Hane, Mikiso. "Early Meiji Liberalism: An assessment." *Monumenta Nipponica* 24:4 (1969): 353–71.

Hashimoto, Bunzô. "Takayama Chogyû: Zassetsu shita Meiji no seishin." In *Nihon no shisôka,* edited by Asahi Jyanaru, 2:162–78. Tokyo: Asahi Shinbunsha, 1963.

Hibbett, Howard S. "Natsume Sôseki and the Psychological Novel." In *Tradition and Modernization in Japanese Culture,* edited by Donald Shively, 305–46. Princeton, NJ: Princeton University Press, 1971.

Hijegata Teiichi. "Takayama Chogyû to shihai suru kaikyû no romanshugi Taoka Reiun." In *Kindai Nihon bungaku hyôronshi,* 22–26. Tokyo: Hôsei University Press, 1973.

Hirao, Michio. *Jiyûminken no keifu.* Kôchi: Kôchi Shimin Toshokan, 1970.

———. *Kôchi ken no rekishi.* Kôchi: Kôchi Shimin Toshokan, 1966.

———. *Risshisha to minken undô.* Kôchi: Kôchi Shimin Toshokan, 1955.

Hirota, Masaki. "Nihon kindai shakai no sabetsu kôzô" [The structure of discrimination in modern Japanese society]. In *Sabetsu no shosô* [Aspects of discrimination]. Tokyo: Iwanami shoten, 1990.

Hisamatsu, Ken'ichi. *The Vocabulary of Japanese Aesthetics.* Tokyo: Center for East Asian Cultural Studies, 1963.

Ichiyô, Higuchi. "Growing Up" [Takekurabe]. Translated by Edward Seidensticker. In *Modern Japanese Literature,* edited by Donald Keene, 70–110. Tokyo: Tuttle, 1957.

———. "Muddy Bay" [Nigorie]. Translated by H. Tanaka. *Monumenta Nipponica* 14:1–2 (1958): 173–204.

Ienaga, Saburô. "Hankindaishugi no rekishiteki seisatsu." In *Nihon kindai shisôshi kenkyû,* 231–61. Tokyo: Tokyo daigaku shuppankai, 1953.

———. *Sûkinaru shisôka no shôgai: Taoka Reiun no hito to shisô* [The career of an unfortunate thinker: Taoka Reiun, the person and his ideas]. Tokyo: Iwanami shoten, 1955.

———. "Taoka Reiun no 'Kokubyaku.'" *Bungaku* 24:6 (1956): 104–6.

Ip, Hung-yok, "The Power of Interconnectivity: Tan Sitong's Invention of Historical Agency in Late Qing China." *Journal of Global Buddhism* 10 (2009): 323–74.

Iriye, Akira. *Global and Transnational History: The Past, Present, and Future.* London: Palgrave Macmillan, 2013.

Iriye, Akira, and Pierre Yves Saunier. *The Palgrave Dictionary of Transnational History.* London: Macmillan, 2009.

Irokawa, Daikichi. *"Bungakkai," Shisô,* April 1962, 123–35.

———. *Kindai kokka no shuppatsu, Nihon no rekishi.* Vol. 21. Tokyo: Chûô kôron sha, 1971.

———. *Kitamura Tôkoku.* Tokyo: Tokyodaigaku Shuppankai, 1994.

———. *Shimpen Meiji Seishinshi.* Tokyo: Chûô kôronsha, 1973.

Ishikawa, Takuboku. *Takuboku zenzhû.* Edited by Kindaichi Kyôsuke et al. 8 vols. Tokyo: Chikuma Shobô, 1967–68.

Itagaki, Taisuke, comp. *Jiyûtôshi.* 2 vols. Tokyo: Aoki bunko, 1958.

Jansen, Marius. *Sakamoto Ryôma and the Meiji Restoration.* Palo Alto, CA: Stanford University Press, 1971.

Josipovici, Gabriel. *What Ever Happened to Modernism?* New Haven, CT: Yale University Press, 2010.

Kano, Masanao. *Kindai kokka o kôsôshita shisôka-tachi* [The intellectuals who shaped the conception of the modern state]. Tokyo: Iwanami Junia shinsho, 2005.

———, ed. *Kuga Katsunan/Miyake Setsurei, Nihon no meicho.* Vol. 37. Tokyo: Chûô kôronsha, 1971.

———. "Kokusuika-tachi no kindaika no kôsô: Jiritsuteki henkaku e no mosaku" [The approach of *kokusui* thinkers to modernization: Groping for self-reliant change]. In *Nihon kindaika no shisô*, 73–78. Tokyo: Kenkyûsha, 1972.

———, "Ienaga Saburô no gakumon to rekishiksi ninshiki [Ienaga Saburô's scholarship and historical awareness] in *Ienaga Saburô tanjô hyakunen* [On the 100th anniversary of Ienaga Saburô's birth], ed. Ienaga Saburô tanjô hyakunen Jikkô-iinkai. Tokyo: Nihon Hyôronsha, 3–23, 2014.

———. *Shihonshugi keiseiki no chitsujo isshiki*. Tokyo: Chikuma shobô, 1969.

Karaki, Junzô. *Gendaishi e no kokoromi*. Tokyo: Chikuma shobô, 1963.

Karube, Tadashi. *Maruyama Masao and the Fate of Liberalism in Twentieth-Century Japan*. Translated by David Noble. Tokyo: International House of Japan, 2008.

Katsumoto, Seiichirô. "Bungaku gainen no bunretsu." *Gunzô*, May 1958, 145–51.

———. "Ichiyô-ware wa onna narikeru mono o." *Jiyû fujin,* August 1948, 19–24; September 1948, 21–27.

———. "Tôkoku no shûkyô shisô." *Bungaku* 24:2 (1956): 8–19.

———, comp. *Tôkoku zenshû*. 3 vols. Tokyo: Iwanami shoten, 1970–73.

Katz, J. B. Review of Raymond Schwab, *La Renaissance Orientale. Journal of Indian Philosophy* 18 (1990): 341–46.

Keene, Donald, ed. *Modern Japanese Literature*. Tokyo: Tuttle, 1957.

———. "The Sino-Japanese War of 1894–5 and Its Cultural Effects on Japan." In *Tradition and Modernization in Japanese Culture*, edited by Donald Shively, 121-175. Princeton, NJ: Princeton University Press, 1971.

———. *The First Modern Japanese: The Life of Ishikawa Takuboku*. New York. Columbia University Press, 2016.

Kinoshita, Naoe. *Pillar of Fire*. Translated by Kenneth Strong. UNESCO Collection of Representative Works. London: Allen and Unwin, 1972.

Kohn, Livia. *Early Chinese Mysticism: Philosophy and Soteriology in the Taoist Tradition*. Princeton, NJ: Princeton University Press, 1991.

Konishi, Sho. *Anarchist Modernity: Cooperatism and Japanese-Russian Intellectual Relations in Modern Japan*. Cambridge, MA: Harvard University Press, 2013.

———. "The People at Rest: The Anarchist Origins of Ogawa Usen's 'Nihonga.'" *World Art* 1:2 (2011): 235–56.

Koschmann, J. Victor. "The Debate on Subjectivity in Postwar Japan: Foundations of Modernism as a Political Critique." *Pacific Affairs* 54:4 (Winter 1981–82): 609–31.

LaFargue, Michael. *The Tao of the Tao Te Ching: A Translation and Commentary*. New York: State University of New York Press, 1992.

Latour, Bruno. *We Never Have Been Modern*. Cambridge, MA: Harvard University Press, 1993.

Lau, D. C. *Lao-tzu/Tao-te Ching*. London and New York: Penguin Books, 1963.

Lears, T. J. Jackson. *No Place of Grace: Antimodernism and the Transformation of American Culture, 1880–1920*. New York: Pantheon Books, 1981.

Levenson, Joseph. *Liang Ch'i-ch'ao and the Mind of Modern China*. Berkeley: University of California Press, 1967.

Lewis, Pericles. *The Cambridge Introduction to Modernism*. Cambridge: Cambridge University Press, 2007.

Lewis, Todd, and Kent Bickness. "The Asian Soul of Transcendentalism." *Education About Asia* 16:2 (Fall 2011): 12–19.

Liu, Lydia. *Translingual Practice: Literature, National Culture, and Translated Modernity in China, 1900–1937*. Palo Alto, CA: Stanford University Press, 1995.

Loftus, Ronald. "Discovering the Other: The East through the Eyes of the Nineteenth Century West." In *Three Rs: Reading as the aRt of Rumination*, edited by William Duvall, 1–20. Supplemental Series, no. 2. Salem, OR: Willamette Journal of the Liberal Arts, 1988.

———. "In Search of Japan's First Modern Autobiography." *Biography* 6:3 (1983): 235–72.

———. "The Inversion of Progress: Taoka Reiun's *Hibunmeiron*." *Monumenta Nipponica* 40:2 (1985): 191–208.

———.*Telling Lives: Women's Self-Writing in Modern Japan*. Honolulu: University of Hawai'i Press, 2004.

Lopate, Phillip. *To Show and to Tell: The Craft of Literary Nonfiction*. New York: Free Press, 2013.

Lu, Xing. *Rhetoric in Ancient China, Fifth to Third Century B.C.E.: A Comparison with Classical Greek Rhetoric*. Columbia: University of South Carolina Press, 1998.

Makeham, John, ed. *Transforming Consciousness: Yogācāra Thought in Modern China*. New York: Oxford University Press, 2014.

Mansfield, Nick. *Subjectivity: Theories of the Self from Freud to Haraway*. New York: New York University Press, 2000.

Maruyama, Masao. "Chûsei to hangyaku" [Loyalty and Treason]. In *Kindai Nihon shisôshi kôza*, 377–471. Tokyo: Chikuma shobô, 1951.

———. "Politics and Man in the Contemporary World." In *Thought and Behavior in Modern Japanese Politics*, edited by Ivan Morris, 321-348. London: Oxford University Press, 1969.

———. "Rekishi isshiki no 'kôsô'" [On the deepest layer of historical consciousness]. In *Rekishi shisôshû, Nihon no shisô*, edited by Maruyama Masao, 1:3–41. Tokyo: Chikuma shobô, 1972.

———. "Theory and Psychology of Ultra-Nationalism." In *Thought and Behavior in Modern Japanese Politics*, edited by Ivan Morris, 1-24. London: Oxford University Press, 1969.

Mathy, Francis. "Kitamura Tôkoku, the Early Years." *Monumenta Nipponica* 18:1–4 (1963): 1–44.

———. "Kitamura Tôkoku, Essays on the Inner Life." *Monumenta Nipponica* 19:1–2 (1964): 66–110.

———. "Kitamura Tôkoku, Final Essays." *Monumenta Nipponica*, 20:1–2 (1965): 41–63.

Matsuda, Michio. "Nihon no chishikijin." In *Kindai Nihon shisôshi kôza*, vol. IV. Tokyo: Chikuma shobô, 1950, 9–57.

Matsumoto, Sannosuke. *Kindai Nihon no seiji to ningen*. Tokyo: Jobunsha, 1966.

———. "*Nihon* oyobi *Nihonjin*." *Bungaku* 24:4 (1956): 513–19.

Macdonald, Simon. "Transnational History: A Review of Past and Present Scholarship." Accessed April 2016. https://www.ucl.ac.uk/cth/objectives/simon_macdonald_tns_review.

McClain, James. *A Modern History of Japan*. New York: Norton, 2002.

McGill, B. J. *Schopenhauer, Pessimist and Pagan*. New York: Brentano, 1931.

Mead, George Herbert. *Mind, Self, and Society*. Edited with an introduction by Charles W. Morris. Chicago: University of Chicago Press, 1962. Originally published in 1934.

———. *Movements of Thought in the Nineteenth Century*. Edited with an introduction by M. H. Moore. Chicago: University of Chicago Press, 1972. Originally published in 1936.

Melzer, Arthur, M. Jerry Weinberger, and M. Richard Zinman, eds. *History and the Idea of Progress*. Ithaca, NY: Cornell University Press, 1995.

Minford, John. *I Ching (Yijing): The Book of Changes*. Translated with an introduction and commentary by John Minford. New York: Viking, 2014.

Mishra, Pankaj. *From the Ruins of Empire: The Revolt against the West and the Remaking of Asia*. London and New York: Penguin Books, 2013.

Mitsuhiro Yoshimoto, *Kurosawa*. Durham, NC: Duke University Press, 2000.

Mitter, Rana. "Modernity." In *The Palgrave Dictionary of Transnational History*, edited by Akira Iriye and Pierre-Yves Saunier, 720–22. London: Macmillan, 2009.

Miyajima, Hajime. *Mejiteki shisôka so no keisei*. Tokyo: Miraisha, 1960.

Moeller, Hans-Georg. *The Philosophy of the Daodejing*. New York: Columbia University Press, 2006.

Monod, Gabriel. "The Political Situation in France." *The Contemporary Review*, 64: 613-28, 1893.

Morgan, Lewis Henry. *Ancient Society*. Cleveland: Meridian Books, World Publishing, 1877.

Morisue Yoshiaki, Hôgetsu Keigo, and Konishi, Shirô eds. *Seikatsushi* III Vol. 17 of *Taikei Nihonshi sôsho*. Tokyo: Yamakawa shuppansha, 1969.

Motoyama, Yukihiko. "Meiji nijû-nendai no seiron ni arawareta nashionarizumu." In *Meiji zenhanki no nashionarizumu,* edited by Sakata Yoshio, 37-87. Tokyo: Miraisha, 1958.

———. "Miyake Setsurei: Zaiya no nashionarisuto." In *Nihon no shisôka*, edited by Asahi jyanaru, 2:59–76. Tokyo: Asahi shinbunsha, 1963.

Munitz, Milton K. *Cosmic Understanding: Philosophy and Science of the Universe*. Princeton, NJ: Princeton University Press, 1986.

Munro, Donald J. *The Concept of Man in Early China*. Palo Alto, CA: Stanford University Press, 1969.

Muses, Charles. *East-West Fire: Schopenhauer's Optimism and the Lankavatara Sutra*. London: John W. Watkins, 1955.

Nagel, Thomas. *Mortal Questions*. London: Cambridge University Press, 1979.

Najita, Tetsuo. "Nakano Seigo and the Spirit of the Meiji Restoration in Twentieth Century Japan." In *Dilemmas of Growth in Prewar Japan*, edited by James Morely, 375–421. Princeton, NJ: Princeton University Press, 1971.

Narita, Ryûichi. *Kingendai Nihonshi to Rekishigaku: Kakikaerarete-kita kako*. Tokyo: Chûô kôronsha, 2012.

Natsume, Sôseki. "Gendai Nihon no kaika." *Natsume Sôseki shû* (1). *Gendai Nihon Bungaku Taikei*, vol. 17. Tokyo: Chikuma shobô, 1968.

Ngai, Mae. "Promises and Perils of Transnational History." In *Perspectives on History*, American Historical Association, October 2012. Accessed April 2016. https://www.historians.org/publications-and-directories/perspectives-on-history/december-2012/the-future-of-the-discipline/promises-and-perils-of-transnational-history.

Nisbet, Robert. *Social Change and History*. London: Oxford University Press, 1969.

———. *The Sociological Tradition*. New York: Basic Books, 1966.

Nishida, Masaru. "Kaisetsu" [Explanatory notes]. In Taoka Reiun and Ogawa Usen, *Yûzo Muzo* (The Voiced and the Voiceless]. Tokyo: Takayamabô, 2000, 1-8.

———. *Kindai bungaku no sensei ryoku* [The latent power of modern literature]. Tokyo: Yagi shoten, 1973.

———. *Kindai wa hitei dekiru ka?* [Can we deny the modern?]. Tokyo: Orijin shuppan sentaa, 1993.

———. "Nihon kindai bungaku to kyûba kakumei." In *Kindai bungaku no sensei ryoku* [The latent power in modern literature]. Tokyo: Yagi shoten, 1973.

———. "*Seinenbun.*" *Bungaku* 24:8 (1956): 105–10.

———, comp. *Byôchû Hôrô* [Wanderings from the Sickbed]. Reprinted Tokyo: Shakai bungaku sôsho, 2000. Originally published by Genyôsha, 1910.

———, comp. "Taoka Reiun mihappyô ikô, (I)." *Bungakuteki tachiba*, no. 1 (July–August 1965): 72–96.

———, comp. "Taoka Reiun mihappyô ikô (II)." *Bungakuteki tachiba*, no. 9 (November–December 1966): 98–119.

———, comp. "Taoka Reiun mihappyô ikô (III)," *Bungakuteki tachiba*, no. 12 (October 1967): 105–27.

———. "Taoka Reiun no daigaku jiyûron." In *Kindai bungaku no sensei ryoku* [The latent power in modern literature], 29–38. Tokyo: Yagi shoten, 1973.

———. "Taoka Reiun no ibun" [Posthumous writings of Taoka Reiun], in *Kindai bungaku no sensei ryoku* [The latent power in modern literature], 16–28. Tokyo: Yagi shoten, 1973.

———. "Taoka Reiun no tennôseikan." In *Kindai bungaku no sensei ryoku* [The latent power in modern literature], 39–51. Tokyo: Yagi shoten, 1973

———. "Taoka Reiun to hisan shôsetsu." *Meiji-Taishô bungaku kenkyû*, no. 15 (February 1955): 46–59.

———. *Kindai bungaku no sensei ryoku*. Tokyo: Yagi shoten, 1973.

———. "*Tenko.*" *Bungaku* 24:9 (1956): 125–28.

Nishida, Taketoshi, ed. *Meiji zenki no toshi kasô shakai*. Tokyo: Kôseikan, 1970.

———. "Yokoyama Gennosuke chaku: 'Nihon kasô shakai' no seiritsu." *Rekishigaku kenkyû*, no. 161 (January 1953): 36–47.

Nordau, Max. *The Conventional Lies of Our Civilization*. Chicago: L. Schick, 1884.

———. *Degeneration*. New York: D. Appleton, 1905.

Notehelfer, F. G. *Kôtoku Shûsui: Portrait of a Japanese Radical*. Cambridge: Cambridge University Press, 1971.

Odagiri, Hideo. *Bungakushi*. Tokyo: Tokyokeizai shimpôsha, 1961.

———, ed. *Ishikawa Takuboku shû*. *Meiji Bungaku zenshû*, vol. 52. Tokyo: Chikuma shobô, 1970.

———. *Kitamura Tôkoku ron*. Tokyo: Yagi shoten, 1970.

———, ed. *Meiji shakaishugi-bungaku shû* (1). *Meiji Bungaku zenshû*, vol. 83. Tokyo: Chikuma shobô, 1965.

———, ed. *Meiji shakaishugi bungaku shû* (2). *Meiji Bungaku zenshû*, vol. 84. Tokyo: Chikuma shobô, 1965.

———. "Taoka Reiun: Meiji shakai to no tairitsu." In *Nihon no shisôka*, edited by Asahi jyanaru, 2:127–44. Tokyo: Asahi Shinbunsha, 1963.

Okabayashi, Kiyomi. *Jiyûminken undô bungaku no kenkyû*. Kôchi: Kôchi shimin toshokan, 1973.

Okuma, Shigenobu, comp. *Fifty Years of New Japan*. Edited and translated by M. B. Huish. 2 vols. London: Smith Elder, 1909.

Ouspensky, P. D. *The Fourth Way*. New York: Vintage, 1957.

Peckham, Morse. *Beyond the Tragic Vision: The Quest for Identity in the Nineteenth Century*. New York: George Braziller, 1962.

———. *Romanticism: The Culture of the Nineteenth Century*. New York: George Braziller, 1965.

Pierson, John D. "The Early Liberal Thought of Tokutomi Sohô." *Monumenta Nipponica* 29:2 (Summer 1974): 199–224.

Pierson, Stanley. "Edward Carpenter, Prophet of a Socialist Millennium." *Victorian Studies* 13:3 (March 1970): 301–18.

Pine, Red, ed. *The Diamond Sutra: The Perfection of Wisdom*. Washington, DC: Counterpoint, 2001. Text and commentaries translated from Sanskrit and Chinese by Red Pine.

Pinkard, Terry. "Taylor, 'History,' and the History of Philosophy." In *Charles Taylor*, edited by Ruth Abbey, 187–213. Cambridge: Cambridge University Press, 2004.

Pyle, Kenneth B. *The New Generation in Meiji Japan*. Palo Alto, CA: Stanford University Press, 1969.

Rowbotham, Sheila. *Edward Carpenter: A Life of Liberty and Love*. London: Verso, 2008.

Ryan, Marleigh. *Japan's First Modern Novel: Ukigumo of Futabatei Shimei*. New York: Columbia University Press, 1967.

Said, Edward. *Orientalism*. New York: Random House, 1978.

Sakata, Yoshio, ed. *Meiji Zenhanki no Nashionarizumu*. Tokyo: Miraisha, 1958.

Sasabuchi, Yûichi. "*Bungakkai*" *to sono jidai*. Tokyo: Meiji shoin, 1959.

———. *Romanshugi bungaku no tanjô*. Tokyo: Meiji shoin, 1958.

Sasagawa, Rimpû. "Reiun shûenki." *Chûô Kôron,* October 1912, 81–88.

Schwab, Raymond. *The Oriental Renaissance: Europe's Rediscovery of India and the East, 1680–1880*. Translated by Gene Patterson-Black and Victor Reinking. New York: Columbia University Press, 1984.

Senuma, Shigeki. "*Taiyô*." *Bungaku* 23:7 (1955): 70–78.

———. "Tôkoku no rekishi isshiki." *Bungaku* 24:2 (1956): 20–25.

Shimazaki, Kiyoshi, ed. *Meiji kiroku bungaku shû. Meiji Bungaku zenshû,* vol. 96. Tokyo: Chikuma shobô, 1967.

Shimizu, Yoshi, comp. *Tetsugakkan jiken to rinri mondai*. Tokyo: Bunmeidô, 1903.

Shively, Donald, ed. *Tradition and Modernization in Japanese Culture*. Princeton, NJ: Princeton University Press, 1971.

Sinnett, Alfred Percy. *Esoteric Buddhism*. London: Trübner, 1883.

———. *The Occult World.* London: Trübner, 1883.

Smith, Nicholas. *Charles Taylor: Meaning, Morals, and Modernity*. Cambridge: Polity, 2002.

Speeth, Kathleen Riordan. *The Gurdjieff Work.* Berkeley, CA: And/Or Press, 1976.

Spiegel, Gabrielle M. "The Task of the Historian." Accessed March 2015 http://www.historians.org/about-aha-and-membership/aha-history-and-archives/presidential-addresses/gabrielle-m-spiegel#fn51.

Squires, Graham, and Itô Yushi. "How Can Literature Be Beneficial to Life? The Yamaji-Kitamura Controversy Reconsidered." Nichibunkan, 1996. Accessed April 2016. http://publications.nichibun.ac.jp/en/item/kosh/1996-03-25-3/pub.

Sumiya, Mikio. *Nihon teikoku no keiren. Nihon no rekishi,* vol. 22. Tokyo: Chûô kôronsha, 1971.

Takahashi, Tadashi. *Taoka Reiun*. Pamphlet no. 3. Kôchi: Kôchishiritsu Jiyûminlenkinenkan, 1994.

Takemura, Noriyuki. "Wang Guowei (王國維) no kyôkaisetsu (境界説) to Taoka Reiun (田岡嶺雲) no kyôkaisetsu" [Wang Guowei's theory of "boundaries" and Taoka Reiun's theory of "boundaries"]. *Studies in Chinese Literature,* December 31, 1986, 127–48. JAIRO (Japan Institutional Repositories Online). Accessed June 2015. http://catalog.lib.kyushu u.ac.jp/handle/2324/9731/p127.

Takayama, Chogyû. *Chogyû zenshû.* 6 vols. Tokyo: Hakubunkan, 1914–15.

Talmon, Jacob L. *Romanticism and Revolt.* New York: Harcourt, Brace and World, 1967.

Tanaka, Hisako, trans. "Muddy Bay (Nigorie)." *Monumenta Nipponica* 14:1–2 (1958): 173–204.

Tanaka, Kotarô. "Taoka Reiun, Kôtoku Shûsui, Okumiya Takeshi no tsuikairoku." *Chûô kôron,* December 1914, 1–26.

Taoka Reiun, "Ippu-ippu wa hatashite tensoku nariya," *Shinsei* 11:4 (March 1904): 87–90.

———. "Indo no shimpisetsu," *Taiyô* 3:10 (May 1897): 170–78.

———. *Urokoun.* Tokyo: Takayamabô, 1905.

Taylor, Charles. *Sources of the Self: The Making of Modern Identity.* Cambridge, MA: Harvard University Press, 1986.

Tierney, Robert Thomas. *Monster of the Twentieth Century: Kōtoku Shūsui and Japan's First Anti-imperialist Movement.* Berkeley: University of California Press, 2015.

Tokutomi, Rôka [Kenjirô]. *Footprints in the Snow.* Translated by Kenneth Strong. London: Allen and Unwin, 1970.

Tôyama, Shigeki. "Nihon kindaika to Tôkoku no kokumin bungaku ron." *Bungaku* 20:5 (1952): 1–8.

Tsuzuki, Tsutomu. *Maruyama Masao e no michi annai.* Tokyo: Yoshida shoten, 2013.

Uete, Michinari. "Kokumin no Tomo/Nihonjin." *Shisô,* no. 453 (March 1962): 112–22.

von Hartmann, Eduard. *Philosophy of the Unconscious.* 3 vols. London: Routledge and Kegan Paul, 1950.

Waizumi, Aki. "*Nihonjin.*" *Bungaku* 23:4 (1955): 91–97.

Walker, Brett. *Toxic Archipelago: A History of Industrial Disease in Japan.* Seattle: University of Washington Press, 2010.

Wang, Keping. "Wang Guowei: Philosophy of Aesthetic Criticism." In *Contemporary Chinese Philosophy*, edited by Chung-ying Cheng and Nicholas Bunnin, 37–56. New York: Wiley, 2008.

Watson, Burton. *Su Tung-P'o.* New York: Columbia University Press, 1965.

Weintraub, Karl J. "Autobiography and Historical Consciousness." *Critical Inquiry* 1:4 (June 1975): 821–48.

———. *The Value of the Individual: Self and Circumstance in Autobiography.* Chicago: University of Chicago Press, 1978.

Wilhelm, Richard. Translated by Cary Baynes. *The I Ching or Book of Changes*. 3rd ed. Princeton, NJ: Princeton University Press, 1967. First published in 1950.

———, Hellmut. *Eight Lectures on the I Ching*. Princeton, NJ: Princeton University Press, 1973.

Wu, John C. H., trans., and Paul Sih, ed. *Lao-tzu/Tao Teh Ching*. New York: St. John's University Press, 1961.

Yamagiwa, Keiji. *Kinoshita Naoe*. Tokyo: Rironsha, 1955.

Yamamoto, Sanehiko, ed., *Miyake Setsurei shû*, *Kindai Nihon shisôtaikei*, vol. 5 (Tokyo: Chikuma shobô, 1975).

Yanagida, Izumi, ed. *Meiji seijishōsetsushû* (1). *Meiji Bungaku zenshû*, vol. 6. Tokyo: Chikuma shobô, 1966.

———, ed. *Miyake Setsurei shû*. *Meiji Bungaku zenshû*, vol. 33. Tokyo: Chikuma shobô, 1967.

———. *Nihon kakumei no yogensha: Kinoshita Naoe*. Tokyo: Shinshû, 1961.

———. *Seiji shôsetsu kenkyû*. vols. 1-3. *Meiji Bungaku kenkyû*. Tokyo: Shunbunsha, 1967.

Yokoyama, Gennosuke. *Nihon no kasô shakai*. Tokyo: Aoki bunko, 1949.

———. *Naichi zakkyo ato no Nihon*. Tokyo: Iwanami shoten, 1954.

Yoshida, Seiichi. *Shizenshugi no kenkyû*. Vol. 1. Tokyo: Tokyodô shuppan, 1955.

Yuasa, Nobuyuki. *Bashô: "The Narrow Road to the Deep North" and Other Travel Sketches*. Middlesex: Penguin, 1966.

Zöller, Günter. "Schopenhauer on the Self." In *The Cambridge Companion to Schopenhauer*, edited by Christopher Janaway, 18–43. Cambridge: Cambridge University Press, 1999.

Zuber, Devin. "The Buddha of the North: Swedenborg and Transpacific Zen." *Religion and the Arts* 14 (2010): 1–33.

INDEX

Abe, Isô 4, 133
Aizan, Yamaji 192, 234-235 n19, 239 n55, 261-262 n15, 265 n62, 269 n96
Altieri, Charles xiv, 78, 221, 224 n6, 252 n138, 289 n23
Ames, Roger (and David Hall) 45, 224 n7, 235 n22, 236 n24
Anarchism 4, 6, 7, 8, 89, 125, 158, 160, 197
Animal magnetism 96, 141, 142, 275 n49
Anquetil-Duperron, Abraham-Hyacinthe 60, 68-69, 73, 74, 248 n116, 251 n125-126, 254-255 n145
App, Urs, *The Birth of Orientalism*, 75, n 133
Arima, Tatsuo, *The Failure of Freedom*, 120 and n 116.
Arnold, Sir Edwin 60, 63
Ashio Mine pollution incident, 106, 133, 171
Asiatick Researches 64, 69, 248 n112, 252 n133
Asiatisches Magazin 68 (see also Friedrich Majer)
Asukai, Masamichi 92
"Autonomous self" (*jishuteki jinkaku*) 214
Aydin, Cemil 2

Bashô 51-53, 57, 74, 84
Batchelor, Stephen 62, 73
Bebel, August 6, 10, 195, 204-06

Berman, Marshall xxi-xxii,11, 14, 147, 213, 216, 220
Bhagavad Gita 37, 69, 96, 148, 238 n39, 249 n118, 276 n62
Besant, Annie 62
Blavatsky, Helena Petrovna 61-62
Böhme, Jakob 10, 53, 58, 69, 96, 196, 241 n68, 244 n94. 254-255 n145
Boxer Rebellion 133, 174
Braid, James 71-72, 96
Buddhism 42, 48, 51, 60, 62, 63, 66, 69, 70, 83, 97, 129-130,148, 196, 197, 238 n139, 253 n139, 277 n75,
Bureaucratic Reforms (*kansei-kaikaku*) 26, 28-29, 31-32, 176
Bunmei (civilization) xii-xv, 107, 116,
Bunmei-kaika ("civilization and enlightenment") xv, 29, 76, 85, 101, 107-108, 118
Byron, Lord George Gordon 8, 10, 49, 52, 55, 57, 58, 76, 78, 93, 107, 128, 136, 139, 157,

Calderón, Pedro 48
Carpenter, Edward 10, 11, 196, 146-147,162-164, 196, 204-205, 207-208, 217, 219
  Civilization: Its Cause and Cure 123, 149-152,
  Love's Coming of Age 208-209
"Cave of the Night Demons" 38
Chaplin, Charlie 213
Chertkov, Vladimir 125

Chikamatsu, Monzaemon 140-141, 207, 209
Chikô (clever reasoning) 11, 129, 135, 279 n107
Chinese Studies (Department) xvi, 7, 8, 34-35, 38, 42-43, 44, 51
Chûgoku Minpô 126
"Clever reasoning" (see *chikô*, 智巧, above)
Colebrooke, Thomas 60-61, 64, 251 n125
Commoner News see *Heimin Shinbun*
Cross, Stephen 50, 247 n109, 248 n114, 265 n61

Daidô-danketsu (grand coalition) 39
Daodejing xiv, 10, 44-45, 47, 51, 84, 172, 224 n7, 229 n26, 235 n22, 236 n123, 236 n124, 236-7 n27, n28, n32, n34, 240 n66, 241 n75, 258 n159, 277 n82, 281 n8 and n9, 288 n17
Daoism 42, 44, 51, 76, 125, 129, 153-154, 196, 229 n26, 234 n15, 236 n23, 24, 241 n75, 277-78 n84, 250 n124
"Dark Undercurrents" 155-158
de Vogüé, Eugene Melchior 72, 250 n123
Degeneration (Max Nordau) 10, 11, 136, 137
Descartes, René 48, 58, 237 n37,
Dôjô (compassion, empathy) 22, 52-53, 56, 102, 105, 218
Dongwen Xueshe (東文学舎) (Eastern Academy of Languages) 128
Doppo, Kunikida 197

Eckhart, Meister 58, 96
Ellis, Havelock 143

Emerson, Ralph Waldo 8, 58, 72, 93
Engels, Friedrich 6, 10, 150, 196, 204-05, 217
Enneads 96. See also Plotinus.
Elshtain, Jean Bethke, 195

Flexner, Simon 212
Freud, Sigmund 65-66, 143, 147, 219
Fujita, Kenpô 38
Fukuzawa, Yukichi 1, 9, 85, 107, 188, 267 n70
Futabatei, Shimei 29, 32, 94, 111-112, 163, 232 n15

Ga, jiga ii-iii, 31. See also Self, Subjectivity.
Gay, Peter 78, 94, 230 n29
Gekka-jiken 26, 176, 282 n17
Genroku era 93, 99, 168, 262 n23
George, Henry 5, 164, 227 n9, 279 n117
Goethe, Johann Wolfgang von 53, 55, 58, 68, 223 n2, 242 n80
Guo Xiang 44
Guyon, Madame Jeanne Marie 10, 53, 58, 69, 96, 196, 255 n145

Hasegawa, Nyozekan 214
100 Day Reforms 128-129, 277, n75. See also Kang Youwei
Heeren, Arnold Hermann Ludwig 69
Hegel, Georg Wilhelm Friedrich 42, 167, 186, 191, 242 n80, 246 n102, 283 n30
Heimin shinbun ("Commoner News") 4-5, 125, 127, 159, 169, 187
Heiminsha ("Commoner Association") 4
Heine, Heinrich 10, 56-58, 78, 84, 107, 139
Hibunmeiron (attack on civilization) 11, 108, 123ff, 126, 144, 154

High Treason Incident 3, 215
 – see also Kôtoku, Shûsui
Higuchi, Ichiyô 102, 106, 107, 120, 121, 126, 265 n57, 267 n63
Hirota, Masaki 101, 264 n48
Hirotsu, Ryûrô 101ff
Hood, Tom 161
Hypnotism 10, 71-72, 76, 97, 141-143, 242 n79, 250 n122

I-ching, see *Yijing, Book of Changes*
Ibaraki News 10, 89, 127, 133
Idealists Band (*Risôdan*) 133
Ienaga, Saburô xviii, 11, 216, 225 n2, 229 n24, 280 n4
Ikioi (勢い) 179-180, 182-184, 187, 191, 218 283 n27
Inner life 78, 84, 90, 93, 126, 261-62 n15, 265 n62
Inner self 14, 16, 18, 31, 32, 48, 49, 83-84, 104-105, 149, 196, 198, 206, 261 n14
"Interconnectivity" 129-130
Iriye, Akira 51
Irokawa, Daikichi xvii, 229 n24, 261 n14, 264 n54
Ishikawa, Takuboku viii, 117, 167, 189, 191, 193, 280 n1
Izumi, Kyôka 101, 103, 212, 264 n47

Janaway, Christopher 56, 65, 254 n145,
Jibun (Contemporary Writing) 88
Jiyû-minken undô. See Popular Rights Movement
Joshi-kaihôron [treatise on women's liberation] 201-202
Journal Asiatiques 70, 249 n119
"Jûkyûseiki ni okeru Tôyô no shisô" ("The Position of Eastern Thought in the Nineteenth Century West") 59ff

Kakuta Kanichirô 200
Kang Youwei 89, 128-129, 277 n75
Kano Masanao xi, xvii, 41, 229 n24
Kant, Immanuel 10, 42, 48, 50, 65-69, 79-81, 119, 128, 229 n24, 239 n45, 252 n138, 253 n 139, 254 n145
Karube, Tadashi 217
Katsu, Ôiso 131
Kawakami, Bizan 101
Kawazu, Tokujirô 176
Ken'yûsha 98, 101, 103, 118,
Kinoshita, Naoe 1, 4, 133, 135, 163, 166, 211 n12
Kitamura, Tôkoku 7ff, 84, 92, 94, 102, 120, 235 n19, 260 n14, 262 n23, 265 n62, 269 n96
Klaproth, Julius (1783–1835) 68
Kôchi (City) 3, 7, 19, 23-28, 31
Kôchi Kyôritsu Gakkô (Kôchi Community School) 23ff
Kohn, Livia 45, 50, 235 n21
Kôko Bungaku 89, 119
Kokumin no Tomo [The Nation's Friend] 32, 234 n19. See also Tokutomi, Sohô
Kokusui-hatsuyô ("enhancement of the nation's special characteristics") 98
Kokusui-hozon ("preserving national essence") 38, 40-41, 75-76, 98, 114, 192, 214
Koku-Byaku 203-204
Konishi, Sho xi, 2, 8, 125, 127, 229 n26, 283 n31
Kôno, Hironaka 176, 187
Kôno, Hiroshi 176, 187
Kosugi, Tengai 101
Kôda, Rohan 93, 103
Kôgi-yôron 180
Kôtoku, Shûsui vii, and Reiun 3ff, 89, 125, 133, 159, 163, 169
Kropotkin, Peter 5, 125, 159

Kuroiwa, Ruikô 126, 133
Kurosawa, Akira xix
Kyakkan(teki) objective xiv
Kyônetsu (狂熱) 99, 102

Laozi xix, 10-12, 38, 42-43, 46, 48, 50, 54, 56, 84, 151, 154, 157-58, 219
La Renaissance Orientale (1950) see also Raymond Schwab 61, 73
Lasalle, Ferdinand 164
Latour, Bruno 173, 193
Lears, T.J. Jackson 13-14, 124
Levenson, Joseph xx
Liang Qichao xx-xxi, 1, 89
Lin Xiyi (1193-1221 CE) 44
Lin Xizhong (ca. 1628-1697) 44
Locke, John 5, 7, 19, 22-23, 42
Lu Deming (556-627 CE) 44
Lu Xiangshan (1139-1192) 44

Magee, Bryan 56
Majer, Friedrich 68
Mannion, Gerard 83
Mansfield, Katherine 87, 90
Mansfield, Nick 224 n4, 287 n2
Maruyama, Kanji 214
Maruyama, Masao xvii, xix, 188, 192, 213, 214
Masaoka, Geiyô 3, 197, 218
Matsubara, Iwagorô 110-111
māyā 62, 65-67, 82
Mead, George H. 78, 252 n138.
Meiji hanshinden [Biographies of Meiji Rebels] 27, 170, 176-77, 180-181, 187, 189, 210
Mesmer, Franz Anton 71-72, 76
Mesmerism 10, 60, 71-72, 76
Mill, John Stuart 5, 7, 13, 19, 23, 29, *Min'yûsha* [Nation's Friend] 32
Mishima, Michitsune 176

Mishra, Pankaj 1, 2
Mitleid (Compassion) 52-53, 56, 102, 105, 218
Mito (Ibaraki Prefecture) 10, 89, 127, 138
Miyake, Setsurei 33, 38, 40, 98, 128, 163, 192, 212
  Tetsugaku kenteki (Vignettes in Philosophy) 42
  Gakan shokei (A Small Portrait of My Views) 42
Monod, Gabriel 72
Morgan, Lewis Henry, *Ancient Society*, 10, 149-50, 162, 204-205
Mori, Ogai 103
Morris, William 6
Muga (無我), "selfless" 155
Muhon (謀反) or "rebellion" 184, 192
Muyoku/wuyu 44-45, 236 n23
Müller, Friedrich Max 70
Munitz, Milton 55, 105
Muses, Charles 83
Mysticism 10, 56, 58, 60-62, 66, 69, 72, 76, 82, 84, 95-97, 119, 148, 152, 165, 196, 217

Nagata Shrine 170-171
"Nagatamura ni te" [At Nagatamura] 170-175, 184, 217
Nakae, Chômin 5, 23, 26, 200, 231 n12.
Nakano, Jirôsaburô 176
Nakano, Seigô 179
Nakano Shôyô 38, 43
Narita, Ryûichi 264 n48
Nietzsche, Friedrich 10, 16, 65, 66, 139, 157, 165, 200, 275 n51
Nihonshugi ("Japanism") 114. See also Takayama, Chogyû

Nihonjin 8, 33, 38, 40, 42, 56, 90, 95, 106, 117
Nisbet, Robert 188
Nishida, Masaru xi, xviii, xix, 13, 101, 128, 199, 201
Nordau, Max 146-147, 151, 165, 203, 204-206, 217
  The Conventional Lies of Our Civilization 10, 11, 136
  Degeneration 10, 147, 149

Odagiri, Hideo 101
Ogawa, Usen 1, 89, 127, 163, 167
Okumiya, Kenshi 176, 282 n17
Osaka Middle School 25-30, 34, 86, 88, 105, 176
Ôsei-fukko 179
Ôsugi Sakae 163, 194
Oupnek'hat 68-69, 96, 247 n110, 254-55 n145, 258 n139, 281 n8. See also, Upanishads
Ozaki, Kôyô 93, 98-99, 101, 118

Paracelsus, Theophrastus 141
Parerga and Paralipomena 50, 69, 79
Paulsen, Friedrich 165
Peace Preservation Law 194
Plato 10, 48, 49, 55, 56, 58;
  Schopenhauer on 65-69, 79-80, 96, 139, 148, 157
  On allegory of shadows on the cave wall 68, 79
Plotinus 58, 69. 96. See also *Enneads*.
Popular Rights Movement 3, 4-5, 17, 19, 25-27, 34, 39-42, 85-86,
  Kitamura Tôkoku and 92-93, 170, 176-177, 189, 184, 186-187,
Pyle, Kenneth 38, 85

Rakugosha ("straggler") 9, 13, 14, 197, 198, 215-216
Risôdan 133. See also "Idealists Band."
Risshishisa (Self-Help Society), 34
Rorty, Richard 167
Rousseau, Jean-Jacques 5, 7, 8, 16, 19, 23, 58, 72, 139, 145, 154-155, 157-158, 163-164, 169, 189, 196, 199, 219
Rowbotham, Sheila 147

Sacred Books of the East 60, 70. See also Friedrich Max Müller
Safranski, Rüdiger 79, 140, 246 n10, 250 n125
Said, Edward 73, 74, 75
Saigô Takamori 1, 23
Saito, Ryûkû 103
Sakai, Toshihiko 4, 123, 133, 163, 274 n40
Sakkiden xviii, 9, 15-17, 19, 31, 42, 128,132,136, 145-46, 155, 180, 199, 203, 215-216, 221, 225,
Sasagawa, Rimpû 38, 43, 103, 119, 203
Schelling, Friedrich Wilhelm 8, 10, 11, 16, 42, 58, 255 n147
Schiller, Johann Christoph Friedrich von 53, 55, 58, 25051 n124
Schopenhauer, Arthur 8,10, 38, 42, 48, 50, 52, 56, 58, 60, 64-68, 79-84, 123, 199
  and pessimism 65, 66, 82, 84, 245 n101, 255 n146
  Manuscript Remains 249 n117, 254 n145, 258 n159-67
  On the Basis of Morality 240 n58
  Parerga and Paralipomena 50, 69, 79
Schwab, Raymond 61, 73, 251 n126
Seiji kara, bungaku e ("from politics to literature") 92

Seinenbun 88-90, 112, 114, 116-119, 122, 125, 138, 198, 231, 260, n2, 280 n4
Sekai no taisei (世界の大勢, global historical trends) 182
self i-ii, xi-xiv, xv, 14, 22-27. See also Subjectivity)
Sempô Yojin 128
Shakai mondai (social problems) 29, 91, 110, 112, 113, 115, 121, 198, 218
Social Problems (Henry George) 5, 164, 279 n117.
Shanghai 75-76, 89, 127-129, 134, 272 n21, 277 n75
Shiga, Shigetaka 33
Shigai 8, 43, 56
Shirakawa, Riyô 9
Shukan(teki), subjective xiv, 119, 152. See also Subjectivity.
Shutaiseironsô (debate over subjectivity) xix, 214,
Shukoh, Prince Dara (1615–59) 60, 69, 248 n114
Sinnett, Alfred Percy 62-63
Social problems 29, 91, 110ff, 112-113, 115, 121-122, 164, 218.
See also "shakai mondai)
Socialism 4-7, 22, 142-143, 145, 148, 158-160, 162-165, 188-189, 197, 228, 231 n6, 276 n60
Sôseki, Natsume 166, 212
Spencer, Herbert 38
Spiegel, Gabrielle xiii. 223 n3
Steiner, Rudolf (1861–1925)
Su, Dongpo 43, 51, 84
Subjectivity xiii, 2, 11, 17, 49, 119, 135, 142, 152, 213, 221. 224 n4, 244-45 n100, 278, 283 n31 n90
debate on (*shutaiseironsô*) 214, 289 n22
Swedenborg, Emanuel 241, 244 n94

Tagore, Rabindrnath 1
Taguchi Ukichi (see also *Shigai*)
Taika Reforms 178-179
Taisei (大勢) 182-183, 185-188
Taiyô [The Sun] 92. See also Takayama Chogyû
Taiji (Supreme Ultimate) 47, 237 n35
Takahashi, Tadashi 122, 197, 225 n13
Takayama, Chogyû 113-114, 121, 197, 268 n85
Talmon, J.L. 110, 218
Tan, Sitong 128-130
Tang, Caichang 129, 272 n20, 277 n75
Tanaka, Kotarô 178, 210,
Tao Hongjing (451-536) 44
Taoka, Ryôichi 201, 273 n55, 244-245 n100
Taylor, Charles 17, 78, 124, 140, 224 n5, 274 n44, 278 n90, 289 n20
Tenko (Heaven's Drum) 11, 126-127, 135-140, 165-166, 169-170, 191, 207, 271 n12, 280-281 n4
The Conventional Lies of Our Civilization (Max Nordau) 10, 11, 136, 146, 203
The Sun. See *Taiyô*
The World as Will and Representation (Schopenhauer) 53, 57, 60, 65, 80-84, 95, 200, 238 n39, 246 n102, 256 n150
Theosophical Society 61-62, 148, 243 n93
Thing-in-itself (Kant) 50, 67, 81
Thoreau, Henry David 8, 58, 72, 78, 165, 250 n124, 280 n118
Tôa Shimpô [East Asian Progress] 203
Tôa Zeirin (East Asian Forum) 8, 38, 43, 59, 77, 234 n17
Tokuda Shûsei 4
Tokutomi, Rôka 26, 192

Tokutomi, Sohô 32, 38, 98, 232 n19, 233 n9
Tolstoy, Lev (Leo) 5-6, 66, 125-126, 139, 157, 159, 165, 197, 199, 217, 229, 250, 279 n117
Tsukimisô na onna. See Katsu Ôiso.
Tsûyama 89, 114, 127, 131, 133, 207
Tat twam asi ("That Art Thou") 48

Uchida Roan
Uchimura, Kanzô 133, 232 n1
Ueki, Emori 23
Ukigumo 29, 32, 232 n15
Upanishads 8, 10, 12, 42, 48, 56, 58, 60, 63, 66-69, 74, 79, 196, 219, 247 n108, 248 n114, 249 n118, 250 n 124, 250 n133, 288 n17

Vasalou, Sophia 81, 220, 239 n45
Vedas 8, 10, 12, 42, 53, 58, 63-68, 196, 219, 250 n124
von Hartmann, Eduard 10-11, 64-65, 123, 136, 242 n79, 243 n93, 244 n100

Wang, Guowei 128, 272 n17
Wang, Kangnian 128, 277 n75
Weber, Max 13, 140
Wen, Tingshi 128
Weintraub, Karl J. xiii
Whitman, Walt 148-149

Xu, Xilin 175

Yamagata, Isô 28, 88
Yi, Jun 175, 282 n13
Yijing (Book of Changes) 10, 44, 47, 67, 76, 84, 129, 191, 247 n106, 273 n 24
Yogācāra Buddhism 48, 129-130, 238 n39, 277 n75

Yokoyama, Gennosuke 1, 29, 110, 267 n76,
Yorzuchôhô (newspaper) 126-127, 133
Yoshida, Seiichi 95
Yûzo muzo [The Voiced and the Voiceless] 127, 272 n14

Zen 76, 84
Zhang Zai (1020-1077) 44
Zhuangzi 10-12, 38, 139, 151, 154, 156, 219, 258 n159
 "Free and Easy Wandering," 43-84
Zhi Daolin (314-366 CE) 44
Zola, Emile 6, 61, 72
Zöller, Günter 82
Zhou Dunyi (1017-1073) 47

GPSR Authorized Representative: Easy Access System Europe, Mustamäe tee 50, 10621 Tallinn, Estonia, gpsr.requests@easproject.com

www.ingramcontent.com/pod-product-compliance
Lightning Source LLC
Chambersburg PA
CBHW030433300426
44112CB00009B/979